Atlas of Hawaii

Atlas of Hawaii

Department of Geography,
University of Hawaii at Manoa

The University Press of Hawaii

Editor and Project Director: R. Warwick Armstrong
Professor of Geography and Public Health, University
of Hawaii, Honolulu.

Cartographer: James A. Bier
Cartographer, Department of Geography, University
of Illinois at Urbana-Champaign.

Gazetteer Compiler: Sen-dou Chang
Professor of Geography, University of Hawaii, Honolulu.

STAFF

Cartographic Draftsman: Jon P. Atwood
Department of Geography, University of Hawaii, Honolulu.

Photo-cartographic Specialist: Everett A. Wingert
Assistant Professor of Geography, University of Hawaii, Honolulu.

Place Name Authority: Samuel H. Elbert
Professor Emeritus of Pacific Languages and Linguistics,
University of Hawaii, Honolulu.

Secretary: Monica Y. Okido
Department of Geography, University of Hawaii, Honolulu.

Technical Assistants: M. Jocelyn Armstrong • Jacqueline Brownlea •
Betty F. Kodama • Mary Ellen Nordyke

CARTOGRAPHIC ASSISTANCE

Linda L. Bogle • Jen-hu Chang • Brian J. Choy • Carolyn L. Corrigan •
Robert J. Earickson • Paul C. Ekern, Jr. • Karen A. Essene •
Robert S. Fegley • James W. Frierson, Jr. • Jon Haitsuka • Jorie Higgins •
George B. Immisch • Virginia C. Ing • James O. Juvik • Sonia Juvik •
Jack H. Katahira • Miranda Lee • Albert L. Lyman •
Curtis A. Manchester, Jr. • Lawrence J. Masterson • Etsuko M. McCrath •
Michael E. McCrath • Melinda Meade • Paul A. Meyer • Brian J. Murton •
Richard T. Naito • T. Stell Newman • Lois Nishimoto • Valiant C. Norman •
Jewel Okumura • Cynthia Oyakawa • Jo Ann Oyakawa • Barry L. Parks •
Helen M. Robinson • Barry D. Root • Richard J. Scudder •
Shingo Shimabukuro • Iris Shinohara • Andrew D. Short •
John D. Schroeder • Paul J. Schwind • John M. Street •
Kevin C. Swenson • Katie Takeshita • Ronald C. Taylor • Naomi Terada •
Lawrence Travers • Vu Dinh Dinh • Gene Ward • Harwood White •
Helen Whitehead •

ATLAS COMMITTEE

Roland J. Fuchs, Chairman, Department of Geography, University of
Hawaii, Honolulu.
Robert W. Sparks, Director, University Press of Hawaii, Honolulu.
R. Warwick Armstrong, James A. Bier, Sen-dou Chang, Abraham Piianaia

To the memory of
Professor Curtis A. Manchester, Jr.
1912-1972

CONTRIBUTING AUTHORS AND COMPILERS

Agatin T. Abbott, Professor of Geology, University of Hawaii, Honolulu.

Wilfrid Bach, Associate Professor of Geography, University of Hawaii, Honolulu.

Harold L. Baker, Director, Land Study Bureau, University of Hawaii, Honolulu.

Andrew J. Berger, Professor of Zoology, University of Hawaii, Honolulu.

David Bess, Associate Professor of Transportation, University of Hawaii, Honolulu.

Robert T. Bobilin, Associate Professor of Religion, University of Hawaii, Honolulu.

John P. Charlot, Director, Museum of American Samoa, Pago Pago.

Edith H. Chave, Marine Programs, University of Hawaii, Honolulu.

Anders P. Daniels, Assistant Professor of Meteorology, University of Hawaii, Honolulu.

Gavan Daws, Professor of History, University of Hawaii, Honolulu.

Jill L. Eveloff, Department of Food and Nutritional Science, University of Hawaii, Honolulu.

P. Bion Griffin, Assistant Professor of Anthropology, University of Hawaii, Honolulu.

D. Elmo Hardy, Senior Professor of Entomology, University of Hawaii, Honolulu.

Bank of Hawaii, Department of Business Research, Honolulu.

John R. Healy, Associate Professor of Geography, University of Hawaii, Hilo.

E. Alison Kay, Professor of General Science, University of Hawaii, Honolulu.

Edgar C. Knowlton, Jr., Professor of European Languages, University of Hawaii, Honolulu.

David H. Kornhauser, Professor of Geography, University of Hawaii, Honolulu.

Charles H. Lamoureux, Professor of Botany, University of Hawaii, Honolulu.

L. Stephen Lau, Director, Water Resources Research Center, University of Hawaii, Honolulu.

Gordon A. Macdonald, Senior Professor of Geology and Geophysics, University of Hawaii, Honolulu.

Ralph M. Moberly, Professor of Geology, University of Hawaii, Honolulu.

Joseph R. Morgan, Department of Geography, University of Hawaii, Honolulu.

Robert E. Mytinger, Professor of Public Health, University of Hawaii, Honolulu.

Robert E. Nelson, Director, Institute of Pacific Islands Forestry, Forest Service, U. S. Department of Agriculture, Honolulu.

Daniel S. Noda, Professor of Education, University of Hawaii, Honolulu.

Abraham Piianaia, Lecturer in Geography, University of Hawaii, Honolulu.

Saul Price, Regional Climatologist, National Weather Service, Pacific Region, National Oceanic and Atmospheric Administration, Honolulu.

Sarah E. Sanderson, Associate Professor of Communication, University of Hawaii, Honolulu.

Robert D. Schmitt, State Statistician, Department of Planning and Economic Development, State of Hawaii, Honolulu.

Yung C. Shang, Assistant Economist, Economic Research Center, University of Hawaii, Honolulu.

Allan Sommarstrom, Assistant Professor of Geography, University of Hawaii, Honolulu.

P. Quentin Tomich, Animal Ecologist, Department of Health, State of Hawaii, Honokaa.

Goro Uehara, Professor of Soil Science, University of Hawaii, Honolulu.

ACKNOWLEDGMENTS

It is not possible to acknowledge individually the help received from a large number of people in the University of Hawaii, government agencies, and private industry, and from many private individuals. Specific contributions to text, maps, and illustrations are acknowledged on the page where they appear in the Atlas.

Special recognition is due authors and cartographic assistants who volunteered their time and talents to the Atlas without remuneration. Their generosity and cooperation made it possible for the small staff to produce the Atlas within the constraining limits of time and money available. The Atlas of Hawaii was of necessity compiled and drafted in eighteen months.

Many government and private organizations contributed information through official publications and personal correspondence. They are listed on this page. Special mention is made of the State Department of Planning and Economic Development which provided a substantial portion of the statistical data. Its staff gave much valuable assistance with clarification of questions on statistics, boundaries, and geographic names.

Office space for cartography and drafting was made available by courtesy of the School of Public Health, University of Hawaii. Drafting equipment was loaned by the university's Pacific Urban Studies and Planning Program. The Social Science Research Institute of the university contributed card punching services for preparation of the gazetteer. Each of these assists is gratefully acknowledged.

The coastlines, geodesy, and most of the place names for Atlas maps were taken from maps of the U. S. Geological Survey and National Ocean Survey. The chief reference was the Geological Survey 7.5-minute quadrangle topographic map series, scale 1:24,000.

The Atlas project was financed primarily by a grant from the University of Hawaii to the Department of Geography for cartography and drafting. Supplementary funds were granted by the Population Institute of the East-West Center and the Environmental Center of the University of Hawaii. Publication was financed by The University Press of Hawaii.

CONTRIBUTING ORGANIZATIONS

United States Government. Bureau of Sport Fisheries and Wildlife, Forest Service (Institute of Pacific Islands Forestry), Geological Survey, National Ocean Survey, National Park Service, National Weather Service, Soil Conservation Service.

State of Hawaii. Department of Agriculture, Department of Defense, Department of Education, Department of Health, Department of Land and Natural Resources, Department of Planning and Economic Development, Department of Social Services and Housing, Department of Taxation, Department of Transportation, Public Utilities Commission, State Foundation on Culture and the Arts, University of Hawaii.

City and County of Honolulu. Board of Water Supply, Civil Defense Agency, Fire Department, Department of Parks and Recreation, Planning Department, Police Department, Division of Sewers.

County of Hawaii. Civil Defense Agency, Planning Department, Research and Development.

County of Kauai. Civil Defense Agency, Fire Department, Planning Department, Water Department.

County of Maui. Civil Defense Agency, Parks Department, Planning Department, Department of Water Supply.

Private Organizations. Bank of Hawaii (Department of Business Research), Bernice P. Bishop Museum, Hawaii Audubon Society, Hawaii Visitors Bureau, Hawaiian Electric Company, Hawaiian Sugar Planters' Association, Hawaiian Telephone Company, Kauai Electric Company, Lanai Lodge, Pineapple Growers Association of Hawaii.

Hawaii

Ocean Depth

☐	0-600 feet (0-100 fathoms)
☐	600-7200 feet (100-1200 fathoms)
☐	7200-10,800 feet. (1200-1800 fathoms)

☐	10,800-13,200 feet (1800-2200 fathoms)
☐	13,200-15,600 feet (2200-2600 fathoms)
■	15,600-18,000 feet (2600-3000 fathoms)

■ More than 18,000 feet (3000-3500 fathoms)

1:4,562,000

0 40 80 120 160 miles

0 40 80 120 160 200 240 kilometers

Source: Bathymetry compiled from various sources by R.M. Moberly, Hawaii Institute
of Geophysics, University of Hawaii, and Lt. Comm. R.L. Crozier, USN,
Hydrographic Programs Officer, Staff, Commander in Chief Pacific.   1972

CONTENTS

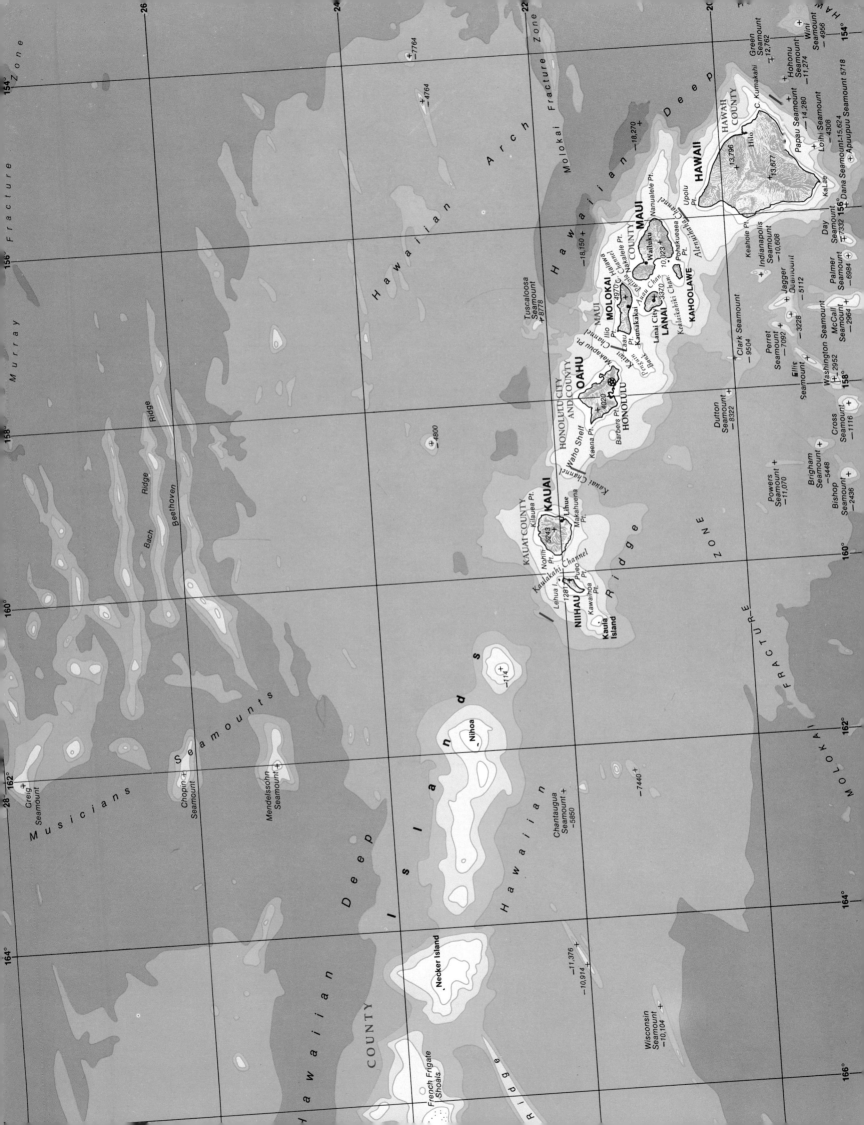

INTRODUCTION

The *Atlas of Hawaii* is a general thematic atlas which treats the State of Hawaii as a whole rather than emphasizing a particular island or area. Since 1825, when the first United States state atlas appeared, for South Carolina, many states have prepared atlases to serve the needs of general reference, resource inventory, education, or promotion. Although the *Atlas of Hawaii* is primarily a general reference work, it is hoped that it will serve these other functions as well. The information is presented primarily in the form of maps, graphs, and other illustrations, supplemented by short discussions in text. Because of Hawaii's diversity of peoples and environments, several topics not usually found in a state atlas, such as languages and religions, find inclusion here.

The Atlas is arranged in five parts. The first contains the reference maps with 3,300 place names for towns, mountains, bays, harbors, and other features.

The second part deals with aspects of the natural environment. Here, the prominence of island and marine environments is demonstrated, with special note of the unique assemblages of plant and animal life in Hawaii and some of the implications of human and natural environmental interactions.

The third part considers the people. The diversity of the State's cultures are treated in sections on history and demography as well as archaeology, languages, religions, and the arts. These topics inevitably overlap with those in the fourth part of the Atlas, which treats elements of the economy and additional topics of the cultural environment.

The fifth part comprises a statistical supplement, bibliography and references cited, a text on place names, and the gazetteer for the reference maps. The statistical supplement includes tables of geographical and climatic data, and conversion factors. The bibliography, in which the entries are arranged by section, is intended as a guide for further reading.

All place names in the Atlas have been checked with official listings of the Advisory Committee on Geographic Names, State Department of Planning and Economic Development, and with existing maps and gazetteers. The pronunciation of all Hawaiian names in the reference map section and gazetteer is clarified by the inclusion of diacritical marks.

Page references in the text refer the reader to related materials elsewhere in the Atlas.

Every effort was made to ensure accuracy and consistency of information throughout the Atlas. Coverage and treatment necessarily vary somewhat due to resource limitations; that is, certain topics are not developed as thoroughly as they could have been or as fully as was initially hoped. Again, as a state atlas the prime objective was to examine Hawaii as a whole. This meant that as far as possible information had to be prepared and presented at levels of generalization appropriate for the State. All maps in the Atlas show the main islands at the same scale, which permits geographical comparisons, especially of areal densities. This helps to illustrate, for example, the true proportion of population and cultural activity concentrated on Oahu in comparison with the other islands. On the other hand, special attention was not given to Oahu or Honolulu despite their relative importance in many respects. While enlarged inset maps of the Honolulu area are employed for clarification of detail, the scale of the maps used is appropriate for a state atlas rather than for a city or island atlas.

Data used in compilation were the most recent available until going to press. A major source of information was the 1970 U. S. Census of Population; most state and county data are for 1971. All maps and diagrams give the source and date of information. In design the Atlas aims for a balance between maps and text. The cartography emphasizes the insular, oceanic setting, with colors suggesting the bright, natural hues of the islands.

HAWAII
THE FIFTIETH STATE

In this map Hawaii appears as the central point on the Earth's surface with the rest of the world surrounding it. Along a part of the perimeter are the antipodes of Hawaii, those places diametrically opposite on the globe, which lie in South West Africa and Botswana, in southern Africa. Hawaii shares the same general latitude of 20°N with a variety of insular and continental environments including Hong Kong, Calcutta, Mecca, the Sahara Desert, and Mexico City. Hawaii comprises 132 islands, reefs, and shoals stretching 1,523 miles southeast to northwest across the Tropic of Cancer between 154°40' and 178°75'W longitude, and 18°54' to 28°15'N latitude. The eight main islands—Hawaii, Maui, Oahu, Kauai, Molokai, Lanai, Niihau, and Kahoolawe (in order of size)—make up over 99 percent of the total land area of 6,425 square miles. The remaining one percent, less than six square miles of land area, is made up of islands off the shores of the main islands and the Northwestern Hawaiian Islands, from Kure Atoll in the north to Nihoa in the south. The State of Hawaii encompasses all these islands except the Midway Islands, which are administered by the United States Navy. Hawaii is the southernmost state in the United States and extends almost as far west as Alaska. It is 4,829 miles west of Washington, D.C., and six hours behind the capital in standard time. The map emphasizes the isolated location of the islands near the center of the Pacific Ocean, far from the original homelands of Hawaii's people. The Marquesas, the probable origin of the early Polynesian Hawaiians, is 2,400 miles to the south; California, the source of most American migrants, is 2,390 miles to the east; Japan, China, and the Philippines, all major sources of Asian settlers, lie 3,850, 4,900, and 5,280 miles to the west. But people have come from all parts of the world to help create the first real multi-ethnic state of the United States. Small and remote though Hawaii may be, it is one of the best-known places on the globe. In the minds of people of many lands it excites the picture of a tropical paradise, one that attracts thousands of visitors each year. It is also an international meeting place for businessmen and scholars from all parts of the globe.

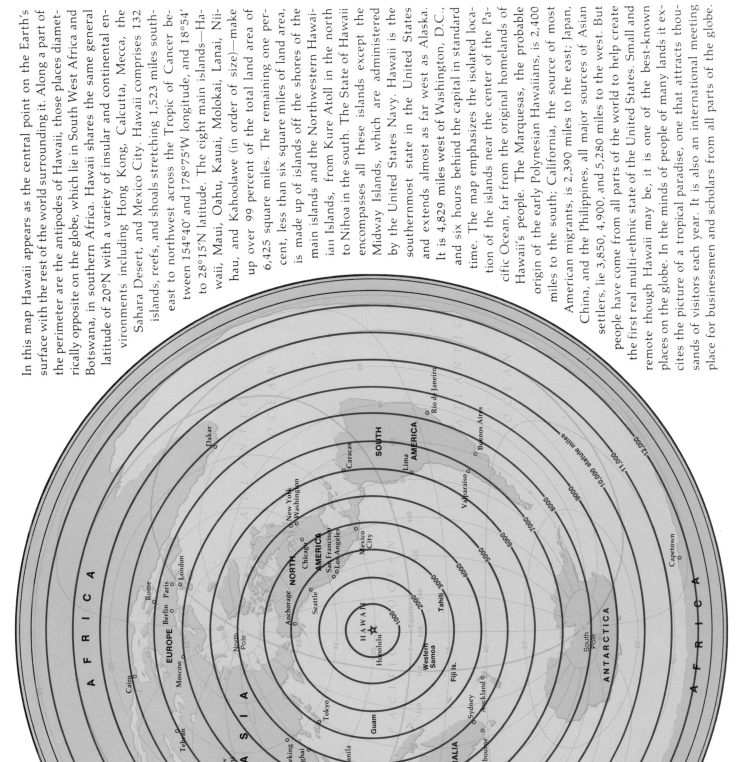

Azimuthal Equidistant Projection

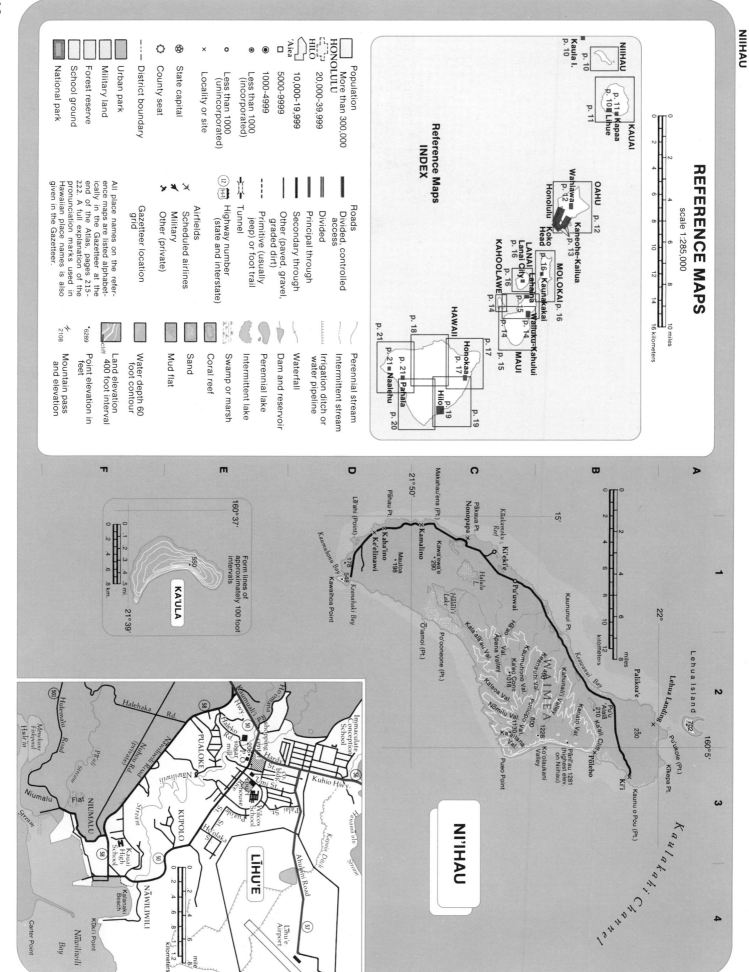

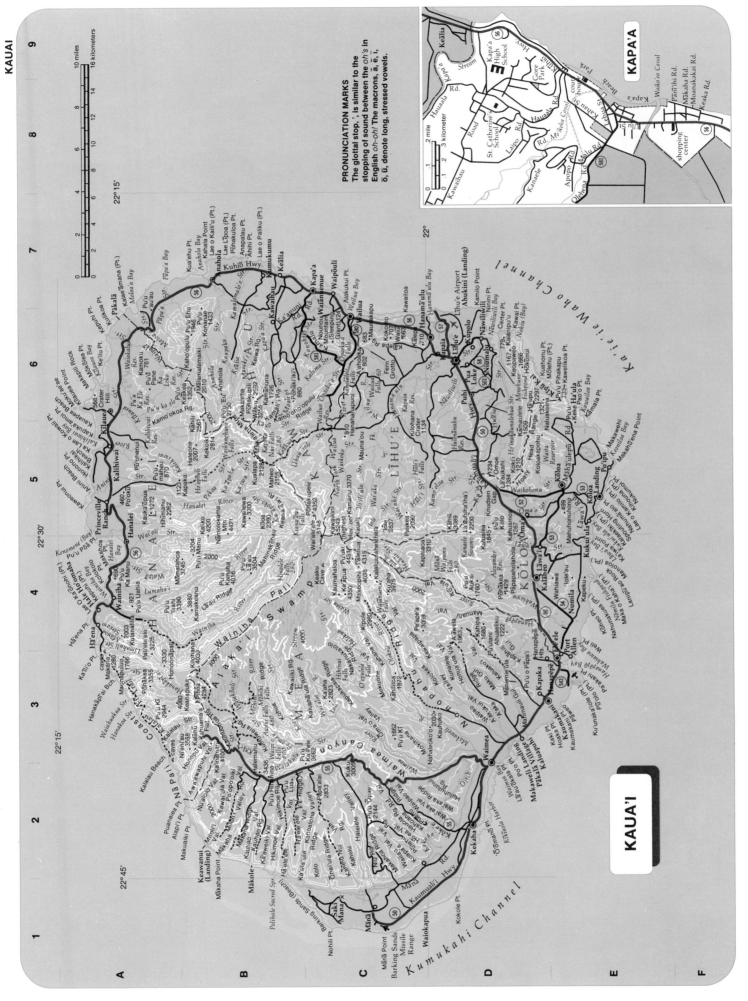

KAUA'I

KAPA'A

PRONUNCIATION MARKS
The glottal stop, ', is similar to the stopping of sound between the *oh*'s in English *oh-oh!* The macrons, ā, ē, ī, ō, ū, denote long, stressed vowels.

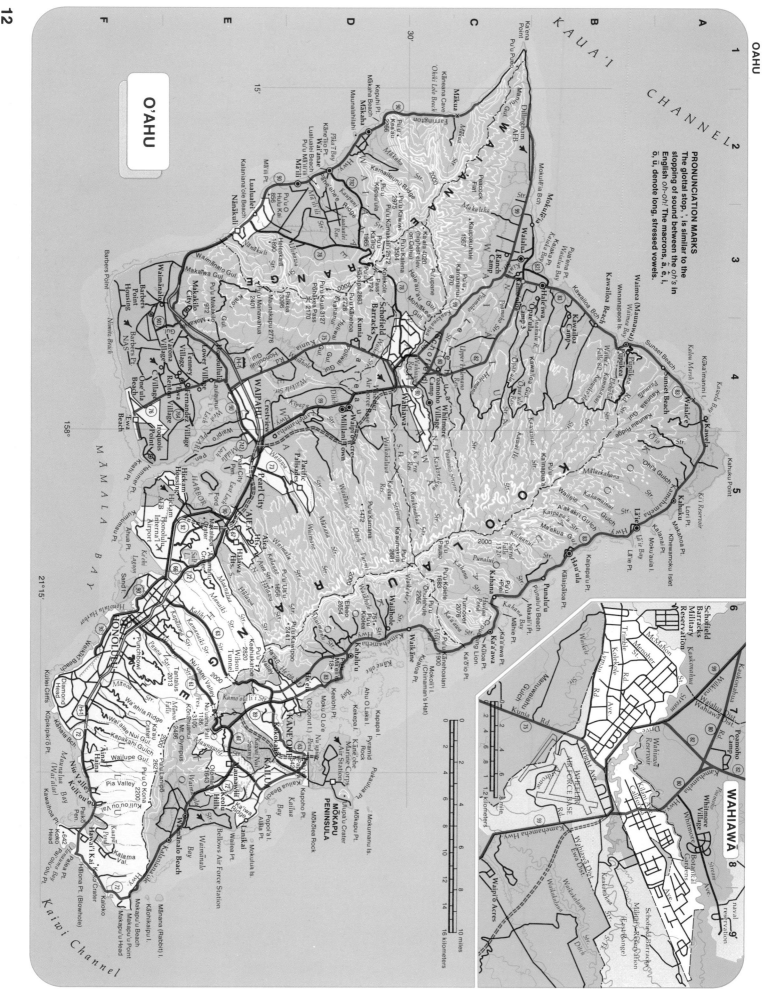

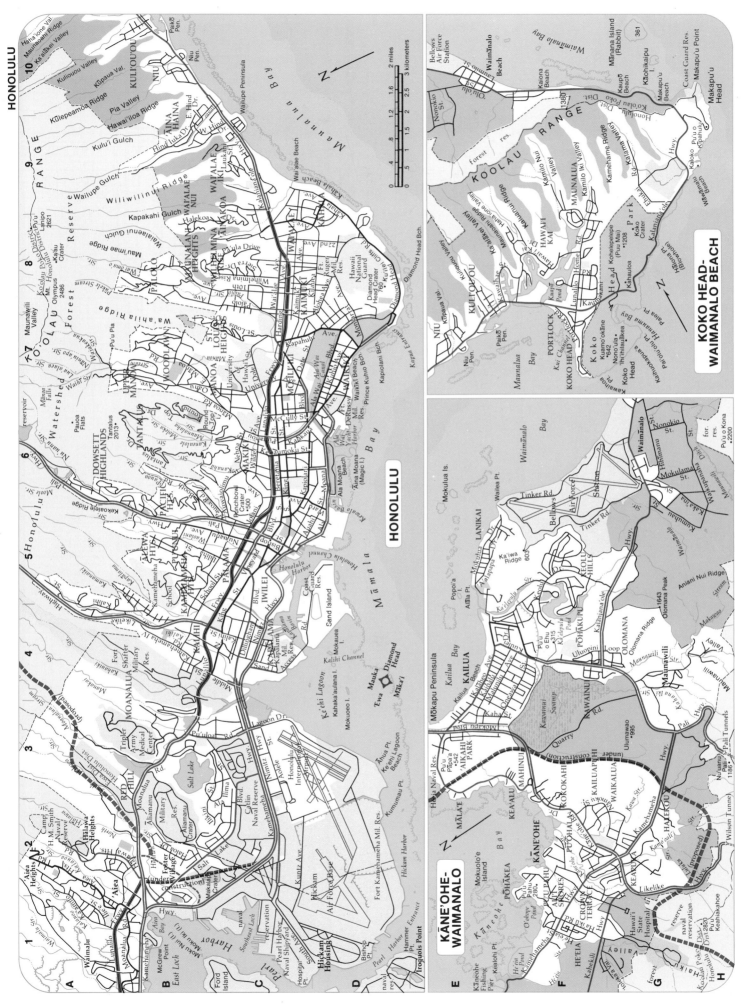

HONOLULU

KOKO HEAD-
WAIMANALO BEACH

KĀNE'OHE-
WAIMANALO

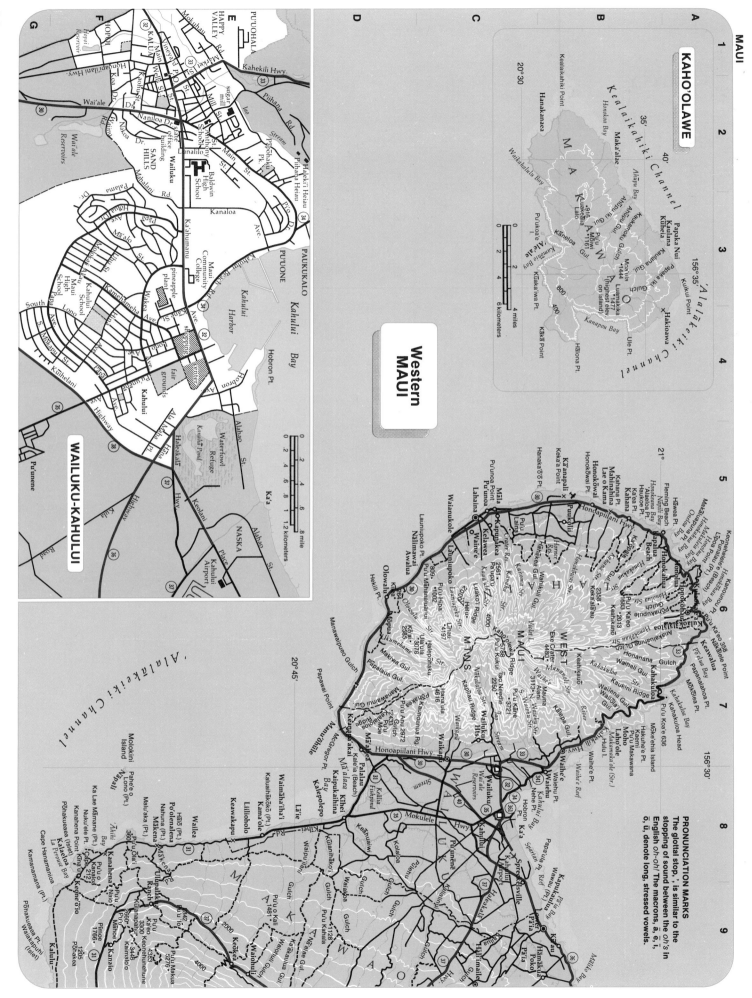

KAHO'OLAWE

Western MAUI

WAILUKU-KAHULUI

PRONUNCIATION MARKS
The glottal stop, ', is similar to the stopping of sound between the oh's in English *oh-oh!* The macrons, ā, ē, ī, ō, ū, denote long, stressed vowels.

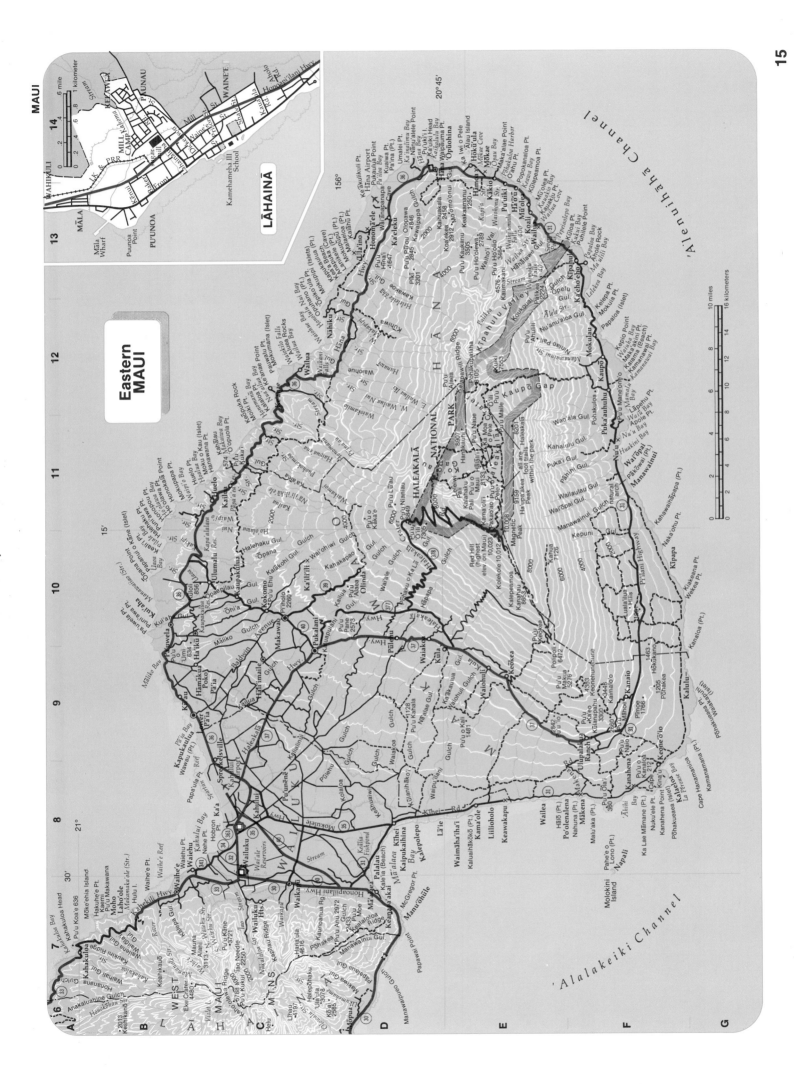

MAUI

14

LĀHAINĀ

Eastern MAUI

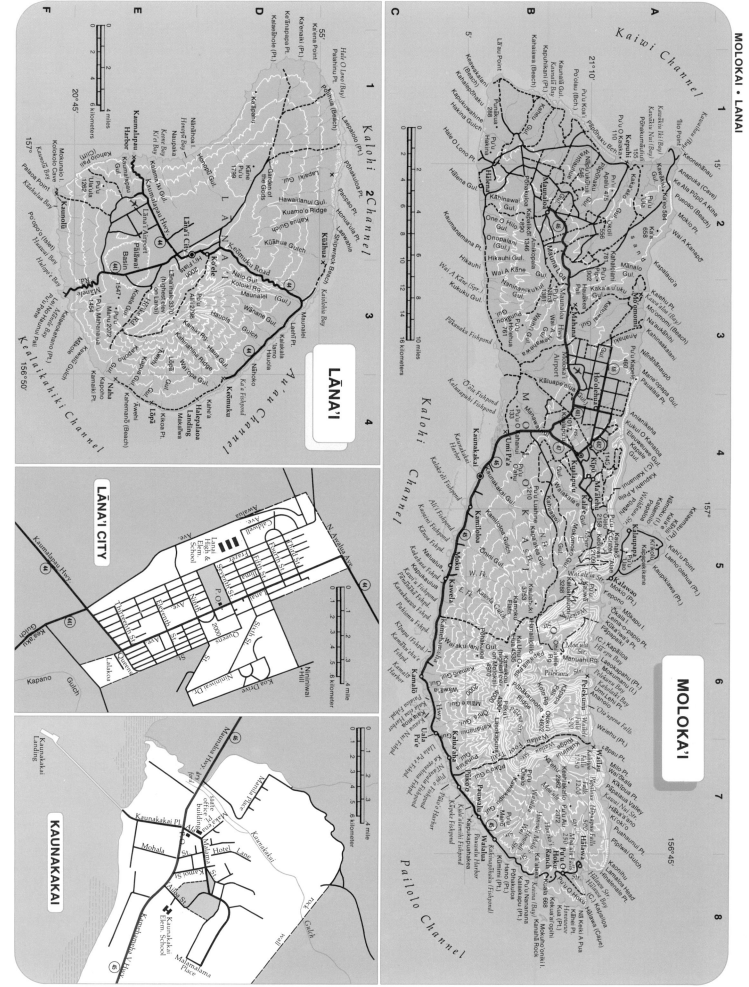

LĀNA'I

LĀNA'I CITY

MOLOKA'I

KAUNAKAKAI

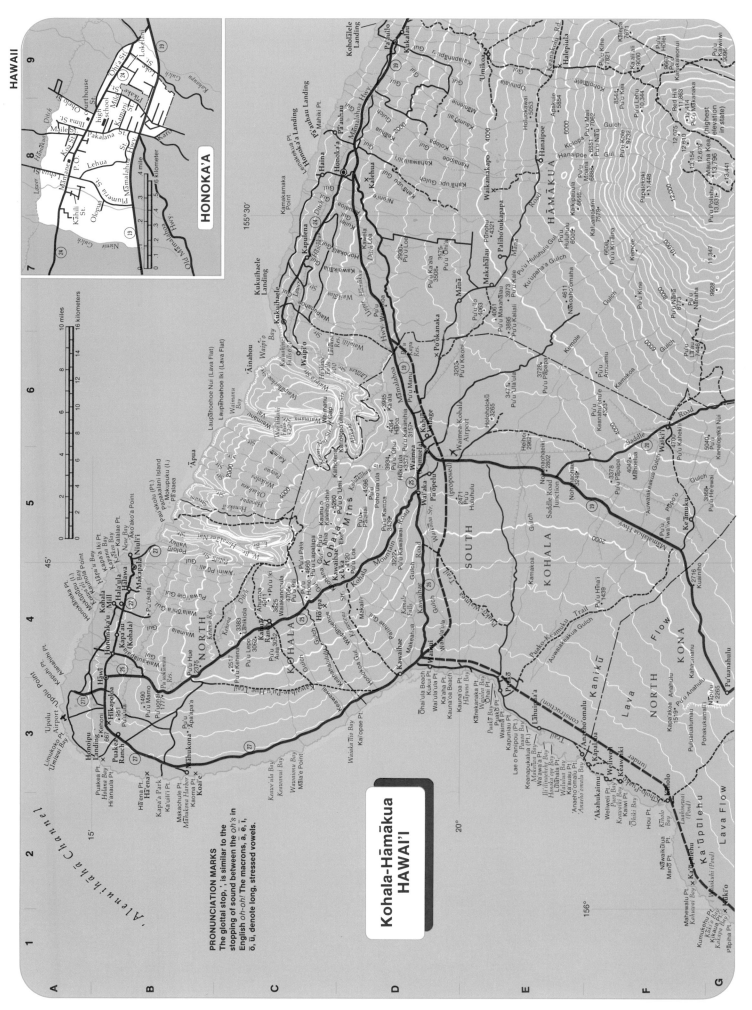

HONOKA'A

PRONUNCIATION MARKS

The glottal stop, ', is similar to the stopping of sound between the oh's in English oh-oh! The macrons, ā, ē, ī, ō, ū, denote long, stressed vowels.

Kohala-Hāmākua
HAWAI'I

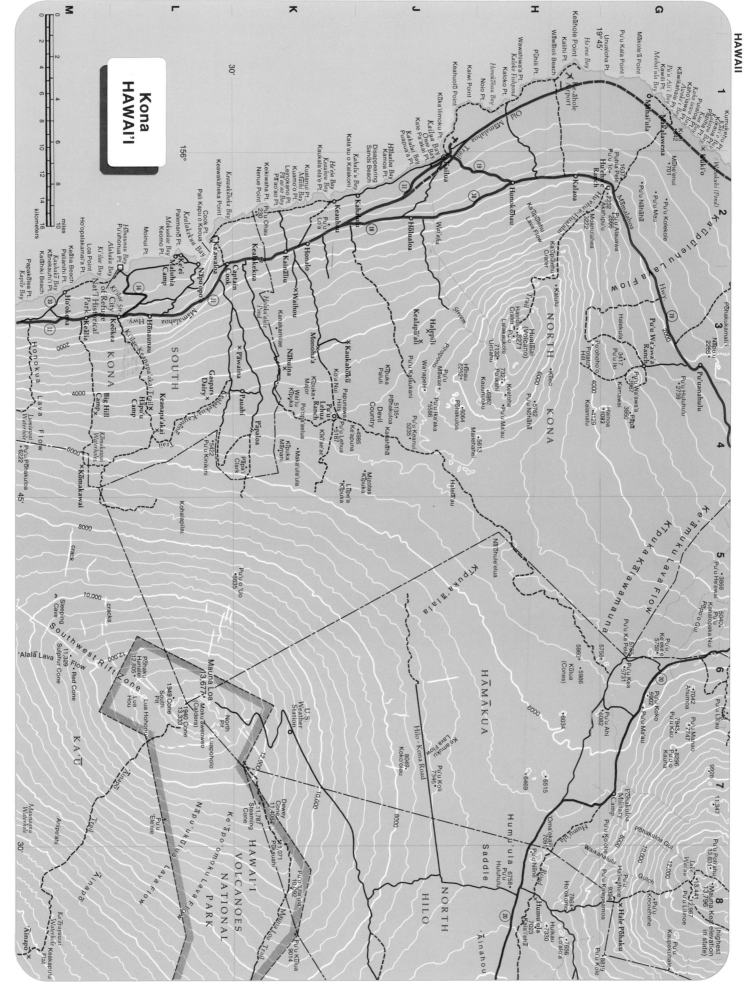

Kona
HAWAI'I

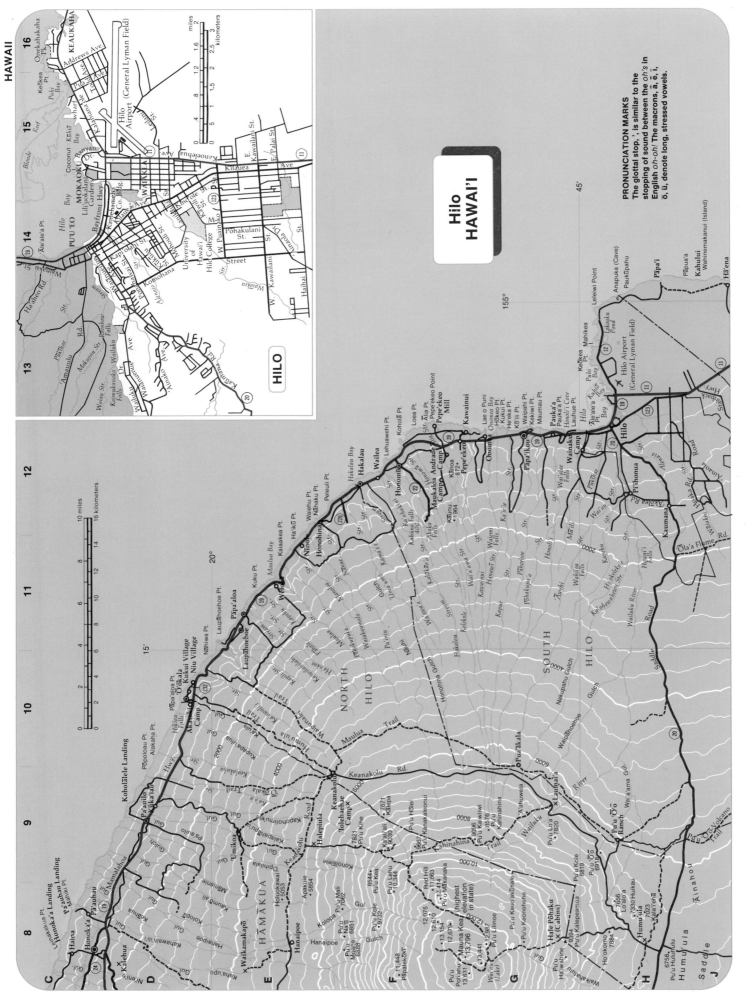

PRONUNCIATION MARKS
The glottal stop, ', is similar to the stopping of sound between the *oh*'s in English *oh-oh!* The macrons, ā, ē, ī, ō, ū, denote long, stressed vowels.

Hilo
HAWAI'I

HILO

Hilo
Airport (General Lyman Field)

KEAUKAHA

MOKAOKU

PU'U'EO

WAIĀKEA

University of Hawai'i Hilo College

SOUTH HILO

NORTH HILO

HĀMĀKUA

Hilo Airport (General Lyman Field)

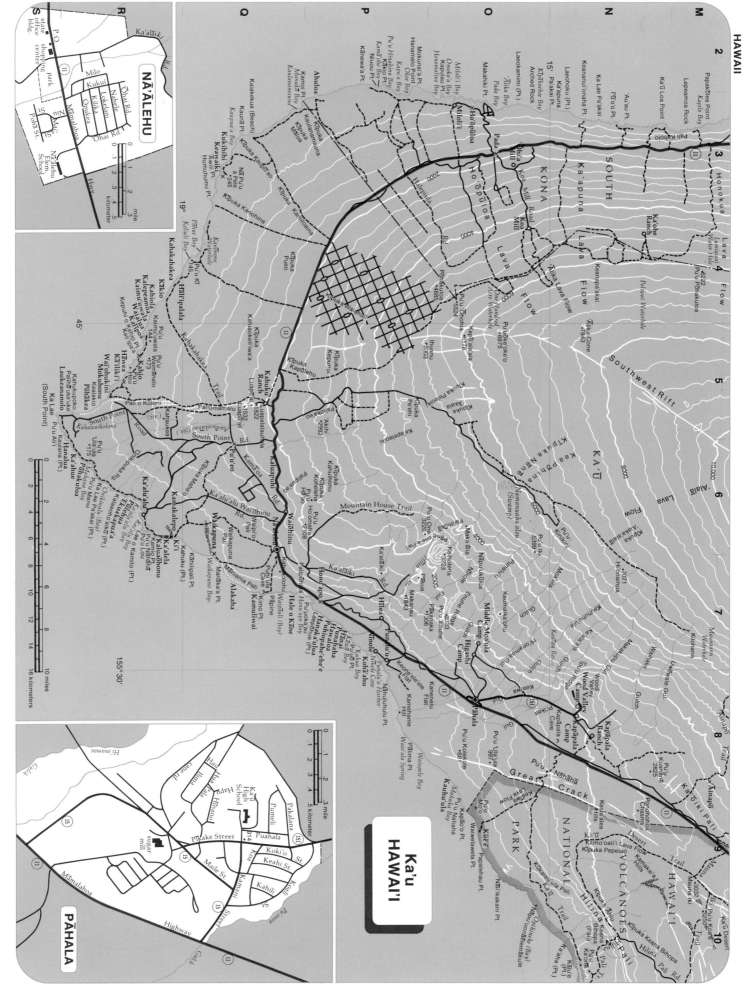

NĀ'ALEHU

State office bldg.
P.O.
S
Shopping center
Park
Milo
Kukui
Nahele
Kalika
'Ōhai Rd.
Lokelani
Opukea
Māmalahoa Hwy
Niu St.
Amy's
Poha St.
Ohai Rd.
Nā'alehu Elem. School

0 1 2 3 mile
0 1 2 3 4 5 kilometer

PĀHALA

Hi'onamoa Gulch
Haao Pali Pl.
Halua Pali
Hāhano
Pakalana St.
Kahi High School
Hapuu
Pumeli
Puahala
Pinake Street
914
Koki'o St.
sugar mill
Maile St.
Keahi St.
Koa
Kamani
Kahili
Pāhala
Keaiwa Street
Māmalahoa Highway

0 1 2 3 4 5 kilometer
0 1 2 3 mile

Ka'u
HAWAI'I

155°30'
19°
45'
15°

0 2 4 6 8 10 mile
0 2 4 6 8 10 12 14 16 kilometers

0 2 4 6 8 10 mile
0 2 4 6 8 10 12 14 16 kilometers

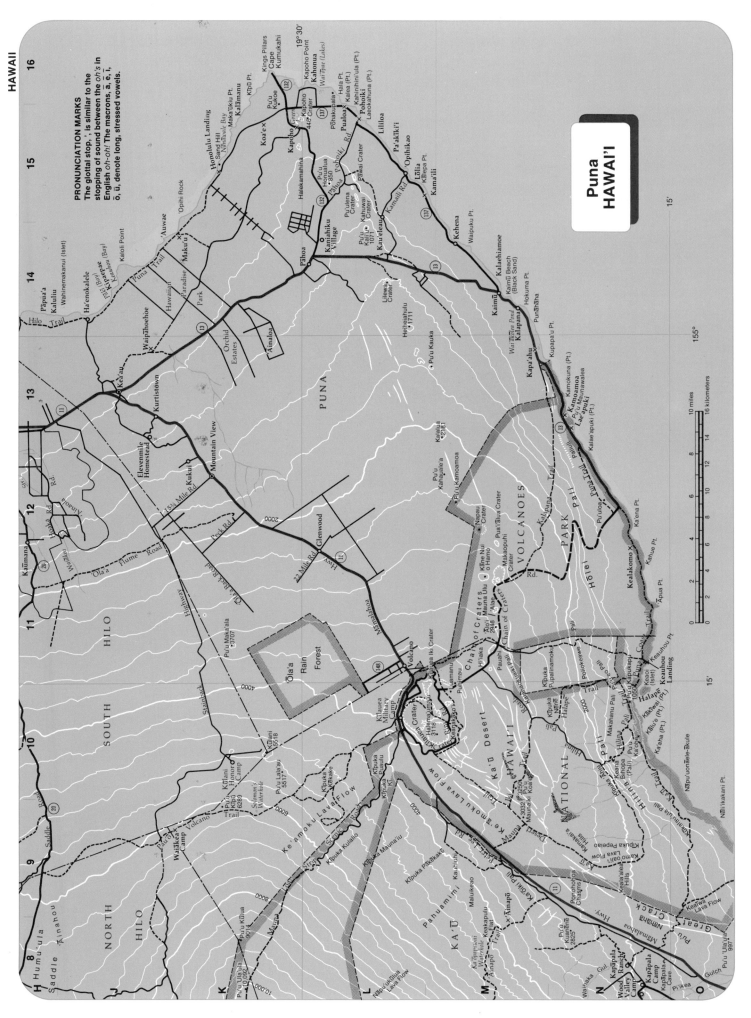

Puna
HAWAI'I

21

PRONUNCIATION MARKS
The glottal stop, ', is similar to the stopping of sound between the oh's in English oh-oh! The macrons, ā, ē, ī, ō, ū, denote long, stressed vowels.

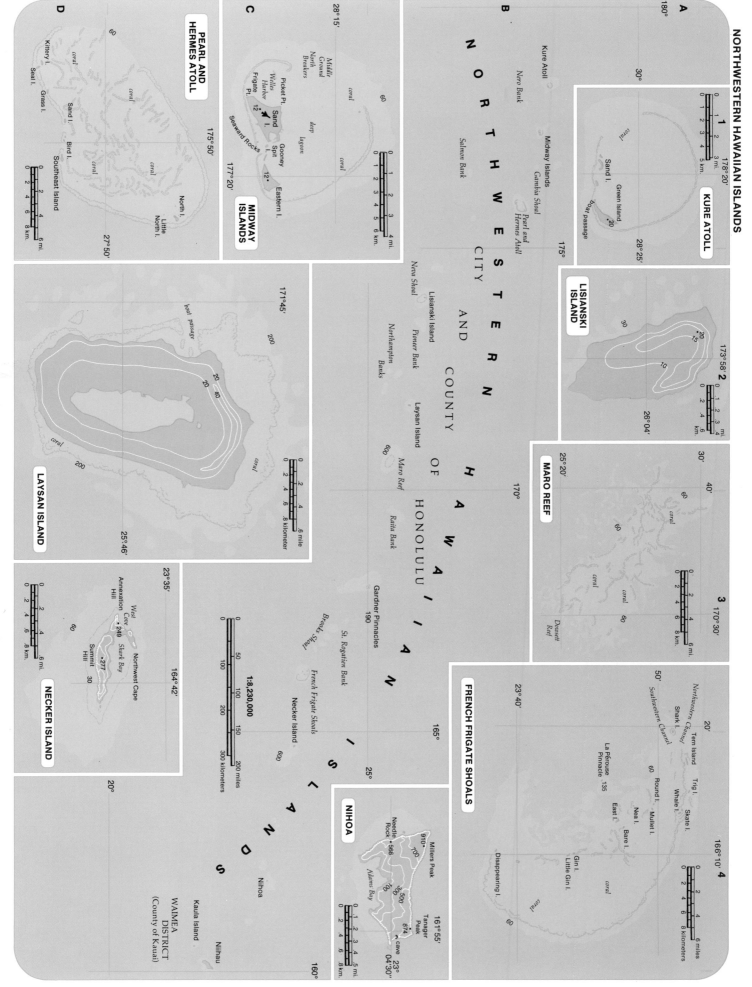

KURE ATOLL

28°25'

178°20'

0 1 2 3 mi.
0 1 2 3 4 5 km.

Kure Atoll

Nero Bank

Green Island
20
boat passage
Sand I.

reef

1

LISIANSKI ISLAND

173°58' 2

26°04'

0 1 2 3 4 mi.
0 1 2 3 4 km.

20
15
30
10

MARO REEF

25°20'

30'

40'

170°30' 3

0 2 4 6 8 mi.
0 2 4 6 8 km.

60
coral
60
coral
coral
Drossett Reef

FRENCH FRIGATE SHOALS

23°40'

50'

20'

166°10' 4

0 2 4 6 mi.
0 2 4 6 8 kilometers

Northwestern Channel
Shark I.
Tern Island
Trig I.
Skate I.
Southwestern Channel
La Pérouse Pinnacle 135
Round I.
Whale I.
Mullet I.
Nea I.
East I.
Bare I.
Disappearing I.
Gin I.
Little Gin I.
coral
60
04'30"
23°

NIHOA

161°55'

23°04'30"

0 1 2 3 4 5 mi.
0 2 4 6 8 km.

Needle Rock
910
Miller Peak
910
700
Tanager Peak
874
cave
566
500
300
Adams Bay

Nihoa

NORTHWESTERN HAWAIIAN ISLANDS

C I T Y   A N D   C O U N T Y   O F   H O N O L U L U

N O R T H W E S T E R N   H A W A I I A N   I S L A N D S

Kure Atoll
Nero Bank
Midway Islands
Gambia Shoal
Salmon Bank
Pearl and Hermes Atoll
Neva Shoal
Lisianski Island
Pioneer Bank
Northampton Banks
Laysan Island
Maro Reef
Raita Bank
600
Gardner Pinnacles
190
Brooks Shoal
St. Rogatien Bank
French Frigate Shoals
Necker Island
600
Nihoa

Kaula Island
Niihau
WAIMEA DISTRICT (County of Kauai)

175°
170°
165°
160°

30°
25°
20°

1:8,230,000

0 50 100 150 200 300 kilometers
0 100 150 200 miles

MIDWAY ISLANDS

28°15'

177°20'

175°50'

0 1 2 3 4 mi.
0 1 2 3 4 5 6 km.

Middle Ground
North Breakers
Picket Pt.
Willis Harbor
Frigate Pt.
12'
Gooney Spit
Sand I.
Eastern I.
12'
Seaward Rocks
deep lagoon
coral
coral
coral
60

PEARL AND HERMES ATOLL

60

0 2 4 6 8 mi.
0 2 4 6 8 km.

Kittery I.
Seal I.
Grass I.
Sand I.
Bird I.
Southeast Island
North I.
Little North I.
coral
coral
coral
coral
deep
60

27°50'

LAYSAN ISLAND

171°45'

25°46'

0 2 4 6 8 mile
0 2 4 6 8 kilometer

boat passage
200
20
40
20
200
200
coral
coral

NECKER ISLAND

23°35'

164°42'

20'

0 2 4 6 8 mi.
0 2 4 6 8 km.

West Cove
Annexation Hill
249
Northwest Cape
Shark Bay
277
Summit Hill
30
60

THE NATURAL ENVIRONMENT

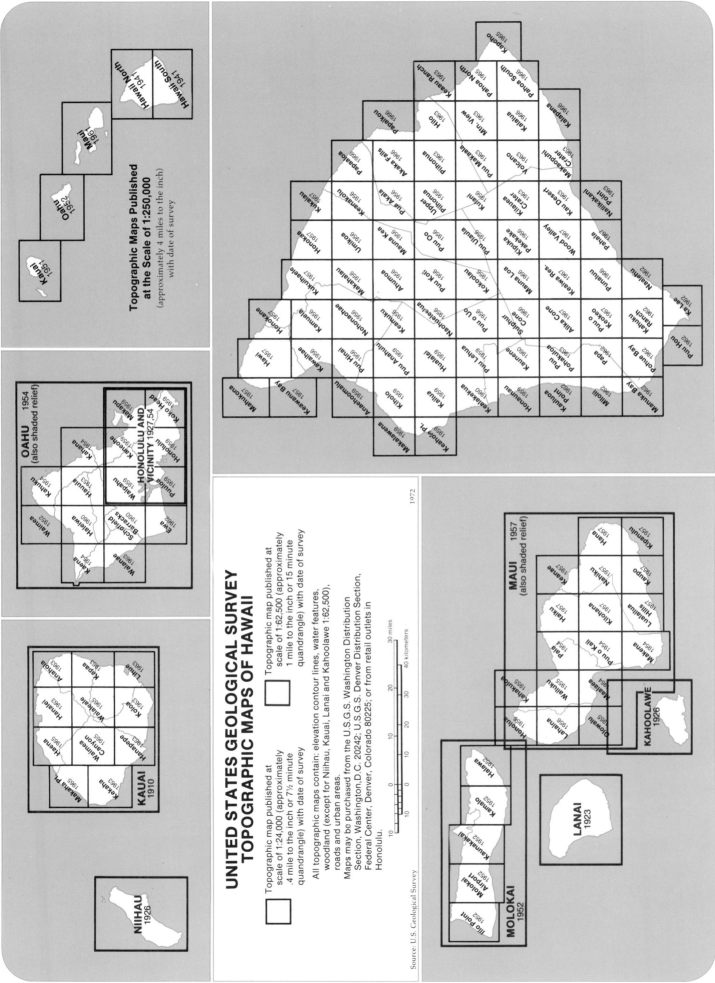

UNITED STATES GEOLOGICAL SURVEY
TOPOGRAPHIC MAPS OF HAWAII

Topographic map published at scale of 1:24,000 (approximately .4 mile to the inch or 7½ minute quandrangle) with date of survey

Topographic map published at scale of 1:62,500 (approximately 1 mile to the inch or 15 minute quandrangle) with date of survey

All topographic maps contain: elevation contour lines, water features, woodland (except for Niihau, Kauai, Lanai and Kahoolawe 1:62,500), roads and urban areas.

Maps may be purchased from the U.S.G.S. Washington Distribution Section, Washington, D.C. 20242; U.S.G.S. Denver Distribution Section, Federal Center, Denver, Colorado 80225; or from retail outlets in Honolulu.

Topographic Maps Published at the Scale of 1:250,000
(approximately 4 miles to the inch) with date of survey

Source: U.S. Geological Survey

1972

0   5   10   20   30 miles
0   10   20   30   40 kilometers

NIIHAU 1926

KAUAI 1910

Haena 1963 | Anahola 1963 | Kapaa 1963
Hanalei 1963 | Waialeale 1963 | Lihue 1963
Haena 1965 | Waimea Canyon 1965 | Koloa 1963 | Hanapepe 1963
Makaha Pt. 1965 | Kekaha 1963

OAHU 1954 (also shaded relief)

Waimea 1952 | Haleiwa 1960 | Kahuku 1953
 | Schofield Barracks 1960 | Hauula 1953 | Kaneohe 1959 | Kahana 1959
Ewa 1962 | Waipahu 1959 | Honolulu 1959 | Koko Head 1959 | Makapuu 1959
Kaena 1954 | Waianae 1959 | Puuloa 1959
HONOLULU AND VICINITY 1927,54

MAUI 1957 (also shaded relief)

Hana 1957 | Kipahulu 1957
Keanae 1957 | Nahiku 1957 | Kaupo 1957
Haiku 1957 | Kilohana 1957 | Lualailua Hills 1957
Paia 1954 | Puu o Kali 1954 | Makena 1954
Kahului 1955 | Wailuku 1955 | Makena 1954
Honolua 1956 | Lahaina 1956 | Olowalu 1955

KAHOOLAWE 1926

LANAI 1923

MOLOKAI 1952

Halawa 1952
Kamalo 1952
Kaunakakai 1952
Molokai Airport 1952
Ilio Point 1952

HAWAII
Kapoho 1965
Keaau Ranch 1963 | Pahoa North 1965 | Pahoa South 1965
Papaikou 1965 | Hilo 1963 | Mtn. View 1963 | Kalalua 1965 | Kalapana 1965
Papaaloa 1965 | Akaka Falls 1965 | Piihonua 1965 | Puu Makaala 1963 | Puu Honuaula 1963 | Makapuhi Crater 1963
Kukuihaele 1957 | Keanakolu 1956 | Pua Akala 1956 | Kilauea Crater 1963 | Kau Desert 1963 | Naliikakani Point 1963
Honokaa 1957 | Umikoa 1956 | Mauna Kea 1956 | Puu Oo 1956 | Puu Ulaula 1956 | Kipuka Pakekake 1965 | Wood Valley 1957 | Pahala 1957
Hawi 1957 | Kawaihae 1957 | Puu Hinai 1957 | Makahalau 1956 | Ahumoa 1956 | Puu Koli 1956 | Kokoolau 1956 | Mauna Loa 1965 | Keaiwa Res. 1957 | Punaluu 1965 | Naalehu 1952
Mahukona 1957 | Keawewai 1957 | Honokane 1957 | Kamuela 1957 | Nohonaohae 1956 | Keamuku 1956 | Naohueleelua 1956 | Puu o Uu 1956 | Sulphur Cone 1957 | Alika Cone 1967 | Puu o Keokeo 1967 | Kahuku Ranch 1952 | Ka Lae 1952
 | Kawaihae 1957 | Puu Hualalai 1959 | Hualalai 1959 | Puu Lehua 1959 | Kaumana 1959 | Pohue Bay 1952 | Puu Hou 1952
 | Keahole Pt. 1959 | Keauhou 1959 | Anaehoomalu 1959 | Kiholo 1959 | Kailua 1959 | Kealakekua 1960 | Honaunau 1959 | Kauulu 1959 | Papa 1959 | Pohakuloa 1963 |
Mahukona 1957 | Keawanui Bay 1957 | Makaiwa Bay 1962 | Milolii 1962 | Manuka Bay 1962 | Makaiwa 1959

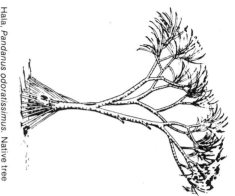

Hala, *Pandanus odoratissimus*. Native tree whose leaves were used by the early Hawaiians for making mats, baskets, and house thatch.

Bishop Museum drawing from Neal (1965:52)

GEODESY

In 1846, during the reign of Kamehameha III, was begun the division of lands which came to be known as the Great Mahele. Part of the division required the survey of small parcels of land (*kuleana*) for distribution and grant of title to former tenants of the king and chiefs. These land parcels were usually irregular in shape, following natural features such as gulches, streams, ridges, and, in the case of the smaller parcels, actual occupancy. It soon became apparent that an accurate and coordinated land survey was needed to replace the many individual surveys being performed. In 1870 the Hawaiian Government Survey was formed under the direction of W.D. Alexander, president of Oahu College.

The first survey of the islands began in 1871 with measurement of a 4-mile baseline on the island of Maui. During 1871 and 1872, triangulation was extended from this baseline over central Maui. Surveying began on Oahu in 1872 with the measurement of a second baseline. By 1900 triangulation of all the islands was substantially complete.

When the Territory of Hawaii was organized in 1900, the islands came under the charting jurisdiction of the U.S. Coast and Geodetic Survey. Hydrographic surveys of the more important harbors and roadsteads were begun, followed by work in the deeper interisland and offshore waters. The earlier surveys were revised and additions were made to the previous triangulation. In 1928, after numerous unsuccessful attempts dating from 1910, a successful connection was made between the triangulation schemes of Oahu and Kauai. Improved signal lamps and favorable weather conditions were important factors in the successful effort.

Under the Hawaiian Government Survey there were six different standards of latitude and four of longitude. The hydrographic adjusted latitude was later calculated from the six original standards and 13 additional latitude determinations of various points in the islands. In 1927 it was decided that a single datum for all the islands was necessary, since two or more islands were sometimes shown on the same nautical chart. The Old Hawaiian

Datum was initially defined in terms of the coordinates of the Oahu baseline using the hydrographic adjusted latitude and the Tupman longitude, one of the four longitudes of the earlier surveys. The Clarke Spheroid of 1866 was adopted as the reference spheroid. Later it was decided to hold fixed the position of station Diamond Head (Leahi) since this was a base station for the connection of the triangulations of Oahu and Molokai, and this necessitated some minor adjustments to the coordinates of the Oahu baseline. The Old Hawaiian Datum is defined in terms of the coordinates of station Oahu west base, which are:

Latitude   21°18'13.89" North
Longitude   157°50'55.79" West
Azimuth to station Oahu east base   291°29'36.0"

At the time of the Hawaiian Government Survey uniform standards of accuracy had not been adopted, and so the accuracy of these older surveys cannot be determined. By today's standards, however, they were almost certainly less than third order.

Modern equipment and improved procedures have greatly increased the accuracy of the Hawaiian survey. The latest horizontal control survey of Oahu, completed during 1969 by the U.S. Coast and Geodetic Survey and the State of Hawaii, consists of first order triangulation and second order traverse. On the accompanying map, the locations of first, second, and third order stations are shown for the principal islands. First order work is of the highest accuracy and precision and normally forms the basic network for national mapping surveys. Second order work is somewhat less precise and accurate. Third order work is the lowest that is suitable for use in topographic mapping. Triangulation diagrams of the principal islands, including the interisland connections, are on file at the Honolulu district office of the National Ocean Survey (formerly U.S. Coast and Geodetic Survey). Also available are geographic positions, plane coordinates, station descriptions of the points utilized in the surveys, and vertical control data.

The geodetic survey forms the basis for other surveys of land subdivisions, boundary demarcations, and calculations of area. The topographic mapping of the U.S. Geological Survey and other civilian and military agencies depends on the geodetic survey for initial horizontal and vertical control. Navigation by sea and air, aerial photogrammetry, astronomy, space travel, and many other activities depend on accurate geodesy of the islands.

J. R. M.

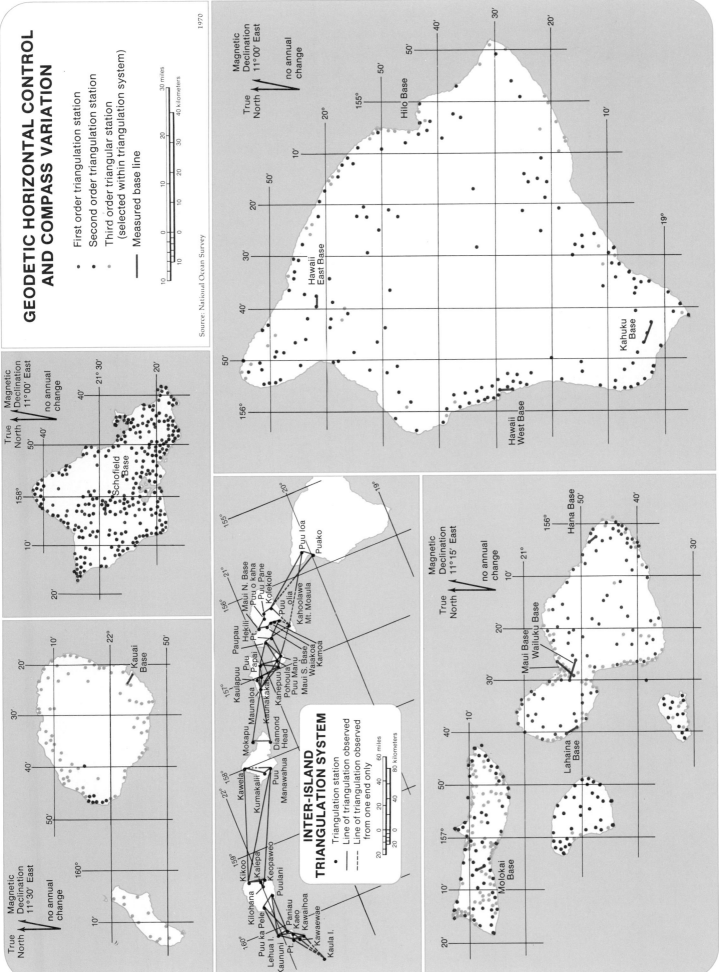

GEODETIC HORIZONTAL CONTROL
AND COMPASS VARIATION

- First order triangulation station
- Second order triangulation station
- Third order triangular station
  (selected within triangulation system)
— Measured base line

1970

Source: National Ocean Survey

INTER-ISLAND
TRIANGULATION SYSTEM

- Triangulation station
— Line of triangulation observed
--- Line of triangulation observed
   from one end only

27

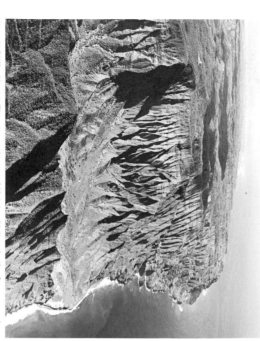

Napali Cliffs, Kauai. The steep slopes of Kalalau Valley, in the foreground, display spectacular erosional effects of running water which has incised the prominent vertical grooves in the face of the palis. Wave erosion is biting deep into the volcanic shield to form the majestic Napali coastline.

Hawaii Institute of Geophysics photograph by A. T. Abbott

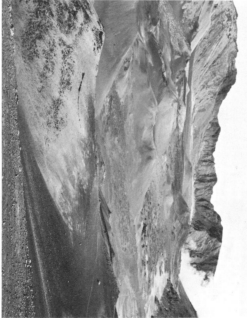

The Mana plain, Kauai. The arid Mana plain, formed by marine erosion at higher stands of the sea and covered by alluvium and sedimentary debris, clings to the southwest corner of Kauai. A former sea cliff cut into the Kauai volcanic shield rises sharply above the plain.

Hawaii Institute of Geophysics photographs by A. T. Abbott,

Haleakala Crater, Maui. Seven miles across to the opposite wall, two miles wide, and one-half mile deep, Haleakala Crater, at an elevation of nearly 10,000 feet, is an erosional depression that was partly filled by lava and cinders extruded during a period of renewed volcanic activity. The highest cinder cone rises about 800 feet above its base.

Hawaii Institute of Geophysics photographs by A. T. Abbott

Kahoolawe Island. Smallest of the eight main Hawaiian Islands, Kahoolawe displays vertical sea cliffs on its southern side. The island is waterless, parched, windswept, dusty, desolate, deserted. It serves as a bombing target for the U.S. Navy. In the distance the shield shape of West Maui volcano shows beneath the clouds.

Hawaii Institute of Geophysics photograph by A. T. Abbott

Lehua Island and Niihau. Lehua Island, in the foreground, is a breached tuff cone which was built during a late stage of volcanic activity. Behind it, on Niihau, the dry Kiekie volcanic plain belongs to the same period, whereas the Paniau upland, in the background, is an erosional remnant of the much older Niihau shield volcano.

Hawaii Institute of Geophysics photograph by A. T. Abbott

leie, *Freycinetia arborea.* Native tree whose leaves were used by the early Hawaiians for mat and basket weaving.

Bishop Museum drawing from Neal (1965:52)

LANDFORMS

The major relief features in Hawaii are the result of building by volcanoes (page 36). Even the lowest of the islands, Niihau, is a volcanic mountain rising more than 13,000 feet above its base on the ocean floor. The tops of the highest mountains, Mauna Kea and Mauna Loa, on the island of Hawaii, are about 6 miles above the bottom of the Hawaiian Deep, just to the northeast (page 49).

Relief features of intermediate size are partly constructional, and partly the result of erosion. Cinder cones and tuff cones, built by moderately explosive volcanic eruptions, reach heights of several hundred feet above their surroundings. For instance, Puu Makanaka, on Mauna Kea, is a cinder cone about 600 feet high; and Diamond Head, in Honolulu, is a tuff cone nearly 800 feet high above its base, which lies a little below sea level.

Valleys formed by stream erosion range in depth from a few feet to more than 2,000 feet. The upper part of Waimea Canyon, on Kauai, is as much as 2,600 feet deep. Waterfalls along the streams commonly are several hundred feet high. Hiilawe Falls, in Waipio Valley on Hawaii Island, with a vertical drop of about 1,000 feet, is one of the highest free falls in the world.

Sea cliffs, cut by waves, range in height from a few to several thousand feet. The cliffs of the Napali Coast, on Kauai, are 300 to 2,000 feet high; and the sea cliff on the north side of East Molokai, one of the highest in the world, is 2,000 to 3,600 feet high.

On the island of Hawaii the Kahuku Pali is a fault scarp (cliff) as much as 600 feet high; and the Hilina Pali is a series of fault scarps, mostly veneered with later lava flows, that rise more than 2,000 feet above the adjacent ocean. Kilauea Crater (a caldera) is bounded on its west side by a fault scarp 400 feet high; and Mokuaweoweo Caldera, on Mauna Loa, has a boundary scarp 600 feet high, also on its west side.

Landforms in Hawaii are the result of construction by volcanoes, living organisms, and sedimentary processes, and of destruction by erosion.

The major constructional landform is the typical, broadly rounded shield volcano built by innumerable thin lava flows. Commonly it has at its summit a large crater (caldera) formed by

collapse of the mountaintop. Similar smaller craters (pit craters) may form on its flanks. Smaller volcanic constructional forms are spatter cones and ramparts, seldom as much as 50 feet high, built where fluid lava erupts at the surface; larger cinder cones, often several hundred feet high, built by more explosive eruptions; and steep-sided hills (domes) formed by viscous lava piling up over the vent. Cinder cones are well seen on Mauna Kea and Haleakala; domes, on West Maui.

Stream erosion first cuts small V-shaped gulches, and eventually great canyons, into the volcanoes. The most characteristic stream-eroded landform is the amphitheater-headed valley, with its steep walls and rounded head. Examples are Manoa Valley on Oahu, Halawa on Molokai, Manawainui on Maui, and Waipio on Hawaii. As adjacent valleys grow larger, their steep walls meet in knife ridges, and sharp-pointed peaks such as Olomana, on Oahu, are formed. Triangular segments of the original shield surface (planezes) may be left between the lower ends of the valleys. The Pali, on windward Oahu, has been formed largely by coalescence of a series of amphitheater-headed valleys. Wave erosion cuts back the edges of the islands and forms sea cliffs (page 28). Waves also erode sea caves and arches, and where the roof of the cave is perforated a spouting horn ("blowhole") may result.

Corals and algae build fringing reefs, and where sea level has later dropped in relation to the land the reef surface may form a plain. Deposition of detrital material by streams forms flat alluvial floors in valleys; and the gravel, sand, and silt may be dropped where mountain streams emerge onto flatter land, building alluvial fans, or be spread over the marginal reef plains, or deposited along the shore to form beaches. Locally, the wind has built sand dunes, especially where beach sand has been blown inland.

G. A. M.

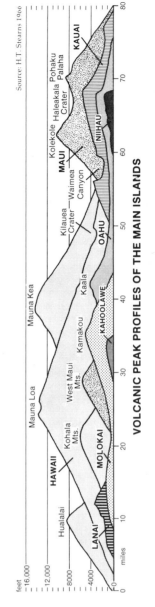

VOLCANIC PEAK PROFILES OF THE MAIN ISLANDS

Source: H.T. Stearns 1966

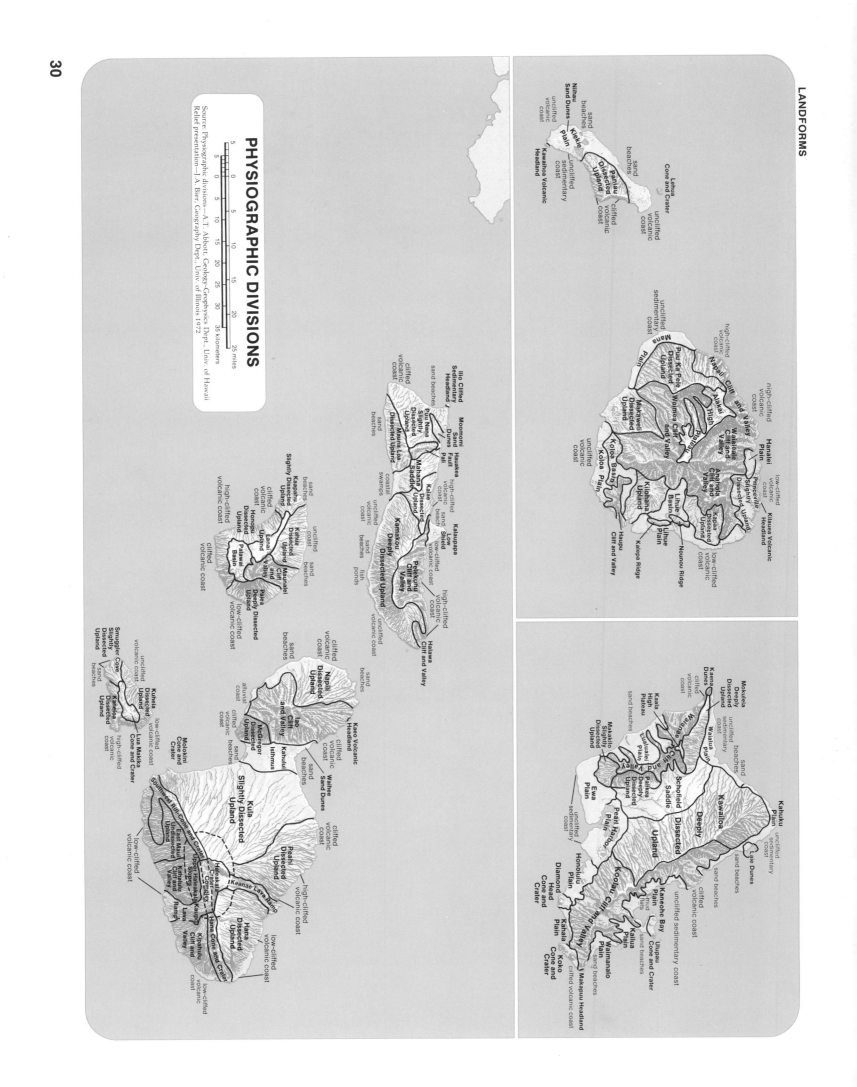

PHYSIOGRAPHIC DIVISIONS

5   0   5   10   15   20   25   30   35 kilometers
5   0   5   10   15   20   25 miles

Source: Physiographic divisions—A.T. Abbott, Geology-Geophysics Dept., Univ. of Hawaii
Relief presentation—J.A. Bier, Geography Dept., Univ. of Illinois 1972

Physiographic Types

Caldera complex. Area having features associated with calderas including craters, cones, bounding faults, fissures, slump blocks, talus heaps, caldera-filling lavas.

Cliff and valley. Area showing little evidence of former slope; with high, nearly vertical cliffs and amphitheater-headed valleys; some valley floors may be gently sloping.

Uncliffed coast. Coastline with little or no cliff along the shoreline.

Low cliffed coast. Coastline with wave-cut cliff—average height about 20 feet.

Cliffed coast. A more mature cliffed coastline—average height about 100 feet.

High cliffed coast. Coast with extreme cliff development up to 2,000 feet in height.

Cone and crater. Volcanic cones and craters of diverse origins, common along volcanic rift zones.

Fault palis. Cliffs resulting from displacement along faults.

Headland. A particularly prominent coastal cliff or promontory.

Isthmus. A low land link between islands.

Lava ramp. A distinctive linear incline formed by lava flows.

Plain. A large area of low relief.

Saddle. Subdued divide between two volcanoes formed where lavas meet or impinge.

Sand dunes. Dunes of loose and/or lithified, wind-blown sand.

Sandy beach. Strips of sand of varying widths at the water's edge.

Undissected upland. Slopes with little or no established surface drainage.

Slightly dissected upland. Slopes cut by widely spaced erosional gullies.

Dissected upland. Slopes cut by numerous major valleys; master drainage patterns established.

Deeply dissected upland. Slopes incised by large, deep valleys; some ridge crests may reflect former slope. Transitional toward the cliff-and-valley type.

Upper slope. A zone above the uplands found only on the highest volcanic shields; characterized by little or no vegetation, late lavas, and barren, rocky terrain.

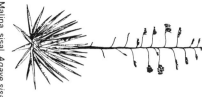

Maiina, sisal, *Agave sisalana*. Introduced as a crop plant and used to make modern hula skirts.

Bishop Museum drawing from Neal (1965:225)

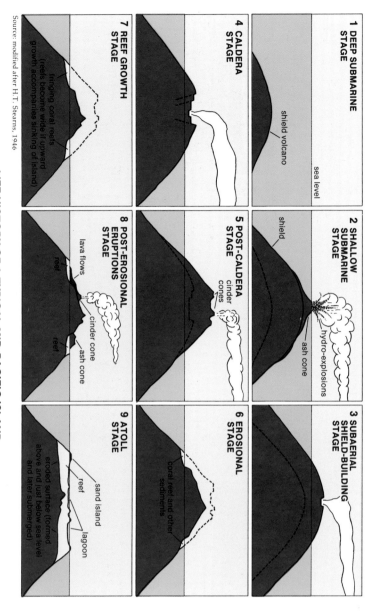

1 DEEP SUBMARINE STAGE
shield volcano
sea level

2 SHALLOW SUBMARINE STAGE
shield
hydro-explosions
ash cone

3 SUBAERIAL SHIELD-BUILDING STAGE

4 CALDERA STAGE

5 POST-CALDERA STAGE
cinder cones
ash cone

6 EROSIONAL STAGE
coral reef and other sediments

7 REEF GROWTH STAGE
fringing coral reefs (reefs become wide if upward growth accompanies sinking of island)

8 POST-EROSIONAL ERUPTIONS STAGE
lava flows
reef
cinder cone
reef
ash cone

9 ATOLL STAGE
sand island
reef
lagoon
eroded surface (formed above and just below sea level and later submerged)

Source: modified after H.T. Stearns, 1946

LIFE HISTORY OF A TYPICAL MID-PACIFIC ISLAND

GEOLOGY

The Hawaiian Islands are almost wholly volcanic. Sedimentary rocks form only a narrow fringe around the edges. The vast majority of the volcanic rocks are *lava flows*, formed by outpouring of liquid *magma*. Only a few percent are *pyroclastic rocks*, formed of fragments thrown out by volcanic explosions.

The volcanoes were built along a line, probably a series of cracks, extending in a northwest-southeast direction across the ocean floor. Starting at the northwest end, at Kure Island, about 25 million years ago, the centers of eruption gradually shifted, until today only the volcanoes at the southeastern end

of the chain are still active. The shifting of the eruptive centers may have resulted from a slow northwestward movement of the earth's upper layer across a point of magma generation in the region beneath, at or near the present island of Hawaii.

The general history of formation of the islands is illustrated by the accompanying figure. Quiet eruptions of very fluid lava on the sea floor gradually built up a broad turtle-backed mountain called a *shield volcano*. As the mountaintop neared the surface, some steam explosions occurred, but as it built above sea level quiet eruptions resumed. Eventually, toward the end of growth of the shield, the top of the volcano sank in to form a big crater called a *caldera*. Continued eruptions gradually filled the caldera.

Then, late in the volcano's history, the frequency of eruption decreased, the composition of the magma changed, and its gas content increased. The lavas became more viscous, the flows were shorter and thicker, and more-explosive eruptions formed larger amounts of pyroclastic rocks. A steep-sided, bumpy cap was built on top of the shield.

As the late-stage eruptions gradually died out, erosion was able to take ever greater bites out of the volcanic mountain. Waves cut high sea cliffs, and streams cut deep valleys, gradually transforming the rounded shield volcano into a jagged range of mountains, such as the Koolau Range on Oahu. The gravel, sand, and clay formed by weathering and erosion were washed down, some into the neighboring ocean, but some deposited on the floors of the valleys and in shallow water around the edge of the island. At the same time colonial corals and algae started to build fringing reefs around the island.

Meanwhile sea level repeatedly rose and fell, at least in part because of changes in the volume of ice on the continents during the glacial period. Glaciation also affected Hawaii more directly, a series of small glaciers occupying the summit of Mauna Kea. At times sea level was as much as 300 feet lower, and at others up to 250 feet higher, than now. During a stand 25 feet above present level, a broad coral reef was built along the south side of Oahu, forming the present Honolulu and Ewa plains. During later and lower sea levels, streams cut valleys into the reef, and as sea level rose again the mouths of the valleys were flooded to form Pearl Harbor.

Finally, after a long period of quiet, volcanic activity resumed, sending lava flows down the valleys and building cones such as Diamond Head and Tantalus. On Haleakala eruptions partly refilled a great cavity carved by streams into the heart of the volcano and formed the present floor of Haleakala Crater.

The Pali, Oahu. The Pali is a continuous line of sheer cliffs resulting from the headward erosion and coalescence of westward migrating valley heads which have reached a common extent at about the same time. The V-shaped gaps of Nuuanu Valley on the left and Kalihi Valley on the right were cut by large streams flowing westward from the former Koolau summit area, which has since been destroyed by erosion.

Hawaii Institute of Geophysics photograph by A.T. Abbott

Maunalei Valley, Lanai. Hidden from casual view, Maunalei Valley slices deep into the east side of Lanai. The steep, deeply grooved slopes and amphitheater head typify Hawaiian valley development. A freshwater well and pump house are located on the floor of the valley.

Hawaii Institute of Geophysics photograph by A.T. Abbott

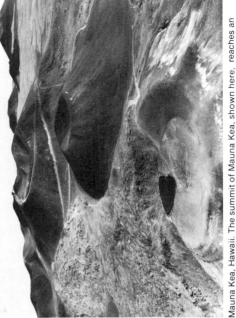

Mauna Kea, Hawaii. The summit of Mauna Kea, shown here, reaches an elevation of 13,796 feet above sea level. Numerous andesitic cinder cones characterize the summit area, which is often snow covered for several months in winter. Lake Waiau, in the foreground, is about 100 yards in diameter and is the highest lake in the United States, with an altitude of 13,020 feet. The astronomical observatory occupies the top of the Summit Cone.

Hawaii Institute of Geophysics photograph by A.T. Abbott

Mauna Kea, Hawaii. The summit of Mauna Kea is surrounded by a light-colored ridge of glacial moraine. In the foreground is the head of Pohakuloa Gulch, on the south side of the mountain.

Hawaii Institute of Geophysics photograph by A.T. Abbott

Waipio Valley, Hawaii, is a great flat-floored chasm cut into the upland of the Kohala shield volcano. Hiilawe Falls cascades a thousand feet over the lip of the precipitous stubby tributary on the left. Note the greater amount of erosional dissection on older Kohala lavas to the right of Waipio Valley as compared with that on the younger Mauna Kea flows to the left.

Hawaii Institute of Geophysics photograph by A.T. Abbott

34

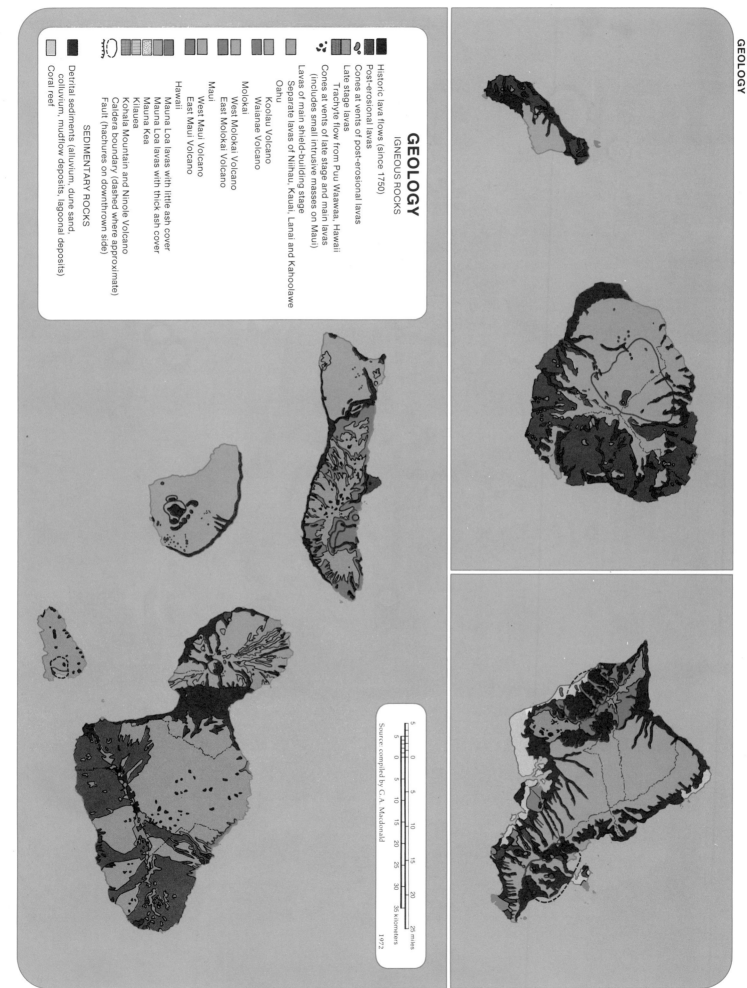

GEOLOGY
IGNEOUS ROCKS

Historic lava flows (since 1750)
Post-erosional lavas
Cones at vents of post-erosional lavas
Late stage lavas
Cones at vents of late stage and main lavas
Trachyte flow from Puu Waawaa, Hawaii
(includes small intrusive masses on Maui)
Separate lavas of Niihau, Kauai, Lanai and Kahoolawe
Lavas of main shield-building stage

Oahu
    Koolau Volcano
    Waianae Volcano

Molokai
    West Molokai Volcano
    East Molokai Volcano

Maui
    West Maui Volcano
    East Maui Volcano

Hawaii
    Mauna Loa lavas with little ash cover
    Mauna Loa lavas with thick ash cover
    Mauna Kea
    Kilauea
    Kohala Mountain and Ninole Volcano
    Caldera boundary (dashed where approximate)
    Fault (hachures on downthrown side)

SEDIMENTARY ROCKS

Detrital sediments (alluvium, dune sand,
    colluvium, mudflow deposits, lagoonal deposits)
Coral reef

Source: compiled by G.A. Macdonald   1972

5
5
0
5   5
10   10
15
20   15
25
30   20
35 kilometers   25 miles

The rocks of the main shield-building stage are **tholeiitic basalts,** rich in magnesium and iron and poor in alkalies (sodium and potassium). Many of them contain visible crystals of green glassy olivine. The matrix is fine grained and stony in appearance. White crystals of feldspar occasionally are visible, but black crystals of pyroxene are rare. Some rocks **(oceanites)** contain as much as 50 percent olivine. Many of the rocks of the late stage also are basalts, but they contain more alkalies than the earlier rocks and are known as **alkalic basalts.** Olivine crystals commonly are visible, and often are accompanied by crystals of the black pyroxene, augite. Feldspar crystals may also be present. Large augite and olivine crystals make up more than half of some rocks **(ankaramites).** Along with the alkalic basalts are other rocks that contain less iron and magnesium and more alkalies. These rocks are **hawaiite** and **mugearite,** the latter being the richer in alkalies. Still richer in alkalies is the rock **trachyte.** On some volcanoes, such as Mauna Kea and Haleakala, the late-stage lavas consist very largely of alkalic basalt and hawaiite; on others, such as Kohala and West Maui, they are mugearite and trachyte. Those of Hualalai are all alkalic basalt except for the trachyte pumice cone of Puu Waawaa and the lava flow from it. The post-erosional lavas are partly alkalic basalt, richer in alkalies and somewhat poorer in silicon than those of the late stage, and partly other rocks still poorer in silicon and richer in alkalies, calcium and magnesium, in which the place of feldspar is taken in part or entirely by nepheline **(basanites** and **nephelinites).** The post-erosional lavas of Niihau, Kauai, and Oahu include alkalic basalts, basanites, and nephelinites; that of Kalaupapa Peninsula on Molokai is alkalic basalt; those of West Maui are basanites; and those of Haleakala (the Hana Volcanic Series) are largely alkalic basalts. Not shown on the map are small post-erosional flows of alkalic basalt in Kolekole Pass, Oahu, and at Kanapou Bay on Kahoolawe.

Volcanism

The main shield-building stage of Hawaiian volcanoes is characterized by gentle eruptions of very fluid lava containing little gas. At the vents fountains of liquid lava may reach heights of more than 1,500 feet, but there is little true explosion, and pyroclastic materials amount to less than one percent. Most of the magma forms thin lava flows that spread freely, often to distances of several miles.

The lava flows are of two types. *Pahoehoe* has a smooth surface that is often wrinkled by dragging of the still-plastic crust by movement of liquid lava beneath it. The flow quickly crusts over, and as it gradually freezes inward from the edges the moving liquid portion becomes narrower until only a stream a few yards across continues to flow through a sort of pipe with solidified walls. At the end of the eruption, part or all of the liquid may drain away, leaving a lava tube. Most lava tubes are only one to 3 feet across, but a few are as much as 50 feet.

As pahoehoe advances downhill, it commonly changes to *aa*, which has a rough surface of jagged fragments of clinker. Some flows start as aa. Usually aa flows are fed by open rivers, and at the end of the eruption the liquid in the river may drain away leaving a trench-like channel several feet deep and a few feet to 50 feet wide. Aa flows usually have layers of clinker at both top and bottom, and a center of massive lava. Both pahoehoe and aa contain many small holes (vesicles) formed by gas bubbles in the liquid lava.

Hawaiian lava flows are more voluminous than those of most other parts of the world. Areas and volumes of flows formed during a few recent eruptions are as follows:

DATE	VOLCANO	AREA OF FLOWS (square miles)	VOLUME OF FLOWS (cubic yards)
1790	Haleakala	2.2	35,000,000
1801	Hualalai	17.7	410,000,000
1840	Kilauea	6.6	281,000,000
1859	Mauna Loa	32.7	600,000,000+
1942	Mauna Loa	10.6	100,000,000
1950	Mauna Loa	35.0	600,000,000+
1955	Kilauea	6.1	120,000,000
1960	Kilauea	4.1	155,000,000

The lava of 1859 flowed more than 35 miles from its vent on Mauna Loa into the sea. Speeds of advance of lava flows may be greater than 5 miles an hour, but are usually between 10 and 1,000 feet an hour.

During historic times Mauna Loa has been active 6.2 percent of the time, erupting, on an average, once every 3.7 years, and has poured out more than 0.7 cubic mile of lava. Kilauea has been active 62 percent of the time, but most of the activity was confined to the inner crater, Halemaumau. Eruptions outside the caldera have occurred, on the average, once every 7.2 years, and have poured out about 0.2 cubic mile of lava. During most of the time from 1823 to 1924, a lake of molten lava existed in Halemaumau. In 1924 a splitting open of the mountain allowed the lava lake to drain away and water from the surrounding rocks to enter the hot lava conduits below the surface, resulting in one of the rare explosive eruptions of the volcano as the water was rapidly transformed into steam. Rock fragments weighing as much as 14 tons were thrown over a large part of the caldera floor.

The late-stage eruptions of Hawaiian volcanoes are more explosive than those of the shield-building stage, because the magma is more viscous and contains more gas. Instead of the small mounds and cones of spatter built around the vents in the earlier stage, late-stage eruptions build cinder cones, some of which are several hundred feet high and as much as a mile across. Most of the flows are of aa type, and are shorter and thicker than those of the earlier stage.

Where the rising magma encounters water the generation of steam brings about explosions which tear the liquid lava into tiny bits and throw them into the air, where they solidify to fragments mostly of sand size, known as *ash*. Most of the ash piles up around the vent to form a cone, and becomes cemented together to form the solid rock called *tuff*. This may happen during any stage, but it was particularly common during the post-erosional eruptions on Oahu. Punchbowl, Diamond Head, Koko Crater, Koko Head, Hanauma Bay, and Ulupau Head are tuff cones. Others are Kilauea Cone on Kauai, Lehua Island near Niihau, Molokini Island near Maui, and Kapoho Cone on Hawaii.

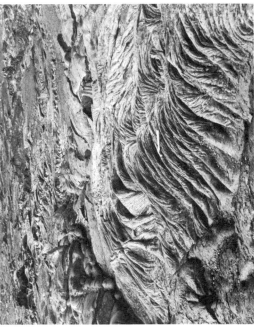

Lava fountain about 300 feet high, with a cinder cone at its base, on the east flank of Kilauea volcano during the eruption of 1955.

U.S. Geological Survey photograph by G.A. Macdonald

Some pahoehoe lava flows can be recognized by the twisted, ropy, billowy, or drapery-like patterns that develop on the crust during final moments of congealing of the fluid lava.

Photograph by C.K. Wentworth

Kilauea eruption. The floor of Halemaumau fire pit is the site of this eruption in November 1967. Small lava fountains in the center of the pit are putting forth a flood of fluid lava which glows through cracks in its cooling crust.

Hawaii Institute of Geophysics photograph by A.T. Abbott

Front of an aa lava flow, 10 to 15 feet high, advancing across cleared land on the east flank of Kilauea volcano. The flow was advancing about 1,000 feet per hour. Flames along the edge of the flow are from burning vegetation.

U.S. Geological Survey photograph by G.A. Macdonald

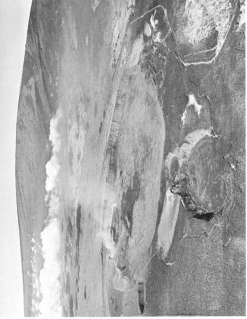

Mauna Loa and Kilauea, Hawaii. In the distance Mauna Loa, a classic example of a shield volcano, rises gently and majestically to an elevation of 13,677 feet. Kilauea's summit at 4,090 feet is marked by a large caldera within which lies Halemaumau Crater, known as the fire pit. On the near side of Kilauea caldera lies Kilauea Iki pit crater, the scene of a spectacular eruption in 1959 which formed a lava lake 365 feet in depth. The thickness of the crust on the lake (in mid-1972) is about 100 feet.

Hawaii Institute of Geophysics photograph by A.T. Abbott

A spatter cone in the Puna district forming during the 1955 eruption of Kilauea. Spatter is molten blobs of lava that congeal and weld themselves to the earlier ejecta thus building a steep-sided cone around the volcanic throat.

U.S. Geological Survey photograph by G.A. Macdonald

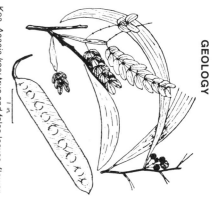

Koa, *Acacia Koa*; true and false leaves, flower heads, pods. Known as Hawaiian mahogany, koa wood is valued for furniture, ukuleles, and carvings.

Bishop Museum drawing from Neal (1965:410)

Earthquakes and Tsunamis

Volcanic eruptions on the island of Hawaii commonly are preceded and accompanied by thousands of earthquakes, but only a few of them are strong enough to be felt, and still fewer do any damage. The quakes result from shifting of segments of the volcano as the mountain swells before eruptions, due to inflation of a shallow magma reservoir beneath, or shrinks during the eruption as magma is drained away. In terms of origin, they are volcanic earthquakes.

Tectonic activity, in the sense of crustal deformation such as that which causes most earthquakes in continental regions, is nearly absent in Hawaii. The entire Hawaiian region is tilting around a fulcrum located approximately at the island of Oahu; Kauai is going up, and Hawaii Island going down at a rate of about one foot per century. The islands are partly surrounded by a trench that appears to be the result of sinking of the adjacent ocean floor, probably at least in part because of the load of the volcanoes resting on it. Minor basins have been formed by sagging of some caldera floors over shallow magma chambers, and some faults pass into monoclines, but no other folding is present.

Major earthquakes, here as elsewhere, are the result of faulting. Some of the faults are on, and probably genetically associated with, the volcanoes. Others are on the ocean floor near the islands. Since 1925, 10 earthquakes with magnitude greater than 5.3 have occurred in the Hawaiian region. Of these, six originated on Hawaii Island and four on faults on the ocean floor. In 1951 a magnitude 6.8 earthquake originated on the Kealakekua fault, just off the Kona Coast of Hawaii. The Maui earthquake of 1938 (magnitude 6.75) had its epicenter about 25 miles north of Pauwela Point on the north shore of Maui, probably on one of the strands of the Molokai fracture zone, a great system of sea-floor faults that trends nearly westward from Baja California to Hawaii.

The greatest Hawaiian earthquake of historic time occurred in April 1868. It was accompanied, and probably was caused, by movements on faults both on- and offshore near the south end of the island of Hawaii. The road near Waiohinu was broken and offset about 12 feet by one of the faults. It is reported that every European-style building in the Kau district was destroyed. The magnitude of the quake was probably around 8.0. In Wood Valley the shaking set off a great mud flow which buried about 500 animals and a village with 31 persons.

The offshore fault movements during the 1868 earthquake caused a huge water wave—a tsunami—which is reported to have come in over the tops of the coconut trees on the south shore of Hawaii. However, most tsunamis that affect the Hawaiian Islands come from sources in the zone of mountain building that borders the Pacific Ocean. Since 1820, eight tsunamis have caused moderate to severe damage on Hawaiian shores, but only the one of 1868 was of local origin. Five came from South America, one from Kamchatka, and one from the Aleutian Islands. Six others, including one of local origin, did a little damage. The Aleutian tsunami of 1946 drove water to heights as great as 55 feet above sea level at some places in Hawaii. At Hilo, where the water reached 32 feet above sea level, 83 lives were lost. The Chilean tsunami of 1960 created a bore in Hilo Bay which struck shore with a speed of 40 miles an hour, drove water to heights as great as 35 feet, and killed 61 persons.

G. A. M.

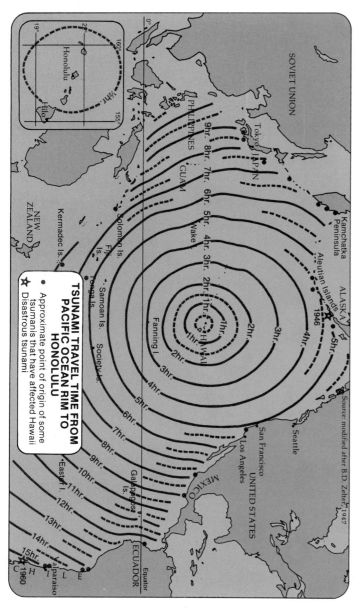

TSUNAMI TRAVEL TIME FROM PACIFIC OCEAN RIM TO HONOLULU

● Approximate point of origin of some tsunamis that have affected Hawaii
☆ Disastrous tsunami

Source modified after B.D. Zetler, 1947

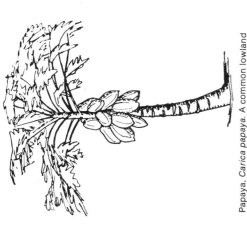

Papaya. *Carica papaya.* A common lowland fruit tree.
Bishop Museum drawing from Neal (1965:600)

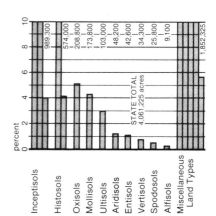

ACREAGE OF STATE SOIL ORDERS

percent	
Inceptisols	
Histosols	989,300
Oxisols	574,000
Mollisols	208,800
Ultisols	173,800
Aridisols	103,000
Entisols	48,200
Vertisols	42,600
Spodosols	34,300
Alfisols	25,800
	9,100
Miscellaneous Land Types	1,852,325
STATE TOTAL 4,061,225 acres	

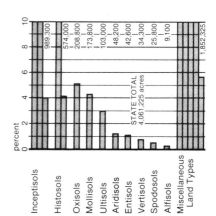

SOILS

Just as there are many different species of plants or animals, there are many different types of soil. Soils differ because of differences in (1) the length of time to which they have been exposed to weathering, (2) the materials from which they have been formed, (3) drainage conditions, (4) the kinds and number of plants and animals that live in and on them, and (5) temperature and rainfall conditions to which the soils are exposed.

It is not surprising then that the soils on the island of Kauai are different from those on the island of Hawaii, for the soils of Kauai have been exposed to weathering for a longer period of time. One would also expect soils that form from alluvium to be different from soils developed from lava rock, and that both would differ from soils developed from volcanic cinders. One need only to compare the soil on valley bottoms with those on adjacent ridge-tops to discover that differences in drainage can cause soil variations. Soils on the windward side of an island differ markedly from those found on the leeward side because climate and vegetation are not the same.

Soils are similar if the factors that contribute to their formation are similar. There are no two identical soils, just as there are no two identical human beings. However, soils are considered to be of the same type if all their measurable and visible properties are alike, that is, if they respond and behave alike. Thus two soils of the same classification, occurring in widely separated parts of the world, could be expected to behave in similar ways.

The soils of Hawaii have been classified and mapped twice in the last 25 years. Field work for the first survey was completed before World War II, but the report was not published until 1955 (Cline, 1955). In that report soils were classified according to the now obsolete Great Soil Group system. In 1960 the Soil Conservation Service of the United States Department of Agriculture published the 7th Approximation to a new comprehensive system of soil classification (Soil Conservation Service, 1960). Hawaii was the first state in the Union to complete a survey of its soil based on this system. The report appeared in two parts, one for the island of Hawaii (Sato et al., 1972), and the other for the remaining islands (Foote et al., 1972).

In this new system there are ten Orders of soils at the highest level of classification. Lower categories are the Suborder, Great Group, Subgroup, Family, and Series. Hawaii is the only state in which all ten Orders are found. There are 190 soil series in Hawaii. The classification of the Wahiawa series, the dominant soil of the Wahiawa-Schofield area of Oahu, is an example:

Series	Wahiawa
Family	clayey, kaolinitic, isohyperthermic
Subgroup	Tropeptic
Great Group	Eutrustox
Suborder	Ustox
Order	Oxisol

A person unacquainted with Hawaii's soil but familiar with the classification scheme would find in this summary a wealth of information about this particular soil. For example, he knows that Oxisols are oxide-rich soils normally found in the tropics. They are the soils which historically have been called lateritic soils or latosols. The designation at the Suborder level indicates that the Wahiawa soil occurs in an area with relatively low rainfall but where the rains coincide with the plant-growing season. The Great Group category provides additional information, which in this case points to the relatively high fertility of this soil. The Subgroup designation suggests that this soil has one or more features not unlike those of soils belonging to the Order Inceptisol. The most useful information from the point of view of management of the Wahiawa soil is found at the Family level. Here one finds information on size distribution of soil particles, the mineral make-up of the soil particles, and soil temperature. The soil series name corresponds to the locality where this soil was first identified.

The table provides details of the land area occupied by the different soil Orders in Hawaii. The two Orders that occur most extensively—the Histosols and Inceptisols, which together comprise almost 40 percent of the area of the State—are largely confined to the island of Hawaii. The remaining eight Orders occupy about 15 percent of the land area. Forty-six percent of Hawaii's land area is classified as "miscellaneous land types"—areas covered by lava or cinders, rough mountainous land, coral outcrops, beaches, and fill-land.

G. U.

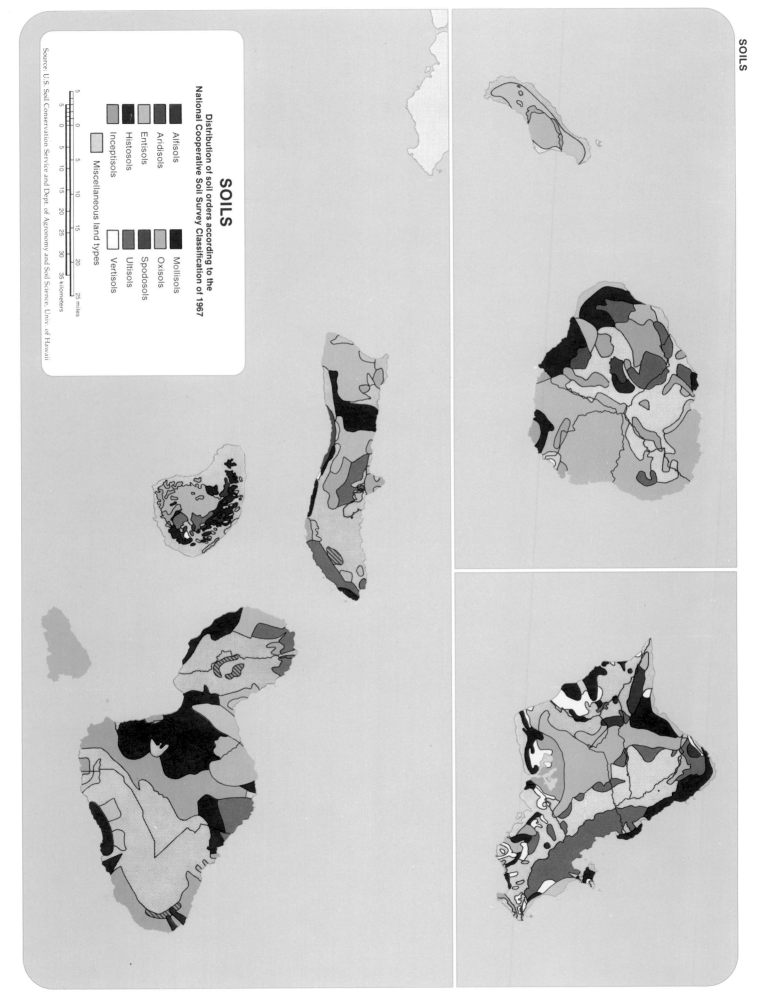

SOILS

Distribution of soil orders according to the
National Cooperative Soil Survey Classification of 1967

Alfisols
Aridisols
Entisols
Histosols
Inceptisols

Mollisols
Oxisols
Spodosols
Ultisols
Vertisols

Miscellaneous land types

5   0   5   10   15   20   25   30   35 kilometers
5   0   5   10   15   20   25 miles

Source: U.S. Soil Conservation Service and Dept. of Agronomy and Soil Science, Univ. of Hawaii

The **Histosols** are organic soils that occur on geologically young but forested lava land. This soil type is characteristically a thin (2 to 8 inch) layer of organic material accumulated on lava rock. It constitutes one of the least exploited resources of the State. The **Inceptisols** are best developed on the thin mantle of volcanic ash which covers extensive areas of the island of Hawaii and East Maui. **Oxisols** and **Ultisols** occur only on old geomorphic surfaces and therefore only on the geologically older islands. Oxisols are found on relatively flat land in the lower elevations, and Ultisols on steeper slopes and the more unstable landscape of the higher elevations. These soils possess exceptional resistance to physical deterioration under intensive mechanized agriculture and are the most important agricultural soils of the State. **Mollisols** are well-drained, relatively young soils that develop on coral, lava, or alluvium. They occur in moderately dry areas of the islands and are generally rich in plant nutrients. **Vertisols**, typical of the dryer regions of talus slopes and floors of the deeply dissected amphitheater-headed valleys, swell and shrink with wetting and drying; they present hazards when highways or homes are built on them. The remaining four soil Orders make up about three percent of the State's land area. As the name suggests, **Aridisols** occur only in very dry regions, and in Hawaii this Order is largely confined to the leeward shores of the Big Island. A **Spodosol** is found only in the Alakai swamp on Mt. Waialeale on Kauai. The **Alfisols** are much like the Ultisols but are less leached of nutrients. And last, the **Entisols** are weakly developed soils found in Hawaii on old beach sand, on volcanic ash near the fringe of the tree line on Mauna Kea, and on recent alluvial deposits.

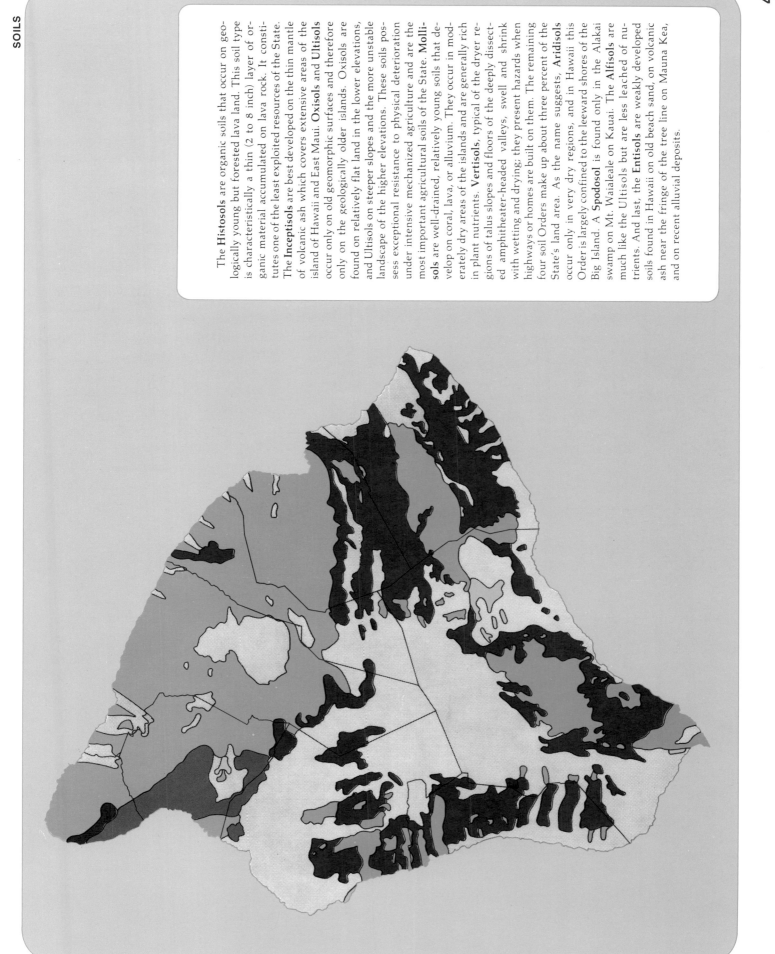

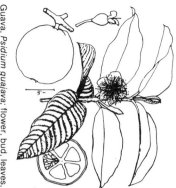

Guava, *Psidium guajava*; flower, bud, leaves, young fruit, ripe fruit. Introduced tree common along roadsides and in waste areas; the fruit is popular and useful.

Bishop Museum drawing from Neal (1965:632)

WATER

Hawaii's water resources are remarkably diversified, not only within each island but from island to island as well. There are perennial streams and flashy streams, rain forests and cactus deserts, groundwater tunnels cutting both into dikes high in the mountains and underground at near sea level. The complex nature of Hawaii's water control and development can be understood only in the context of the climate and geology of the islands (pages 32 and 53).

Hydrology. Over the State, the average annual rainfall is approximately 73 inches, about three times that over the nearby open sea—or 5,000 billion gallons of water a year in addition to what would be expected to fall over the surrounding ocean. Despite rainfalls that commonly exceed 200 inches a year in the mountainous portions of several of the islands in the Hawaiian chain, most streams are very flashy, but only a very few carry water throughout the year. The flashy condition is caused in part by the generally small area of the watersheds or drainage basins, but it is primarily caused by the extremely high permeability of the volcanic rocks and soils that make up the Hawaiian Islands. In particular, the permeability of some of the younger volcanic rocks is so great that virtually no rainwater flows on the land surface as runoff, and few, if any, well-defined stream channels exist in these areas. Basalts are among the most permeable rocks on earth, and the Hawaiian basalts are especially permeable because they are generally very young and, probably even more important, because the individual lava flows occur in thin layers. The high permeability of Hawaiian lavas results primarily from major flow structures such as clinker zones in aa, lava tubes and gas vesicles in pahoehoe, vertical contraction joints formed by the cooling of the lavas, and irregular openings of the surfaces between separate layers of flows.

The rift zones of Hawaiian volcanoes contain many vertical or steeply dipping dikes which cut through the lava flows. In the central portions of the rifts, the dikes are closely spaced and almost completely replace the lava flows. Toward the outer edges of the rift zones, the dikes are more widely spaced and form large compartments which enclose permeable lavas. Because the dikes are dense and have low permeabilities, groundwater may be impounded within the compartments they create.

On the older islands, especially Kauai and Oahu, the margins of the volcanic mountains are covered by coastal-plain sediments of alluvial and marine origin, called sedimentary caprock, which were deposited during periods of volcanic quiescence or inactivity. The greatest thickness of coastal-plain sediments occurs on southern Oahu beneath the Honolulu and Pearl Harbor areas, where the sediments have a maximum thickness of over 1,000 feet. Although the permeability of the sediments varies widely, the overall effect is one of low permeability compared with the basalts. The coastal sediments contain large quantities of water, varying from fresh water to seawater. Compared with the basalt aquifers (the porous, underground water-bearing basalts), however, the capacity of the sediments to store and transmit water is small. Consequently, the sediments act as a caprock retarding the seaward movement of fresh groundwater from the more permeable underlying basaltic aquifers.

Fresh water also occurs as high-level groundwater in Hawaii. The compartments formed by the dikes are commonly filled with water to levels of several hundred feet above sea level, and the overflow gushes out of the mountainside as high-level springs. Although only in very small quantities, water is also found at high levels perched on beds of weathered ash, tuff, soil, and thick sills or flows.

The principal source of fresh water in the State is the lens-shaped basal groundwater body, commonly called the Ghyben-Herzberg lens, which floats on denser salt water under the islands. The Hawaiian basal water body is largely unconfined. However, where the basaltic aquifer is bounded by sedimentary caprock along parts of the coast, artesian heads of a few feet to over 20 feet above sea level may occur because the caprock prevents the fresh water from escaping into the ocean. Because of vertical fluctuating motions caused by ocean tides, water entering the underground as recharge, and the outflow of groundwater as discharge by pumping, the salt and fresh waters mix and form a "zone of transition." In Hawaii the depth to the bottom of the fresh water is normally a few tens to many hundreds of feet, and the thickness of the zone of transition varies from

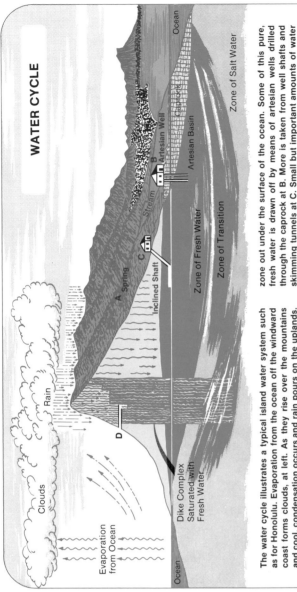

WATER CYCLE

Clouds

Rain

Evaporation from Ocean

Ocean

A Spring

C

Inclined Shaft

D

Dike Complex Saturated with Fresh Water

B Artesian Well

Stream

Artesian Basin

Zone of Fresh Water

Zone of Transition

Zone of Salt Water

Ocean

The water cycle illustrates a typical island water system such as for Honolulu. Evaporation from the ocean off the windward coast forms clouds, at left. As they rise over the mountains and cool, condensation occurs and rain pours on the uplands. Some of the water filters down through the water-tight dike complex; much of the rest trickles through the mass of rock into the zone of fresh water underlying the island. Below this zone is salt water. A small amount goes into springs at A, and into surface streams. A blanket of caprock thickens the fresh-water zone out under the surface of the ocean. Some of this pure, fresh water is drawn off by means of artesian wells drilled through the caprock at B. More is taken from well shafts and skimming tunnels at C. Small but important amounts of water are tapped from the dike complex at D. The water is brought to the surface, used, returned to the sea through sewer mains and other disposal methods, and the cycle begins again.

Source: City and County of Honolulu, Board of Water Supply

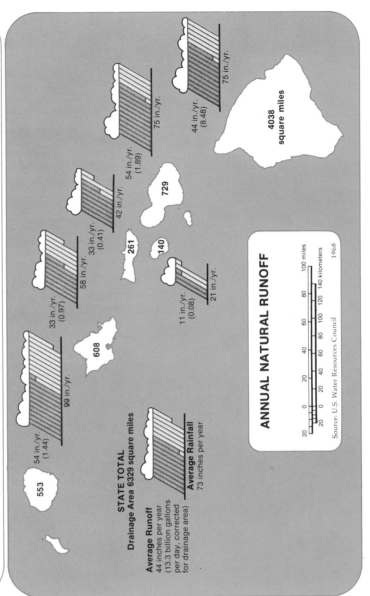

ANNUAL NATURAL RUNOFF

553

608

261

140

729

4038 square miles

99 in./yr.

54 in./yr. (1.44)

33 in./yr. (0.97)

11 in./yr. (0.08)

58 in./yr.

33 in./yr. (0.41)

42 in./yr.

54 in./yr. (1.89)

21 in./yr.

44 in./yr. (8.48)

75 in./yr.

75 in./yr.

STATE TOTAL
Drainage Area 6329 square miles

Average Runoff
44 inches per year
(13.3 billion gallons per day, corrected for drainage area)

Average Rainfall
73 inches per year

Source: U.S. Water Resources Council   1968

only a few tens of feet in relatively undisturbed areas to as much as 1,000 feet in parts of southern Oahu. The accompanying diagram of a cross section of Oahu from Honolulu to Kaneohe shows in a generalized way the occurence of groundwater on the island.

The Water Resource. Approximately 45 percent of the fresh water used in Hawaii is diverted from streamflow, which occurs abundantly in windward areas of the islands. Typically, perennial streams occur on steep northeast trade-wind slopes and flow directly to the sea through relatively short channels. On the longer, more gentle leeward slopes, few streams flow perennially to the sea, but many have continuous flows at upper elevations where rainfall is greatest. All streams are subject to phenomenal flash flooding during heavy rains. However, within a few hours after the rain stops, the streams recede to their normal flow levels because of their short channels and the porous soils of the islands.

Water that flows over land surface as natural runoff (page 43) amounts to about 60 percent of the annual rainfall. This estimate of average annual natural runoff includes surface- and groundwater discharges. Of the total annual discharge, approximately 28 percent is surface runoff in streams and 72 percent is groundwater, including tidal springs.

Water Uses. From earliest times, irrigation has been the dominant water use in Hawaii. Hawaiians built ditches to carry water for the paddy cultivation of taro, their staple crop. Since the latter part of the nineteenth century, several sugar plantations in leeward areas of the islands have irrigated cane fields with streamflow diverted from windward watersheds and conveyed by elaborate and extensive networks of tunnels and ditches.

Sugarcane uses from 6 to 9 feet of water per year. The irrigation of diversified crops consumes from 2.5 to 4 feet per year, and occasionally as much as 5 feet. Consumptive use for pineapples averages 1 to 1.5 feet per year. Irrigation requirements for these crops vary from locality to locality and from season to season. The heaviest requirements occur in the leeward areas during summer months. Much of the planted acreage is not irrigated; for example, of 233,000 acres planted to sugarcane in 1965, only 54 percent was irrigated. Saline water containing 1,300 to 2,000 parts per million of chloride has been successfully used for irrigation of crops, golf courses, and grazing land.

Industrial use of water is primarily for milling sugar, processing pineapples and other food products, and manufacturing. About 364 million gallons per day are used for generating hy-

WATER

droelectric power at 20 small-capacity plants, most of which are operated by sugar plantations to supply electric power for their own use. Water used for cooling in steam electric power plants comes primarily from saline sources.

The latest tabulation of water withdrawal and consumption in Hawaii is summarized in the table on page 45.

Chemically and bacteriologically, most of the groundwater used in Hawaii is of high quality. Its chloride content depends not only on local geologic factors, but also on the amount of withdrawal from the basal aquifer. Although 90 percent of the drinking water used on Oahu for public and private needs comes from basal aquifers, on many of the neighbor islands surface water provides nearly half of the water consumed. In periods of heavy rainfall, surface waters are often turbid, restricting their use.

Navigable harbor channels in Hawaii total 58.4 miles; navigable freshwater channels, 45.3 miles. In-stream water uses other than for boating are minimal. Some streams are stocked by the State with game fish, and ditches and reservoirs on some plantations are stocked with fish to control aquatic plant growth. Waterfowl are relatively uncommon.

Projected water requirements for the respective islands have been made on the assumption that present economic and population distinctions between Oahu and the other islands will generally continue through 2020. For projection purposes, it is expected that the population of Hawaii will increase to 1,086,000 in 1980, 1,680,000 in 2000, and 2,610,000 in 2020 (page 45).

L.S.L.

At an elevation of about 700 feet in the dike zone of windward Oahu, groundwater emerges as springs to become the headwaters of streams. A tributary of Waihee Stream starts as a 75-foot-high waterfall.

Photograph by Alex Williams Photography

Vertical dikes exposed on Puu Pueo near Waikane. Dikes control the movement of groundwater in windward Oahu.

Photograph by Alex Williams Photography

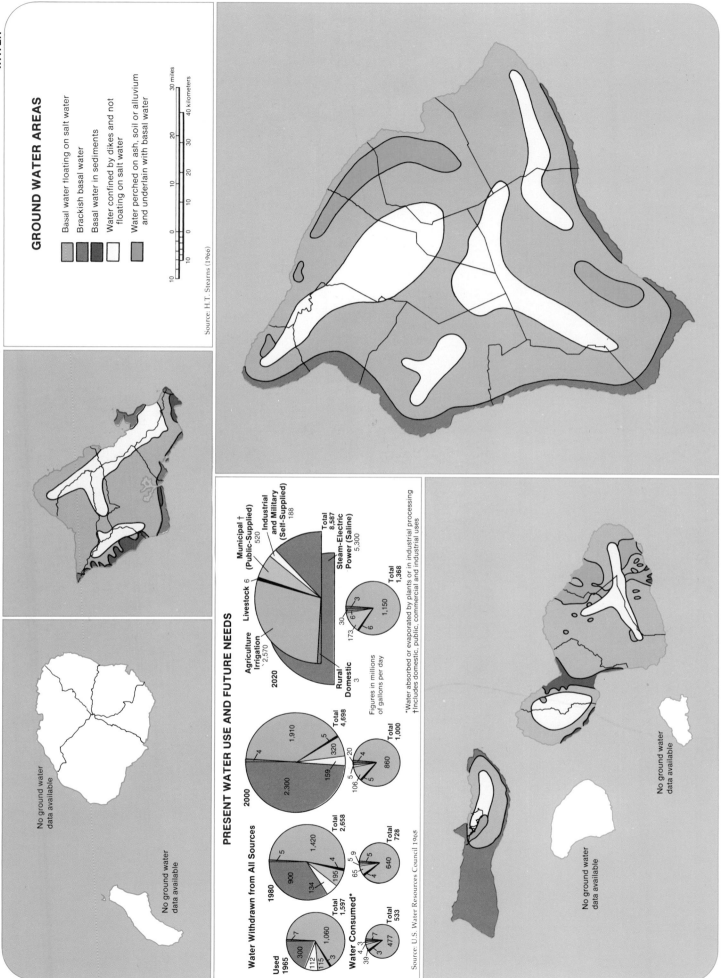

GROUND WATER AREAS

Basal water floating on salt water

Brackish basal water

Basal water in sediments

Water confined by dikes and not floating on salt water

Water perched on ash, soil or alluvium and underlain with basal water

10   0   10   20   30 miles

10   0   10   20   30   40 kilometers

Source: H.T. Stearns (1966)

No ground water data available

No ground water data available

No ground water data available

No ground water data available

PRESENT WATER USE AND FUTURE NEEDS

Water Withdrawn from All Sources

Used 1965
Total 1,597
300   7
112
115   3
1,060

1980
Total 2,658
900   5
134   4
195
1,420

2000
Total 4,698
2,300   4
159   5
320
1,910

2020
Total 8,587
Agriculture Irrigation 2,570
Livestock 6
Municipal † (Public-Supplied) 520
Industrial and Military (Self-Supplied) 188
Rural Domestic 3
Steam-Electric Power (Saline) 5,300

Water Consumed*

1965
Total 533
39   3
3   7
477

1980
Total 728
65   5
4
5
640

2000
Total 1,000
106   5   20
4
5
860

2020
Total 1,368
173   30
6   6
6
1,150

Figures in millions of gallons per day

*Water absorbed or evaporated by plants or in industrial processing
†Includes domestic, public, commercial and industrial uses

Source: U.S. Water Resources Council 1968

45

Kipapa Stream, Oahu, responds quickly to rainfall but loses flow rapidly during dry periods. The minimum flow of the stream is less than one million gallons per day, and the flow is 10 million gallons or more per day for only 40 days of the year.

Photographs by Alex Williams Photography

Kahana Valley, Oahu, looking toward the crest of the Koolau Range. The average annual rainfall at the head of the valley is 250 inches.

Photograph by Alex Williams Photography

Rain forest of the Kaukonahua drainage basin, Oahu.

Photograph by Alex Williams Photography

THE OCEAN

Regional. The Hawaiian Islands, along with numerous banks, guyots, and seamounts, rise from a linear swell of the Pacific sea floor, the Hawaiian Ridge (see maps on endpapers). Thus they resemble the Society, Line, Samoan, and several other linear chains in the Central Pacific. The islands and seamounts are volcanoes, or volcanoes now capped by coralline limestone. Volcanism appears to have been localized where the trend of the ridge has crossed branches of great east-trending fractures. From the junction of the Emperor Seamount chain and the Hawaiian Ridge, volcanism progressed 1,600 miles southeastward past Midway Islands, active about 18,000,000 years ago, to Mauna Loa and Kilauea, active today. The suboceanic lithosphere subsides under the mass of the volcanoes, so that a moat, the Hawaiian Deep, extends part of the way around the islands. Beyond the Deep the elastic lithosphere is flexed gently upward as the Hawaiian Arch.

Northeast trade winds generate the dominant waves in the region around Hawaii and also drive surface currents generally westward at 0.4 to 0.6 knots (20 to 30 cm sec⁻¹). Patterns of the currents, as well as characteristics of waves, salinity, and water temperature in this part of the North Pacific gyre, vary moderately with the seasons, as the cyclonic storms of the Northern Hemisphere move closer to the Hawaiian Islands in winter (page 48).

Nearshore. The original volcanic slopes of the islands have been modified by subaerial erosion of canyons and valleys, by the shaping of terraces near sea level by littoral processes including reef building, and by later episodes of volcanism. Many of these geomorphic features were drowned as the islands sank, and they now characterize the bathymetry (page 49). Submarine canyons are best developed north of Molokai, northeast of Oahu, and northwest of Maui. The deepest and most extensive terrace, named the Waho Shelf, is tilted to the north and ranges between 3,000 and 3,600 feet (900 and 1100 m) in depth. Muds washed as detritus from the islands, and calcareous sands, muds, and gravel of shallow-water origin, are the principal sediments near the islands, whereas pelagic brown clays cover most of the deep-sea floor (page 50).

Surface currents are modified by the shapes of the islands and, very close to shore, by the tides as well (page 51). Eddies in the lee of islands, especially west of Hawaii, are common and probably result from high winds funneled between Maui and Hawaii. Waves near the islands have sources in sea and swell which vary seasonally and which affect different exposures of the coasts. Hawaii has a mixed tide with a low range. Spring tides nowhere exceed 3 feet (1 m). Tsunami waves have ranged up to 28 feet (9 m) high in Hilo and 55 feet (16 m) elsewhere in the State (page 52).

Economic Aspects. The ocean-formed, nonliving resource of greatest value to Hawaii is its shoreline and in particular its beaches. Generally, beaches are larger on older islands, and on a given island they are larger on coasts exposed to the North Pacific swell (page 49). Precious coral has been discovered at various localities along the Hawaiian Archipelago at depths between 1,000 and 1,600 feet, ferromanganese deposits are common on old terraces below 1,200 feet, and a few billion cubic yards of sand are present at depths shallower than 100 feet. These are the principal potential offshore mineral deposits of the Hawaiian Islands (page 50).

R. M. M.

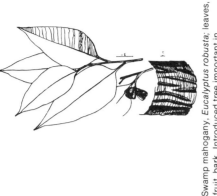

Swamp mahogany, *Eucalyptus robusta*; leaves, fruit, bark. Introduced tree important in Hawaiian forestry.

Bishop Museum drawing from Neal (1965:639)

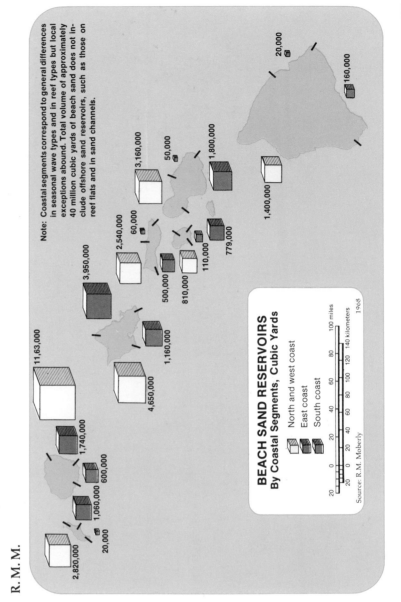

BEACH SAND RESERVOIRS
By Coastal Segments, Cubic Yards

- North and west coast
- East coast
- South coast

Note: Coastal segments correspond to general differences in seasonal wave types and in reef types but local exceptions abound. Total volume of approximately 40 million cubic yards of beach sand does not include offshore sand reservoirs, such as those on reef flats and in sand channels.

Source: R.M. Moberly
1968

PHYSICAL OCEANOGRAPHY OF THE NORTH CENTRAL PACIFIC

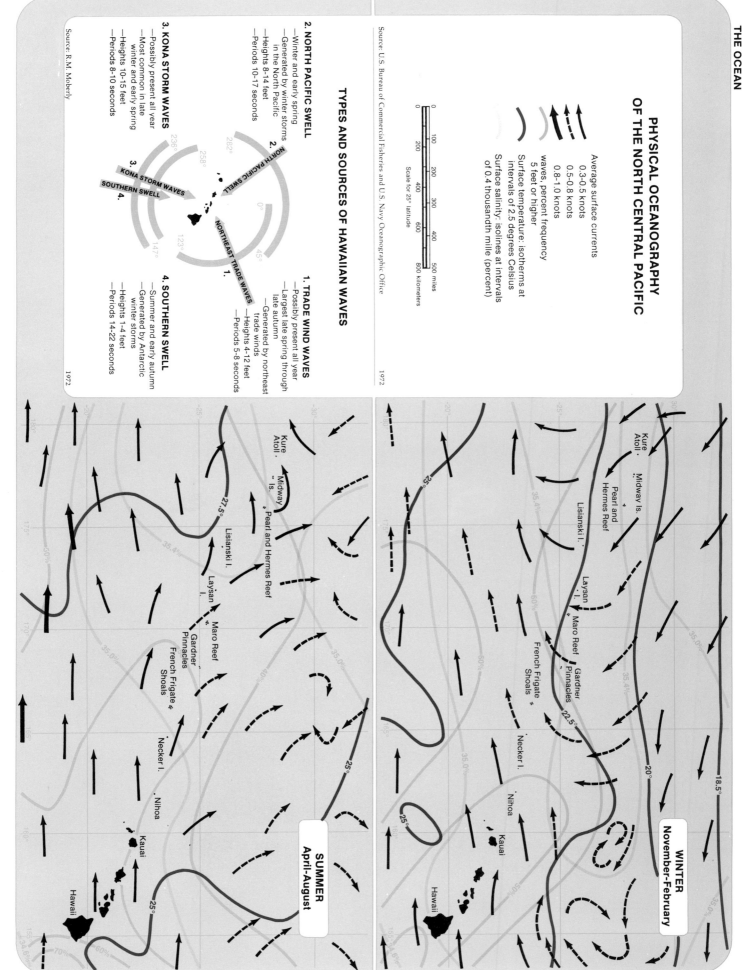

Average surface currents

0.3-0.5 knots
0.5-0.8 knots
0.8-1.0 knots

waves, percent frequency
5 feet or higher

Surface temperature: isotherms at intervals of 2.5 degrees Celsius

Surface salinity: isolines at intervals of 0.4 thousandth mille (percent)

Scale for 25° latitude

0   100   200   300   400   500 miles
0   200   400   600   800 Kilometers

Source: U.S. Bureau of Commercial Fisheries and U.S. Navy Oceanographic Office   1972

TYPES AND SOURCES OF HAWAIIAN WAVES

1. TRADE WIND WAVES
—Possibly present all year
—Largest late spring through late autumn
—Generated by northeast trade winds
—Heights 4-12 feet
—Periods 5-8 seconds

2. NORTH PACIFIC SWELL
—Winter and early spring
—Generated by winter storms in the North Pacific
—Heights 8-14 feet
—Periods 10-17 seconds

3. KONA STORM WAVES
—Possibly present all year
—Most common in late winter and early spring
—Heights 10-15 feet
—Periods 8-10 seconds

4. SOUTHERN SWELL
—Summer and early autumn
—Generated by Antarctic winter storms
—Heights 1-4 feet
—Periods 14-22 seconds

Source: R.M. Moberly   1972

WINTER November-February

SUMMER April-August

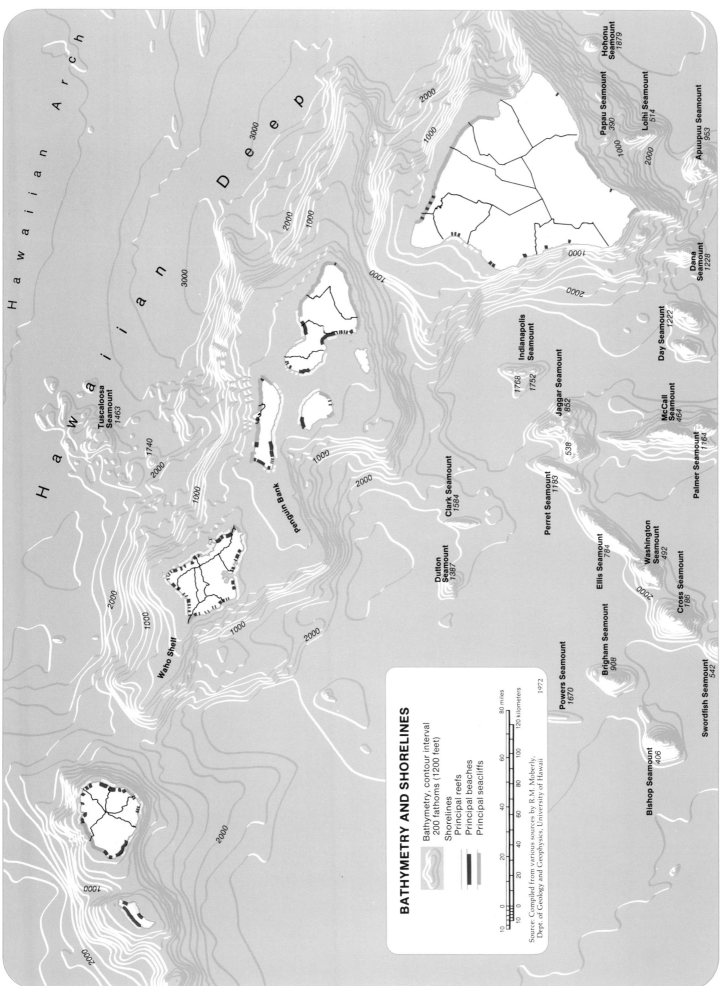

BATHYMETRY AND SHORELINES

Bathymetry, contour interval
200 fathoms (1200 feet)

Shorelines
Principal reefs
Principal beaches
Principal seacliffs

1972

Source: Compiled from various sources by R.M. Moberly,
Dept. of Geology and Geophysics, University of Hawaii

Hawaiian Arch

Hawaiian Deep

Hawaiian Arch

Tuscaloosa
Seamount
1463

1740

Penguin Bank

Waho Shelf

Hohonu
Seamount
1879

Papau Seamount
390

Loihi Seamount
514

Apuupuu Seamount
953

Dana
Seamount
1228

Day Seamount
1222

Indianapolis
Seamount
1768   1752

Jaggar Seamount
852

538

McCall
Seamount
464

Palmer Seamount
1164

Clark Seamount
1584

Perret Seamount
1183

Dutton
Seamount
1387

Ellis Seamount
784

Washington
Seamount
492

Cross Seamount
186

Brigham Seamount
908

Powers Seamount
1670

Swordfish Seamount
542

Bishop Seamount
406

80 miles

120 kilometers

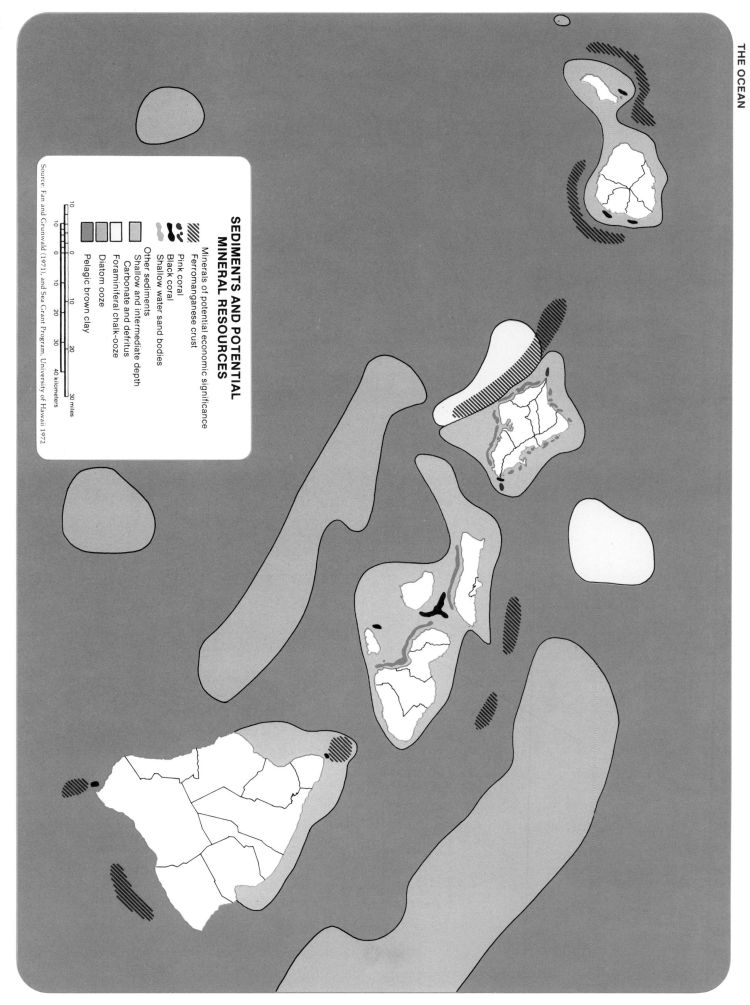

SEDIMENTS AND POTENTIAL MINERAL RESOURCES

Minerals of potential economic significance

Ferromanganese crust

Pink coral

Black coral

Shallow water sand bodies

Other sediments

Shallow and intermediate depth

Carbonate and defritus

Foraminiferal chalk-ooze

Diatom ooze

Pelagic brown clay

Source: Fan and Grunwald (1971), and Sea Grant Program, University of Hawaii 1972

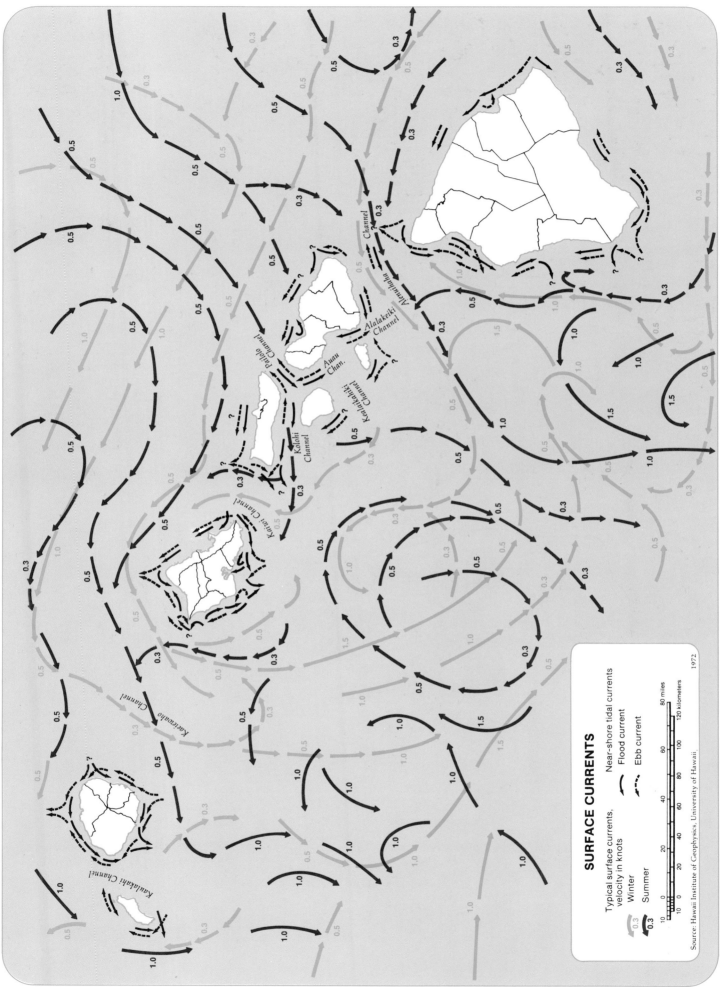

SURFACE CURRENTS

Typical surface currents,
velocity in knots

Near-shore tidal currents

Winter

Flood current

Summer

Ebb current

0.3

0.3

| 0 | 10 | 20 | 40 | 60 | 80 miles |

| 0 | 20 | 40 | 60 | 80 | 100 | 120 kilometers |

1972

Source: Hawaii Institute of Geophysics, University of Hawaii.

Alenuihaha Channel

Alalakeiki Channel

Auau Chan.

Pailolo Channel

Kealaikahiki Channel

Kalohi Channel

Kaiwi Channel

Kaieiewaho Channel

Kaulakahi Channel

52

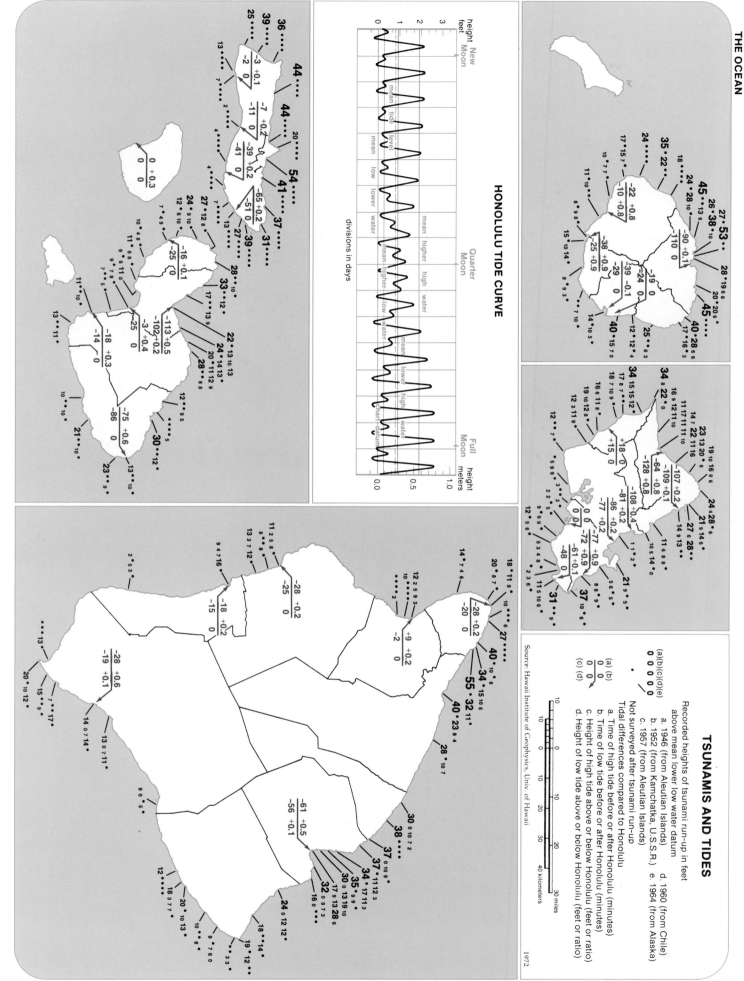

TSUNAMIS AND TIDES

Recorded heights of tsunami run-up in feet above mean lower low water datum

  a. 1946 (from Aleutian Islands)   d. 1960 (from Chile)

  b. 1952 (from Kamchatka, U.S.S.R.)   e. 1964 (from Alaska)

  c. 1957 (from Aleutian Islands)

• Not surveyed after tsunami run-up

Tidal differences compared to Honolulu

  a. Time of high tide before or after Honolulu (minutes)

  b. Time of low tide before or after Honolulu (minutes)

  c. Height of high tide above or below Honolulu (feet or ratio)

  d. Height of low tide above or below Honolulu (feet or ratio)

Source: Hawaii Institute of Geophysics, Univ. of Hawaii

1972

HONOLULU TIDE CURVE

divisions in days

Kou, *Cordia subcordata*: leaf, flowers, fruit.
The wood was used by the early Hawaiians for
making cups, dishes, and calabashes.
Bishop Museum drawing from Neal (1965:714)

CLIMATE

The climate of an area can best be thought of as a composite or frequency distribution of the various kinds of weather that occur there. The outstanding features of Hawaii's climate include mild and equable temperatures the year round, moderate humidities, persistence of northeasterly trade winds, remarkable differences in rainfall within short distances, and infrequency of severe storms.

In most of Hawaii there are only two seasons: "summer," between about May and October, when the sun is more nearly overhead, the weather warmer and drier, and the trade winds most persistent; and "winter," between about October and April, when the sun is in the south, the weather cooler, and the trade winds more often interrupted by other winds and by intervals of widespread cloud and rain.

Hawaii's climate reflects chiefly the interplay of four factors: latitude, the surrounding ocean, Hawaii's location relative to the storm tracks and the Pacific anticyclone, and terrain.

Latitude. Hawaii is well within the tropics, which accounts for the relative uniformity throughout the year in length of day and received solar energy, and hence in temperature.

Hawaii's longest and shortest days are about 13½ and 11 hours, respectively, as compared with 14½ and 10 hours for Southern California, and 15½ and 8½ hours for Maine. The sun at noon is never more than 45° from the zenith and is directly overhead twice during the year—toward the end of May, as it travels to its farthest north, and again in late July, as it returns south.

Uniform day lengths and sun angles result in correspondingly small seasonal variations in incoming solar radiation. Level ground in Hawaii receives at least two-thirds as much solar energy between sunrise and sunset of a clear winter's day as on a clear day in summer, while at latitude 40° the ratio is only one-third, and at latitude 50°, only one-fifth. Owing to the clarity of Hawaii's atmosphere, nearly three-fourths of the incident solar energy penetrates to sea level on a clear day.

The Surrounding Ocean. The ocean supplies moisture to the air and acts as a giant thermostat, since its own temperature varies little compared with that of large land masses. The seasonal range of sea surface temperature near Hawaii is only about 6°, from a low of 73° or 74° between late February and March to a high near 80° in late September or early October. The variation from day to night is only one or two degrees.

Because Hawaii is more than 2,000 miles from the nearest continental land mass, air that reaches it, regardless of its source, spends enough time over the equable ocean to moderate the harsher properties with which it may have begun its journey. In fact, Arctic air reaching Hawaii during the winter is sometimes warmed by as much as 100°F during its passage over the waters of the North Pacific. Hawaii's warmest months are not June and July, when the sun is highest, but August and September; and its coolest month, not December, when the sun is farthest south and days are shortest, but February and March—reflecting the seasonal lag in the ocean's temperature.

Storm Tracks and the Pacific Anticyclone. The so-called storm tracks, the paths taken by eastward-migrating high- and low-pressure areas, generally lie between 35°N and 65°N, and so these are the latitudes of changeable weather. But to the south, and particularly over the subtropical oceans, we often find a different breed of atmospheric eddy, one that changes its position so little that it is referred to as "semi-stationary" and lasts so long that it is called "quasi-permanent."

These relatively well anchored eddies include the large subtropical high pressure systems or anticyclones, and places in their vicinity can expect to have correspondingly stable weather. One of these—the Pacific High or anticyclone—generally lies northeast of Hawaii, so that the air moving outward from it streams past the islands as a northeasterly wind. This is in fact the northeasterly trade wind, whose persistence directly reflects

CLIMATE

that of the Pacific High from which it comes.

Together with the storm tracks, the Pacific High follows the seasonal shift of the sun, moving northward in summer, southward in winter, and tends to be stronger and more persistent in summer than in winter. So in winter, with the weakening and occasional absence of the Pacific High and the closer approach of the storm tracks, the trade winds may be interrupted for days or even weeks at a time by the invasion of the fronts or migratory cyclones of more northerly latitudes and by Kona storms forming nearer by. Hence, winter in Hawaii is the season of more frequent cloudiness and rainstorms, and of southerly and westerly winds replacing the trades for shorter or longer periods.

Terrain. Hawaii's mountains profoundly influence every aspect of its weather and climate. Their endless variety of peaks, valleys, ridges, and broad slopes, each presenting a different aspect to the wind, not only give Hawaii as a whole a climate in some respects markedly different from that of the surrounding ocean, but create within the small compass of the islands a climatic variety that would not exist here if these were flat islands of the same size.

The mountains obstruct, deflect, and accelerate the flow of air. Where the warm, moist winds are forced to rise over windward coasts and slopes, cloudiness and rainfall are much greater than over the nearby open sea; while leeward areas, where the air descends, tend to be sunny and dry. In places sheltered by terrain, local air movements arise quite at variance with winds in exposed localities. And since temperature decreases with elevation by about 3° per thousand feet, Hawaii's mountains, which extend from sea level to nearly 14,000 feet, encompass a climatic range from the tropic to the sub-Arctic.

The climate of Hawaii is defined not only by what it has but by what it seems to lack: the extremes of winter cold and snow on the one hand and summer heat waves, hurricanes, and hailstorms on the other. Yet Hawaii's tallest peaks do get their share of winter blizzards, ice, and snow; highest temperatures reach into the 90s; and thunderstorms, lightning, hail, floods, and droughts—and even hurricanes and tornadoes—are not unknown. But usually these are on a minor scale, less frequent and less severe than their counterparts in continental regions.

Rainfall. Over the open sea near Hawaii, rainfall averages between 25 and 30 inches a year. Yet the islands themselves receive up to 15 times this amount in some places and less than one-third of it in others. The cause of this remarkable variability, and of yearly totals which rival the greatest on earth, is princi-

---

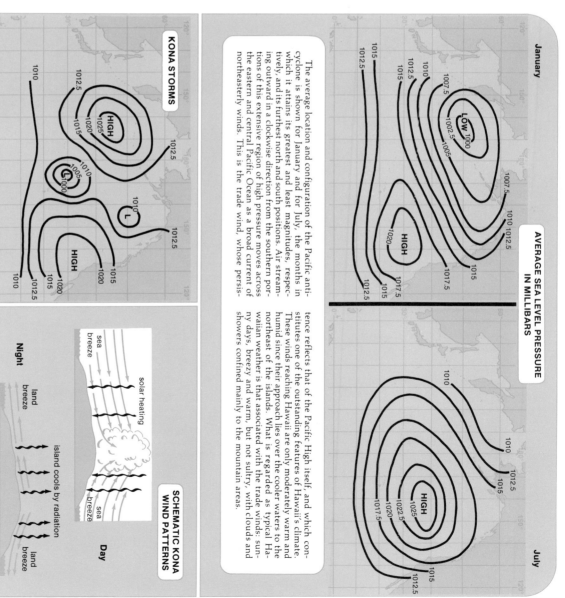

AVERAGE SEA LEVEL PRESSURE IN MILLIBARS

January

July

The average location and configuration of the Pacific anticyclone is shown for January and for July, the months in which it attains its greatest and least magnitudes, respectively, and its furthest north and south positions. Air streaming outward in a clockwise direction from the southern portions of this extensive region of high pressure moves across the eastern and central Pacific Ocean as a broad current of northeasterly winds. This is the trade wind, whose persistence reflects that of the Pacific High itself, and which constitutes one of the outstanding features of Hawaii's climate. These winds reaching Hawaii are only moderately warm and humid since their approach lies over the cooler waters to the northeast of the islands. What is regarded as typical Hawaiian weather is that associated with the trade winds: sunny days, breezy and warm, but not sultry, with clouds and showers confined mainly to the mountain areas.

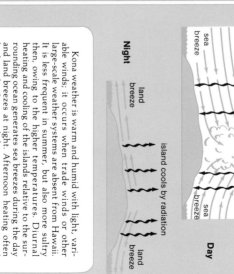

KONA STORMS

Kona storms are low pressure areas (cyclones) of subtropical origin which usually develop northwest of Hawaii in winter and move slowly eastward, accompanied by southerly winds from whose direction the storm derives its name (kona means "leeward" in Hawaiian) and by the clouds and rain that have made Kona storms synonymous with bad weather in Hawaii. Kona storms vary in number from year to year. Some winters have had none, others five or more.

SCHEMATIC KONA WIND PATTERNS

solar heating

sea breeze

land breeze

island cools by radiation

Day

Night

sea breeze

land breeze

Kona weather is warm and humid with light, variable winds; it occurs when trade winds or other large-scale weather systems are absent from Hawaii. It is less frequent in summer, but also more sultry then, owing to the higher temperatures. Diurnal heating and cooling of the islands relative to the surrounding ocean generates sea breezes during the day and land breezes at night. Afternoon heating often leads to cloudiness and showers over mountains and interiors.

CLIMATE

pally the "orographic" (mountain-caused) rains which form within the moist trade-wind air as it moves in from the sea and overrides the steep and high terrain of the islands. Over the lower islands the resulting average rainfall distribution resembles closely the topographic contours: amounts are greatest over upper slopes and crests and least in the leeward lowlands. On the higher mountains the belt of maximum rainfall lies at only 2,000 to 3,000 feet, and amounts drop off rapidly with further elevation, so that the highest slopes are relatively dry.

Another source of rainfall is the towering cumulus clouds that build up over mountains and interiors on sunny calm afternoons. Although such convective showers may be intense, they are usually brief and localized.

Hawaii's heaviest rains are brought by winter storms during the October-to-April season. While the effects of terrain on storm rainfall are not as pronounced as on trade-wind showers, large differences over small distances do occur, due both to topography and to the location of the rain clouds; but these differences vary from storm to storm.

Frequently, the heaviest storm rains do not occur in localities having the greatest average rainfall; nor is it uncommon during such storms for relatively dry areas to receive within a day, or even a few hours, totals exceeding half their mean annual rainfall. For example, downtown Honolulu, with an average yearly rainfall of only 24 inches, has had more than 17 inches in a single day. During storms, 3 inches or more may fall in a single hour, and Hawaii's record rains—more than 11 inches in an hour and nearly 40 inches in 24 hours—rank near the world's greatest.

Since the lowland lees and other dry areas obtain their rainfall chiefly from a few winter storms, and only negligibly from trade-wind showers, their rainfall is strongly seasonal, their summers being arid. In the wetter regions, on the other hand, where rainfall comes from both winter storms and year-round trade-wind showers, seasonal differences are much smaller.

At the opposite extreme, drought is not unknown in Hawaii, although it rarely affects even an entire island at one time. Drought may occur when either the winter storms or the trade winds fail. If the winter storms fail, the normally dry leeward areas are hardest hit; and two successive dry winters, with the intervening normally dry summer, can have serious effects. The failure of the trades most affects windward and upland regions, which receive a smaller proportion of their rain from winter storms.

S. P.

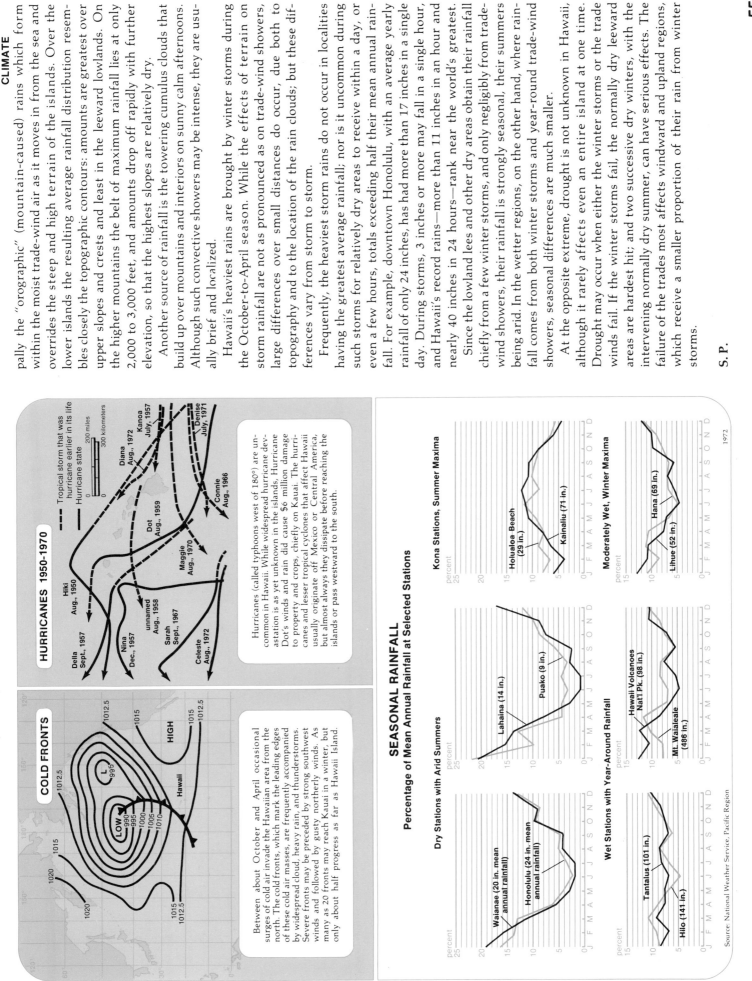

HURRICANES 1950-1970

- - - Tropical storm that was hurricane earlier in its life
——— Hurricane state

0 200 miles
0 300 kilometers

Della Sept., 1957
Hiki Aug., 1950
Nina Dec., 1957
unnamed Aug., 1958
Sarah Sept., 1967
Celeste Aug., 1972
Maggie Aug., 1970
Dot Aug., 1959
Diana Aug., 1972
Kanoa July, 1957
Denise July, 1971
Connie Aug., 1966

Hurricanes (called typhoons west of 180°) are uncommon in Hawaii. While widespread hurricane devastation is as yet unknown in the islands, Hurricane Dot's winds and rain did cause $6 million damage to property and crops, chiefly on Kauai. The hurricanes and lesser tropical cyclones that affect Hawaii usually originate off Mexico or Central America, but almost always they dissipate before reaching the islands or pass westward to the south.

COLD FRONTS

1012.5
1015
1012.5
1020
1015
1012.5
HIGH
1015
1012.5
Hawaii
L 995
LOW 990
995
1000
1005
1010
1020
1015

Between about October and April occasional surges of cold air invade the Hawaiian area from the north. The cold fronts, which mark the leading edges of these cold air masses, are frequently accompanied by widespread cloud, heavy rain, and thunderstorms. Severe fronts may be preceded by strong southwest winds and followed by gusty northerly winds. As many as 20 fronts may reach Kauai in a winter, but only about half progress as far as Hawaii Island.

SEASONAL RAINFALL
Percentage of Mean Annual Rainfall at Selected Stations

Dry Stations with Arid Summers

Waianae (20 in. mean annual rainfall)
Honolulu (24 in. mean annual rainfall)

Kona Stations, Summer Maxima

Holualoa Beach (29 in.)
Kainaliu (71 in.)
Lahaina (14 in.)
Puako (9 in.)

Wet Stations with Year-Around Rainfall

Tantalus (101 in.)
Hilo (141 in.)

Hawaii Volcanoes Nat'l Pk. (98 in.)
Mt. Waialeale (486 in.)

Moderately Wet, Winter Maxima

Hana (69 in.)
Lihue (52 in.)

1972

Source: National Weather Service, Pacific Region

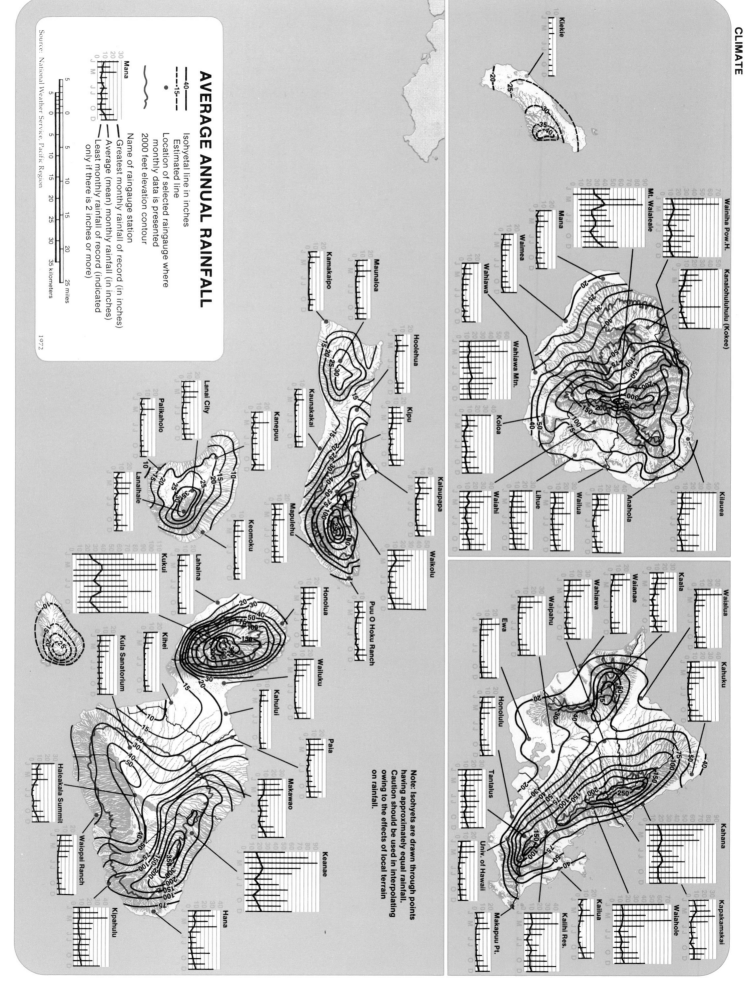

AVERAGE ANNUAL RAINFALL

—40— Isohyetal line in inches
––15–– Estimated line
• Location of selected raingauge where monthly data is presented

〜〜〜 2000 feet elevation contour

Name of raingauge station
Greatest monthly rainfall of record (in inches)
Average (mean) monthly rainfall (in inches)
Least monthly rainfall of record (indicated only if there is 2 inches or more)

Source: National Weather Service, Pacific Region

1972

Note: Isohyets are drawn through points having approximately equal rainfall. Caution should be used in interpolating owing to the effects of local terrain on rainfall.

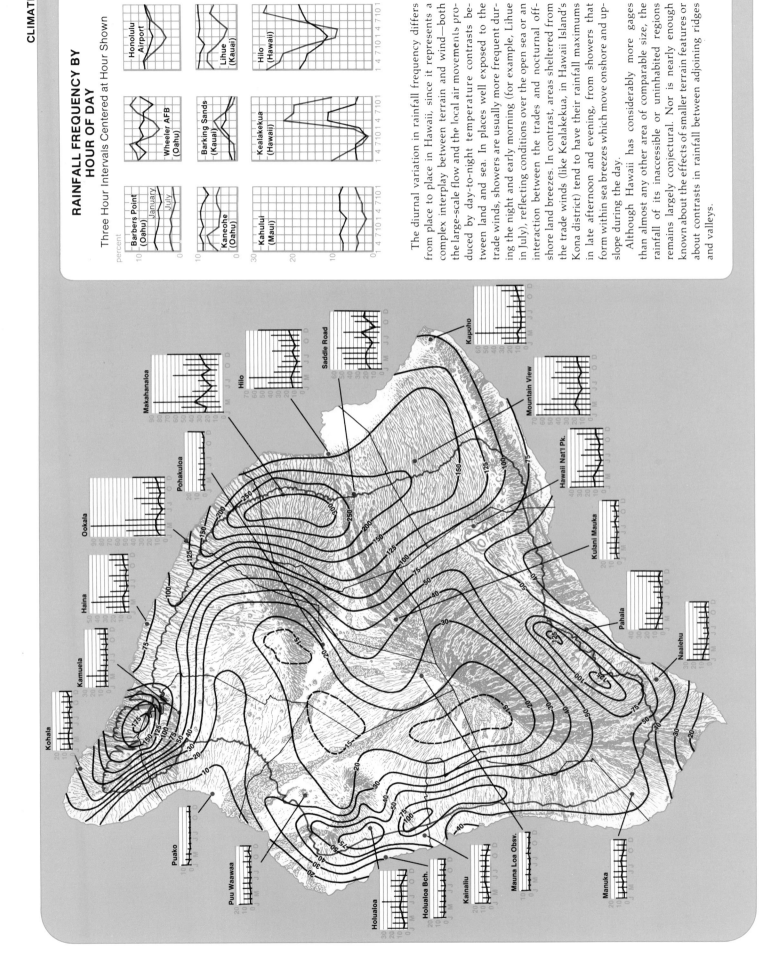

RAINFALL FREQUENCY BY HOUR OF DAY

Three Hour Intervals Centered at Hour Shown

Honolulu Airport

Lihue (Kauai)

Hilo (Hawaii)

Wheeler AFB (Oahu)

Barking Sands (Kauai)

Kealakekua (Hawaii)

Barbers Point (Oahu)

January

July

Kaneohe (Oahu)

Kahului (Maui)

percent

The diurnal variation in rainfall frequency differs from place to place in Hawaii, since it represents a complex interplay between terrain and wind—both the large-scale flow and the local air movements produced by day-to-night temperature contrasts between land and sea. In places well exposed to the trade winds, showers are usually more frequent during the night and early morning (for example, Lihue in July), reflecting conditions over the open sea or an interaction between the trades and nocturnal off-shore land breezes. In contrast, areas sheltered from the trade winds (like Kealakekua, in Hawaii Island's Kona district) tend to have their rainfall maximums in late afternoon and evening, from showers that form within sea breezes which move onshore and up-slope during the day.

Although Hawaii has considerably more gages than almost any other area of comparable size, the rainfall of its inaccessible or uninhabited regions remains largely conjectural. Nor is nearly enough known about the effects of smaller terrain features or about contrasts in rainfall between adjoining ridges and valleys.

58

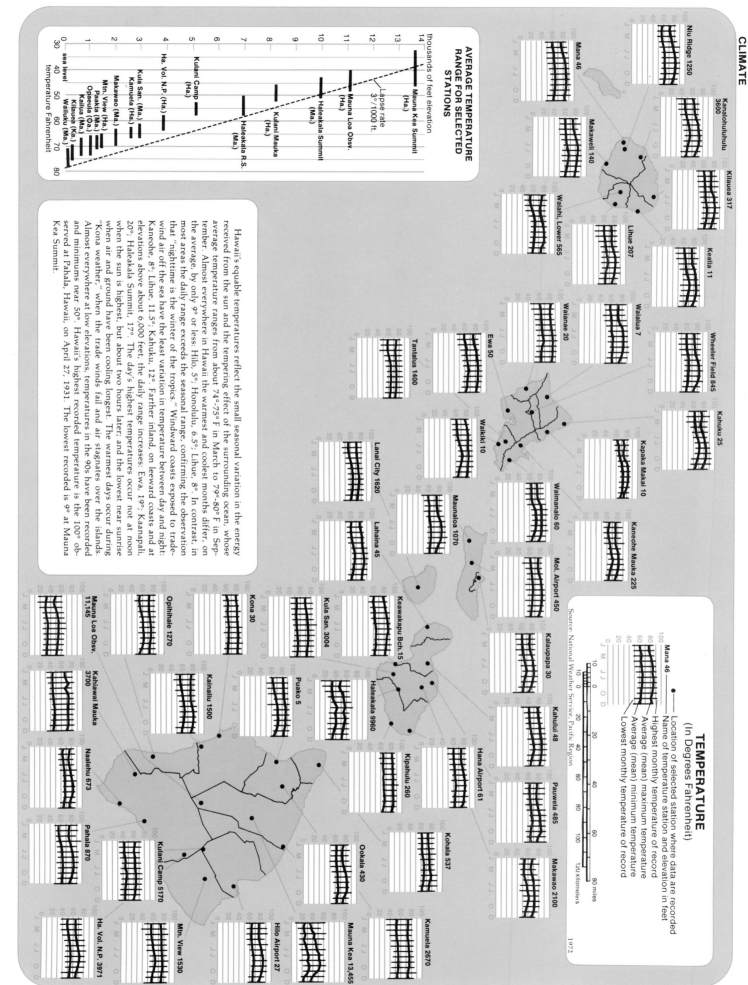

AVERAGE TEMPERATURE RANGE FOR SELECTED STATIONS

Lapse rate 3°/1000 ft.

Mauna Kea Summit (Ha.)
Mauna Loa Obsv. (Ha.)
Haleakala Summit (Ma.)
Kulani Mauka (Ha.)
Haleakala R.S. (Ma.)
Ha. Vol. N.P. (Ha.)
Kulani Camp (Ha.)
Kula San. (Ma.)
Kamuela (Ha.)
Makawao (Ma.)
Mtn. View (Ha.)
Paakia (Ma.)
Opaeula (Oa.)
Kailua (Ma.)
Kilauea (Ka.)
Wailuku (Ma.)

thousands of feet elevation
sea level
temperature Fahrenheit

TEMPERATURE
(In Degrees Fahrenheit)

Mana 46 —— Location of selected station where data are recorded
Name of temperature station and elevation in feet
Highest monthly temperature of record
Average (mean) maximum temperature
Average (mean) minimum temperature
Lowest monthly temperature of record

Source: National Weather Service, Pacific Region

1972

Hawaii's equable temperatures reflect the small seasonal variation in the energy received from the sun and the tempering effect of the surrounding ocean, whose average temperature ranges from about 74°-75° F in March to 79°-80° F in September. Almost everywhere in Hawaii the warmest and coolest months differ, on the average, by only 9° or less: Hilo, 5°; Honolulu, 6.5°; Lihue, 8°. In contrast, in most areas the daily range exceeds the seasonal range, confirming the observation that "nighttime is the winter of the tropics." Windward coasts exposed to trade-wind air off the sea have the least variation in temperature between day and night: Kaneohe, 8°; Lihue, 11.5°; Kahuku, 12°. Farther inland, on leeward coasts and at elevations above about 6,000 feet, the daily range increases: Ewa, 19°; Kaanapali, 20°; Haleakala Summit, 17°. The day's highest temperatures occur not at noon when the sun is highest, but about two hours later; and the lowest near sunrise when air and ground have been cooling longest. The warmest days occur during "Kona weather," when the trade winds fail and air stagnates over the islands. Almost everywhere at low elevations, temperatures in the 90s have been recorded and minimums near 50°. Hawaii's highest recorded temperature is the 100° observed at Pahala, Hawaii, on April 27, 1931. The lowest recorded is 9° at Mauna Kea Summit.

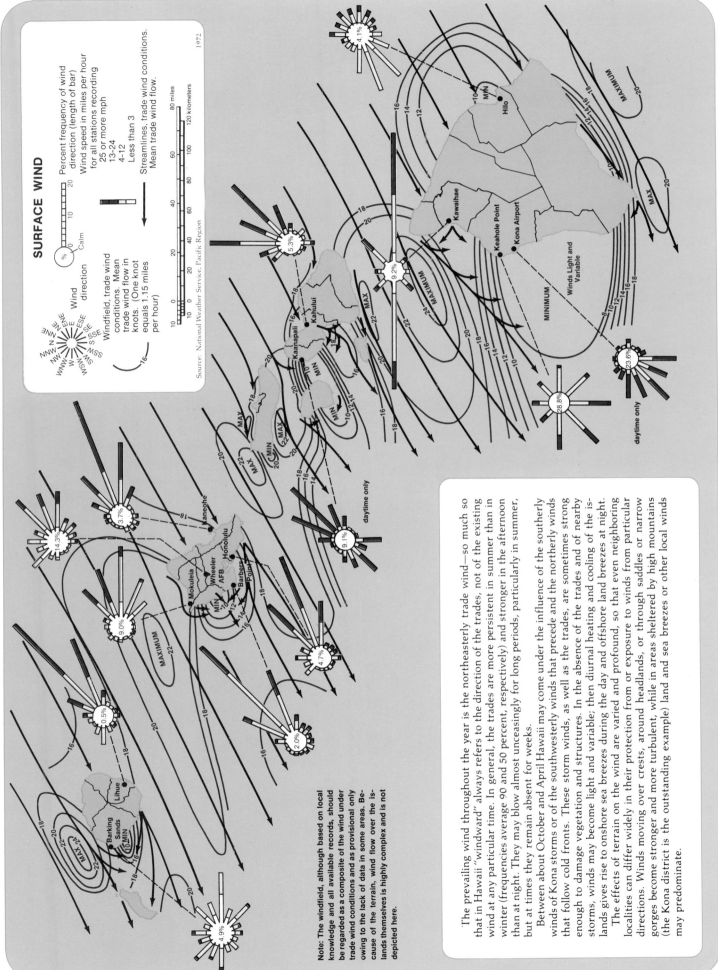

SURFACE WIND

Wind direction

NNW NNE
NW N NE
WNW ENE
W E
WSW ESE
SW SE
SSW SSE
S

Windfield, trade wind conditions. Mean trade wind flow in knots. (One knot equals 1.15 miles per hour)

16

% Wind direction
Calm

Percent frequency of wind direction (length of bar)

Wind speed in miles per hour for all stations recording
25 or more mph
13-24
4-12
Less than 3

0 10 20

Streamlines, trade wind conditions. Mean trade wind flow.

1972

miles
10 0 10 20 40 60 80 miles

10 0 20 40 60 80 100 120 kilometers

Source: National Weather Service, Pacific Region

Note: The windfield, although based on local knowledge and all available records, should be regarded as a composite of the wind under trade wind conditions and as provisional only owing to the lack of data in some areas. Because of the terrain, wind flow over the islands themselves is highly complex and is not depicted here.

The prevailing wind throughout the year is the northeasterly trade wind—so much so that in Hawaii "windward" always refers to the direction of the trades, not of the existing wind at any particular time. In general, the trades are more persistent in summer than in winter (frequencies average 90 and 50 percent, respectively) and stronger in the afternoon than at night. They may blow almost unceasingly for long periods, particularly in summer, but at times they remain absent for weeks.

Between about October and April Hawaii may come under the influence of the southerly winds of Kona storms or of the southwesterly winds that precede and the northerly winds that follow cold fronts. These storm winds, as well as the trades, are sometimes strong enough to damage vegetation and structures. In the absence of the trades and of nearby storms, winds may become light and variable; then diurnal heating and cooling of the islands gives rise to onshore sea breezes during the day and offshore land breezes at night.

The effects of terrain on the wind are varied and profound, so that even neighboring localities can differ widely in their protection from or exposure to winds from particular directions. Winds moving over crests, around headlands, or through saddles or narrow gorges become stronger and more turbulent, while in areas sheltered by high mountains (the Kona district is the outstanding example) land and sea breezes or other local winds may predominate.

SEASONAL AND DIURNAL WIND
DIRECTION AND PERCENT FREQUENCY
At Four Selected Stations

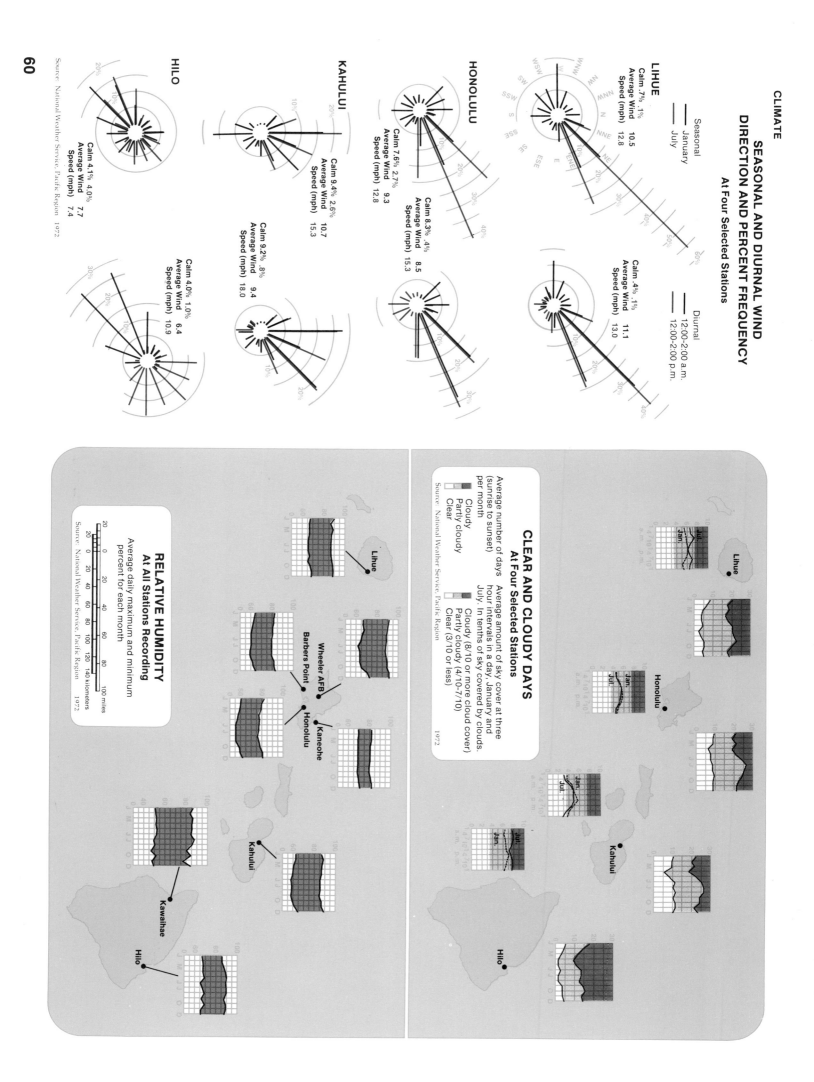

Seasonal
— January
— July

Diurnal
— 12:00-2:00 a.m.
— 12:00-2:00 p.m.

LIHUE
Calm .7%, .1%
Average Wind   10.5
Speed (mph)   12.8

Calm .4%, .1%
Average Wind   11.1
Speed (mph)   13.0

HONOLULU
Calm 7.6% 2.7%
Average Wind   9.3
Speed (mph)   12.8

Calm 8.3%, .4%
Average Wind   8.5
Speed (mph)   15.3

KAHULUI
Calm 9.4% 2.6%
Average Wind   10.7
Speed (mph)   15.3

Calm 9.2% .8%
Average Wind   9.4
Speed (mph)   18.0

HILO
Calm 4.1% 4.0%
Average Wind   7.7
Speed (mph)   7.4

Calm 4.0% 1.0%
Average Wind   6.4
Speed (mph)   10.9

Source: National Weather Service, Pacific Region   1972

CLEAR AND CLOUDY DAYS
At Four Selected Stations

Average number of days
(sunrise to sunset)
per month

Average amount of sky cover at three
hour intervals in a day, January and
July. In tenths of sky covered by clouds.

Cloudy
Partly cloudy
Clear

Cloudy (8/10 or more cloud cover)
Partly cloudy (4/10-7/10)
Clear (3/10 or less)

Source: National Weather Service, Pacific Region   1972

Lihue
Honolulu
Kahului
Hilo

RELATIVE HUMIDITY
At All Stations Recording

Average daily maximum and minimum
percent for each month

Source: National Weather Service, Pacific Region   1972

Lihue
Wheeler AFB
Barbers Point
Kaneohe
Honolulu
Kahului
Kawaihae
Hilo

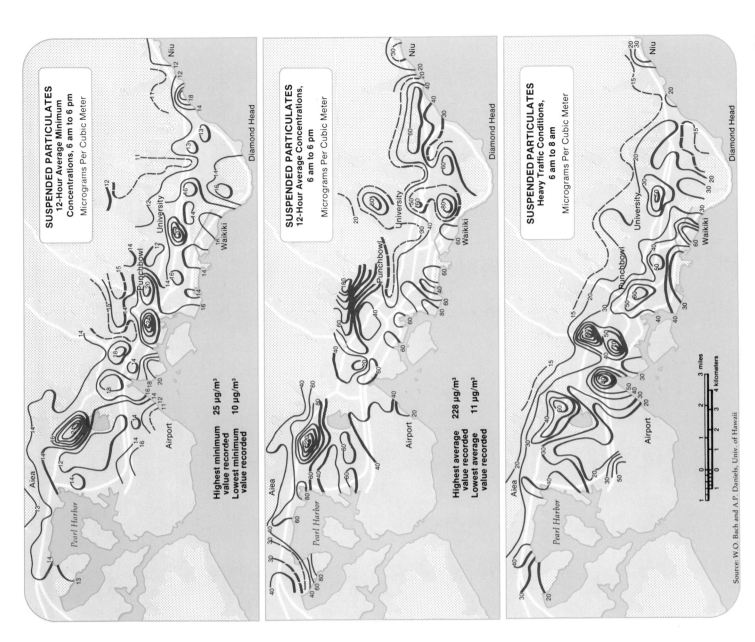

Source: W.O. Bach and A.P. Daniels, Univ. of Hawaii

SUSPENDED PARTICULATES
12-Hour Average Minimum
Concentrations, 6 am to 6 pm
Micrograms Per Cubic Meter

Highest minimum value recorded   25 µg/m³
Lowest minimum value recorded   10 µg/m³

SUSPENDED PARTICULATES
12-Hour Average Concentrations,
6 am to 6 pm
Micrograms Per Cubic Meter

Highest average value recorded   228 µg/m³
Lowest average value recorded   11 µg/m³

SUSPENDED PARTICULATES
Heavy Traffic Conditions,
6 am to 8 am
Micrograms Per Cubic Meter

AIR QUALITY

While the air over Hawaii in general is relatively clean and low in pollution, certain areas are cause for serious concern. Chief among them is the urban area of Honolulu where large numbers of motor vehicles (page 169) daily pour tons of exhaust gases and particulates into the air. Industrial air pollution is comparatively minor. Natural pollution from volcanic action can be severe under certain wind conditions, but it is a rare occurrence. Many physical and meteorological factors combine to allow motor vehicle pollutants to concentrate at high levels in certain parts of the city. These include: the site of the city in the lee of the trade winds and occasional long periods of light and variable wind flow; modified local air circulation due to tall buildings and higher surface temperatures caused by buildings, pavements, and traffic; and large amounts of sunshine.

Some air pollutants, such as suspended particulates, can be measured directly in order to forecast spatial and temporal patterns over a city. Other pollutants, such as carbon monoxide, which are more difficult to measure directly on a mobile continuous basis, are best forecast through a meteorological diffusion model.

The maps on page 61 present data for suspended particulates. The measurements were made with an integrating nephelometer, an instrument which can be attached to a car or aircraft to give instantaneous recordings of air quality at any location. It measures concentrations of particles in the small size range of 0.1 to 1.0 micrometers, a range critical to human respiratory health.

For the purpose of sampling suspended particulates, the Honolulu urban area was subdivided into 3,500 squares of 250 x 250 meters each. The mobile sampling was conducted from 6 a.m. to noon on one day, and from noon to 6 p.m. on the following day, from July through September 1971. During the six-hour sampling periods, which covered some 120 miles and produced some 40 feet of chart paper with continuous data, it was arranged that as many squares as possible were sampled during different two-hour time periods. About 20 six-hour sampling runs were made. Thus each two-hour sampling run is based on about 1,000 data, and each 12-hour sampling map is constructed from about 6,000 data. This constitutes one of the most detailed monitorings of an air pollutant conducted in any urban area. However the maps reflect only trade-wind conditions, which produce the best dispersion conditions for pollutants in Hawaii.

The first map on page 61 shows the lowest concentrations of suspended particulates recorded during any of the 20 separate runs, which can be taken as indicative of Honolulu's background pollution levels. The lowest values are characteristically found on the exposed residential hilltops of St. Louis Heights and Maunalani Heights. The highest values are found in congested downtown areas and along Moanalua Road.

The second map depicts maximum suspended particulate concentrations averaged for each grid square from vehicular sources only. It is important to note that vehicular emission can raise the suspended particulate levels more than ten times above the 12-hour average background level to 228 micrograms per cubic meter. Again, the busy intersection of Moanalua Road and Hale Street, the Nuuanu Pali Highway, and congested streets in Waikiki stand out as the most polluted areas.

The third map shows the morning rush-hour conditions from 6 a.m. to 8 a.m. Since this map includes data for suspended particulates from all

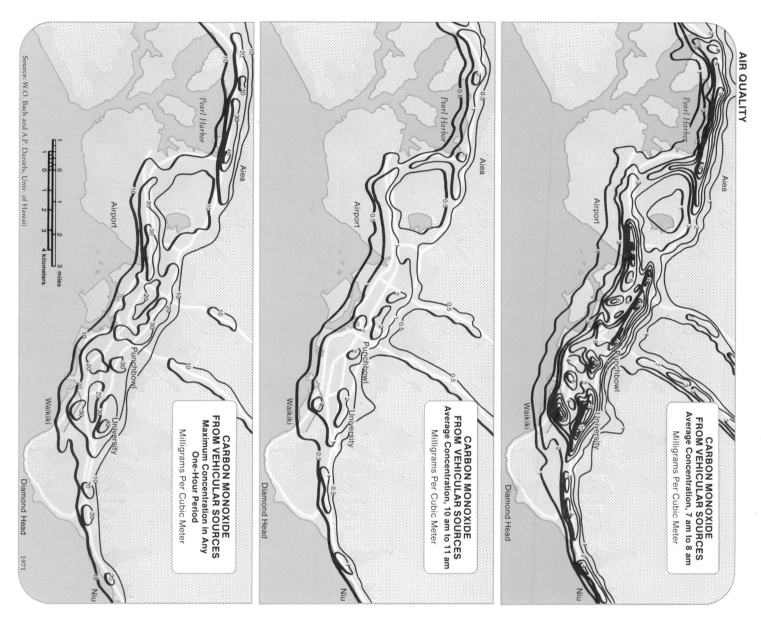

CARBON MONOXIDE FROM VEHICULAR SOURCES
Average Concentration, 7 am to 8 am
Milligrams Per Cubic Meter

CARBON MONOXIDE FROM VEHICULAR SOURCES
Average Concentration, 10 am to 11 am
Milligrams Per Cubic Meter

CARBON MONOXIDE FROM VEHICULAR SOURCES
Maximum Concentration in Any One-Hour Period
Milligrams Per Cubic Meter

Source: W.O. Bach and A.P. Daniels, Univ. of Hawaii

1971

sources during the rush-hour period, including any background values, the mean values are somewhat lower than those reflecting maximum average concentrations produced by vehicular sources only. Again it is clear that the highest concentrations cluster around the busiest intersections. It is now generally accepted that particles of a size range that penetrate deeply into the lungs are produced in cities by automobile exhausts, tire wear, and turbulent dust-blowing enhanced by the moving vehicles.

Meteorological Diffusion Models. Because of the current technical difficulties in direct measurement of certain gases, meteorological diffusion models can make the most realistic assessment of air quality in urban areas where there is a combination of fixed and mobile sources of air pollution. The main purposes of such a model are to: (1) predict the spatial and temporal patterns of air pollution concentrations, (2) determine the minimum number necessary and the best locations for monitoring devices, (3) supply information on which to base a rational permit and variance system, and (4) provide the necessary input data for economically and socially optimum air-quality control.

Results of diffusion modeling for carbon monoxide (CO) in Honolulu are shown in maps on page 62. Data for the model for the 1970–1971 period included sample measurements of CO, estimated emissions from motor vehicles, traffic densities, and street lengths. The first map shows the average concentration of CO for the morning rush-hour period. The CO-concentration patterns coincide closely with those of traffic and highway density. The second map shows the average CO concentration two hours later. Increased ventilation and decreased traffic density produce in some areas as much as a five-fold reduction in CO concentration.

The accuracy of air-quality prediction models must be validated by comparison with actually recorded data. The hourly CO data measured in September 1971 by the Department of Health at Punchbowl and Beretania Streets in Honolulu are compared with the calculated data in the following tabulation:

Morning Hours	Average 1-hour CO values (mg per cubic meter)	
	At Dept. of Health	Predicted from model
6–7	4.7	5.0
7–8	6.9	6.9
8–9	4.2	4.6
9–10	2.8	2.6

The close agreement between the measured and calculated values would in this case justify the application of the diffusion model in air quality control.

Since the Hawaii Air Quality Control Region, like most other control regions, does not attempt to control average concentrations, but rather the frequency of occurrence of a selected maximum concentration, such maxima are presented in the third map. The one-hour maximum air quality standard for CO has been set at 10 mg/m³ for Hawaii. This standard is already exceeded in Honolulu and surrounding urban areas. In some areas the magnitude of the standard is exceeded almost five times.

W. B. and A. P. D.

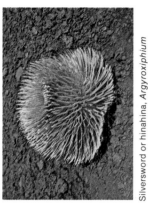

Silversword or hinahina, *Argyroxiphium sandwicense*. A spectacular plant from Haleakala, Maui.

Photograph by C.H. Lamoureux

Mao or Hawaiian cotton, *Gossypium sandwicense*. A rare plant from dry coastal regions.

Photograph by C.H. Lamoureux

Ohai, *Sesbania tomentosa*. A small shrub from coastal areas that is becoming very rare.

Photograph by C.H. Lamoureux

Mamani, *Sophora chrysophylla*. A dominant tree in drier forests at high elevations.

Photograph by C.H. Lamoureux

PLANTS

Hawaii has a fascinating and unique collection of plant life. There are more than 2,500 kinds of higher plants that occur only in the Hawaiian Islands and nowhere else. Yet most visitors and many residents of the State are not aware of these unique plants and see very few of them. The coconuts, orchids, sugarcane, and pineapples of the tourist advertisements are recent immigrants to Hawaii, neither native nor unique. The native plants are common today only in such remote places as the headwalls of deep valleys, on steep cliffs, and on mountain ridges and peaks.

A brief review of the history of Hawaii's plant life will help us understand why this is so. When the Hawaiian Islands first reached above the surface of the sea they were without land plants. Gradually, over long periods of time, living seeds and spores of plants from elsewhere reached the islands, borne by winds, drifting on the sea, or carried by birds. Each time a different seed or spore happened to land in a place where the young plant developing from it could survive, grow, and produce a new crop of seeds or spores, then another kind of plant had become established in Hawaii. Through time, gradual changes have occurred in these isolated Hawaiian populations, and many have evolved to a point at which they differ enough from all other plants that they can be classified as distinct species or varieties.

The plant geographer uses the term *native* to refer to a plant, the ancestors of which reached the area where it now grows by natural means without help from man. He distinguishes between native and *introduced* (or *exotic*) species—those plants that reached a given geographic area only with the assistance of man, whether such assistance was intentional or inadvertent. The term *endemic* is applied to a group of organisms native to a single small geographic area. Thus a species endemic to the Hawaiian Islands is one that occurs naturally only in this group of islands. An *indigenous* organism is one that is native to a larger geographic area—thus a species which is native to Hawaii, the Society Islands, the Marquesas, Samoa, and Fiji would be described as indigenous to Hawaii, but not endemic.

The most recent compilation of Hawaiian plants (St. John, 1972) lists 1,381 native species of flowering plants, of which 96.6 percent are endemic and 3.4 percent indigenous. When subspecies, varieties, and forms are included, there are 2,656 recognized taxonomic groups of which 99.1 percent are endemic. Other work has indicated that all of these plants have evolved from about 275 species of successful natural immigrants which have arrived in Hawaii on the average of once every 70,000 years or so since the time when the islands emerged from the sea. Most of these original immigrants seem to have come from the Indo-Pacific area to the south and west of Hawaii, but about 20 percent probably came from the east, from the Americas.

The isolation of the Hawaiian island chain from other land masses, the isolation between the separate islands in the chain, the equable but variable climate, the topography which leads to isolation of small populations in deep valleys or separate mountain peaks, and isolation brought about by lava flows and formation of kipukas are all factors which have permitted evolution to occur at an especially rapid rate.

The products of these evolutionary processes as we can observe them in Hawaii today include a series of botanical novelties. There are several groups that have woody species in Hawaii although they are members of a family which elsewhere in the world consists mostly of small herbs. Such woodiness occurs in violets (*Viola, Isodendrion*), lobelias (*Lobelia, Trematolobelia, Cyanea, Clermontia, Delissea, Rollandia*, and *Brighamia*), plantains (*Plantago*), amaranths (*Charpentiera*), and chenopods (*Chenopodium*). In some families, adaptive radiation has occurred—several species and genera have evolved from a common ancestor and now occupy a series of different ecological niches. Examples can be found among the lobelias, but perhaps the most striking example is a group of members of the sunflower family closely related to the tarweeds of western North America. In this group are several species of *Dubautia* ranging from small rain-forest trees to shrubs of open dry lava flows, species of *Argyroxiphium* (the silverswords and greenswords), and species of *Wilkesia* (the iliau or Kauai greenswords). While some otherwise herbaceous plants seem to have developed the woody habit in Hawaii, others are giant herbs such as the apeape (*Gunnera*) with circular leaves up to 6 feet in diameter.

Very few native plants have spines or thorns, even those whose continental ancestors probably possessed them. The akala or Hawaiian raspberry (*Rubus*) is usually almost without prickles although some individuals do exhibit them. This lack of spininess can probably be explained by the fact that the native plants

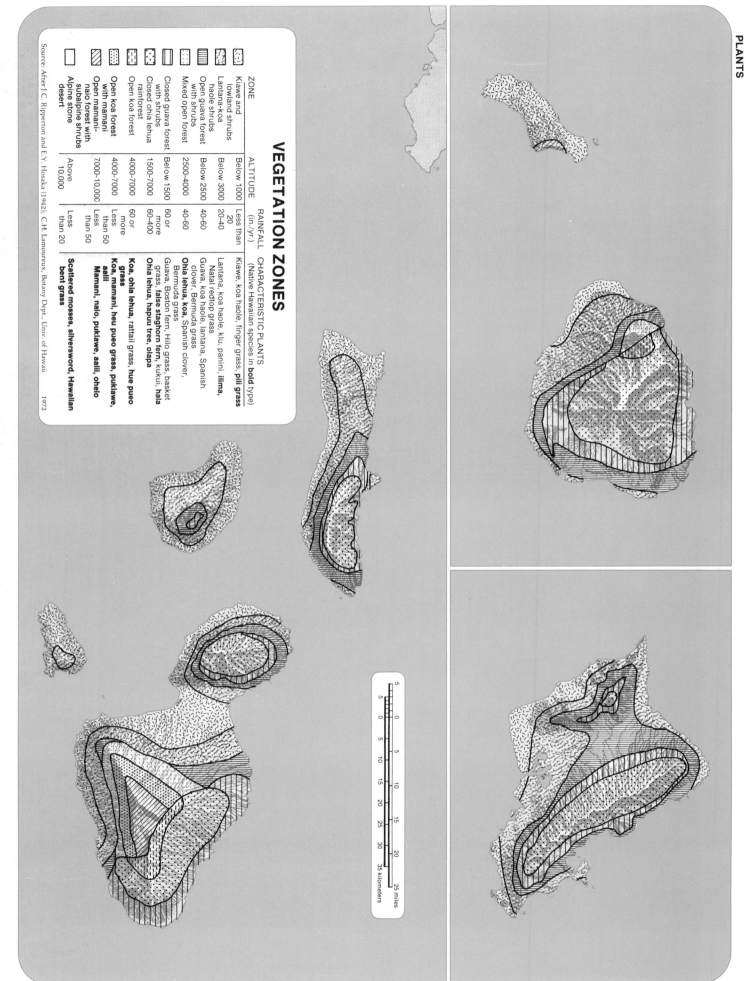

VEGETATION ZONES

ZONE	ALTITUDE	RAINFALL (in./yr.)	CHARACTERISTIC PLANTS (Native Hawaiian species in **bold** type)
Kiawe and lowland shrubs	Below 1000	Less than 20	Kiawe, koa haole, finger grass, **pili grass**
Lantana-koa haole shrubs	Below 3000	20-40	Lantana, koa haole, klu, panini, **ilima,** Natal redtop grass
Open guava forest with shrubs	Below 2500	40-60	Guava, koa haole, lantana, Spanish clover, Bermuda grass
Mixed open forest	2500-4000	40-60	**Ohia lehua, koa,** Spanish clover, Bermuda grass
Closed guava forest with shrubs	Below 1500	60 or more	Guava, Boston fern, Hilo grass, basket grass, **false staghorn fern, kukui, hala**
Closed ohia lehua rainforest	1500-7000	60-400	**Ohia lehua, hapuu tree, kukui, hala**
Open koa forest	4000-7000	60 or more	**Koa, ohia lehua,** rattail grass, hue pueo grass
Open koa forest with mamani	4000-7000	Less than 50	**Koa, mamani,** heu pueo grass, puklawe, **aalii**
Open mamani-naio forest with subalpine shrubs	7000-10,000	Less than 50	**Mamani, naio,** puklawe, **aalii, ohelo**
Alpine stone desert	Above 10,000	Less than 20	Scattered mosses, **silversword, Hawaiian bent grass**

Source: After J.C. Ripperton and E.Y. Hosaka (1942); C.H. Lamoureux, Botany Dept., Univ. of Hawaii   1972

The map shows the distribution of vegetation zones in Hawaii today. It is adapted from the one developed by Ripperton and Hosaka (1942). Vegetation is a term used for the physiognomy of the plant cover of an area, for example, a forest or a grassland. Generally the vegetation type is further characterized by reference to the dominant species. As can be seen from the map, the dominant or characteristic plants in all the vegetation zones at lower elevations are species introduced to Hawaii since 1778. What is actually shown is potential vegetation, that is, the vegetation that one might predict could develop in an area, given the climate and the plant species currently present in that area. It does not take into account the vegetation, or lack thereof, in urban areas and does not depict modifications resulting from plantation agriculture, pasture development, and similar factors. Also, it does not reflect differences in vegetation as related to different ages of lava flows or different stages of soil development. Although such factors are of considerable importance in governing the distribution of vegetation types, they cannot be depicted accurately on maps at this scale.

The zonation of plants is closely related to climatic factors, as a comparison of the vegetation map with climate maps (pages 56 and 58) will reveal. The most important climatic factors governing plant distribution in Hawaii seem to be average annual rainfall at elevations below about 5,000 feet, and temperature and rainfall at higher elevations.

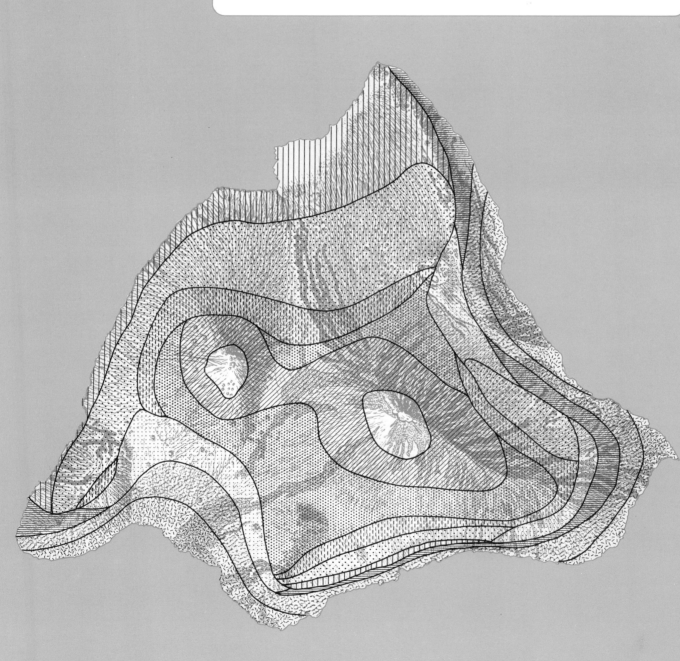

Uluhe, *Dicranopteris linearis*. A fern that forms dense tangled patches in forest openings at lower elevations.

Photographs by C.H. Lamoureux

Kolea lau nui, *Myrsine lessertiana*. An endemic tree, found frequently as an understory tree in rain forests.

Night-blooming cereus, *Hylocereus undatus*. This cactus, introduced from Mexico, has been widely planted in Hawaii.

Ohia lehua, *Metrosideros collina* subsp. *polymorpha*. The most common and most widely distributed native Hawaiian tree.

evolved in Hawaii when there were no grazing or browsing mammals present. Therefore there was no evolutionary pressure resulting in retention or development of such protective mechanisms as spines or thorns.

As a consequence of the isolation of the islands, several major groups of plants did not become successfully established in Hawaii until they were brought in by man. For example, Hawaii has no native conifers, no native mangroves, no native aroids, and no native banyans or figs, although all these groups are native throughout most of the tropics.

Other large groups of plants are poorly represented in the native flora. There is only one native genus of palms, the loulu (*Pritchardia*). There are only four native species of orchids—the lowest number of native orchids in any of the 50 states. Of the hundreds of species of palms and orchids grown in Hawaii today, essentially all have been introduced by man since 1800 from tropical parts of America, Africa, and Asia and from other Pacific islands.

The intentional introduction of plants to Hawaii was begun by early Polynesian voyagers, who brought with them about 25 species of plants used for food, fiber, shelter, and medicine. Among these plants were taro (*Colocasia*), coconut (*Cocos*), wauke (*Broussonetia*), kukui (*Aleurites*), breadfruit (*Artocarpus*), sugarcane (*Saccharum*), yams (*Dioscorea*), and ti (*Cordyline*). The Polynesians also brought the pig, the first herbivorous mammal to be introduced, as well as the dog, the jungle fowl, and the rat. This was the beginning of a series of ecological and environmental changes in Hawaii which continue at an ever-accelerating rate today. Land was cleared, crops were planted, native species of plants were replaced with introduced species. It is probable that some species of native plants became extinct, especially in the lowlands where the Hawaiian had the greatest environmental impact. There are no records, of course, to help modern scientists determine exactly what plants may have become extinct in the period between initial Polynesian colonization and the arrival of Captain Cook in 1778, but it is doubtful that the number was very great in comparison with the number which have become extinct since that time.

Cook released goats in Hawaii, and shortly thereafter other European explorers brought sheep, cattle, and horses. These hoofed, grazing, and browsing mammals had an especially severe impact on Hawaiian plants, which had no effective defenses against being either eaten or trampled by the animals. While the native plants were disappearing from large areas, new waves of European immigrants were busily introducing potentially useful plants. Some of these did prove useful, others escaped from cultivation and eventually became pests; still other weedy plants were unintentionally introduced along with the desirable species. As land was cleared for plantations and ranches, as sandalwood (*Santalum*) forests were destroyed for commercial purposes, and as other areas were stripped of native plants by feral animals, many of the newly introduced plants were able to spread into these areas and quickly became established. Some of these, such as klu (*Acacia farnesiana*), panini (*Opuntia megacantha*), and lantana (*Lantana camara*), possessed spines or thorns and were thus less susceptible to destruction by feral mammals.

By 1900 the native plant cover below about 1,500 feet elevation had been almost completely destroyed and replaced by a plant cover consisting largely of introduced species. At higher elevations, in some areas, larger numbers of native species persist but they are declining in numbers and being replaced by introduced competitors. The plants one sees in Honolulu today are the same widely planted ornamental species to be found in any city in the tropics—monkeypods (*Samanea*) and jacarandas (*Jacaranda*) from tropical America, tulip trees (*Spathodea*) and sausage trees (*Kigelia*) from tropical Africa, royal poincianas (*Delonix*) from Madagascar, and shower trees (*Cassia*) from India and tropical Asia.

C.H.L.

Amaumau, *Sadleria cyatheoides*. The young fronds of this fern are frequently reddish; they become green as they mature.

Photograph by C.H. Lamoureux

Poinsettia, *Euphorbia pulcherrima*. A shrub, introduced from Mexico, which produces masses of brightly colored floral bracts during the winter months.

Photograph by C.H. Lamoureux

Hoary bat from the island of Hawaii.
Photograph by P. Q. Tomich

MAMMALS

Because Hawaii is far from any continent and because geologically the present islands are very young, few land mammals have arrived through natural dispersal and become established. It is likely that truly marine mammals, the whales and dolphins, have been numerous in Hawaiian waters since very early times inasmuch as they are widely distributed in the oceans and are of ancient origin. When the seafaring Polynesians first came to Hawaii the only mammals associated with the land were a seal and a small bat. The domestic dog and pig and a commensal rat accompanied the Polynesians.

Most of the impressive variety of land mammals found in the Hawaiian Islands today have arrived since the rediscovery of the group by Cook in 1778. These aggressive introduced species have had a pronounced effect on the face of Hawaii—its vegetation, its birds, and in one way or another on all terrestrial life of the islands. However, this brief discussion will summarize only what is known of the mammals of earlier periods and their place in the island ecosystem, as a background to more familiar present-day conditions.

Bat. The most remarkable example of a land-based mammal reaching Hawaii under its own power is the hoary bat (*Lasiurus*). Flights that brought bats to Hawaii may have been rare, and the local population probably has been isolated from its parent stock for tens of thousands of years. Our bat is a small reddish form, distinct at the subspecies level from its larger, grizzled brown continental relatives. There are two continental populations, one in North America and one in South America. The hoary bat is strongly migratory and regularly reaches the Farallon Islands off California, the Galápagos, and the Bermudas. Specimens have been captured in Iceland, and there is one

probable record for the Orkney Islands, near Scotland. Thus the hoary bat of Hawaii is from a hardy stock with a proved potential for dispersal. Long flights must depend on adequate supplies of fuel, in the form of fat, for sustained energy. Even now, the resident bat of Hawaii lays in a reserve of body fat late in summer, although its migratory instincts are suppressed. The principal breeding population is on the island of Hawaii, but another exists on Kauai. Bats are reported occasionally on Oahu and on Maui, but it is not known whether they are resident there or whether bats move regularly between the islands.

Seal. The seal of Hawaii is one of the monk seals (*Monachus*). It is a relict species that became isolated from close relatives in the Caribbean and Mediterranean when the Isthmus of Panama was formed some 200,000 years ago. The Hawaiian monk seal somehow made its way to the Hawaiian Archipelago, and very possibly it was the first mammal to live on these shores. It is now endemic to Hawaii; that is, it is found nowhere else in the world. The principal breeding population frequents the region from French Frigate Shoals to Kure Atoll. Although this monk seal ranges at sea, it is typically a creature of sandy beaches and adjacent shallows. Rarely, one is seen in the vicinity of the main islands. The ancient Hawaiians probably did not regularly hunt the monk seal. By about 1900, however, it was near extinction as a result of exploitation by explorers and other seafarers who killed the animals for food and perhaps for their skins and oil. Remarkably, it was unknown to science until 1905. Under careful protection in the Hawaiian Islands National Wildlife Refuge it has made an encouraging recovery, and there are now well over a thousand individuals.

Rat. The Polynesian rat (*Rattus*) that accompanied the colonizers of Hawaii some 1,000 to 1,500 years ago is widely distributed in the Pacific wherever Polynesian peoples settled. Like them, it originated in Southeast Asia. Because of its minor importance in Hawaiian culture, the Polynesian rat is generally supposed to have come as an accidental stowaway and not as an intentional introduction. It was not eaten in Hawaii, as it was in New Zealand, although it was used in a formalized contest or sport in which rats were placed in an arena and shot with bows and arrows. This singular pastime is authenticated only for Hawaii. The Polynesian rat in Hawaii is justly referred to as a native rat; it has evolved into an assemblage of populations distinct from those in other regions of the Pacific, and is considered a separate subspecies or geographic race.

Rodents in modern Hawaii, including the Polynesian rat, have been a serious problem in wildlife conservation, in the

Hawaiian monk seal at Laysan Island.
Photograph by P.Q. Tomich

Tamed feral piglet. Traces of wild-type coat stripings are evident.

economy, and in public health. A specific example of wildlife predation is the direct extinction of the Laysan rail (*Porzanula*) when the roof rat invaded its last refuge at Midway Islands in World War II. We may never know the toll that rats have taken of birdlife on the larger islands, and it is remarkable that forest-inhabiting native birds survive at all in the presence of these rodents. Sugarcane and other crops are damaged by rats in the fields, and annual losses are estimated in millions of dollars. Rats have been reservoirs of bubonic plague in Hawaii for more than half a century, from 1899 until at least 1957, but this fear-some disease of man probably has now been eradicated from the islands. Intensive research in Hawaii during the past 15 years has helped find means to alleviate many rodent-caused problems.

Dog. The domestic dog (*Canis*), like the domestic pig, was important in Polynesian cultures as a pet, for food, for barter, in religious ritual, and as a source of raw materials for arts and crafts. Both animals were available, fully domesticated, in an earlier Asian homeland of the Polynesians, and they would cer-tainly have been brought to Hawaii eventually by voyagers who intended to settle in the islands. Dogs were a staple item of food; they were kept in pens and reared on a vegetable diet. At large feasts in the early 1800s as many as 200 to 400 dogs would be served. The Polynesian dog was evidently a small, dull-witted, and unaggressive beast that most likely did not survive away from the villages. There is no evidence that it developed a pre-dator-prey relationship with the pigs that may have roamed in the forests. Rather, it was probably dependent on man for both care and shelter and was not man's companion nor a protector of the home, as is the dog of Western cultures. The original Hawaiian breeds of dogs have been gradually submerged by repeated crossings with those brought from other regions of the world. The introduction of suitable prey species made it possible for these new aggressive strains to live in the wild. Domestic and feral sheep have been the most important food of feral dogs, and such dogs are still found in outlying areas where they are a menace to poultry, wild birds, game mammals, and livestock. Dogs breed in the wild on all the major islands, but packs of uniform character seldom are formed because of the frequent infusion of new blood from strays. Dogs reared in the wild recognize man as potential prey rather than as either friend or foe, and are prone to attack him on sight.

Pig. It is probable that pigs (*Sus*) lived free in the moun-tains before European times in Hawaii, but the evidence is in-direct and scanty. Certainly, the omnivorous pig should have had no difficulty making its living in the lush forests, much as it does today. However, there is no tradition which suggests that the Hawaiians were hunters or that they made use of forest animals other than birds. Captain Cook made the pointed re-mark that he could get no pigs larger than 50 to 60 pounds when he bartered for them as provender for his ships in 1779. Total impact of pigs on the indigenous vegetation may have been slight. The pig of early times has been modified or perhaps totally replaced by more recently imported domestic breeds that readily took to the wild. After many generations, these feral pigs have selectively reverted to types that resemble the European wild boar and are generally large in size. This newer stock of pigs certainly has placed its mark on native forest vegetation through direct damage to the forest floor and by the spread of exotic plants, to an extent that is only now being assessed.

It can be inferred that the early Polynesians lived in har-mony with the community of mammals then established in Ha-waii, and with the natural ecosystem. Their technology was poorly developed; they had no large, hoofed mammals; and they depended heavily on the resources of the sea. It is no credit to European man and those who followed him to Hawaii that several introduced land mammals were permitted to revert to nature and to form uncontrolled feral populations (e.g., cat-tle, goats, and sheep), or came as uninvited immigrants on his ships (a mouse and additional species of rats), or were unwise introductions in the first place (mongoose, axis deer). The frag-ile terrestrial ecosystems of Hawaii, with assemblages of plants, birds, and insects that are unique in the world, have suffered accordingly. Today there are encouraging signs that more in-telligent action will prevail in the future in perpetuating our in-valuable biological assets. The keys to the problem are com-munity education toward better understanding of the natural environment, and continued preservation of significant natural habitats. Great effort must be made to halt unwise exploitation of land resources for short-term gain, and to enforce strict con-trol of the browsers, the tramplers, and other predators on natural plant and animal communities.

P.Q.T.

MAMMALS CLASSED ACCORDING TO PERIOD OF ARRIVAL, MEANS OF ARRIVAL, AND CULTURAL SIGNIFICANCE

Marine mammals that may have ranged into the area before the islands arose, and are currently found in Hawaiian waters

Rough-toothed dolphin	*Steno bredanensis*
Slender-beaked dolphin	*Stenella attenuata*
Spinner dolphin	*Stenella longirostris*
Common dolphin	*Delphinus delphis*
Common bottlenose dolphin	*Tursiops truncatus*
Pacific bottlenose dolphin	*Tursiops gillii*
Pacific white-sided dolphin	*Lagenorhynchus obliquidens*
False killer whale	*Pseudorca crassidens*
Killer whale	*Orcinus orca*
Pilot whale	*Globicephala melaena*
Hawaiian dolphin	*Peponocephala electra*
Pygmy killer whale	*Feresa attenuata*
Pygmy sperm whale	*Kogia breviceps*
Sperm whale	*Physeter catodon*
Blainville's beaked whale	*Mesoplodon densirostris*
Cuvier's beaked whale	*Ziphius cavirostris*
Hump-backed whale	*Megaptera novaeangliae*

Land-based mammals with specialized abilities for reaching Hawaii from continental shores before the arrival of man in Hawaii

Hoary bat	*Lasiurus cinereus*
Hawaiian monk seal	*Monachus schauinslandi*

Species that accompanied the Polynesian peoples and were associated with their cultures

Polynesian rat	*Rattus exulans*
Domestic dog	*Canis familiaris*
Pig	*Sus scrofa*

Immigrant species that arrived accidentally with shipping and developed commensal and wild populations

Roof rat	*Rattus rattus*
Norway rat	*Rattus norvegicus*
House mouse	*Mus musculus*

Domesticated mammals brought by man in post-contact times and developed significant feral populations

European rabbit	*Oryctolagus cuniculus*
Domestic dog	*Canis familiaris*
House cat	*Felis catus*
Domestic horse	*Equus caballus*
Donkey	*Equus asinus*
Pig	*Sus scrofa*
Domestic cattle	*Bos taurus*
Domestic goat	*Capra hircus*
Domestic sheep	*Ovis aries*

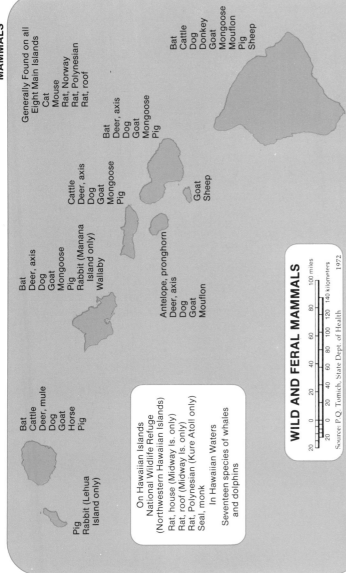

Pig
Rabbit (Lehua Island only)

On Hawaiian Islands
National Wildlife Refuge
(Northwestern Hawaiian Islands)
Rat, house (Midway Is. only)
Rat, roof (Midway Is. only)
Rat, Polynesian (Kure Atoll only)
Seal, monk
   In Hawaiian Waters
Seventeen species of whales
and dolphins

Antelope, pronghorn
Deer, axis
Dog
Goat
Mouflon

Cattle
Deer, axis
Dog
Goat
Mongoose
Pig

Goat
Sheep

Bat
Deer, axis
Dog
Goat
Mongoose
Pig
Rabbit (Manana Island only)
Wallaby

Bat
Deer, axis
Dog
Goat
Mongoose
Pig

Generally Found on all
Eight Main Islands
Cat
Mouse
Rat, Norway
Rat, Polynesian
Rat, roof

Bat
Cattle
Dog
Donkey
Goat
Mongoose
Mouflon
Pig
Sheep

WILD AND FERAL MAMMALS

20 0   20   40   60   80   100 miles
20 0 20 40 60 80 100 120 140 kilometers

Source: P.Q. Tomich, State Dept. of Health   1972

Wild mammals brought for zoo display, rat control or sport hunting, and which produced stable free-ranging populations

Brush-tailed rock-wallaby	*Petrogale penicillata*
Small Indian mongoose	*Herpestes auropunctatus*
Axis deer	*Axis axis*
Mule (black-tail) deer	*Odocoileus hemionus*
Pronghorn antelope	*Antilocapra americana*
Mouflon sheep	*Ovis musimon*

Petroglyph figure of a dog from the island of Hawaii (chalked for contrast).

Photograph by P.Q. Tomich

Polynesian rat feeding on sugarcane. This rodent is abundant in lowland agricultural areas.

Photograph by P.Q. Tomich

Feral goats feeding near an experimental enclosure fence in Hawaii Volcanoes National Park. The rank vegetation that sprang up inside the fence after 17 months is largely of native grasses and a previously unknown native bean. Land outside the fence is cropped bare by goats. It is hoped that a current control program will eliminate goats from the park.

Photograph by P.Q. Tomich

Koloa or Hawaiian duck, *Anas wyvilliana.*
Photograph by E. Kridler

Io or Hawaiian hawk, *Buteo solitarius.*
Illustration from Wilson and Evans (1890–1899)

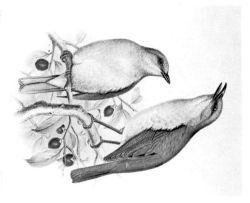

Omao or Hawaiian thrush, *Phaeornis obscurus.*
Illustration from Wilson and Evans (1890–1899)

Nene or Hawaiian goose, *Branta sandvicensis.*
Photograph by E. Kridler

BIRDS

Native Hawaiian Birds. Hawaii's isolated location in the middle of the Pacific Ocean, far from the continental land masses of North America and Asia, has made possible the evolution of many unique Hawaiian land birds. Ten families of world birds have representatives on the Hawaiian Islands, and one family is found only in Hawaii.

Some of Hawaii's native birds are adapted for spending most of their lives in the vicinity of streams, ponds, marshes, or tidal flats. These include the Koloa or Hawaiian duck (*Anas wyvilliana*), Laysan duck (*Anas laysanensis*), gallinule (*Gallinula chloropus sandvicensis*), coot (*Fulica americana alai*), and the black-necked stilt (*Himantopus himantopus knudseni*).

The State bird of Hawaii is the Nene or Hawaiian goose (*Branta sandvicensis*). Unlike its relatives in other parts of the world, the Nene has become adapted to life on rugged lava flows far removed from either standing or running water. The Nene carries on its nesting activities at elevations between about 5,000 and 8,000 feet on Mauna Loa on the island of Hawaii. The State Division of Fish and Game released more than 200 pen-reared Nene in Haleakala Crater, Maui, between 1962 and 1969. Reproductive success of these birds has been exceedingly low, however, and a maximum of three young birds were known to have been raised to independence as of 1972.

The largest number of Hawaii's native birds inhabit dense forests, but three species usually are found in pastures, scrubland, and cutover forests. Two of these are found only on the island of Hawaii—the Hawaiian hawk or Io (*Buteo solitarius*) and the Hawaiian crow or Alala (*Corvus tropicus*). The Hawaiian short-eared owl or Pueo (*Asio flammeus sandvichensis*) is a permanent resident on all of the main inhabited islands; it is found in open grassland, pastures, and forests, on lava flows and in residential areas. The true forest birds of the main islands belong to four different bird families, and a fifth family (Sylviidae, Old World warblers) is represented by the Nihoa millerbird (*Arocephalus familiaris kingi*), whose total world range is confined to the 156-acre volcanic remnant called Nihoa Island.

The Hawaiian thrush or Omao (*Phaeornis obscurus*) is a common inhabitant of the relatively undisturbed native forests on Hawaii and Kauai. The small Kauai thrush (*Phaeornis palmeri*) lives only in the Alakai Swamp on Kauai.

The Elepaio (*Chasiempis sandvichensis*), an important bird in Hawaiian mythology, is found on Kauai, Oahu, and Hawaii. The Elepaio has been the most adaptable of all the native land birds, and on Oahu it can be found in some areas (such as upper Manoa Valley and Moanalua Valley) where nearly all of the vegetation is composed of introduced plants. It also inhabits the very wet native ohia forests and the relatively dry mamani-naio forests on Mauna Kea. The Elepaio is a member of a large family (Muscicapidae) consisting of Old World flycatchers. Another Old World family contains birds called honeyeaters (Meliphagidae). The center of abundance of this family is Australia and New Guinea, but five species once lived in Hawaii. Separate species of Oo (genus *Moho*) occurred on the islands of Kauai, Oahu, and Molokai as recently as the 1890s, but all are now thought to be extinct except for the Kauai Oo (*Moho braccatus*). This rare species is to be found only in the depths of the Alakai Swamp.

Hawaii is best known among ornithologists around the world for the endemic family of Hawaiian honeycreepers (Drepanididae). From a single ancestral species that reached the Hawaiian Islands in the remote past, 22 species and 24 subspecies or geographical races evolved on the various islands of the chain. This family of birds demonstrates better than any other bird family the evolutionary process of adaptive radiation. The bills of the several species vary from extremely heavy, seed-crushing and wood-tearing bills to long, decurved bills suited for obtaining the nectar from lobelia flowers and short,

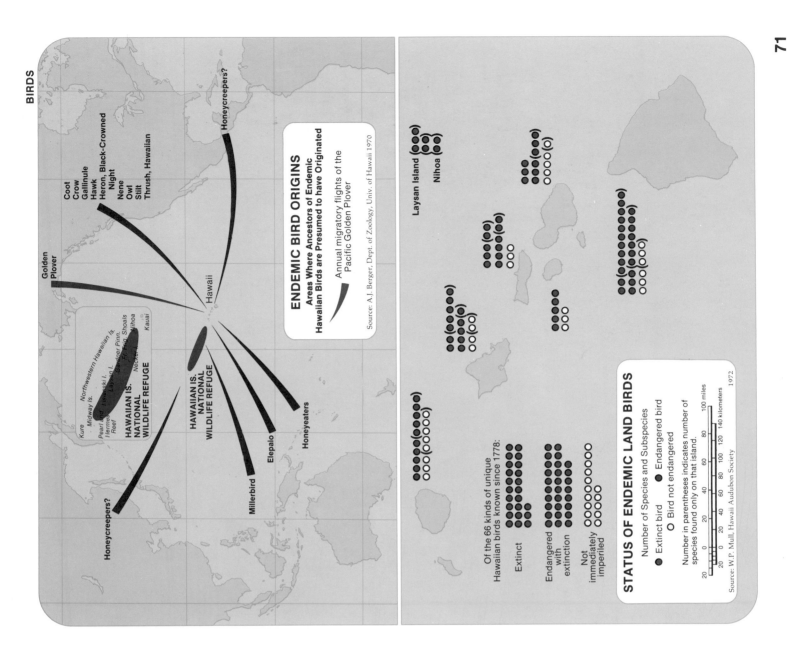

ENDEMIC BIRD ORIGINS
Areas Where Ancestors of Endemic
Hawaiian Birds are Presumed to have Originated

Annual migratory flights of the
Pacific Golden Plover

Source: A.J. Berger, Dept. of Zoology, Univ. of Hawaii 1970

Honeycreepers?

Golden
Plover

Coot
Crow
Gallinule
Hawk
Heron, Black-Crowned
Night
Nene
Owl
Stilt
Thrush, Hawaiian

Hawaii

Honeycreepers?

Kure Northwestern Hawaiian Is.
Midway Is.
Pearl and Hermes I. Laysan I. Gardner Pinn.
Reef Fr. Frig. Shoals Nihoa
Necker Kauai
HAWAIIAN IS.
NATIONAL
WILDLIFE REFUGE

HAWAIIAN IS.
NATIONAL
WILDLIFE REFUGE

Honeyeaters

Elepaio

Millerbird

STATUS OF ENDEMIC LAND BIRDS

Number of Species and Subspecies

● Extinct bird   ● Endangered bird
○ Bird not endangered

Number in parentheses indicates number of
species found only on that island.

Of the 66 kinds of unique
Hawaiian birds known since 1778:

Extinct

Endangered
with
extinction

Not
immediately
imperiled

Laysan Island

Nihoa

0 20 40 60 80 100 miles
20 0 20 40 60 80 100 120 140 kilometers

1972

Source: W.P. Mull, Hawaii Audubon Society

---

delicate bills that can be used either for catching insects or sipping nectar. In fact, so diverse in their bill structure are the honeycreepers that the first European ornithologists who studied them placed different species in several different bird families. In plumage pattern, the many species vary from the brilliant, vermilion-colored Iiwi (*Vestiaria coccinea*), with black wings and tail, to the yellow and yellowish green Anianiau (*Loxops parva*).

Some species of honeycreeper were confined to a single island—for example, the Anianiau to Kauai, and the Akiapolaau (*Hemignathus wilsoni*) and the Mamo (*Drepanis pacifica*) to Hawaii. By contrast, the Apapane (*Himatione sanguinea*) was found on all of the inhabited islands, and a subspecies inhabited Laysan Island.

Unfortunately, of the 66 different kinds of unique Hawaiian land birds that were known during the nineteenth century, about 35 percent are thought to be extinct, and 42 percent are considered to be rare and endangered. These endangered Hawaiian birds account for more than *one-half* of all the birds listed by the United States Bureau of Sport Fisheries and Wildlife in the Red Book of rare and endangered species! In fact, four times as many birds have become extinct in Hawaii as in the entire North American continent, or any other area of the world with the possible exception of the Mascarene Islands.

Indigenous Hawaiian Birds. These are birds that are native to Hawaii but also to a much wider geographical area. The black-crowned night heron (*Nycticorax nycticorax hoactli*), for example, has inhabited the main Hawaiian Islands for an unknown, but very long, period of time. However, this heron is not considered to be an endemic species because ornithologists do not recognize it as having any distinctive characteristics that would justify separating it from the continental subspecies, which has a breeding range extending from Washington and Oregon southward to northern Chile and Argentina.

The black-crowned night heron occurs on all of the main islands, where it inhabits ponds, marshes, and lagoons. It feeds on aquatic insects, fish, frogs, and mice. The birds roost and nest in trees. The future of this species in Hawaii is completely dependent upon the preservation of suitable feeding habitat. With the rapid expansion of Hawaii's population and the consequent demand for housing and commercial buildings, the marshland habitat required by the heron, coot, and gallinule has been reduced drastically in recent years, and these birds are classified as endangered species.

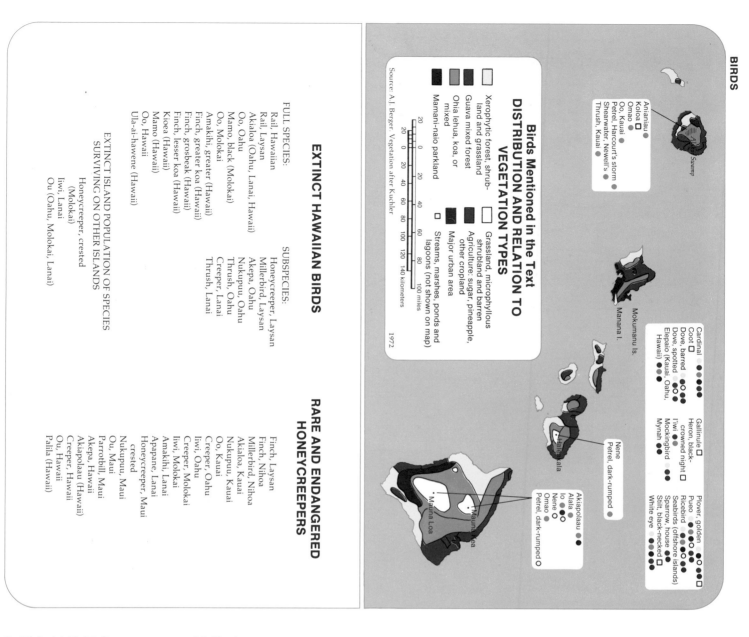

**Birds Mentioned in the Text
DISTRIBUTION AND RELATION TO
VEGETATION TYPES**

Xerophytic forest, shrub-land and grassland
Guava mixed forest
Ohia lehua, koa, or mixed
Mamani-naio parkland
Grassland, microphyllous shrubland and barren
Agriculture; sugar, pineapple, other cropland
Major urban area
Streams, marshes, ponds and lagoons (not shown on map)

Source: A.J. Berger: Vegetation after Kuchler   1972

Aniani au
Koloa
Omao
Oo, Kauai
Petrel, Harcourt's storm
Shearwater, Newell's
Thrush, Kauai

Swamp

Mokumanu Is.
Manana I.

Cardinal
Coot
Dove, barred
Dove, spotted
Elepaio (Kauai, Oahu, Hawaii)
Mynah

Gallinule
Heron, black-crowned night-
I'iwi
Mockingbird

Plover, golden
Pueo
Ricebird
Seabirds (offshore islands)
Sparrow, house
Stilt, black-necked
White eye

Nene
Petrel, dark-rumped

Akiapolaau
Alala
Io
Nene
Omao
Petrel, dark-rumped

Mauna Loa
Mauna Kea
Haleakala

EXTINCT HAWAIIAN BIRDS

FULL SPECIES:
Rail, Hawaiian
Rail, Laysan
Akialoa (Oahu, Lanai, Hawaii)
Oo, Oahu
Mamo, black (Molokai)
Oo, Molokai
Amakihi, greater (Hawaii)
Finch, greater koa (Hawaii)
Finch, grosbeak (Hawaii)
Finch, lesser koa (Hawaii)
Kioea (Hawaii)
Mamo (Hawaii)
Oo, Hawaii
Ula-ai-havene (Hawaii)

SUBSPECIES:
Honeycreeper, Laysan
Millerbird, Laysan
Akepa, Oahu
Nukupuu, Oahu
Thrush, Oahu
Creeper, Lanai
Thrush, Lanai

**EXTINCT ISLAND POPULATION OF SPECIES
SURVIVING ON OTHER ISLANDS**
Honeycreeper, crested (Molokai)
Iiwi, Lanai
Ou (Oahu, Molokai, Lanai)

RARE AND ENDANGERED HONEYCREEPERS

Finch, Laysan
Finch, Nihoa
Millerbird, Nihoa
Akialoa, Kauai
Nukupuu, Kauai
Oo, Kauai
Creeper, Kauai
Creeper, Oahu
Iiwi, Oahu
Creeper, Molokai
Iiwi, Molokai
Creeper, Molokai
Amakihi, Lanai
Apapane, Lanai
Honeycreeper, Maui crested
Nukupuu, Maui
Ou, Maui
Parrotbill, Maui
Akepa, Hawaii
Akiapolaau (Hawaii)
Creeper, Hawaii
Ou, Hawaii
Palila (Hawaii)

The so-called seabirds or oceanic birds comprise the largest group of indigenous birds. Twenty-two different species belonging to six families and three orders of birds return to the Hawaiian Islands each year to carry on their nesting activities. Many of these species spend the nonbreeding season flying over the open ocean, obtaining their food (fish and squid) from the ocean and resting on its surface. Some species, such as the sooty tern (*Sterna fuscata*), however, are thought to fly continuously for months at a time during the nonbreeding season, not once alighting on land or on the surface of the ocean to rest.

The majority of seabirds in Hawaii nest on the Northwestern Hawaiian Islands. All of these islands, except Midway and Kure, form the Hawaiian Islands National Wildlife Refuge. Several million seabirds nest on these tiny islands where the only mammalian predator is man himself. Three small passerine birds also live out their lives on two of these islands: the Laysan finch (*Psittirostra cantans cantans*) and Nihoa finch (*P. cantans ultima*), both finch-billed honeycreepers, and the Nihoa millerbird, an Old World warbler.

Some of the offshore islands of the main chain also provide suitable nesting areas for seabirds. Two of the most important are Mokumanu and Manana Island off the coast of Oahu. Twelve different species are known to have nested on Mokumanu in recent years and four species on Manana Island. Sooty terns and common noddies (*Anous stolidus*) nest on Manana Island by the tens of thousands.

Some species of seabirds probably nested on all of the high inhabited islands, and it is known that the Hawaiians used both the adults and the fat nestlings for food. Two species are believed now to nest only in the remote mountains of Kauai: Newell's shearwater (*Puffinus puffinus newelli*), whose nesting grounds were not discovered until 1967, and Harcourt's storm petrel (*Oceanodroma castro cryptoleucura*), whose nesting grounds still had not been discovered as of 1971. The dark-rumped petrel (*Pterodroma phaeopygia sandwichensis*) nests in Haleakala Crater, Maui, and, in much smaller numbers, on Mauna Loa and Mauna Kea on the island of Hawaii.

Also included in the category of indigenous birds is a group of migratory species that spend the nonbreeding season on the Hawaiian Islands but nest 2,000 or more miles north of the islands in Alaska or Siberia. The best known of these is the Pacific golden plover (*Pluvialis dominica fulva*), a shorebird that is a common winter resident on all of the islands. It inhabits the lawns and golf courses of residential areas and also is found at elevations up to about 10,000 feet on the mountains of Hawaii.

Mamo, *Drepanis pacifica.*
Illustration from Wilson and Evans (1890-1899)

Apapane, *Himatione sanguinea.*
Illustration from Wilson and Evans (1890-1899)

Akohekohe, crested honeycreeper,
Palmeria dolei.
Illustration from Wilson and Evans (1890-1899)

Blue-faced booby, *Sula dactylatra.*
Photograph by E. Kridler
U.S. Sport Fisheries and Wildlife

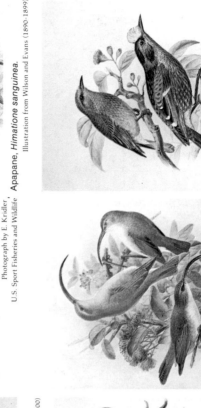

Laysan albatross, *Diomedea immutabilis.*
Photograph by E. Kridler,
U.S. Sport Fisheries and Wildlife

Kauai Akialoa, *Hemignathus procerus.*
Illustration from Rothschild (1893-1900)

Elepaio, *Chasiempis sandwichensis.*
Illustration from Rothschild (1893-1900)

Kauai Oo, *Moho braccatus.*
Illustration from Rothschild (1893-1900)

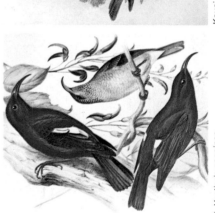

Iiwi, *Vestiaria coccinea.*
Illustration from Wilson and Evans (1890-1899)

Other species of shorebirds and ducks also migrate to Hawaii at the end of their breeding seasons in northern areas.

Introduced Birds. There is no way of being certain what kind of vegetation covered the lowlands of the main Hawaiian Islands when the first Polynesians landed. Whatever the vegetation had been, it was largely replaced by the introduced plants that the Hawaiians used for food and fiber. We do know that the naturalists who accompanied Captain Cook found some native birds at no great elevation above sea level. Cook and later visitors unintentionally caused the destruction of much of the native flora by releasing cattle, goats, pigs, sheep, and other grazing animals (page 67). Protected by a kapu declared by Kamehameha the Great, and in the absence of any of their normal predators, these feral animals multiplied exceedingly fast. They destroyed many native forests by trampling the ground and by eating the seedlings of the trees. Being dependent upon the endemic plants for food, shelter, and nesting sites, the native birds either had to move or perish, and many perished. As a result, when foreigners from many lands made a new home in Hawaii during the nineteenth century, there were no songbirds in the lowlands. It was natural that the settlers should want to import familiar birds from their homelands, and, when sugarcane, pineapple, and cattle became important economically, an effort was made to introduce birds that would feed upon the insect pests of the crops and cattle.

Records of foreign bird introductions in Hawaii have always been scanty, but we know that a minimum of 156 different kinds of exotic birds had gained their freedom in the Hawaiian Islands between 1796, when the first pigeons or rock doves (*Columba livia*) were released, and 1970. We know that other species were released, but, if any records at all were made, they consisted only of a common name in a newspaper article.

Available evidence suggests that, of the 156 foreign introductions, 108 species failed to survive and 48 species are now established as breeding populations. The most familiar of the established species are the common mynah (*Acridotheres tristis*), white-eye (*Zosterops japonica*), cardinal (*Richmondena cardinalis*), red-crested cardinal (*Paroaria coronata*), mockingbird (*Mimus polyglottos*), house sparrow (*Passer domesticus*), barred dove (*Geopelia striata*), and spotted dove (*Streptopelia chinensis*). These exotic species were brought to Hawaii from many parts of the world: North America, South America, Europe, Japan, India, China, and other parts of Asia.

A. J. B.

73

Fig. 1. Citrus swallowtail, *Papilio xuthus* Linnaeus (female and male).

Photograph by Ron Mau

Fig. 2. Kamehameha butterfly, *Vanessa tameamea* Eschscholtz.

Photograph by Ron Mau

Fig. 3. Blackburn's butterfly, *Vaga blackburni* (Tuely).

Photograph by W. Gagne

Fig. 4. The coconut leafroller, *Hedylepta blackburni* (Butler).

Photograph by Ron Mau

INSECTS

Insects were probably the first terrestrial animals to reach the Hawaiian Islands. Long before man came, there were many thousands of insect species established.

When the Hawaiians first arrived there were no pestiferous forms present and no insects which would damage plants used as human food. But the situation changed rapidly as the early immigrants brought body lice, some domestic flies, and probably fleas. The first published reference to Hawaiian insects was made by William Ellis (1783:156), the assistant surgeon on Cook's voyage of 1778, when he indicated that house flies were troublesome to the natives. He reported that flyflaps, or brushes, made of a bunch of feathers fixed to the end of a thin piece of polished wood or bone, were used to brush away flies. The kahilis, as the brushes were called, gradually became symbols of rank among the Hawaiians, and kahili bearers usually accompanied royalty. The flyflaps evolved into the immense symbolic kahilis which were used at funerals and royal occasions, and which are still seen at special Hawaiian ceremonies.

With the arrival of Europeans came mosquitoes, cockroaches, ticks, termites, flies, ants, grasshoppers, bugs, and other destructive and pestiferous insects. As transport became faster and as more people arrived in the islands the number of new immigrant insects increased rapidly. In spite of strict quarantine measures over the past 20 years an average of 16 new insect species have become established each year, but fortunately relatively few of these have been injurious species. Nevertheless, in the last 10 years Hawaii has received one new mosquito, several plant-eating bugs, defoliating grasshoppers and caterpillars, leafminers, and other pests. A recent arrival that has become established is a beautiful swallow-tail butterfly (Fig. 1) whose caterpillars do serious damage as they feed on leaves of citrus. The constant influx of new insects creates a threat to the local economy, and the State needs to be prepared to combat dangerous species as soon as they are discovered.

These invasions of insects from other areas over the years and the tremendous changes brought about by man—urbanization, destruction of the forests, depredation by introduced deer, goats, pigs, cattle, sheep, and rats—have caused the native Hawaiian insects, almost without exception, to disappear from the

lowland areas, as is the case with the native plants, birds, and land snails. The endemic forms are now found only at higher elevations, in deep valleys, and in areas where native plants are still found. The native flora and fauna are closely associated and interdependent; when one disappears the other soon follows.

One of the most unusual features of the Hawaiian Islands is the remarkable fauna of insects—as well as of birds and land snails—which has evolved. Probably nowhere else in the world has such a profusion of different forms and unusual adaptations developed in such a short period of geological time. Hawaii is indeed one of the most ideal places in the world for evolutionary studies. Compared with those of continental areas, the biotic factors affecting speciation, or change, are rather simple in oceanic situations, and research technics now being used should begin to explain why evolution has proceeded at such a rapid pace, how and why animals evolve, and how long a period is required for speciation to occur. But the islands are changing rapidly, and many native species have already been lost and many others are endangered; it is vital that the unusual opportunities for research on this remarkable fauna be exploited as rapidly as possible.

It appears evident that nearly 10,000 species of insects occur throughout Hawaii of which about 98 percent are found nowhere else in the world. It has been estimated that this total fauna probably originated from as few as 150 ancestral species. The 10,000 estimated species are divided roughly into the following groups: approximately 3,000 beetles; 1,500 flies; 1,250-1,500 wasps and bees; 1,250-1,500 moths and butterflies; 1,000 bugs; 750-1,000 leafhoppers and scale insects; and nearly 1,000 grasshoppers, crickets, lacewings, bark lice, and miscellaneous groups of insects. It is apparent that many thousands of new species remain to be discovered, named, and described.

The layman is usually unaware of Hawaii's remarkable biota, especially its insects. The native species are mostly confined to areas relatively unmolested by man and are seldom encountered except by the biologist. For the most part, they are cryptic, often small, well camouflaged, and inconspicuous; they are often found in only certain types of habitats.

The Hawaiian insect fauna is described by biologists as disharmonic—that is, many major groups which would be found in continental areas are completely lacking in Hawaii, and their places are taken by forms that evolved in the islands. The ancestral types were mostly small species carried to Hawaii by cyclonic winds or perhaps in the jet stream; others may have been carried on the feet or bodies of migratory birds; and still others may

Fig. 5. The "fabulous green sphinx of Kauai," *Tinostoma smaragditis* (Meyrick).

Photograph by W. Gagne

Fig. 6. Native Drosophila with common "garbage can" species, *Drosophila nigrofacies* (Hardy) and *D. simulans* Sturtevant.

Photograph by D.E. Hardy

Fig. 7. Native *Drosophila*, *D. mimica* Hardy.

Photograph by H. Stalker

Fig. 8. Native *Drosophila*, *D. crucigera* Grimshaw.

Photograph by H. Stalker

have traversed the ocean on driftwood. The chances of survival were indeed slim. It has been estimated that ancestral species arrived and became established at the rate of about one every 25,000+ years. The majority of the immigrants came from Asia and the southwest Pacific. The foun? ecies found ample un-occupied habitats in whi? le or no competition, predation, or para⸱¹ ts, and a favorable climate. Nev? s had to be made to ena¹¹ One of the un-

completely different habitats and ways of life from those of related forms in other parts of the world. Deviations from the usual are common in all orders.

Some visitors to the islands are disappointed not to find large, showy butterflies and other "exotic" insects in evidence. The butterfly fauna is sparse; there are only eleven species, of which only two are native. One is rather large, brightly colored, orange-red and black marked (Fig. 2). It feeds on mamaki (*Pipturus*) and related plants in the mountains. This species was named for King Kamehameha. The other, a small hairstreak, blue-brown above (Fig. 3) and bright green on the underside of the wings, feeds on leaves of koa. Well over a thousand species of moths have developed throughout the islands. Most are small, rather nondescript (Fig. 4), rarely seen creatures associated with a wide assortment of native plants. The hawk, or sphinx, moths, however, are large, showy insects, some having a wingspread of 4 inches and marked with bright colors. One has been referred to as "the fabulous green Sphinx" or "the elusive green Sphinx of Kauai" (Fig. 5). It is apparently the only green species of these large moths known in the world, and few specimens have been collected. It seems to be confined to the tops of ohia trees in the Kokee region of Kauai.

Most people are acquainted with *Drosophila* (pomace flies, or vinegar gnats), the small flies attracted to overripe or fermenting fruits, or to vinegar. These flies are used widely throughout the world in the study of genetics, and until about 1950 a large portion of the knowledge of this field was based on laboratory studies of these animals. An astonishing number of species of drosophilids occur in Hawaii, and nearly 500 species have now been described. It is estimated that the total number of species will reach 700. This is the greatest concentration of species known in the world, and the flies exhibit many modifications of structures and habits not found in other areas. Since 1963 a major research project at the University of Hawaii has been the study of their evolution and genetics.

The Hawaiian flies are ideal for studies of evolution and genetics since many of them are gigantic in size, many times larger than normal. They have giant chromosomes from the study of which a great deal of evolutionary information can be obtained. Many can be reared in artificial media for study and manipulation under laboratory conditions. Conspicuous markings over the wings characterize many species (Figs. 6–9), and most exhibit extraordinary sexual dimorphism, including, in the males, unusual structural developments on the legs and other parts of the body. Courtship and mating behavior is most elaborate. Each species has its distinctive behavior, and relationships and evolutionary trends can be determined by studying the courtship and mating patterns.

From studies of the chromosomes, behavior, morphology, and ecology, the relationships and evolution of approximately 100 of the picture-winged species have been ascertained. The degrees of relationship have been narrowed until it is now possible to identify newly formed species and incipient species. Some that can be demonstrated to be valid biological species cannot be differentiated by morphological characters.

It is evident that approximately 97 percent of the species are restricted to single islands, and most are plant specific. The representatives of ancestral types have been traced to Kauai, and the typical route of distribution has been shown to be from Kauai directly to Maui, bypassing Oahu in most cases. At least in the case of drosophilid flies it seems apparent that Maui has been the main center of diversification—that this is the area where the greatest number of species have developed. It has been clearly demonstrated that many major species groups arose on Maui and spread from there to the other Hawaiian Islands, although only rarely have they gone back to Kauai.

Beetles are the most abundant group of Hawaiian insects. This is a vast assemblage of highly diversified animals which in most parts of the world are among the most common and conspicuous of insects. In Hawaii, however, the native species are secretive and not readily seen. They are predominantly small creatures living in and under bark, as borers in wood of native trees, in mosses, and in ground litter and decaying plant materials. The largest and most ornate are the longhorned beetles (Figs. 10–11). These are wood borers which are highly host specific, and each different type is usually restricted to a certain species of native tree or woody shrub. Over 100 species have been described, and there are apparently many new species still to be discovered. Even though these beetles are large and often brightly marked—they often measure 3 or more inches in length with the antennae

Fig. 9. Native *Drosophila*, *D. picta* (Grimshaw).
Photograph by H. Stalker

Fig. 10. Native longhorned beetle, *Plagithmysus bilineatus* (Sharp).
Photograph by D.E. Hardy

Fig. 11. Native longhorned beetle, *Plagithmysus vitticollis* Sharp.
Photograph by D.E. Hardy

Fig. 12. Native damselfly, *Megalagrion* sp?
Photograph by D.E. Hardy

(feelers) extended—the adults are rarely seen, even by entomologists. The specialist working on these insects collects them by searching through the forests, finding trees or shrubs that have been damaged by the boring of the larvae; he cuts off these twigs and branches and brings them into the laboratory to rear the adult beetles.

Perhaps the most obvious of the native Hawaiian insects are the dragonflies and damselflies. The former are commonly seen all the way from sea level to the mountaintops; they are very strong fliers and represent one of the few groups whose ancestors probably reached Hawaii on their own power. The damselflies (Fig. 12) are among the most unusual in the world. In Hawaii they have evolved from aquatic to terrestrial animals; in other parts of the world the nymph stage of these insects lives in ponds and slow-moving streams. Twenty-seven species are known in Hawaii, many living in the leaf axils of certain forest plants, and one in the ground litter under dense fern growth.

Flightlessness has developed in a number of cases; certain insects, which have evolved from winged, actively flying ancestors, have lost their power of flight and have developed entirely different habits from those of relatives in other areas. Several lacewings have lost their ability to fly and have become rather bizarre creatures. Zimmerman (1957:80) referred to one of these (Fig. 13) as "one of the marvels of creation." A group of small predaceous flies have also lost their wings, except for a narrow strip along each front margin. They hop about like fleas on ground litter in the forest.

A recent discovery of immense biological importance is the presence of cave-dwelling insects and related animals in Hawaii. Howarth (1972), of the Bishop Museum, found an entirely new fauna living in lava tubes. About a dozen forms have been discovered which have lost most of the attributes that are normally essential for life on the surface, such as eyes, wings, and jumping powers. From an evolutionary standpoint this is an exciting discovery since, in terms of geological time, these adaptations must have occured very recently; these insects may provide rather precise data concerning the time required for new forms of animals to evolve. An eyeless and flightless planthopper lives on tree roots that dangle in the caves and apparently finds its food by means of refined senses of touch and smell. Two kinds of crickets walk on the floors and walls instead of jumping, as their surface relatives do. Their antennae are greatly elongated, three times longer than their bodies. Another specialized member of the community is a water-treading bug. Unlike its surface relatives which live near or on water, it lives on the damp walls and

preys on worms and fly larvae. A tiny beetle captures the springtails and mites that scurry on the walls, and the larger insects are preyed on by a large, blind wolf spider. It is probable that many other animals, still to be discovered, live in the total darkness of island caves.

The same pattern of profuse speciation and unusual adaptation occurs in many other different groups of Hawaiian insects (Figs. 14,15). The brief space available here has allowed discussion of only a few examples of a truly remarkable fauna. To date, 13 volumes of the series *Insects of Hawaii* have been prepared dealing with the major orders except for Coleoptera (beetles) and Hymenoptera (wasps and bees).

D. E. H.

Fig. 13. Flightless hemerobiid, *Pseudosectra swezeyi* Zimmerman.
Photograph by W. Gagne

Fig. 14. The Koa bug, *Coleotichus blackburniae* White.
Photograph by Ron Mau

Fig. 15. Native antlion, *Eidoleon wilsoni* (McLach).
Photograph by D.E. Hardy

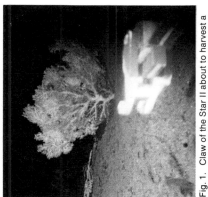

Fig. 1. Claw of the Star II about to harvest a living specimen of precious coral at a depth of 1,200 feet off Makapuu, Oahu.

Photograph by R. Grigg

FISH AND MARINE INVERTEBRATES

Communities of colorful seaweeds, fishes, and corals and other invertebrates occur throughout the Hawaiian Islands. In the deep blue waters offshore, pelagic fishes such as tuna and mahimahi roam the open sea, feeding on smaller fishes which make up part of the planktonic community. At depths of 100 meters and more, precious corals (Fig. 1) and the bivalve *Pinna* are bottom-dwelling forms which live where there is little or no light and which maintain themselves on detritus and plankton falling through the water column. Island shorelines are ringed with basalt benches and tide pools, calcareous benches, fringing and subtidal coral reefs, and sandy beaches. All these places offer recreational opportunities for people to fish, hunt octopus and lobster, pick opihi and limu, and observe and collect a host of useful and colorful organisms.

There are about 700 species of fishes, 400 seaweeds (algae), 1,000 mollusks, and 1,350 other kinds of invertebrates in the shallow waters around the islands. Most of these organisms are representatives of species distributed through the tropical Indian and Pacific oceans from the east coast of Africa to Hawaii. Perhaps 20 percent of the fish and mollusks are found only in Hawaii. How and when marine organisms reached Hawaii's remote shores are still matters of speculation: perhaps millions of years ago when the first island appeared above the surface of the sea, they came by rafting, drifting, or swimming.

High rocky shorelines, reached only by spray, are inhabited by relatively few species, which are dull gray or black in color and which can withstand long periods without water. The littorines (pupu kolea) among the mollusks, and the scuttling black grapsid crab (a'ama) are the most conspicuous members of this community, but in shallow, sun-warmed pools there may also be a blenny and a goby. Seaward of the littorines and the crab, but still above the reach of the tide, are the black nerite (pipipi) and a narrow band of a pulmonate limpet, *Siphonaria*.

Seaward of the spray zone the variety of animals and plants increases. Much of the surf-swept lava coast is painted pink by

the alga *Porolithon* and studded by the dark, domelike shingle urchin *Colobocentrotus* (Fig. 2) and the opihi (*Cellana* spp.). Subtidally, surf-swept cliffs are inhabited by other rather dark-colored and heavy-shelled animals, such as the muricids *Thais* and *Drupa* on the surface of the substrate and the brown and white cowries *Cypraea mauritiana* and *C. maculifera* in crevices. Fishes in these areas are strong swimmers and often dark in color like the Achilles tang shown in Figure 3.

Tide pools are most conspicuous and best developed on tide-level lava shorelines. The substrate is matted with green and brown seaweeds in which are cones, miters, and some of the smaller cowries. There is often a tangle of spaghettilike tentacles of the worm *Terebellum* (Fig. 4), and the bottom of the pools may be littered with sea cucumbers (loli). The common fish of tide pools are young silver perch (aholehole), damselfish (kupipi), surgeonfish (manini), and small blennies.

Along many areas of the shorelines of Kauai, Oahu, and Maui, water-leveled calcareous benches jut 100 feet or more from the shore into the sea. The flat surface of the benches is turfed with a thick algal mat in which are found at least eight species of cone shells, two or three miters, the small snakehead cowry, and a black *Morula*. Common algae forming this mat include *Sargassum*, *Laurencia*, and *Halimeda*. *Codium* and *Gracillaria*, the limu we eat, may also be present. The wave-pounded frontal ramparts of the benches are studded with the short-spined sea urchin *Echinometra*, and in the crevices there are often small drupes and morulas among the mollusks and xanthid crabs. At high tide surgeonfishes (manini and palani), parrotfishes (uhu) and wrasses (hinalea) feed on the algae or on the invertebrates of these benches (Fig. 5).

Along the shoreline, usually back of fringing reefs, are sandy beaches. Ghost crabs (*Ocypode*) run along the water line and excavate their burrows in beach sand, and auger shells (*Terebra* spp.) burrow where the waves wash up the beach. Subtidally, a variety of organisms are found over or in the sand. Razorfishes hover over it, diving into it when disturbed, and goatfishes (weke) stir up the sand with their barbles. The kona crab, helmet shell, and some of the cones, miters, and auger shells are other sand-dwelling forms occurring in these areas of depths of 3 to 50 feet and more.

The most conspicuous, diverse, and colorful of the shallow water communities are those of the corals which form both fringing and subtidal reefs. Coral communities are variously developed in the island chain: to the north Kure, Midway, and Pearl and Hermes Reef are complex calcareous structures capping

Euchelus corrugatus.
×7

Parashiela beetsi.
×14

Thalotia rubra.
×14

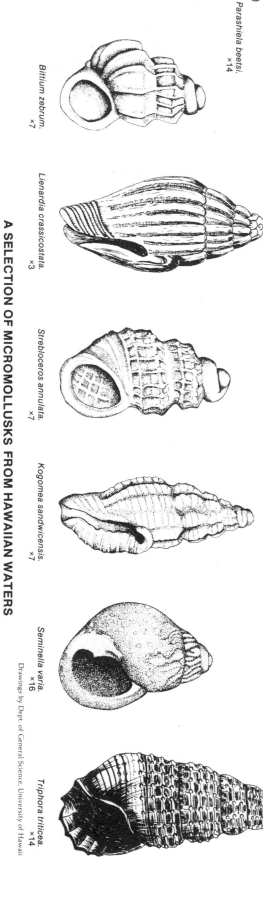

Merelina sp.
×14

Bittium zebrum.
×7

Lienardia crassicostata.
×3

Strebloceros annulata.
×7

Kogomea sandwicensis.
×7

Seminella varia.
×16

Triphora triticea.
×14

volcanoes which may have been above the sea more than 20 million years ago; farther south Kauai, Oahu, Maui, Molokai, and Lanai are partially ringed by fringing reefs (Fig. 6). The island of Hawaii has no fringing reef, but extensively developed subtidal reefs occur off the Kona Coast. Reef growth in Hawaii may be slower than elsewhere, perhaps because the water surrounding the islands is cooler than that of other Pacific reefs. Hawaii lacks the main reef-building coral of the Pacific, *Acropora*. *Porites* and *Pocillopora* are our most common reef-building corals.

Although the most conspicuous members of coral communities are the corals themselves, reefs are complex structures comprised of many other invertebrates, fishes, and plants. Indeed, living corals may comprise less than half the mass of the reef itself, and the brilliant colors of corals are due in large part to the minute algae which live symbiotically in the tissues of coral polyps.

Coral reefs are unique in that they have the ability to construct and maintain shore habitats where none existed previously. Fringing reefs are topographically and biologically complex structures. The active, growing part of the reef is the seaward edge where most of the live corals are found. Just shoreward of this front there is a ridge which may rise above sea level; it is comprised largely of pink calcareous algae and is termed the algal ridge. Shoreward of the algal ridge is the most extensive part of the reef—the reef flat—sand covered, channeled, sometimes showing masses of the frondose brown alga *Sargassum*, and stud-

ded with rubble; only an occasional live coral head is seen in the reef flat. The reef includes many distinctive biological communities. At the seaward edge where there is much living coral are the sea urchins, especially the slate-pencil urchin (Fig. 7) and long-spined urchins (wana). Here too are some of the cowries and cones and the coral-eating mollusk, *Coralliophila*. Among the reef fishes frequenting this area are the brilliantly hued butterflyfishes, parrotfishes, wrasses, and surgeonfishes. Many of these forms feed on coral polyps. On the algal ridge there are a number of mollusks, especially reef-building forms such as vermetids or worm-shells and the limpetlike *Hipponix*. On the reef flat damselfishes and wrasses predominate among the fishes. And in crevices and caves are octopus, the spiny lobster (Fig. 8), and squirrelfishes (menpachi and u'u).

Subtidal reefs exhibit an even greater diversity of animal life than do fringing reefs, for it is in the branching and encrusting corals that are found most of Hawaii's larger and more beautiful shells: the tiger cowry, *Cypraea tigris*, and most of the endemic Hawaiian cowries, miters, cones, and triton shells. Studded among the brilliant colors and diverse shapes of the corals are sea urchins such as the slate-pencil and long-spined wana, and nibbling on the coral polyps are the brilliantly colored butterflyfishes and the tangs (Figs. 9 and 10). Many of the fishes of this community are yellow, matching the coloration of the reef corals.

E. A. K. and E. H. C.

A SELECTION OF MICROMOLLUSKS FROM HAWAIIAN WATERS

Drawings by Dept. of General Science, University of Hawaii

FISH AND MARINE INVERTEBRATES

Fig. 2. Opihi (*Cellana*) and the shingle urchin (*Colobocentrotus*) on the wave-beaten face of a rocky coastline.

Photograph by E.A. Kay

Fig. 4. Tide pool at Honaunau, Hawaii, with manini and the tentacles of the worm *Terebellum*.

Photograph by E.A. Kay

Fig. 3. Achilles tang among basalt boulders at Mahukona, Hawaii.

Photograph by J.A. Maciolek

Fig. 6. Fringing reef off Diamond Head, Oahu.

Photograph by E.A. Kay

Fig. 7. *Pocillopora* heads with the yellow coral *Porites* and a slate-pencil sea urchin at Kealakekua Bay, Hawaii.

Photograph by E.H. Chave

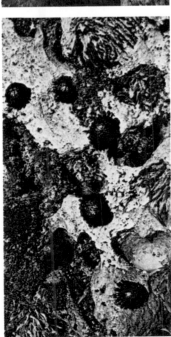

Fig. 5. Manini feeding on filamentous algae near Palaau, Molokai.

Photograph by J.A. Maciolek

Fig. 8. Lobster under a rock encrusted with *Porites* and sponges at Pearl and Hermes Reef.

Photograph by J.A. Maciolek

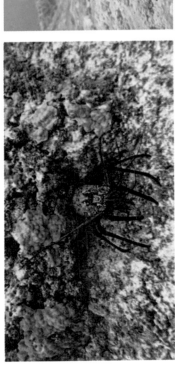

Fig. 9. Four butterflyfishes and a surgeonfish near a well-developed head of *Porites* at Pearl and Hermes Reef.

Photograph by J.A. Maciolek

Fig. 10. Moorish idol and striped wrasse in lava and coral rubble at Pokai Bay, Oahu.

Photograph by E.H. Chave

Hanauma Bay

Hanauma is a unique crater bay on Oahu's southeastern tip. It is both a state park and a marine conservation district. The latter designation was awarded in 1967 to protect the bay's diverse marine life from excessive exploitation. Restrictions prohibiting the taking of any plants, animals, or substrate materials were imposed at that time, allowing marine life to be only viewed and photographed. With this protection, fishes, corals, and other animals have flourished.

Hanauma Bay has become a popular recreational area because of its natural attributes and nearness to Honolulu (a 20-minute drive from Waikiki). Its clear, blue waters lie deep within a double, steep-sided volcanic crater that opens southeasterly to the sea. The inner edge of the bay is bordered by an attractive sandy beach. Beach park facilities are provided and lifeguards are on duty daily. Although it is only a hundred or so acres in area, the bay contains a variety of habitats, ranging from a protective barrier reef and calm-water swimming areas at the inner end, through submerged, coral-studded lava ledges and sand patches to a depth of nearly 100 feet at

its mouth. Seaweeds, fishes, corals, urchins, and many other organisms abound. At least 90 species of fishes have been recorded in the bay. They appear to have increased in numbers and tameness since protective restrictions were imposed. Among the common ones are parrotfishes (uhu), surgeonfishes (manini, palani, kole, etc.), and goatfishes (weke, kumu, etc.). Colorful butterflyfishes (kikakapu) and wrasses (hinalea) are easily approached and photographed with an underwater camera.

The novice snorkeler or diver may find many species of seaweeds, fishes, and invertebrate animals in nearshore swimming areas and pools in the barrier reef. Proficient, properly equipped divers desiring to explore deeper waters should enter and exit from the water at a small cove at the north end of the bay or from the wave bench area (see map). Swimmers and divers should avoid those areas indicated on the map as hazardous because of currents, eddies, and large waves. Attractive corals and fishes are more abundant in the center of the bay, away from these danger zones.

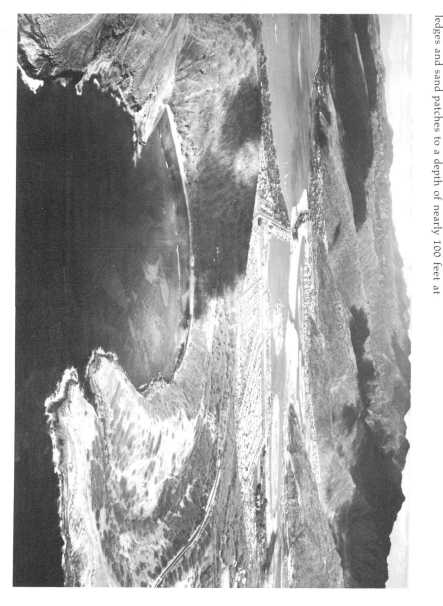

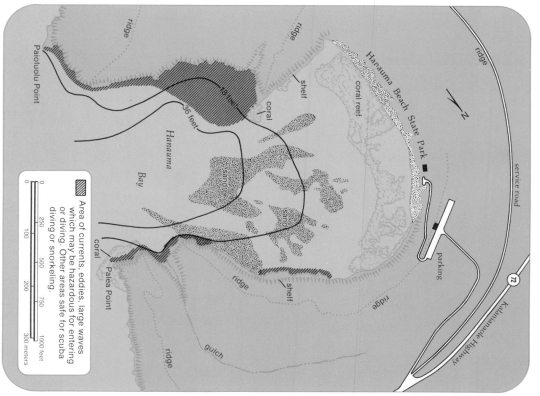

HANAUMA BAY. View across the entrance to the bay looking northwest to Maunalua Bay and the residential suburbs of Portlock, Hawaii Kai and Kuliouou. Koko Head is to the left (out of the photograph). Photograph by Agatin T. Abbott, Hawaii Institute of Geophysics; map and text by Edith H. Chave and John A. Maciolek, Marine Programs, University of Hawaii.

Area of currents, eddies, large waves which may be hazardous for entering or diving. Other areas safe for scuba diving or snorkeling.

THE CULTURAL ENVIRONMENT

Ti, *Cordyline terminalis*. Its leaves can be used for hula skirts, sandals, food wrappings, and animal fodder; its root, for making okolehao (local brandy).

Bishop Museum drawing from Neal (1965:203).

GEOGRAPHIC OVERVIEW

The preceding sections of the Atlas deal with natural aspects of the environment, and subsequent sections with cultural aspects. In a sense, the first part is an overview of the physical and biological characteristics of the environment within which the population has developed and continues to develop its culture, and on which it depends for land, air, water, food, and other essentials of life. The second part is a survey of the people, their social and economic institutions, technology, and patterns of environmental use. This distinction between "natural" and "cultural" is arbitrary; everything in the environment may at certain times and places become part of those particular organizations called ecosystems.

Earlier sections refer to some of the interactions between the natural and the cultural in the environment—some disruptive, others protective. For example, the introduction of certain mammals and the expansion of agriculture and urban settlement have led to the extinction of several species of native birds and endangered many others (page 72). Pollution of the air by exhaust gases poses a health problem in urban areas (page 61). Efforts to offset these adverse results of cultural activities may be seen in the establishment of conservation districts and air pollution controls.

The natural environments of islands provide many advantages for human development, but they also present limitations and it is vital that these constraints be accommodated in ways that are protective of the environment as a whole. First, there is the matter of limited area which imposes constraints on the use of land for cities, agriculture, recreation, and conservation—that is, on the carrying capacity of the environment for people and their activities. In 1960 there were 6.6 acres of land for every person in Hawaii; in 1970 this had been reduced to 5.2 acres per person. Secondly, the islands are relatively isolated, which has the advantage of separation from other more aggressive places, but also disadvantages, like the high cost of importing needed sup-

plies and consequent higher living costs. Thirdly, the equable and generally warm climate maintains higher annual increments of most biogeochemical cycling than is the case in latitudes having more definite seasons. This is good for soil development and plant growth but becomes a debit when it accelerates soil erosion or aggravates air and water pollution.

The islands are limited or lacking in many resources such as oil, coal, metallic ores, lumber, and water sources suitable for generation of power. This is turn places restrictions on economic activities. But Hawaii is rich in aesthetic resources—the beaches, scenery, and varied cultural attractions.

In the past, isolation limited diversity of plants and animals. Hence interspecies competition was minimized, the preservation of archaic and poorly adapted forms was fostered. Ecologically, the islands proved extremely vulnerable to disruption when isolation was broken down. Introduced plants quickly dominated native species in most areas, and introduced insects, birds, and mammals have posed serious threats to the stability of many ecosystems. The human societies that precipitated most of the disturbances have themselves undergone great social and economic change as successive exotic cultures have been introduced.

The limitations of the physical and biological aspects of the island ecosystem are more serious today because the risks of catastrophic instability appear to increase disproportionately with increase in the human population and its technology. The margins for human error are smaller on islands.

The maps in the Atlas show geographical distributions of elements of the natural and cultural environment and in synthesis form a descriptive geography of the individual islands, and illustrate many of Hawaii's geographic characteristics; the nature of its climate, geology, plant and animal life, the multi-ethnic composition of the population, the diversity of languages, religions, and arts, and an economy based primarily on military, agricultural, and tourist activities. The maps convey less readily the geography of the individual islands, and the following sketches (presented in order of island size) are an attempt to summarize island-specific characteristics.

Hawaii, the Big Island, has an air of relative space and distance. It is 123 miles from Hilo to Kailua via Volcano, around the great domes of Mauna Kea and Mauna Loa that crest over 13,000 feet and are snow-capped in winter. Hawaii is an island of extensive sugar plantation and cattle range, including the Parker Ranch of over 200,000 acres, plus many small farms raising coffee, nuts, flowers, fruits, and poultry. It has Hawaii Volcanoes

Hawaiian arts and crafts: stamp designs for clothing.
Bishop Museum drawing from Te Rangi Hiroa (1964:195)

National Park, where volcanic activity can be seen more often than not; barren expanses of lava from old and new eruptions; and dense ohia, koa, and fern forests. Almost half its people live in the city of Hilo, and the majority of the others in small towns. Tourism and land subdivision for potential residential expansion dominated economic development in the decade 1960–1970, while the sugar industry faced a less certain future. Pressures of people on land are less marked on this largest island, but conflicts of interest and problems in planning environmental use are not.

Maui's two mountains are connected by a broad isthmus. On the isthmus and adjoining northern slopes are great sugar and pineapple plantations with their plantation villages; there, too, are the expanding commercial and residential areas of Wailuku and Kahului. With Hawaii, Maui shares a contrasting pattern of busy tourist activities centered around beaches and other scenic attractions—as at Lahaina, Kaanapali, and Kihei—and sparsely populated areas where life is quieter and more unhurried. Most of the spectacular summit area of 10,000-foot Haleakala is now a national park.

Oahu, with 82 percent of the population, is the social, political, and economic hub of the State. Higher densities of population and consequent pressures on land prevail. Land use is intensive: urban industrial and residential functions must be served; sugar and pineapple plantations and truck farms must be supported; forest watershed reserves must be protected. Oahu is Honolulu, Kailua, and Kaneohe—clusters of tall buildings among expanses of low buildings and a profusion of trees and flowers. Oahu is Pearl Harbor and other military establishments. It is shipping, aircraft, and hordes of motor vehicles. It combines enclaves of the quiet and pristine with excesses of noise and pollution. It is the center of government, commerce, industry, medical and social services, entertainment and the arts. It is fine hotels and restaurants, Waikiki, a circle of beaches, and a constant flow of visitors from around the world. Opportunities for employment, education, and communication are greatest on Oahu; so, too, are extremes of poverty and affluence, social problems and achievements, environmental disruptions and improvements.

Kauai has been eroded into a spectacular scenery of peaks, ridges, canyons, and palis, of which Na Pali coast and Waimea Canyon are best known. Mt. Waialeale receives the world's heaviest rainfall, which feeds numerous streams and waterfalls and helps preserve a central, high wilderness of swamp and forest that is sanctuary for some of the last surviving native plants, insects, and birds. On its coastal lowlands, Kauai has sugar and pineapple plantations, and large mill towns. Here, again, is the hyperactivity of hotel-resorts and beaches, but also the more relaxed pace of rural island life—of fishing village, taro patch, and small farm.

Molokai has two distinct parts: a wet eastern region of rugged, largely inaccessible mountains and sea cliffs, and a drier, flatter, western region that supports the island's pineapple plantations and most of the ranches and small farms. Plantation settlements, fishing villages, and small tourist resorts are the foci of population. Molokai remains an essentially quiet, rural place with more traditional styles of living, but its relative isolation from the State's overall growth shows signs of changing.

Lanai is a miniature blending of elements of the other islands in mountain, valleys, forest, scrub, cliffs, and beaches. It is dominated by one crop—pineapple; one company with sole ownership of its lands; and one town—the most sophisticated plantation settlement in the islands.

Niihau (page 28) is an island of low hills, dry and streamless and mostly covered with scrub forest and grass. It is a privately owned cattle and sheep ranch, and its few people are of largely Hawaiian stock. On this island with its two small villages, one school, single road, and no commerce unconnected with the ranch, they live a separate and secluded life.

Kahoolawe (page 28), mostly barren and waterless, is uninhabited. It once supported a small Hawaiian population, and in recent years, sheep and cattle. With the introduction of goats the already sparse plant cover was destroyed, and this disruption continues. Now under military tenure the island serves as a target for aerial bombing practice. Because in an island state all land is precious, Kahoolawe must be restored to take a constructive place in Hawaii's future.

The Northwestern Hawaiian Islands, extending over almost 1,200 miles of ocean, are low tiny islets, reefs, and shoals that are mostly barren, sparsely vegetated, windswept, and pounded by the sea. Since 1909 the islands from Nihoa to Pearl and Hermes Atoll have been set apart as the Hawaiian Islands National Wildlife Refuge, a sanctuary for myriads of seabirds, for a few surviving species of native land birds, and for the Hawaiian monk seal and the green sea turtle. About 50 people live in two military stations—one on French Frigate Shoals and the other on Kure Atoll.

Staff

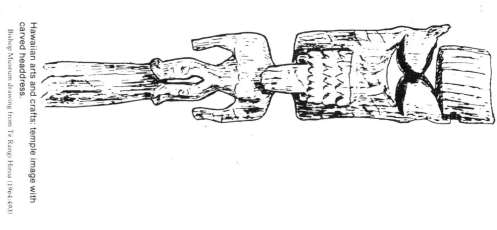

Hawaiian arts and crafts: temple image with carved headdress.

Bishop Museum drawing from Te Rangi Hiroa (1964:493)

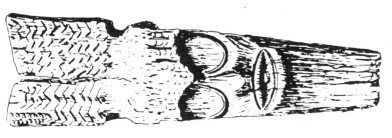

Hawaiian arts and crafts: carved temple slab.
Bishop Museum drawing from Te Rangi Hiroa (1964:526)

ARCHAEOLOGY

Archaeology in Hawaii has two foci. The preservation and enhancement of Hawaii's cultural heritage is one. The student of prehistoric archaeology does for precontact (A.D. 1778) Hawaii what the historian and anthropologist do for postcontact times: study and report to the public the places, events, and changes in Hawaiian culture. The archaeologist continually provides new discoveries and conclusions to the public so that all Hawaii may share the precontact heritage. Secondly, archaeology operates as a part of the science called anthropology, with goals of understanding the how and why of processes of change in Hawaiian culture. For example, the development of the chiefly *alii* class, perhaps long after Polynesian colonists originally came to the islands, might be investigated in the light of population growth pressure and changing use of food resources. Actually, the two foci are not separable, but are perspectives aimed at different audiences. A brief discussion of several recent projects will illustrate the aims and the products of archaeological study (page 87). Fortunately, the results of the research will become more available to the public through park development, site restorations, and publications.

The district of Kohala on the island of Hawaii is one of the richest in historical, archaeological, and legendary materials in the State. The dry leeward coast, just south of Mahukona, has been the site of University of Hawaii archaeological investigations into colonization, population growth, subsistence activities, and general culture change before A.D. 1800. In the *ahupuaa* (a native territorial unit) of Lapakahi, three years' work has indicated that Koaie hamlet, on the coast, was founded about A.D. 1300. A small group of fishermen lived in houses built on the bare ground and supported by large posts. About A.D. 1500 the hamlet changed in character: the houses were built on stone platforms with fine pebble floors, and perhaps a high-status residential area was set off by a huge stone wall. At the same time people moved upland and began growing sweet potatoes and building small C-shaped dwellings or shelters. Eventually, the uplands were intensively cultivated, and the lowland coastal

area became a strip of nearly continuous settlement characterized by clusters of family-sized residential units. Between 1700 and 1778 or 1800, a maximum number of people may have been fully exploiting all available food resources and may have united into a district-based political and economic network. *Ahupuaa* remained the center of most people's lives, but they were bound by trade and the *alii* authority system to the world outside their residence. Lapakahi today contains the archaeological evidence of these changes; plans are proceeding to restore sections for public display in a state park. For reading see Newman (1970).

Kohala is also the land of Kamehameha I. His "birth stones" are near Upolu Point, and above Hapuu Bay is, reputedly, his family heiau. Mookini heiau, famous in legend, was rededicated by Kamehameha. Other important heiau are Kukuipahu, nearly unique with its dressed stone and looking most "un-Hawaiian," and Kupalaha heiau. Just to the south near Kawaihae is the imposing Puu Kohola heiau, where Kamehameha killed a sacrificial victim, thereby effecting one more step in his rise to power. Beside Puu Kohola is another heiau, Mailekini (page 87).

South of Kohala, in Kona, is the famous Honokohau settlement, known for prehistoric and historic occupation, and for its fishponds (Aiopio, Aimakapa, and Kaloko) and heiau. Archaeological research suggests large populations reaching well back into prehistory, and use by high *alii* until close to the twentieth century.

In Kau, around the South Point area, archaeologists from the Bishop Museum have excavated several sites that suggest early dates for these fishing stations, shelters, heiau, salt pans, and canoe mooring holes. Occupation began as early as A.D. 700, and continued into historic times. Handy and Pukui (1958) describe historic Hawaiian culture in Kau.

Other Big Island sites of importance include the Puako petroglyphs, the Anaehoomalu petroglyphs, and nearby Kuualii fishpond. On the top of Mauna Kea is a basalt quarry which furnished the raw material for adzes, a basic wood-working tool of the Hawaiians. The City of Refuge National Historical Park at Honaunau is the most striking and best restored of all Hawaiian site complexes. Once a place of sanctuary for refugees and the location of several heiau, it has been rebuilt to approximate its early historic appearance. The thatched house, Hale o Keawe, atop a stone platform was the sacred storage place of deified bones of *alii*. *Holua*, or slides, are also present. Kealakekua Bay is the place where Captain Cook met his death. At the villages of Napoopoo and Kaawaloa, heiau and burial caves can still be seen, as well as extensive agricultural fields above the cliffs.

Hawaiian arts and crafts: digging sticks.
Bishop Museum drawing from Te Rangi Hiroa (1964:12)

Of all the islands, Oahu has seen the destruction of the greatest number of sites, but several locales are important in terms of archaeological knowledge and cultural heritage. Makaha Valley, in Leeward Oahu has undergone excavation by the Bishop Museum. While much of the lower valley has been altered, middle and upper portions contained the remains of agricultural systems, residences, and Kaneaki heiau. The latter is now restored and topped by a thatched house. On the windward side, Kahana Valley, the site of a future state park, is fronted by Huilua fishpond, a beautiful example of the once-numerous man-made fishponds of Oahu. The valley interior is rich in sites. To the south on the windward coast are Molii, Kahaluu, and Heeia fishponds. Remnants of others exist along Kaneohe Bay. The Mokapu fishponds, on Mokapu peninsula, are good examples of large ponds. Nearby in Kailua is Ulupo heiau, an interesting, easily accessible structure. Bellows Beach in Waimanalo is one of the earliest sites in the State. Excavated by the University of Hawaii, it contained residences on top of old sand dunes, and burials within. A date of approximately A.D. 600 reinforces the hypothesis that the early colonists, upon reaching Hawaii, settled in wet environments where both fishing and agriculture could best be pursued. At Maunalua Bay, southeast Oahu, Kuliouou and Makaniou shelters were two of the first sites excavated in the State. An important and easily seen heiau on Oahu is Puu o Mahuka, a gigantic site on a bluff above Waimea Bay.

Molokai is rich in sites. Most notable may be the numerous fishponds along the south coast, the phallic rock, the five heiau of Hokukano (Iliiliopae is very striking), and the settlement complex in Halawa Valley. Excavated by the University of Hawaii and the Bishop Museum, Halawa is one of our best-known valleys. A sand dune fishing hamlet was established as early as A.D. 600. With population growth, a gradual movement into the valley occurred, wet taro terraces were built, and dry taro was grown wherever possible. Residential clusters appeared along each side of the valley on ridges extending down the valley sides. Two major heiau, Mana and Papa as well as lesser shrines, were also built on the valley sides. Most of these sites are observable today.

Maui has undergone little recent excavation. Among its impressive heiau are Loaloa, near Kaupo, and Piilanihale near Hana. The latter is the largest heiau in Hawaii and is in good condition although difficult to reach. Waianapanapa State Park, also near Hana, contains several small sites ranging from caves to shrines and burial mounds. The Kahikinui complex is a large, well-preserved series of hamlets and sites now being studied.

Kauai has several excavated and unexcavated sites of importance, as well as areas of considerable potential for future excavation. The Wailua complex of heiau includes a city of refuge, Puuhonua Hikinaakala, and associated heiau. Several other sites are close by. The Menehune irrigation ditch by the Waimea River is a remnant example of dressed-stone masonry and a reminder of the complex water-movement systems built before 1778.

Lanai is best represented by Kaunolu, a well-preserved village complex of numerous house platforms, pens, and other stone features. Halulu heiau, canoe sheds, petroglyphs, and burial mounds complete this example of an early historic fishing village. The islands of Niihau, Nihoa, Necker, and Kahoolawe all contain archaeological sites. Of the four, only Niihau is unknown and unexcavated, but all are now closed to the public.

Several museums in the State display artifacts and reconstructions of Hawaiian life. The displays at the Bishop Museum in Honolulu are outstanding, complementing the archaeological sites located throughout the islands. For those who are interested, the famous sites such as Puu Kohola heiau on Hawaii and the complexes are especially valuable. Complexes are groups of sites of many kinds—for example, a village with its houses, heiau, canoe sheds, holua slide, fields for crops, and burial mounds. Each year archaeological excavations are conducted at various locations throughout the islands. The excavation teams are generally hospitable to the interested public and, when field conditions permit, will discuss their research. The Bishop Museum's department of anthropology and authorities at the several campuses of the University of Hawaii should be consulted for information concerning the whereabouts of work in progress. Usually, most of the work will be found on the island of Hawaii, with small but interesting and accessible "digs" on each of the other islands.

P. B. G.

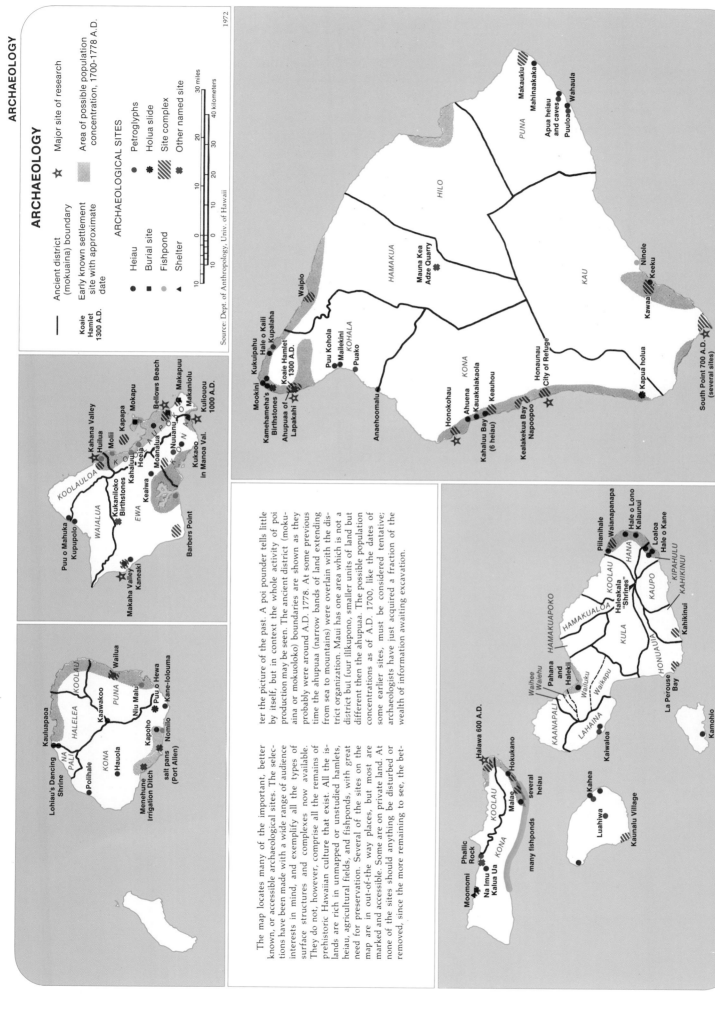

ARCHAEOLOGY

Ancient district (mokuaina) boundary

☆ **Major site of research**

▦ **Area of possible population concentration, 1700–1778 A.D.**

Koale Hamlet 1300 A.D. Early known settlement site with approximate date

ARCHAEOLOGICAL SITES

● Heiau   ● Petroglyphs
■ Burial site   ✳ Holua slide
● Fishpond   ▨ Site complex
▲ Shelter   ✳ Other named site

1972

Source: Dept. of Anthropology, Univ. of Hawaii

Scale: 10 0 10 20 30 miles / 10 0 10 20 30 40 kilometers

The map locates many of the important, better known, or accessible archaeological sites. The selections have been made with a wide range of audience interests in mind, and exemplify all the types of surface structures and complexes now available. They do not, however, comprise all the remains of prehistoric Hawaiian culture that exist. All the islands are rich in unmapped or unstudied hamlets, heiau, agricultural fields, and fishponds, with great need for preservation. Several of the sites on the map are in out-of-the-way places, but most are marked and accessible. Some are on private land. At none of the sites should anything be disturbed or removed, since the more remaining to see, the bet-

ter the picture of the past. A poi pounder tells little by itself, but in context the whole activity of poi production may be seen. The ancient district (mokuaina or mokuoloko) boundaries are shown as they probably were around A.D. 1778. At some previous time the ahupuaa (narrow bands of land extending from sea to mountains) were overlain with the district organization. Maui has one area which is not a district but four Ilikupono, smaller units of land but different then the ahupuaa. The possible population concentrations as of A.D. 1700, like the dates of some earlier sites, must be considered tentative; archaeologists have just acquired a fraction of the wealth of information awaiting excavation.

87

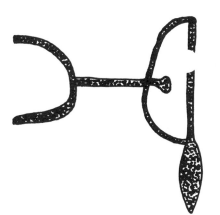

Petroglyph: paddle man, Puako, Hawaii.

HISTORY

The Post-Contact Period, 1778 to 1972

The discovery of the Hawaiian Islands by Europeans, a thousand years or more after the original settlement by Polynesians, was the work of the English naval captain James Cook, certainly the greatest seagoing explorer of his century, perhaps the greatest in the history of Western expansion. In the course of his third major voyage in the Pacific, Cook was taking his two ships, HMS *Resolution* and HMS *Discovery*, from the South Pacific to the northwest coast of America when, on January 18, 1778, he sighted the island of Oahu. On January 20 his ships anchored off Waimea, Kauai, and Cook and his men spent several days there and at Niihau, leaving on February 2.

Making his way south again from the American coast late in 1778, Cook sighted Maui on November 25, and Hawaii on November 30. He needed a safe anchorage where he could refit the ships, take on supplies, and allow his men some relaxation. In search of such a place, he took the *Resolution* and the *Discovery* along the north and east coasts of Hawaii, around the southern point, and up the west coast as far as Kealakekua Bay, where on January 18, 1779, the ships dropped anchor.

By chance, Cook's two visits—to Kauai and Niihau in 1778 and Hawaii in 1779—occurred at the time of an annual religious festival in honor of the Hawaiian god Lono. The priests of Lono's cult at Kealakekua Bay honored Cook in a way that identified him with Lono, and on this basis the men of the expedition were treated with great respect and hospitality for the more than two weeks of their stay.

Cook left Kealakekua Bay on February 4 but was forced to return on February 11, when the *Resolution's* foremast was damaged in a storm. For whatever reason, the white men had evidently outstayed their welcome, and the protection and sponsorship of the priests of Lono were at an end. On the night of February 13, some Hawaiians stole a ship's boat from the *Discovery*. Next morning, Cook went ashore with a party of marines,

about a dozen armed men in all, to take a chief hostage against the return of the boat. This was a strategy that Cook had used to good effect in other island groups, but here it misfired, fatally for him. Things went wrong on the shore at Kaawaloa village, and in fighting that flared up too suddenly to be comprehended, Cook was killed, along with some of his men.

Violence and tragedy were enough to cloud somewhat among Europeans the initial reputation of the Hawaiian Islands. No Western ship put in again for several years. Just the same, Cook's discovery was of great potential usefulness. In all the Pacific north of the equator, there was no other island group so well placed to serve as a way station in the developing commerce between Asia and the west coast of the American continent. Contact was reestablished in 1785, and merchantmen trading between Canton and the American northwest began wintering at the Hawaiian Islands. At the turn of the nineteenth century sandalwood, in demand at Canton, was discovered, first on Kauai and then on the other islands, and this made the Hawaiian group even more attractive to ships' captains.

The Hawaiian high chiefs, on their side, had a use for Westerners—as suppliers of firearms. In the generations before Cook's appearance, power among the chiefs had evidently become concentrated among the regional rulers of the two biggest islands, Maui and Hawaii. At no time, though, were all the islands under a single ruler. For one thing, the agriculture of the islands did not produce a big enough surplus to allow chiefs to take men away from the taro patches to fight their wars indefinitely on islands separated by wide channels. Furthermore, in a war technology of nothing but spears, clubs, daggers, and slingshots, no chief had the weight of arms to impose convincing and permanent defeat upon his competitors for power.

Within one generation of Cook's appearance, however, the islands were united by means of war. It is hard to escape the conclusion that the introduction of Western arms was one important element in making unification possible. It is equally hard to escape the conclusion that the unifying chief, Kamehameha, was a remarkable man. The west coast of the island of Hawaii, where he emerged as a leader to be reckoned with, was frequented by Western ships, and thus he had the chance to make an early assessment of the usefulness of guns. But then, so did all the other chiefs of his time and place. All traded for firearms when they could; each used them in his own interest. It was Kamehameha who fought his way to supremacy, first on Hawaii, then on the other islands. The Battle of Nuuanu, fought on Oahu in the spring of 1795, made him ruler of all the islands

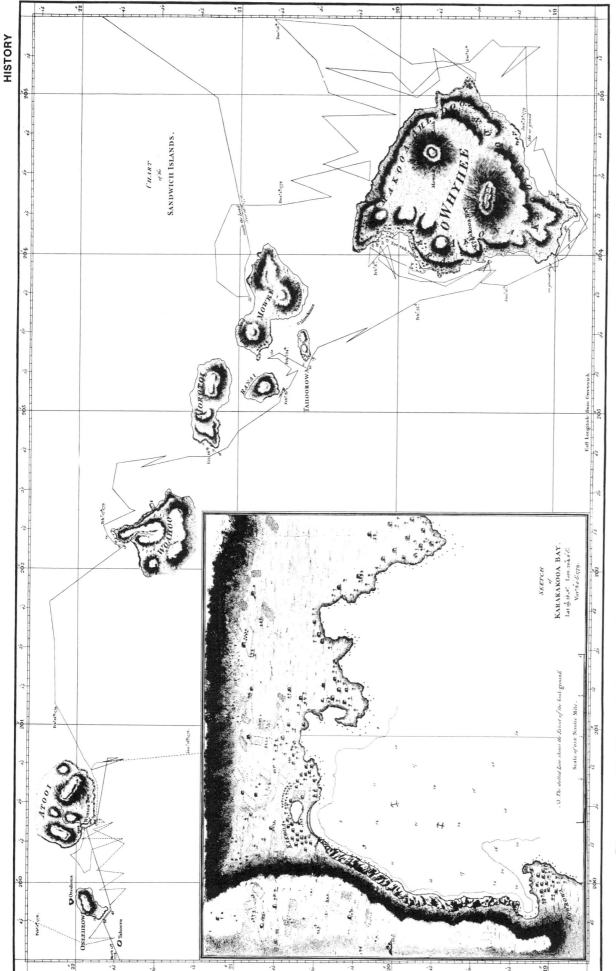

This reproduction of Captain James Cook's map of the Sandwich Islands—as he called them—is the earliest historic map of Hawaii. The dashed line traces Cook's first arrival, in January 1778 from Tahiti, and his landing at Waimea, Kauai. The solid line marks his course on the return visit in November 1778 from North America. Cook's ships cruised off Maui and Hawaii for seven weeks before landing on January 18, 1779 at Kealakekua Bay (inset map). The spelling of names on the map is the navigator's transliteration of local pronunciation and does not conform to modern spelling.

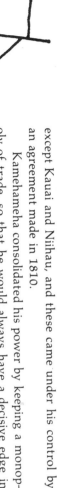

Petroglyph: ship, Kapalaoa, Hawaii.

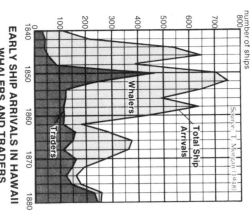

number of ships

EARLY SHIP ARRIVALS IN HAWAII WHALERS AND TRADERS

Source: T. Morgan (1948).

Whalers

Total Ship Arrivals

Traders

except Kauai and Niihau, and these came under his control by an agreement made in 1810.

Kamehameha consolidated his power by keeping a monopoly of the use of resources. Chiefs who might challenge him were brought to live under his surveillance, away from their lands and followers; and each island was put under the administration of a governor appointed by and responsible to Kamehameha. Kamehameha was extremely quick, as well, to learn how to handle white men. Before the conquest, he had a number of them working for him as gunners and ship handlers; afterward, the most competent became his governors, harbormasters, and political advisers.

Kamehameha's power remained essentially unchallenged from the Battle of Nuuanu in 1795 until his death at Kailua, Hawaii, in May 1819; he was in his sixties. The dynasty he founded survived his death, but in altered form. The kapu system, upon whose maintenance he insisted all his life, was deliberately discarded six months after his death by two of his surviving wives, Kaahumanu and Keopuolani, and his successor as king, his son Liholiho, who reigned as Kamehameha II (1819-1824).

The abolition of the kapu, four decades after Cook's death, has been variously explained. One likely interpretation of events is that with the coming of the white man the sources of power in the Hawaiian world changed, and governing systems changed accordingly. Before the white man's arrival, high chiefs ruled on the basis of their claim to closeness to divinity. The kapu operated as a constant reaffirmation of this claim. That is to say, power was ritually defined, expressed, and maintained. The obviously powerful white man drew his power from sources other than the kapu, and some of the instruments of this power —ships, guns, metal, money—could be acquired by chiefs in trade. A dynasty basing its right to rule on an accumulation of power of a Western sort did not need the kapu. Indeed, the old religion, involving a numerous and unproductive priesthood, the practice of rituals which consumed time and resources, including the maintenance of large, laboriously constructed temples, might be nothing more than a drain on the strength of the dynasty. Then, too, female chiefs of whatever exalted rank were ritually excluded from the making of the highest political decisions. Once the kapu was gone, however, women like Kaahumanu could use their great personal influence directly in the ruling politics of the nation.

The 1820s opened a new era in more ways than one. The Pacific whaling industry was moving into the northern oceans,

and whalers, principally American ships from New England ports, began putting in at the islands twice a year, spring and fall, in ever-increasing numbers. At the same time, the islands came within the orbit of Christian missionary work, also directed from Protestant New England.

This New England influence—more broadly, American influence—became the outstanding fact of Hawaii's experience with the outside world. To be sure, nations other than the United States had interests in the Pacific. From the late 1820s to the 1850s, France pushed its powers and privileges in Hawaii. For six months in 1843, the islands were under the British flag as the result of a hasty annexation by a naval captain (an action later countermanded by the British Foreign Office). At no time in the nineteenth century, in fact, was Hawaii's independence secure; and if arms were the test, a single warship of a foreign power could command the situation, as the 1843 annexation showed. Hawaii retained its political independence through the mingled forbearance and mutual suspicion of the great powers. In the meantime, American commercial and social influence created ties between the islands and the United States which made it next to inevitable that, if and when annexation came, it would be American annexation.

Whaling, in its effect on Hawaii, far outstripped the earlier trade in sandalwood and ships' supplies. In general terms, it urbanized the islands. Honolulu on Oahu, with its protected deep water harbor, and Lahaina on Maui, with its open but usable roadstead, became port towns, centers of commercial exchange and social change, attracting by mid-nineteenth century between a quarter and a third of all Hawaiians as more or less permanent residents. Lahaina all but died with the whaling industry in the 1870s. Honolulu, named the capital in 1850, continued to grow relative to all the other towns during the nineteenth century and into the twentieth. It was true enough throughout that period to say that what happened in rural Oahu and on the outer islands might have nothing but local significance; what happened in Honolulu might very well affect all Hawaii.

Honolulu was the place where the white population was concentrated: transients, like sailors off merchant ships and whalers; sojourners, like the earliest traders; residents, like the established businessmen and the missionaries. The most concentrated attempt to bring Hawaiians into some sort of long-range working relationship with the West was organized by the Protestant missionaries from New England, beginning with the arrival of the first contingent in March 1820. They were joined—

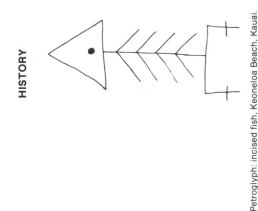

Petroglyph: incised fish, Keoneloa Beach, Kauai.

or, rather, challenged—in 1827 by French Roman Catholics of the Congregation of the Sacred Hearts of Jesus and Mary. Then Mormons appeared in 1850 and Anglicans in 1862. But without question it was the Protestant influence that was decisive. From the beginning, they made it their business to be close to the chiefs. Within a few years they were rewarded with converts among the *alii*. In the reign of Kauikeaouli, Kamehameha III (1824–1854), all but a very few of the important chiefs became church members. In the late 1830s a religious "awakening" among the commoners brought new members by the thousand. In terms of statistics, the Hawaiian mission was certainly the most successful of its era in the Pacific. And in terms of influence on national policy, the most important white men of that era were certainly men who came to the islands with the mission. Hiram Bingham, the mission leader of the 1820s and 1830s, was the unofficial but constant adviser of the chiefs, from Kaahumanu on; and when in the 1840s the kingdom modernized its government along constitutional lines, a handful of men left the mission to take up cabinet appointments or judicial posts—William Richards, Richard Armstrong, Lorrin Andrews, and Gerrit P. Judd, the last of whom was preeminent in policy making until 1853.

The Protestant view of the ideal Hawaii involved the following elements: an independent nation governed according to a constitution which would embody as much American republicanism as was compatible with the continuance of monarchy; a people literate, Westernized in culture, politically well-informed, enjoying the modest fruits of honest labor on the land, and living in the Protestant faith. The actual Hawaii came some of the way to meeting these specifications, but by no means all the way. The missionary accomplishment was impressive by the standards of the time, sufficient for the governing body in Boston to phase the mission out of existence in the 1850s and 1860s in favor of an independent Hawaiian church. At the same time, other influences of a broad cosmopolitan nature among both whites and Hawaiian commoners served to dilute the attempted strict Puritanism of the early mission days, and there was a drift away from American Protestantism toward Anglicanism in the ruling house under Alexander Liholiho, Kamehameha IV (1854–1863). For the rest of the nineteenth century, American Protestantism as a strictly religious force declined in strength, until by 1900 Protestants among the Hawaiians were far outnumbered by Catholics and Mormons.

height it had brought 500 or more ships to Hawaii a year, put thousands of crewmen on leave on the streets of Honolulu and Lahaina in the spring and fall seasons, and left $1,000,000 or more at a time to circulate in the islands. Then in 1859 petroleum came into production in the United States, and the demand for whale oil lessened. The Civil War disrupted seagoing commerce, and the whaling industry recovered somewhat only to be virtually ended in 1871 by a disaster which trapped a good part of the American fleet in the Arctic ice.

Sugar succeeded whaling as the economic mainstay of the islands. As early as 1802 attempts had been made to boil sugar from wild cane. In 1835 the first Western-style plantation was

By the 1860s, whaling, which for 40 years had been the basis of the money economy of Hawaii, was in decline. At its

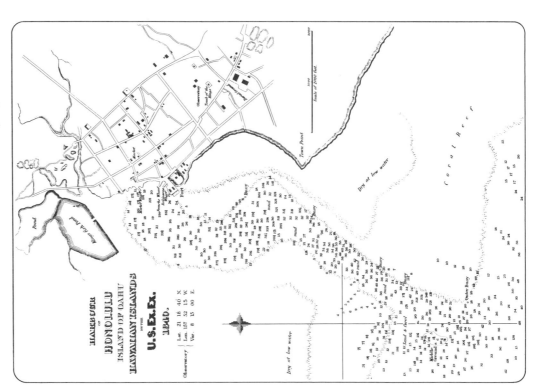

This map of Honolulu Harbor in 1840 is reproduced from the original prepared by the U.S. Exploring Expedition of 1838-1841, led by Charles Wilkes.

Reproduced from U.S. Exploring Expedition (1844)

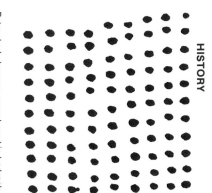

Petroglyph: konane game board in bedrock, Honokohau, Hawaii.

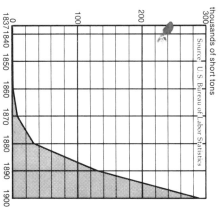

thousands of short tons

EARLY HAWAII SUGAR PRODUCTION

Source: U.S. Bureau of Labor Statistics

established, on Kauai. Small cargoes of sugar were shipped to California as part of the increasing agricultural export trade that peaked with the gold rushes. The Civil War, which kept the American whaling fleet away from Hawaii, at the same time allowed Hawaiian sugar into the mainland market in quantity, as a replacement for sugar no longer produced in the wartime South. The year 1869 was significant: thanks to sugar, Hawaii achieved, for the first time, a favorable balance of trade.

Once it became clear that sugar could do for the economy what other products could not (coffee, silk, wheat, indigo, and beef were among the many tried), the great aim of economic policy became the guaranteeing of the American market. This was accomplished in 1875-1876, when a treaty of commercial reciprocity was negotiated. It provided for the duty-free entry of Hawaiian sugar to the United States, giving the islands a great advantage over other foreign producers competing in that market.

In political terms, reciprocity bound Hawaii's general interests more closely still to the United States. Domestically, reciprocity turned Hawaii into a plantation society, which it remained in substance until well into the twentieth century.

For sugar, the large plantation was the logical producing unit. The idea of Hawaii as a nation of small independent farmers became obsolete without ever having been realized. Changes in land ownership inaugurated in the 1840s (the Great Mahele) introduced the idea of land held in fee simple. In 1850 a new law permitted foreigners to buy and sell land. This was the beginning of the era of large estates in Western hands. Sugar made big landholdings necessary; the reciprocity treaty made them, with good management, highly profitable. Just before the reciprocity treaty was passed, Hawaii was exporting about 25 million pounds of sugar; by 1890, 250 million pounds. By 1900, Hawaii was supplying 10 percent of the United States sugar market.

This process of accumulation and exploitation of land for sugar set the course of politics as well as commerce, and in addition transformed society at large. One part of the transformation was directly observable in human terms. The cultivation of sugar demanded a large labor force. The Hawaiians themselves would certainly not supply it. Disease had made terrible inroads among them. The Hawaiian population at the time of Cook was between 200,000 and 300,000. A century later, at the time of reciprocity, it was less than 60,000. According to one estimate made in the 1870s there were no more than 5,000 able-bodied Hawaiian men available for plantation work.

A good part of the ingenuity of government and private enterprise was directed toward ensuring a steady supply of labor. Two lines of thought, not always compatible, emerged. First, the plantations had to be served. Second, it would be good if the population of Hawaii could somehow be replenished at the same time. Pacific islanders were tried, briefly and unsuccessfully, as laborers. Inquiries were made about India as a possible source of supply. Malaysia was discussed. Periodically, the argument was made that the islands would be better off with more white men; but it was generally acknowledged (and unsuccessful experiments bore it out) that plantation labor was not suitable work for imported whites, except perhaps for Mediterranean types such as Portuguese, some thousands of whom were recruited.

Out of all this, in the end, grew the practical consensus that first China and then Japan would have to be the sources of labor. The first Chinese under contract arrived in 1852. By the mid-1860s there were more Chinese males in the islands than white males. The first group of Japanese arrived in 1868, but not until 1887 did the large-scale, continuous importation of laborers from the southern provinces of Japan begin. Recruitment of Japanese stemmed, in fact, from the planters' dissatisfaction with Chinese. Contracts ran for several years; at the end of the term, a good many Chinese chose not to renew their work agreements. Unable in most cases to pay their way back to China, they went to the towns, especially Honolulu, looking for work. The Japanese in their turn followed much the same pattern of movement. Among neither the Chinese nor the Japanese in the nineteenth century was there a good balance between men and women—it was in the interest of the planters to recruit young single men as laborers—and so the question of population as against labor supply remained unsettled.

The establishment of the sugar industry—more exactly, the emergence of a white planter class with its affiliates of businessmen and professional men in Honolulu—began to work changes in the mood of Hawaiian politics from the 1860s on. In crude terms, the influential white man in the islands was finding less and less of worth and usefulness in the native Hawaiian. Earlier in the century, missionary orthodoxy held that the Hawaiian possessed many good qualities, and that with Christian help he could very likely be saved from himself. The orthodoxy of the sugar planter, the businessman, the lawyer, and the white civil servant of the prosperous reciprocity era was that Western industry and ingenuity produced all that was good in the islands. Hawaiians, by contrast, could not sustain themselves—as work-

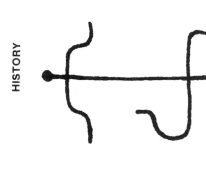

Petroglyph: runner, Pohue Bay, Hawaii.

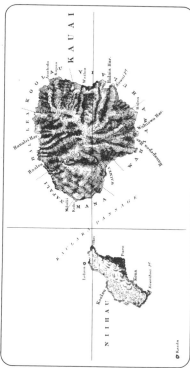

This map of the island of Kauai, dated 1841, is reproduced from a map of the Hawaiian Islands prepared by the U.S. Exploring Expedition of 1838-1841, led by Charles Wilkes. Other portions of the map appear on pages 94 and 97.
Reproduced from U.S. Exploring Expedition (1844)

ers, as taxpayers, as useful citizens, even as a people: they appeared, indeed, to be dying out. Toward the end of the nineteenth century, the rationale of social Darwinist thinking began to be applied in the islands: perhaps the Hawaiians were unfit to survive, biologically, culturally, and historically; perhaps the whites were fated to rule.

The fifth and last of the Kamehamehas, Lot (1863-1872) died without an heir. His successor, William Lunalilo (1872-1873), chosen in a royal election, was a bachelor. On his early death, a new election returned as king David Kalakaua (1874-1891). In his reign, which spanned almost exactly the years of reciprocity under the kingdom, the question of the political control of the islands became acute, and as often as not the question was put in racial terms.

The planters had a point. It was their productivity that kept the kingdom going. The Hawaiians had a point, too. They were, they felt, being pushed off the land by whites. Kalakaua reigned over a polarized citizenry, white and brown (for political purposes, the alien Orientals, though increasing in numbers, were negligible). He emerged more and more, in white eyes at least, as a champion of brown against white. He was, in addition, a king of expensive tastes and strong monarchical principles, or at least practices.

For several years, Kalakaua and his leading adviser Walter Murray Gibson were allied with the wealthy sugar grower, steamship owner, and financier, Claus Spreckels, who had made his millions in California and used his money to get a toehold, then a foothold, then a near stranglehold on the political economy of Hawaii. The majority of the planters, and especially those descended from Protestant missionary families, regarded Spreckels as a dangerous interloper, and Gibson and Kalakaua together as the embodiment of irresponsible government.

Throughout the 1880s, the political situation became more and more unstable. Eventually, the rule of Kalakaua and Gibson became intolerable to the leading taxpayers of the kingdom and their adherents. On June 30, 1887, in a bloodless revolution involving a few hundred men under arms but no shots fired in anger, Gibson was ousted and Kalakaua was compelled to assent to a new constitution, which reduced him to not much more than ceremonial status. Legislative, executive, and judicial power were lodged with the propertied (largely white) minority, and the vote was denied to about two-thirds of the native population.

From this time on, talk of annexation of Hawaii by the United States was heard more and more openly. The year of the

revolution, 1887, was also the year of the renewal of the reciprocity treaty. The revolutionary Reform Party negotiated, along with the renewal, an agreement by which the United States would have exclusive rights to the use of Pearl Harbor as a naval station. In July 1889, an abortive counterrevolution took place at Honolulu. A part-Hawaiian named Robert Wilcox and several dozen followers occupied Iolani Palace briefly and had to be driven out by gunfire and explosives. Wilcox's politics were by no means clear, but he was certainly anti-Reform. In 1890 the United States revised its tariff policy, to the great detriment of the Hawaiian sugar industry, and in the depression that followed in the islands, the arguments for annexation were renewed.

Kalakaua did not live to see the outcome. He died in February 1891, in the course of a visit to California. His successor was his sister Liliuokalani (1891-1893), first queen of Hawaii in her own right and last ruler of the monarchy. Liliuokalani, even more than Kalakaua, was insistent that the reigning monarch should control the kingdom on behalf of the Hawaiian people. For this purpose, the Reform constitution was an unsuitable instrument. The queen's views were well known among her

enemies, and for them this was a powerful political reason to be added to their economic reasons for wanting annexation to the United States. Early in 1892 Lorrin Thurston, one of the leading revolutionaries of 1887, formed a secret Annexation Club.

Between mid-1892 and early 1893, legislative affairs were more than ordinarily confused, with four changes of cabinet and innumerable arguments over two pieces of legislation favored by the queen as means to improve the revenues of the crown—a national lottery and a scheme to license the sale of opium.

On Saturday, January 14, 1893, the queen prorogued the

HISTORY

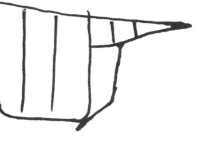

Petroglyph: church, Anaehoomalu, Hawaii.

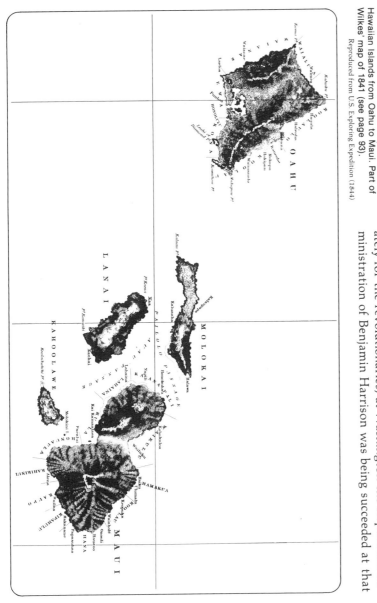

Hawaiian Islands from Oahu to Maui. Part of Wilkes' map of 1841 (see page 93). Reproduced from U.S. Exploring Expedition (1844).

legislature and prepared to make public her new constitution. Lorrin Thurston and the other annexationists formed themselves into a revolutionary Committee of Safety. They consulted United States Minister to Hawaii John L. Stevens and the commander of USS *Boston*, a warship stationed at Honolulu, and composed a proclamation announcing the end of the monarchy and the formation of a provisional government, with the aim of annexation.

The revolutionaries armed themselves and took to the streets of Honolulu on Tuesday, January 17, to secure the government buildings. American troops from the *Boston* were ashore; Minister Stevens was more than ready to recognize the revolutionary regime. The proclamation was read. Resistance was minimal: the only casualty was one man shot in the shoulder. By nightfall on Tuesday the revolution was over; the queen had surrendered, as she put it, to superior force, under protest, and in the expectation that the United States Congress would not countenance the support given the revolutionaries by Minister Stevens.

The provisional government immediately proposed the joining of Hawaii and the United States by annexation. Unfortunately for the revolutionaries, at Washington the Republican administration of Benjamin Harrison was being succeeded at that moment by the Democratic administration of Grover Cleveland. Investigations were ordered by Cleveland, and the report convinced him that the monarchy would not have been overthrown without the aid of Minister Stevens. On this basis, Cleveland found the revolutionaries' offer of annexation unacceptable and directed that the monarchy be restored.

The revolutionaries refused to retrace their steps. They repeated their wish for annexation and, while waiting for a change of heart at Washington, brought into being their own republic under the presidency of Sanford B. Dole, a highly regarded politician descended from a Protestant missionary family. The new regime was inaugurated on July 4, 1894.

The royalists, regarding themselves as unjustly abandoned by the Cleveland administration, plotted a counterrevolution. For ten days following a shooting on January 6, 1895, Honolulu was under arms again. The royalists were easily defeated and their leaders tried for treason. Liliuokalani, under house arrest, signed a document of abdication and was sentenced, in her married name of Mrs. John O. Dominis, to five years at hard labor and a fine of $5,000. The sentence was later reduced. By November 1896 she was free, a citizen with full rights once more.

By then, too, the prospects for annexation were better. At Washington, Cleveland was being succeeded by the Republican William McKinley, whose administration was sure to be cordial to the acquisition of the islands. The United States Senate discussed an annexation treaty, and when it appeared as though a majority favored it, but not the essential two-thirds majority, the idea of a joint resolution of annexation by simple majority in each house of Congress was substituted.

Arguments against acquiring Hawaii centered on the idea that the United States was traditionally a continental power, without noncontiguous territories. Then, too, it was pointed out that the racially mixed population of Hawaii, where whites of American origin were a small (if powerful) minority, was not traditionally regarded as the best raw material for American politics and society.

It would take some powerful arguments to overcome these negative propositions. In the end, annexation was one product of war between the United States and Spain in 1898. The United States went to war with Spain over Cuba, then a Spanish holding in the Caribbean. Part of the United States' broad strategy was to embarrass the Spanish empire in its Pacific holdings, particularly the Philippines. The spectacular success of the United States Navy in this arena brought into national prominence for the first time the possibility that the United States could enter

the twentieth century as a great Pacific power, with territories spread across the ocean all the way to Asia. In this reading of the "manifest destiny" of the American people, Hawaii assumed a strategic and geopolitical importance outweighing its demographic doubtfulness. The joint resolution of annexation, which had been hanging fire, quickly passed both houses of Congress, and President McKinley signed it on July 7. The transfer of sovereignty took place on August 12 in Honolulu. Under organic legislation which took effect in 1900, Hawaii became a territory of the United States.

The revolutionaries of 1887 and 1893 and the annexationists of the period up to 1898 could congratulate themselves. They would always have said that, in opposing and then overthrowing the monarchy, they were basing their actions on American ideas of what was good in government. The planters as well could be pleased, in one sense at least. Now that Hawaii was a domestic rather than a foreign producer of sugar, the great industry of the islands was no longer at the mercy of changes in American tariff policy. From the point of view of labor supply, however, annexation might mean difficulty for the sugar men. The United States, late in the nineteenth and early in the twentieth century, was moving toward ending the admission of Oriental immigrants. Once Hawaii became part of the nation, this policy would apply in the islands as on the mainland. In practice, at annexation, Chinese were already barred from immigrating. The likelihood was that Japanese in their turn would be excluded: no more new migrants would be permitted.

The planters responded by bringing in as many Japanese workers as possible before any ban might take effect, more than 70,000 between 1896 and 1907. Even this was not enough to supply the still-expanding sugar industry (and the relatively new pineapple industry, which at its height later in the twentieth century would provide about 75 percent of the world's canned pineapple). Looking for yet another source of cheap field labor, the planters turned to the Philippines—a highly suitable place, since it had fallen under the American flag in the war with Spain in 1898, and thus no problems existed in bringing in Filipinos. Between 1907 and 1946, some 120,000 Filipino workers were recruited.

The idea put forward at times in the nineteenth century that "cognate races" could be found, similar to the Hawaiian, to strengthen the native element of the population, seemed merely strange by the twentieth century. Chinese married Hawaiians in some numbers; so did Filipinos in their turn; Japanese too, but in fewer numbers. The result of this, together with the growth of a second generation of Orientals, children of migrants, was a distinctively local population; but the simple days of a population composed only of Hawaiians and whites were gone forever.

As for the Hawaiian proper, his fate was still very much in doubt. The population figures of the twentieth century showed a diminishing pure Hawaiian group, an increasing part-Hawaiian group. For a variety of reasons, it was felt that special provision should be made for those who identified themselves as Hawaiians. One expression of this feeling was the establishment of the Kamehameha Schools, begun in 1887, lavishly endowed from the revenues of the Bishop Estate, whose landholdings, the most extensive in the islands, were derived from the former estates of the Kamehameha dynasty. Another program designed especially for Hawaiians came into being with the Hawaiian Homes Commission Act of 1920. It was intended to rehabilitate Hawaiians disadvantaged by urban society, by giving them the chance to farm on homesteads held on long leases at nominal rents.

Whatever directions the various ethnic groups took in the early decades of the twentieth century, political, economic, and social leadership remained very much in the hands of the men who had engineered revolution and annexation, together with their associates and descendants. The era of reciprocity had centralized the sugar industry greatly. The twentieth century carried centralization further, until a complex of firms, popularly known as the Big Five, emerged with almost total control. These five—Castle and Cooke, Alexander and Baldwin, C. Brewer, Theo. H. Davies, and American Factors—produced and marketed 75 percent of the sugar crop in 1910, 96 percent in 1933. They also controlled, by stock ownership and interlocking directorates, the bulk of the territory's banking, insurance, utilities, wholesale and retail commerce, and transportation.

Inevitably, they controlled politics as well. Their brand of business conservatism was stamped on the policies of every gubernatorial administration from annexation to World War II. Eight out of every ten legislators elected during the same period were Republicans.

As paternalistic societies went, Hawaii was sufficiently enlightened. Agricultural workers were paid, on the average, more than many unskilled industrial workers on the mainland. Management was ready to make some concessions in matters of health and welfare (largely, of course, in order to turn aside attempts at labor organization). Public education up to a certain level was available to the children of immigrant laborers. Still,

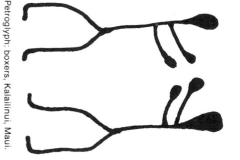

Petroglyph: boxers, Kalalinui, Maui.

until World War II the territory could by no means be described as an open society. The plantation was the model for all other institutions, and its hierarchies of power were ethnically determined.

Some extremely serious long-term issues could not be damped down by such a society. If Hawaiians, perforce, accepted in large numbers their position as clients of the ruling white minority, Orientals in larger numbers did not. As, increasingly, the immigrant laboring population was supplemented by a second generation of Orientals born in the islands and thus American by citizenship, the prospect of basic social change became apparent. It could be seen in the population figures, census period by census period.

The issue was essentially simple. The original Oriental plantation laborer was not expected to be a full member of society. The second generation, citizens by birth, could not constitutionally be denied full membership in that society. If the Orientals came into their own politically, this would mean the end of the era of unchallenged control by the Big Five. By 1936 one out of every four voters was Japanese.

Increasingly, the Japanese population became the focus of the problem. First, it was by far the biggest single element in the Oriental population. Second, its percentage of the total population kept growing because of births in the islands, even after immigration from Japan was halted, and this meant that the proportion of citizen Japanese to alien Japanese was growing. Third, and this was a great complication, Japan and the United States, by mid-thirties, were headed toward war.

The Japanese attack on Pearl Harbor at 7:55 a.m. on Sunday, December 7, 1941, opened another era in Hawaii's history. The damage to the Pacific Fleet at Pearl Harbor and to airplanes on the ground at nearby bases constituted the worst military disaster in American history. Martial law was declared immediately, and the islands remained under curfew and blackout restrictions until close to the end of the war.

Military courts took over law enforcement, and though their legality was challenged periodically, it was not until 1946 that the United States Supreme Court ruled against the military in this respect.

The apparent justification for the harshness of the military government was, of course, the presence of such a large population of Japanese, citizen and alien. They were too numerous by far to be interned, as were California's Japanese, and at the same time their loyalty was regarded as so problematic that martial law seemed necessary. Among Japanese of military age

there were very few aliens. It was this group that settled, actually and symbolically, the question of loyalty. A volunteer fighting force composed of Nisei, or Americans of Japanese ancestry (AJAs), was formed, called the 100th Battalion, later incorporated in the 442nd Regimental Combat Team. This unit distinguished itself greatly in the European theater, becoming the most highly decorated unit in the armed forces of the United States.

The veterans of the 442nd, many of them with law degrees earned under the GI Bill of Rights, became the nucleus of the postwar Democratic Party, challenging and finally—in 1954—dislodging from power the long-entrenched Republican Party. In the territorial legislature of that year, one out of every two members was an AJA.

This was one great victory in the general postwar emancipation of the Oriental. Another great change, associated with the political victory, was the rise of an extremely powerful labor movement. There had in fact been strikes against sugar and pineapple management since early in the century, some of them involving violence, and one, in 1924 on Kauai, resulting in the deaths of sixteen strikers by gunfire. As late, almost, as World War II, the general basis of labor organization had been ethnic identity; thus there had been Japanese strikes or Filipino strikes, often limited to a handful of plantations. Ethnic divisions in the labor force made it easier for management to break strikes. Not until class solidarity was substituted for ethnic identity as an organizing principle did the labor movement succeed. This substitution was accomplished within the framework of federal labor legislation of the New Deal period. The union leader of note during this period, indeed from the late thirties to the late sixties, was Jack Hall of the ILWU. His union, considered as a political and economic force, came to equal the Big Five in influence. With more than 30,000 members in a total population of 500,000 in the late forties, it had decisive strength, as was shown by a paralyzing dock strike in 1949.

At the height of the cold war, during the McCarthy period of American politics, the ILWU was regarded as being the instrument of a Communist conspiracy in Hawaii. On the basis of congressional hearings held by the House Un-American Activities Committee, Jack Hall and six others, most of them with union connections, were charged under the Smith Act with conspiring to teach the overthrow of the United States government by force and violence. They were convicted in 1953. Their appeals were eventually sustained in 1958, by which time the issue of Communism within the United States was generally rather

Petroglyph: rainbow man, Nuuanu, Oahu.

less heated than it had been earlier in the fifties.

The Communist issue in Hawaii became embroiled with the issue of statehood, which assumed greater importance every year in the postwar period. The islands had been American soil since 1898, with territorial status. The question of statehood for Hawaii began to be raised seriously before World War II, with congressional hearings in the islands in 1935 and 1937. That the question was not resolved in Hawaii's favor until 1959 can be attributed to the issue of Communism as much as to anything else (except, perhaps, a residual distrust of Hawaii's multi-racialism, manifesting itself among some Southern senators).

There was never anything in the exhaustive public record to show that the problem of Communism in Hawaii was more serious than that on the mainland at the same time. In itself, then, if logic had prevailed, the problem should not have interfered with Hawaii's progress toward statehood. It was such a powerful emotional issue, however, that it tended to obscure other considerations put forward in Hawaii's favor.

At the time of annexation, no arrangements were made for Hawaii's ultimate transition from territory to state. This in itself was somewhat unusual: in the past, new areas had been acquired on the assumption that they would become states. Hawaii, though, was such an unusual acquisition that past practices apparently did not hold. Thus, even as Hawaii met one test after another regarding statehood, there was a lingering reluctance on the part of Congress to grant the islands equal status with the mainland states.

Territorial status carried with it certain disabilities. American citizens in Hawaii, for example, could not vote in presidential elections. Hawaii had an elected delegate to Congress, but he had no vote. Hawaii thus had virtually no formal voice at Washington, no bargaining power, no way of ensuring (to take one case which mattered) that Hawaii got its reasonable share of federal tax disbursements. Washington controlled Hawaii's local affairs more closely than it did those of sovereign states.

Governors of Hawaii were appointed by the president; so were high court judges. The basis of all this was the organic legislation framed for Hawaii by Congress after annexation. This organic law itself could be altered at any time by Congress.

Two episodes in the thirties, each in its own way, prompted reconsideration of Hawaii's status. First, the Massie case of 1931, involving the alleged rape of a Navy officer's wife by five young men of nonwhite ancestry and the subsequent killing of one of the men by the woman's family, was given nationwide publicity. Hawaii was portrayed in the sensational press as un-

civilized, unsafe, unfit for self-determination. Congressional committees for a time discussed putting the islands under a naval commission, which would have been a retrograde step from territorial status. Second, in 1934, Congress passed the Jones-Costigan Act, under which Hawaii was classed for sugar importation purposes with offshore and foreign producers. Hawaii's share of the mainland market was cut, and it was made vulnerable to future cuts. The Big Five, up to this time, had considered territorial status generally satisfactory: with a powerful lobby at Washington, big business had been able to protect its interests, have a voice in presidential appointments to Hawaii, and so on. From the time of the Jones-Costigan Act onward, some businessmen, and more as time went on, argued that the only real guarantee for the sugar industry would be statehood—indisputable equality of status.

World War II gave the supporters of statehood positive evidence of Hawaii's readiness. Hawaii suffered Pearl Harbor, bore martial law, and supplied some of the best fighting men on the Allied side. These arguments were marshalled by the Hawaii Statehood Commission, together with more prosaic figures about population, literacy, earning power, and tax contributions

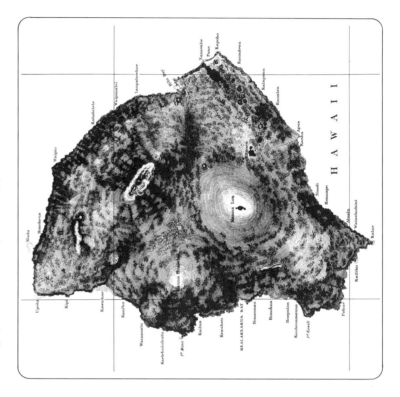

HAWAII

Island of Hawaii. Part of the Wilkes map of 1841 (see page 93).

Reproduced from U.S. Exploring Expedition (1844)

Petroglyph: human figure, Puuloa, Hawaii.

to the federal treasury, all showing that Hawaii ranked with a number of already established states.

Not until the middle fifties was a strategy developed that would give the islands a better than even chance of admission. This involved linking Hawaii with Alaska, another candidate for statehood. In the end, Alaska was admitted before Hawaii, in 1958. This was a disappointment for Hawaii in a sense, but it also made further delays over Hawaii next to indefensible. The Senate finally passed a Hawaii statehood bill on March 11, 1959, and the House passed it on March 12. On June 27 a plebiscite in the islands ratified the congressional vote by a margin of 17 to one, indicating overwhelming approval. Admission day was set for August 21, and Hawaii became the fiftieth state.

In the ten years that followed statehood, Hawaii experienced unparalleled growth and prosperity. The great money earners at the end of the sixties were the same as at the start: sugar, pineapple, federal spending (principally in defense), and tourism. But the relative importance of these industries changed sharply, and in this change was reflected Hawaii's experience of statehood, an increasing—and apparently irreversible—assimilation with the mainland.

Sugar and pineapple together were worth about $390,000,000 in 1970, a 37 percent increase from 1960. The rate of increase was much higher in defense spending over the same period: it rose from $373,100,000 to $660,200,000. Tourists spent $131,000,000 in 1960, and $570,000,000 in 1970, an increase of almost 450 percent. The total number of tourists staying overnight or longer in 1970 was 1,800,000, up about 600 percent since 1960.

Sugar was in a reasonably stable world market, regulated by a quota system. Pineapple's future appeared less than good. Cheap labor elsewhere in the world was pricing Hawaii out of its share of the market. Increased defense spending was based on American strategy in the Pacific generally and the Vietnam war in particular. It was in tourism that the greatest transformation took place, and that was the result, first, of statehood, with a growing awareness of the islands among travelers, and second, of the introduction of passenger jet service from the mainland to Hawaii.

The infusion of money from these and other sources made for great activity in the economy and great social changes. Per capita income rose from $2,380 in 1960 to $3,928 in 1970. Assessed value of real property more than doubled in the same period from $3,174,073 to $6,555,382. Tax collection more than doubled between 1964 and 1970, reaching $1,055,004,000. Use of electricity more than doubled; use of gas almost doubled. Motor registrations almost doubled, to 404,000 in a total population of 769,913, which itself was up from 632,772 in 1960. Toward the end of the sixties, an average of 40,000 intended residents arrived each year to add to the natural increase. During the sixties, for the first time, whites outnumbered Japanese as the largest single group in the State, though still a minority of the total population. Hawaii remained a culture of ethnic minorities in an increasingly Americanized physical and social environment.

Throughout the sixties, the voters of Hawaii consistently returned the Democratic Party to power with large majorities. In the process, the party of the postwar social revolution became the party of the post-statehood establishment. It was as wealthy and powerful in its way as the Republican Party of the Big Five had once been. Indeed, big business, as well as big labor, was among the interest groups which together made up the consensus regime of John A. Burns, principal architect of the postwar Democratic Party and governor of the State since 1962.

Previously insulated by distance and cultural difference from the mainland, Hawaii was now far more involved in and vulnerable to national movements of short- and long-term consequence. As the seventies opened, the statehood boom appeared to be slackening, slowing down with the national economy. The national concern with the environment began to make an impact locally, on the basis that Hawaii could not afford to put its environment too far in pawn to growth along mainland lines, especially when that growth had speculative elements, particularly in land development. There even appeared, with the seventies, a narrowly based but strong radical reexamination of Hawaii's economy and society, linking the persistence of nineteenth-century patterns of landholding among the big estates with ethnic advantage and disadvantage, and linking the rise of the white population with the destruction of local cultural patterns.

Hawaii, evidently, had come of age as a state at what turned out to be perhaps the most difficult time in the nation's history. What Hawaii could manage to do in putting the past, present, and future together was problematical. In 1972, close to the bicentenaries both of the nation and of Cook's appearance at the islands, Hawaii was the only state with a governor's commission on the year 2000, and the only state without a comprehensive plan for historical preservation.

G. D.

POPULATION

NUMBER AND DISTRIBUTION OF INHABITANTS

The total resident population of Hawaii in 1970 was 769,913, according to final results of the decennial U.S. Census. It was probably three times as large as the population of two centuries earlier, on the eve of Captain Cook's arrival, and it was more than fourteen times the total in 1876, when Hawaii's population reached its lowest level in modern times.

Nobody knows the exact population of the Hawaiian Islands when they were first seen by Europeans. Captain Clerke, who assumed leadership of the expedition after Cook's death, published an all-island estimate of 400,000, but one of his officers, Lt. William Bligh, guessed 242,200, and Captain George Dixon, a visitor in 1787, preferred a contact total of only 200,000. Most modern authorities have recommended estimates for 1778 ranging from 200,000 to 300,000.

Whatever the correct total at that time, it soon fell off precipitously and continued to decline for almost a century. In 1823 the newly arrived American missionaries estimated that there were about 140,000 inhabitants in the islands. They conducted actual censuses in 1831–1832 and 1835–1836, counting 130,313 the first time and 108,579 the second time. The first complete census taken by the Hawaiian government reported 84,165 in 1850. The low point was reached early in 1876, when only an estimated 53,900 persons lived in the Hawaiian Kingdom.

There were many reasons for this decline. The early navigators introduced gonorrhea, which caused sterility, and syphilis, which resulted in stillbirths. Many Hawaiians died in epidemics of previously unknown diseases, including *okuu* (probably cholera) in 1804, influenza in the 1820s, mumps in 1839, measles, whooping cough, and influenza in 1848–1849, and smallpox in 1853. Kamehameha's wars late in the eighteenth century resulted in battlefield deaths and famine. Fertility was surprisingly

low, and infant mortality (some of it from infanticide) was exceptionally high.

Government and business leaders were deeply concerned about this rapid depopulation and took various steps to counteract it. A Board of Health was created in 1850, and the first modern hospital was built in 1859. The decline in the labor force was stemmed by importing plantation labor from abroad: Chinese beginning in 1852, Japanese from 1868, Portuguese starting in 1878, Puerto Ricans in 1901, Koreans in 1904, and Filipinos initially in 1907, as well as a number of smaller groups from other countries. This organized immigration, together with a growing number of foreigners arriving on an individual basis, became sufficient by the mid-1870s to counterbalance the natural decrease in population, and the total count began to rise.

Growth was rapid from 1876 until the end of World War II as birth rates rose, mortality dropped, and immigrants poured into the island chain. The population had increased to 80,578 in 1884, 154,001 in 1900, 255,881 in 1920, and 422,770 in 1940. War in the Pacific forced this curve sharply upward, and by mid-1944 there were an estimated 859,000 persons in the Territory, including 407,000 members of the armed forces and 65,000 civilian defense workers.

Petroglyph: birth scene, Kahaluu, Hawaii.

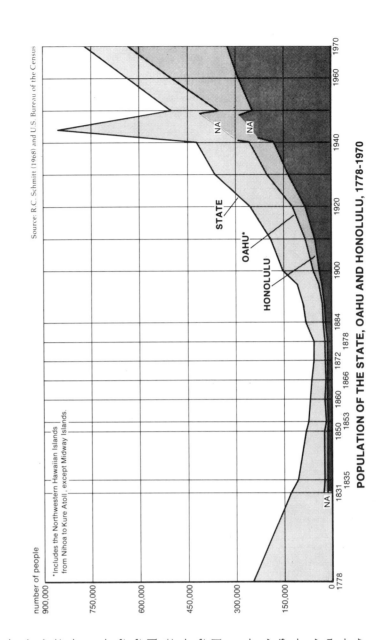

number of people

POPULATION OF THE STATE, OAHU AND HONOLULU, 1778-1970

*Includes the Northwestern Hawaiian Islands from Nihoa to Kure Atoll, except Midway Islands.

Source: R.C. Schmitt (1968) and U.S. Bureau of the Census

STATE

OAHU*

HONOLULU

The quarter century following the end of World War II witnessed an initial period of decline followed by a resumption of past growth trends. Military cutbacks, extensive strikes in sugar, pineapple, and shipping industries, and the effects of a mainland recession triggered a sizeable net out-migration during the late 1940s and early 1950s, resulting in a postwar low of 498,000 reached in mid-1950. Increased military expenditures and burgeoning tourism reversed this net outflow after 1954, and the population increased from 505,000 in that year to 622,000 on the eve of statehood and 788,000 by mid-1971.

Recent totals appear even greater if the population is defined on a de facto basis. As indicated, the total resident population on April 1, 1970, was 769,913. This figure included 55,142 members of the armed forces (including many aboard Navy and Coast Guard ships home-ported in Hawaii), 61,858 civilian dependents of these island-based personnel, and 652,913 other civilians. It also included an estimated 10,469 Hawaii residents temporarily out of the State on business or vacation, but excluded an estimated 37,864 tourists and other visitors temporarily present. If the number of persons actually in the State on the census date is calculated, it comes to 797,308.

More than four-fifths of Hawaii's residents live on Oahu, an island which accounts for only 9.2 percent of total land area of the State. This concentration has been building up for more than a century: Oahu had 22.9 percent of the all-island total in 1831, 38.0 percent in 1900, 61.0 percent in 1940, and 81.9 percent in 1970. The population of the other islands has declined not only in relative terms but also, until recently, in absolute terms. Their combined total reached a modern peak in 1930 with 165,413, and then, with mechanization of agriculture, it fell quickly to 132,363 by 1960. Resort development sparked a resurgence of growth thereafter, and their 1970 population was 139,385. Long-term trends in some percentage distributions are as follows:

	1831	1878	1910	1940	1960	1970
Oahu	23%	35%	43%	61%	79%	82%
Honolulu	10	24	27	42	46	42
Rest of Oahu	13	11	16	19	33	40
Other islands	77	65	57	39	21	18
Urban	10	24	31	63	76	84
Rural	90	76	69	37	24	16

About half the current population of Oahu lives in Honolulu, the urban cluster officially described (for statistical purposes) as the area between Red Hill and Makapuu Point, between the crest of the Koolau Mountains and the southeastern shore of the island (page 120). The population of Honolulu proper has grown from 13,344 in 1831 to 39,306 in 1900 and 324,871 in 1970. The Honolulu Urbanized Area, a statistical entity defined for census purposes, consists of Honolulu itself and also the adjacent built-up area beyond Honolulu International Airport as far as Waipahu, Ewa, and Ewa Beach. The Urbanized Area, thus defined, had a 1970 population of 443,749. The Honolulu Standard Metropolitan Statistical Area, another federally defined statistical unit, is the same as the City and County of Honolulu, and had 630,528 inhabitants in 1970.

Other urban places in the State are considerably less populous. In order of 1970 size they are: Kailua, 33,783; Kaneohe, 29,903; Hilo, 26,353; Waipahu, 24,150; Pearl City, 19,552; Wahiawa, 17,598; and Schofield Barracks, 13,516. The twin cities of Wailuku and Kahului, Maui, had 7,979 and 8,280 residents, respectively. The largest towns on Kauai were Kapaa (3,794) and Lihue (3,124). Kaunakakai, Molokai, with 1,070, and Lanai City, Lanai, with 2,122, were the largest communities on those islands. Niihau is completely rural, and Kahoolawe is uninhabited. For the State as a whole, the urban population was 643,222 in 1970, or 83.5 percent of the total (page 120).

Population densities vary widely—from island to island and within major cities. For the State as a whole, the 1970 density was 119.8 persons per square mile, or about the same as California or Florida. The City and County of Honolulu, however, had a density of 1,058.5 (3,751.4 in Honolulu proper and 600.4 for the rest of Oahu), while the neighbor islands averaged only 23.9, and ranged from zero on Kahoolawe and 3.4 on Niihau to 53.8 on Kauai. The 161 census tracts into which Oahu has been divided had 1970 densities as high as 60,064 in tract 54 (Mayor Wright Homes) and 35,198 in tract 24 (McCully-Moiliili), and as low as 24.8 in tract 100 (Haleiwa-Kawailoa). These are resident densities rather than de facto densities, which would often be far higher. Waikiki, for example, had a 1970 resident population of 13,124 in its 602 acres, but this figure took no account of the 10,717 wage- and salary-workers employed in the area (according to a 1964 survey), or the 25,000 or so nonresident guests in its 16,000 hotel rooms at peak times in 1970. The gross density of Waikiki could thus be given as either 13,962 or 53,000 per square mile, depending on the definition of "population."

R.C.S.

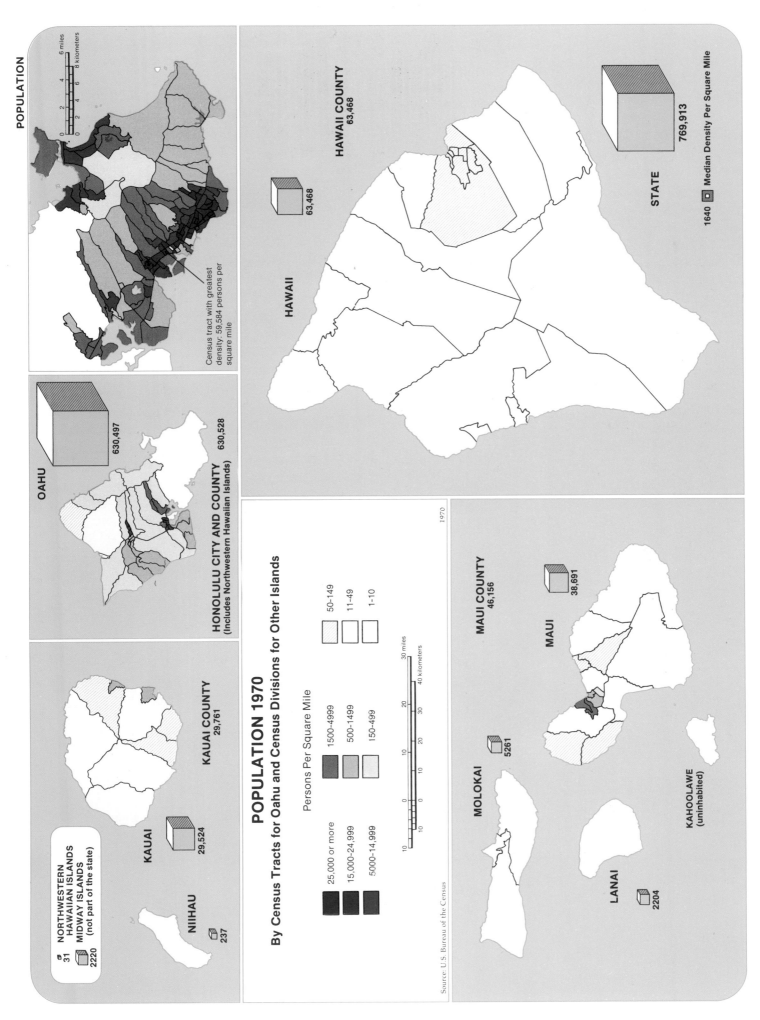

6 miles
8 kilometers

Census tract with greatest density: 59,584 persons per square mile

OAHU
630,497

HONOLULU CITY AND COUNTY
(Includes Northwestern Hawaiian Islands)
630,528

HAWAII COUNTY
63,468

HAWAII
63,468

STATE
769,913

1640 □ Median Density Per Square Mile

NORTHWESTERN HAWAIIAN ISLANDS
31
MIDWAY ISLANDS
(not part of the state)
2220

KAUAI
KAUAI COUNTY
29,761
29,524

NIIHAU
237

POPULATION 1970
By Census Tracts for Oahu and Census Divisions for Other Islands

Persons Per Square Mile

50-149
11-49
1-10

25,000 or more
15,000-24,999
5000-14,999

1500-4999
500-1499
150-499

10   0   10   20   30 miles
10 0 10 20 30 40 kilometers

1970

MAUI COUNTY
46,156

MAUI
38,691

MOLOKAI
5261

LANAI
2204

KAHOOLAWE
(uninhabited)

Source: U.S. Bureau of the Census

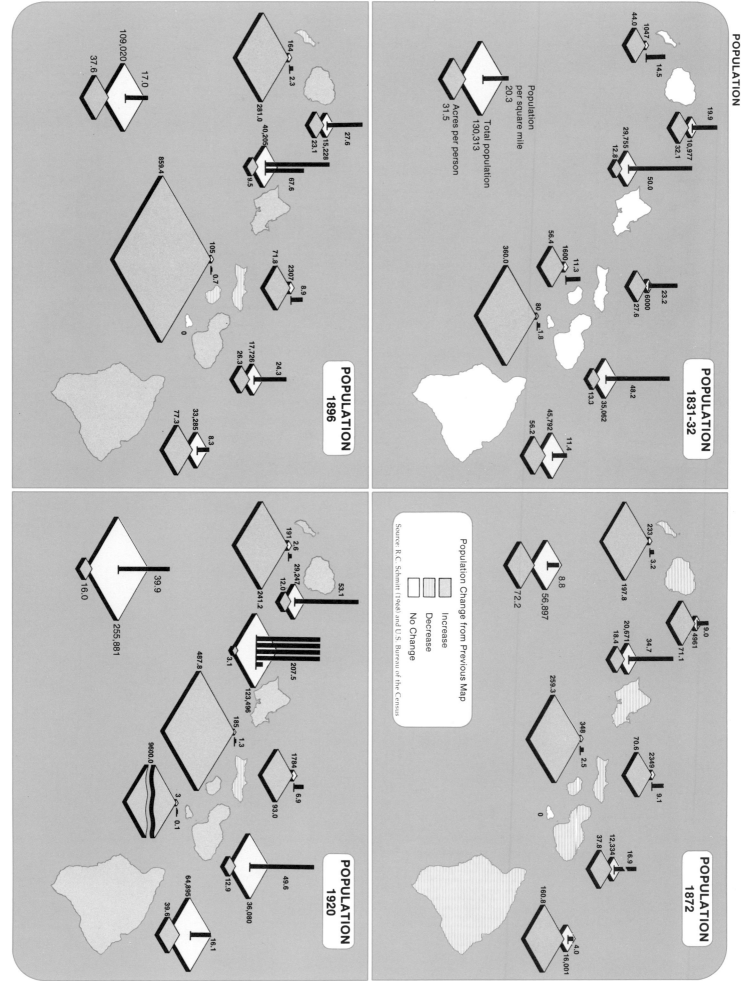

POPULATION
1831-32

Total population 130,313
Population per square mile 20.3
Acres per person 31.5

POPULATION
1872

Population Change from Previous Map

Increase

Decrease

No Change

Source: R.C. Schmitt (1968) and U.S. Bureau of the Census

POPULATION
1896

POPULATION
1920

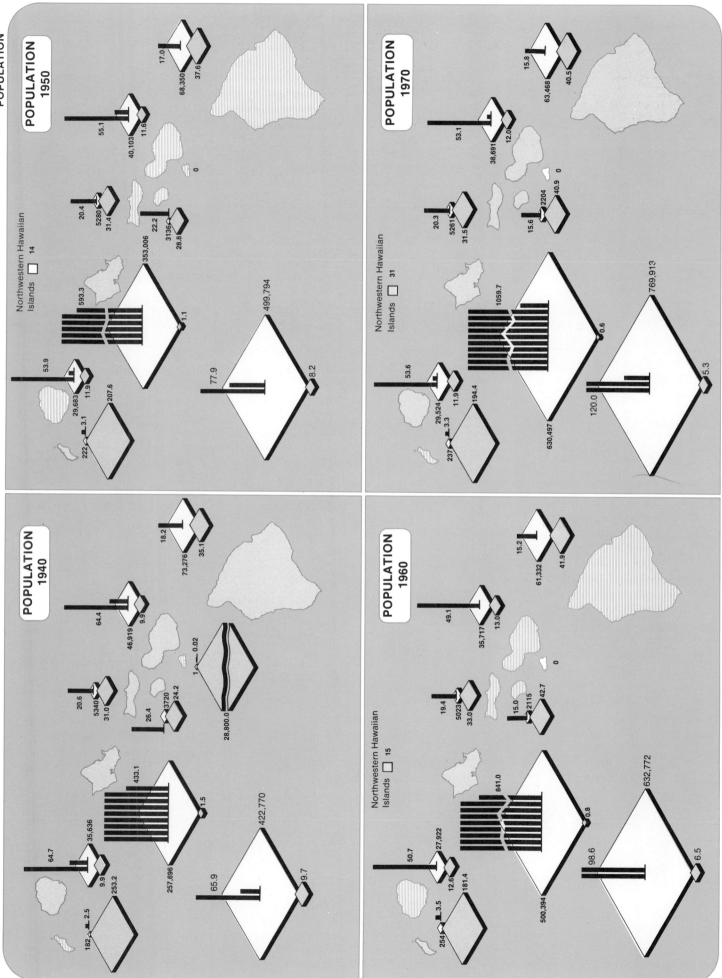

POPULATION 1940

POPULATION 1950

POPULATION 1960

POPULATION 1970

Northwestern Hawaiian Islands 14

Northwestern Hawaiian Islands 15

Northwestern Hawaiian Islands 31

DEMOGRAPHIC CHARACTERISTICS

The population of Hawaii is relatively youthful; it has a surplus of males and includes a wide range of ethnic and national origins.

There were 108.1 males per 100 females in the 1970 resident total. The relative abundance of males was due in part to the large military population of the State and in part to the large number of older plantation workers who came to the islands as single men many years ago and never found wives.

Half of the residents in 1970 were under 25 years of age. Fully 35.7 percent were less than 18, 58.5 percent were between 18 and 64, and only 5.7 percent were 65 years of age or older. The statewide median age rose from 21.7 years in 1930 to 23.2 in 1940 and 24.9 in 1950, dropped to 24.3 in 1960, and then increased to 25.0 in 1970. It was 24.6 on Oahu, 28.9 on the Big Island, 29.0 in Maui County, and 29.7 in Kauai County. In local areas, median ages ranged from 17.3 years on Niihau to 43.6 in Puunene and 52.0 at Kalaupapa settlement.

The major ethnic groups are Caucasian and Japanese (pages 105-110). According to the preliminary results of a sample survey conducted by the Hawaii State Department of Health in 1970, approximately 33.5 percent of the resident population was Caucasian (including Puerto Rican), 26.8 percent was Japanese, 16.2 percent was Part Hawaiian, 7.9 percent was Filipino, 7.9 percent was mixed other than Part Hawaiian, 3.9 percent was Chinese, 1.0 percent was unmixed Hawaiian, 0.9 percent was Korean, 0.8 percent was Negro, 0.8 percent was Samoan, and 0.4 percent was other or unknown. These figures differ considerably from 1970 census totals, which arbitrarily combine all persons of mixed race (a fourth of the population and 46.7 percent of all births in 1969) with the race of the father.

Ethnic distributions have changed greatly over the years. In 1853, 95.8 percent of the population was Hawaiian, 1.3 percent was Part Hawaiian, and 2.9 percent was non-Hawaiian. By 1910, only 13.6 percent was Hawaiian, 6.5 percent was Part Hawaiian, and almost 80 percent non-Hawaiian, chiefly Japanese (41.5 percent) and Caucasian (23.0 percent). Recent growth has been greatest for the Caucasians, Samoans, and persons of mixed race.

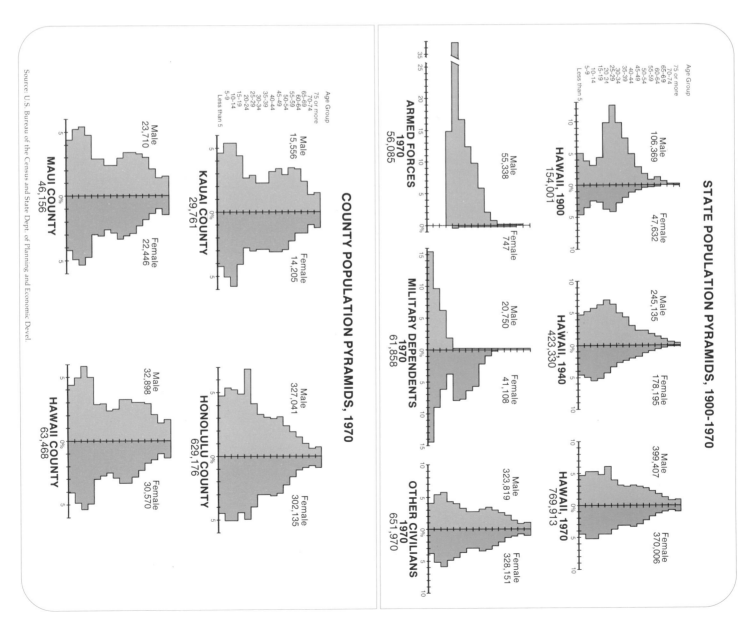

STATE POPULATION PYRAMIDS, 1900-1970

HAWAII, 1900
154,001
Male 106,369
Female 47,632

HAWAII, 1940
423,330
Male 245,135
Female 178,195

HAWAII, 1970
769,913
Male 399,407
Female 370,006

ARMED FORCES
1970
56,085
Male 55,338
Female 747

MILITARY DEPENDENTS
1970
61,858
Male 20,750
Female 41,108

OTHER CIVILIANS
1970
651,970
Male 323,819
Female 328,151

COUNTY POPULATION PYRAMIDS, 1970

KAUAI COUNTY
29,761
Male 15,556
Female 14,205

HONOLULU COUNTY
629,176
Male 327,041
Female 302,135

MAUI COUNTY
46,156
Male 23,710
Female 22,446

HAWAII COUNTY
63,468
Male 32,898
Female 30,570

Source: U.S. Bureau of the Census and State Dept. of Planning and Economic Devel.

There are few ethnic enclaves in Hawaii. The best known are Niihau, a privately owned island populated entirely by Hawaiians and Part Hawaiians; Nanakuli, Waimanalo, and other communities under the jurisdiction of the Department of Hawaiian Home Lands, and thus given to concentrations of ethnic Hawaiians; and the large military bases on Oahu, with their clusters of mainland Caucasians and Negroes. The plantation "camps," once made up of single ethnic groups, have largely disappeared.

Most Hawaii residents were born in the islands, although a sizeable fraction is of mainland origin. The 1970 census reported that 59.2 percent were Hawaii-born, 23.2 percent mainland-born, and 9.8 percent foreign-born, with the rest from outlying U.S. possessions or not reported. Forty years earlier, when the foreign-born were at their absolute peak at 121,209 (compared with 75,595 in 1970), they accounted for almost a third of the total:

	1872	1900	1930	1970
Born in Hawaii	92.1%	38.3%	58.2%	59.2%
Born on the mainland	1.6	2.8	8.2	23.2
Foreign born	6.4	58.9	32.9	9.8

Of 256,172 Hawaii residents classified as either foreign-born or having foreign-born parents, four-fifths were of Asiatic origin, chiefly Japanese.

The State had 203,088 households and 170,358 families in 1970 (page 120). Average household size was 3.59 individuals, compared with 3.87 in 1960 and 4.14 in 1950. Average household size ranged from 1.19 in downtown Honolulu and 1.51 in Chinatown to 6.08 on Niihau.

Among persons 14 years of age and over, 58.8 percent of the males and 63.0 percent of the females were currently married in 1970. These percentages have changed radically over the years with the changing balance of the sexes. In 1896, for example, only 34.4 percent of the males but 71.0 percent of the females were married. The number of unattached males per 1,000 unattached females rose from 1,919 in 1866 to 8,200 in 1900, then fell to 2,162 in 1940 and 1,217 in 1970.

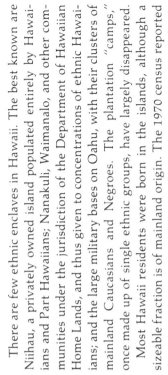

Source: A.W. Lind (1967) and State Dept. of Planning and Economic Devel.

POPULATION, 1778-1970, BY ETHNIC GROUPS

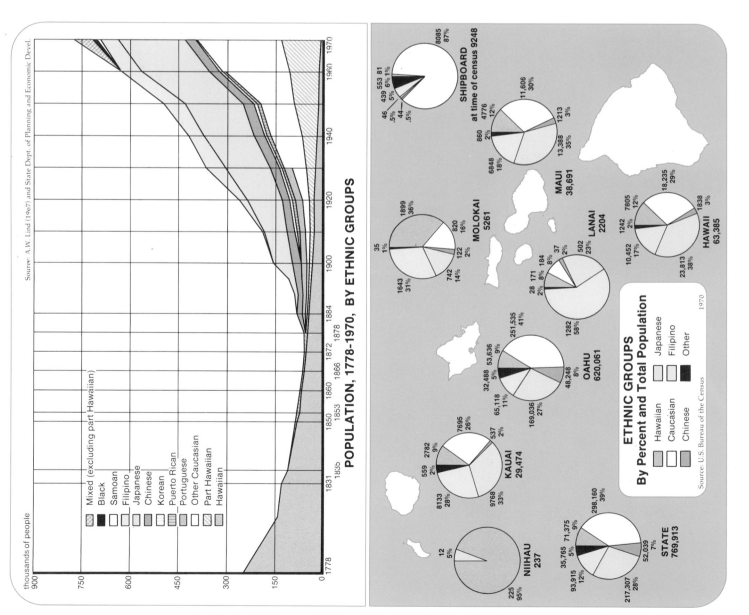

ETHNIC GROUPS
By Percent and Total Population

Source: U.S. Bureau of the Census   1970

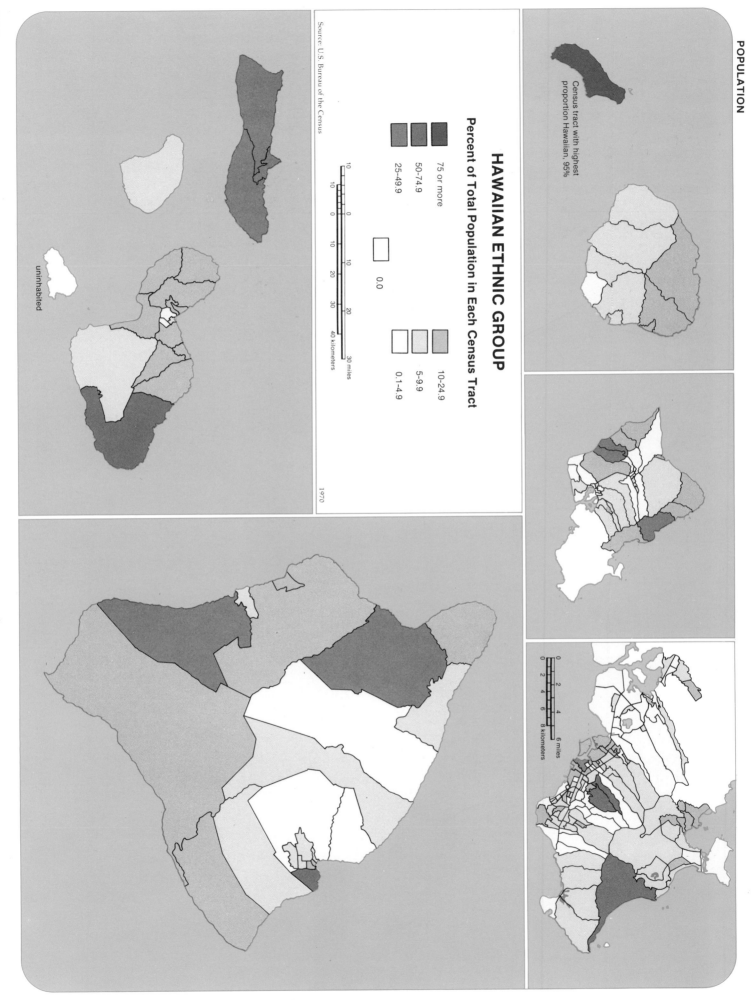

HAWAIIAN ETHNIC GROUP
Percent of Total Population in Each Census Tract

Census tract with highest
proportion Hawaiian, 95%

75 or more

50-74.9

25-49.9

10-24.9

5-9.9

0.1-4.9

0.0

uninhabited

Source: U.S. Bureau of the Census

1970

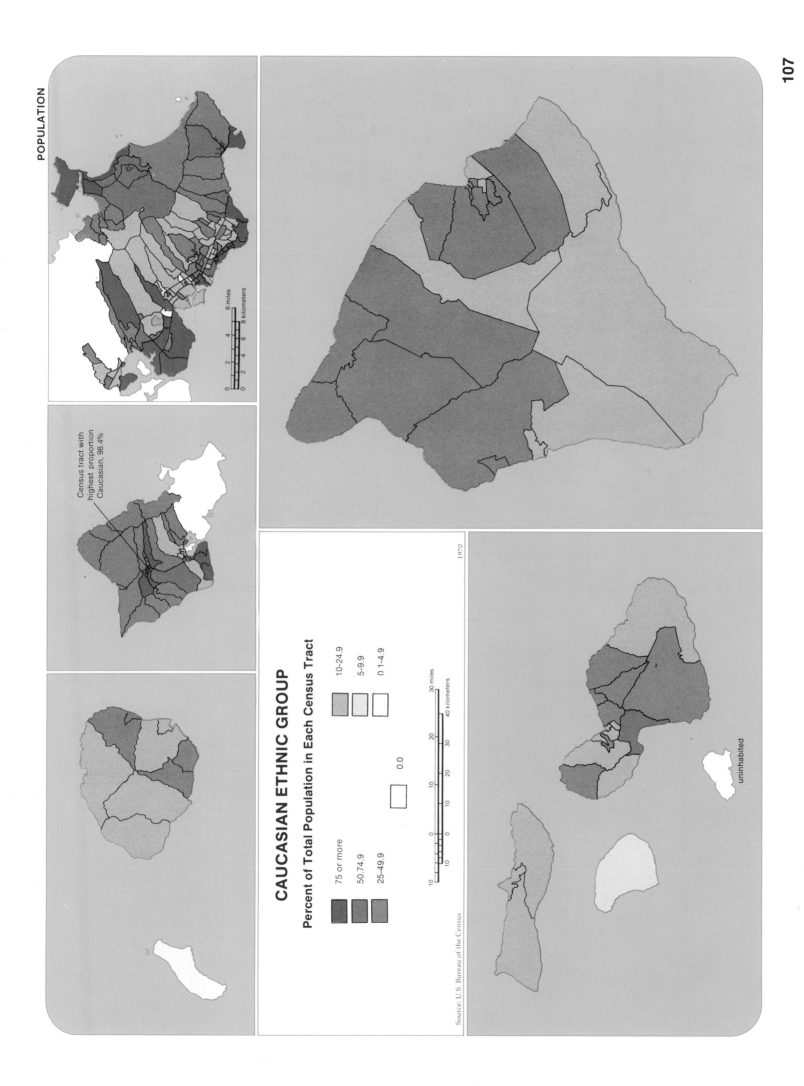

CAUCASIAN ETHNIC GROUP

Percent of Total Population in Each Census Tract

Census tract with highest proportion Caucasian, 98.4%

75 or more	10-24.9
50-74.9	5-9.9
25-49.9	0.1-4.9

0.0

uninhabited

0   10   20   30 miles

0   10   20   30   40 kilometers

1970

Source: U.S. Bureau of the Census

6 miles

0   2   4   6   8 kilometers

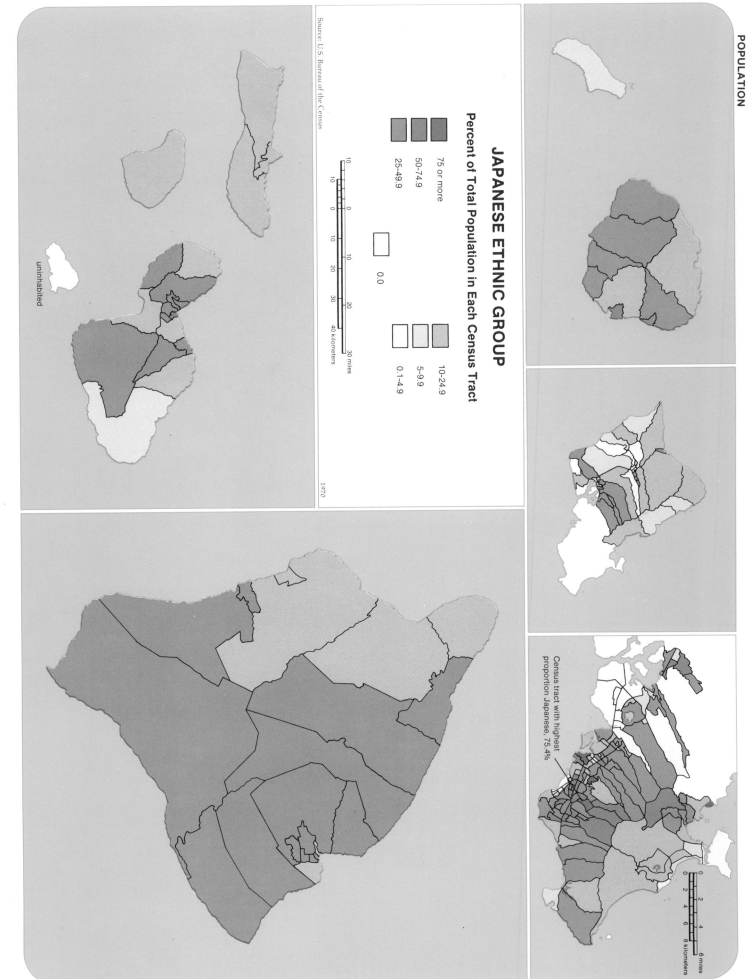

JAPANESE ETHNIC GROUP

Percent of Total Population in Each Census Tract

75 or more

50–74.9

25–49.9

0.0

10–24.9

5–9.9

0.1–4.9

uninhabited

Census tract with highest proportion Japanese, 75.4%

Source: U.S. Bureau of the Census

1970

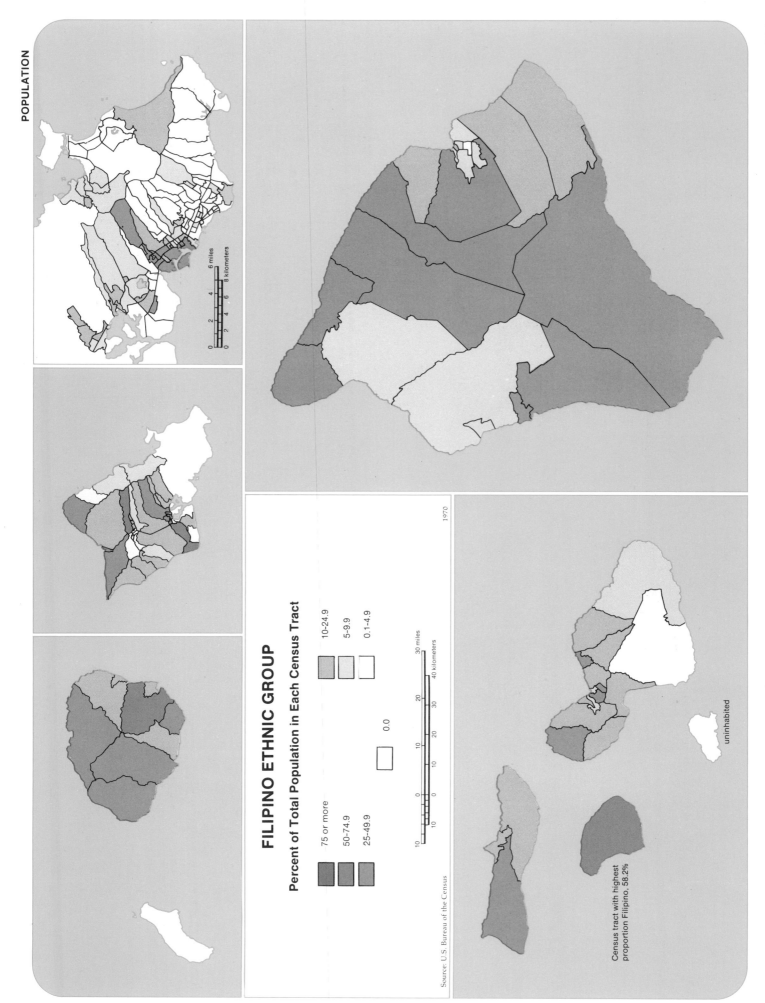

FILIPINO ETHNIC GROUP

Percent of Total Population in Each Census Tract

75 or more

50-74.9

25-49.9

10-24.9

5-9.9

0.1-4.9

0.0

Source: U.S. Bureau of the Census

1970

uninhabited

Census tract with highest
proportion Filipino, 58.2%

6 miles

8 kilometers

30 miles

40 kilometers

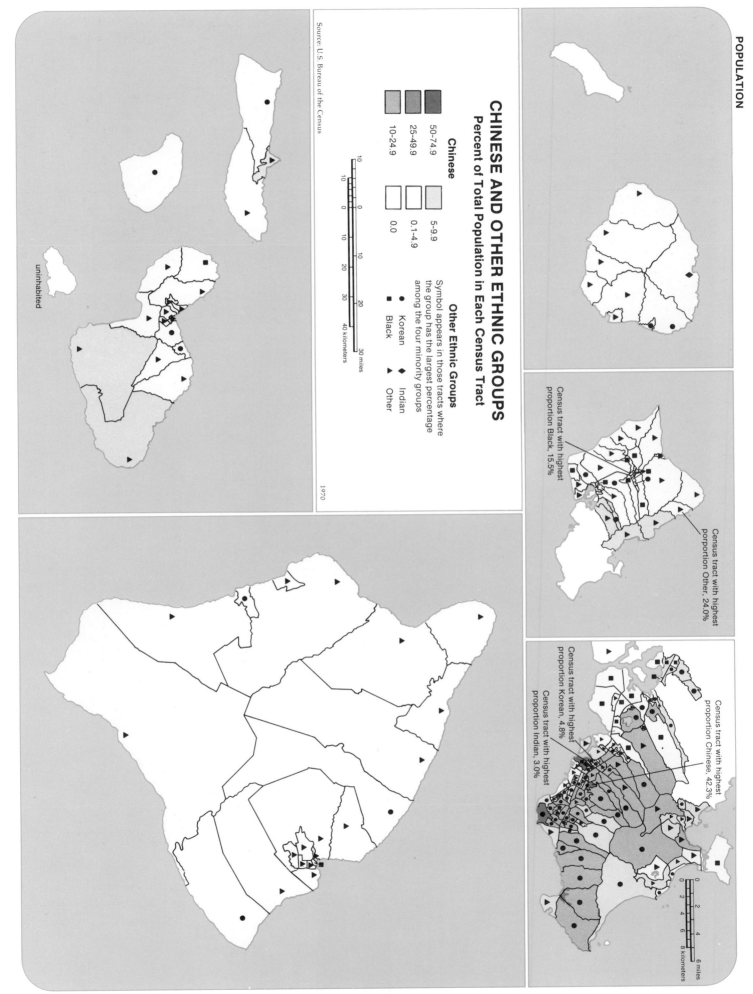

CHINESE AND OTHER ETHNIC GROUPS
Percent of Total Population in Each Census Tract

Chinese

50-74.9	5-9.9
25-49.9	0.1-4.9
10-24.9	0.0

Other Ethnic Groups

Symbol appears in those tracts where the group has the largest percentage among the four minority groups

● Korean	◆ Indian
■ Black	▶ Other

Source: U.S. Bureau of the Census

1970

uninhabited

Census tract with highest proportion Black 15.5%

Census tract with highest proportion Other, 24.0%

Census tract with highest proportion Chinese, 42.3%

Census tract with highest proportion Korean, 4.8%

Census tract with highest proportion Indian, 3.0%

SOCIAL AND ECONOMIC CHARACTERISTICS

Residents of Hawaii are in general characterized by relatively high educational attainment, by high rates of participation in the labor force, by concentration in government and service employment, and by high family incomes (pages 112 and 132).

According to census reports, more than 228,000 persons attended school in 1970—virtually everyone of school age in the islands. Among those in elementary school, one out of nine attended parochial or other private schools. In the 14- to 17-year age group, 93.4 percent were enrolled, a ratio that varied surprisingly little from place to place within the State. Among persons 25 years old and over, the median number of school years completed was 12.3, with a range between 10.3 on Kauai and 12.4 on Oahu (page 180).

Forty-nine percent of all females 16 years old and over were in the labor force in 1970. Among married women with husband present, the ratio was 48.1 percent, and among those with their own children under six, it was 37.8 percent. Five-sixths of the males 18 to 24 years of age were in the labor force, as were 22.0 percent of all males 65 and older. Only 3.0 percent of the civilian labor force was unemployed at the time of the 1970 census.

The plantation economy of the past has given way to today's service- and government-oriented economy. In 1900 agricultural workers outnumbered those in other civilian activities 57,125 to 32,802. The total in agriculture reached its peak in 1930 (at 63,478), then dropped, falling to 31,806 by 1950 and 13,283 in 1970. Nonagricultural employment meanwhile soared, to 74,317 in 1930, 135,765 in 1950, and 274,527 in 1970. By 1970, 10.9 percent of all employed persons were in manufacturing industries (chiefly food processing), 49.9 percent had white-collar occupations, and 24.7 percent worked for the federal, state, or county government (pages 112 and 134).

Family incomes were relatively high, with a median of $11,554 annually in 1969 compared with $6,366 in 1959, $3,568 in 1949, $742 in 1910, and about $50 in the 1840s. By county, the 1969 median ranged from $9,643 in Maui County to $12,035 on Oahu (page 112).

These measures of advancing prosperity must, however, be interpreted in the light of increased prices. The Honolulu consumer price index in 1970 was 32 percent above its 1960 level, 71 percent over 1950, and 182 percent greater than 1940. Living costs in Honolulu, moreover, were at least 20 percent above the mainland urban average in 1970, according to a survey by the U.S. Bureau of Labor Statistics.

Source: R.C. Schmitt (1968) and U.S. Bureau of the Census

*Population 15 years and older before 1900; 14 years and older 1900-1970.

Not in Labor Force

Total Working-Age Population

Total Employed

Armed Forces

Non-Agriculture

Agriculture

WORKING-AGE POPULATION, 1872-1970*; TOTAL EMPLOYED, 1878-1970; MILITARY STATUS OR ACTIVITY, 1900-1970

EDUCATION By County

12.4 Median school years completed, persons 25 years and older

Percent in school, of persons 14 to 17 years of age

Percent in private school, of all children in elementary school

Source: U.S. Bureau of the Census

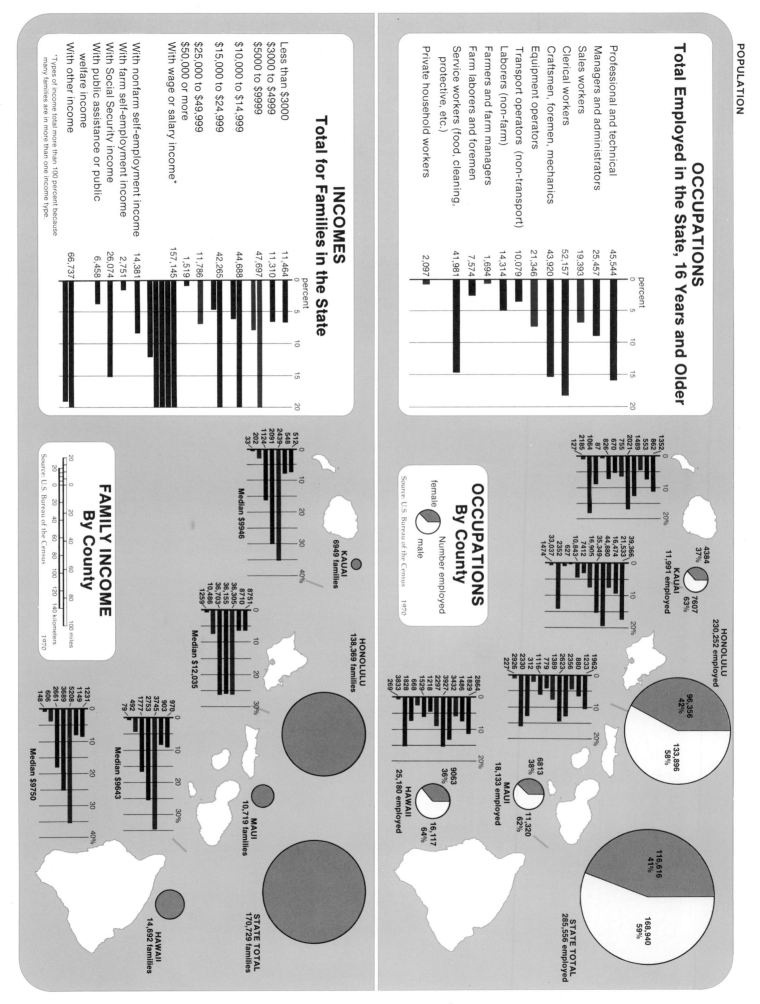

OCCUPATIONS
Total Employed in the State, 16 Years and Older

Professional and technical	45,544
Managers and administrators	25,457
Sales workers	19,393
Clerical workers	52,157
Craftsmen, foremen, mechanics	43,920
Equipment operators	21,346
Transport operators (non-transport)	10,079
Laborers (non-farm)	14,314
Farmers and farm managers	1,694
Farm laborers and foremen	7,574
Service workers (food, cleaning, protective, etc.)	41,981
Private household workers	2,097

Source: U.S. Bureau of the Census 1970

OCCUPATIONS
By County

female / male — Number employed

KAUAI 11,991 employed — 4384 37% / 7607 63%

HONOLULU 230,252 employed — 96,356 42% / 133,896 58%

MAUI 18,133 employed — 6813 38% / 11,320 62%

HAWAII 25,180 employed — 9063 36% / 16,117 64%

STATE TOTAL 285,556 employed — 116,616 41% / 168,940 59%

KAUAI: 1352, 862, 553, 1489, 2021, 755, 670, 826, 87, 1064, 2185, 127

HONOLULU: 39,366, 21,533, 16,474, 44,880, 35,349, 16,905, 7412, 10,843, 627, 2352, 33,037, 1474

MAUI: 2864, 1829, 1486, 3432, 392, 2297, 1218, 1529, 668, 1828, 3833, 269

HAWAII: 1962, 1233, 880, 2356, 2623, 1389, 779, 1116, 312, 2330, 2926, 227

INCOMES
Total for Families in the State

Less than $3000	11,464
$3000 to $4999	11,310
$5000 to $9999	47,697
$10,000 to $14,999	44,688
$15,000 to $24,999	42,265
$25,000 to $49,999	11,786
$50,000 or more	1,519
With wage or salary income*	157,145
With nonfarm self-employment income	14,381
With farm self-employment income	2,751
With Social Security income	26,074
With public assistance or public welfare income	6,458
With other income	66,737

*Types of income total more than 100 percent because many families are in more than one income type.

FAMILY INCOME
By County

KAUAI 6949 families — Median $9946 — 512, 548, 2439, 2091, 1124, 202, 33

HONOLULU 138,369 families — Median $12,035 — 8751, 8710, 36,305, 36,155, 36,703, 10,486, 1269

MAUI 10,719 families — Median $9643 — 970, 903, 3745, 2753, 1777, 492, 79

HAWAII 14,692 families — Median $9750 — 1231, 1149, 5208, 3689, 2661, 606, 148

STATE TOTAL 170,729 families

Source: U.S. Bureau of the Census 1970

0 20 40 60 80 100 kilometers
0 20 40 60 80 100 miles

VITAL STATISTICS

Birth and death rates have shifted significantly during Hawaii's two hundred years of recorded history. Fertility has fluctuated in response to new diseases, immigration patterns, war, depression and prosperity, and contraceptive procedures. A more consistent trend is seen in mortality rates during the last hundred years, as improved public health measures, medical discoveries, and better living conditions have gradually overcome the effects of introduced diseases and epidemics, high infant mortality, famine, and other conditions responsible for the high death rates of earlier periods.

Reproduction and survival were chancy matters in nineteenth-century Hawaii. Venereal diseases caused sterility or stillbirths. Some women resorted to abortion, using the crudest of procedures. There is considerable evidence of infanticide among Hawaiians, a practice that persisted until the middle of the nineteenth century. Early missionary doctors in the 1820s estimated that more than half of all infants died before they were two years of age. Childhood diseases were common and far more severe among the previously unexposed Hawaiians. Epidemics killed perhaps 15,000 children and adults in 1804, 10,000 in 1848-1849, 5,000 or 6,000 in 1853, and 1,700 as late as 1918-1920. Crude birth rates before 1900 ranged from 16 to 41 per 1,000 inhabitants; crude death rates, from 19 to 105—with an unknown, but obviously high and variable, degree of underregistration. The average length of stay in The Queen's Hospital in 1877-1879 was 59 days, at an average daily cost of 61 cents. The average expectation of life at birth for babies born in Honolulu in 1884-1885 was only 36.5 years.

The crude birth rate rose during the first quarter of the twentieth century, in response as much to shifts in the age and sex distribution of the population as to any increase in completed fertility per married woman; the peak seems to have been 43.3 births per 1,000 inhabitants in 1925. Urbanization, increased knowledge of contraceptive techniques, and economic decline brought the rate down to 23.1 during the 1930s, but it recovered rapidly during and after World War II, reaching a postwar high of 34.8 in 1953. Partly because of the introduction of contraceptive pills in 1960 and legalized abortion in 1970, the rate again dropped, and by 1971 was only 21.4.

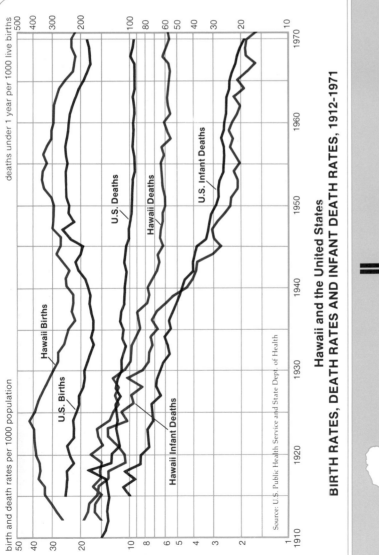

Hawaii and the United States
BIRTH RATES, DEATH RATES AND INFANT DEATH RATES, 1912-1971

Source: U.S. Public Health Service and State Dept. of Health

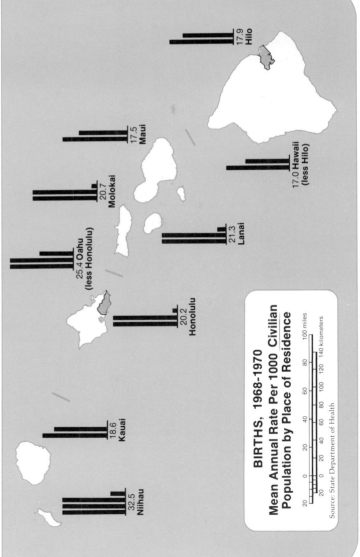

BIRTHS, 1968-1970
Mean Annual Rate Per 1000 Civilian Population by Place of Residence

Source: State Department of Health

Mortality rates in Hawaii declined sharply in the late nineteenth and early twentieth centuries, then began to level off (page 113). Whereas one of every three babies died before its first birthday during the first decade of the present century, in 1971 the infant death rate had dropped to an all-time low of 16.2 per 1,000 live births—one of the lowest rates in the United States and the Pacific (pages 113 and 184). Life expectancy for males rose from 47.8 years in 1919-1920 to 67.8 in 1949-1951 and 70.5 in 1970; corresponding averages for females were 47.3, 71.3, and 77.2. The 1970 crude death rate of 5.6 per 1,000 population is also one of the lowest among the 50 states. A contributing factor is the larger proportion of young people in Hawaii compared with most states. The differences in death rates between islands (see below) are also partly due to age differences in island populations (page 104). The crude death rates used on these pages have not been adjusted statistically for age, sex, health, or other population differences, but they have the advantage of indicating the actual probability of death among their respective populations.

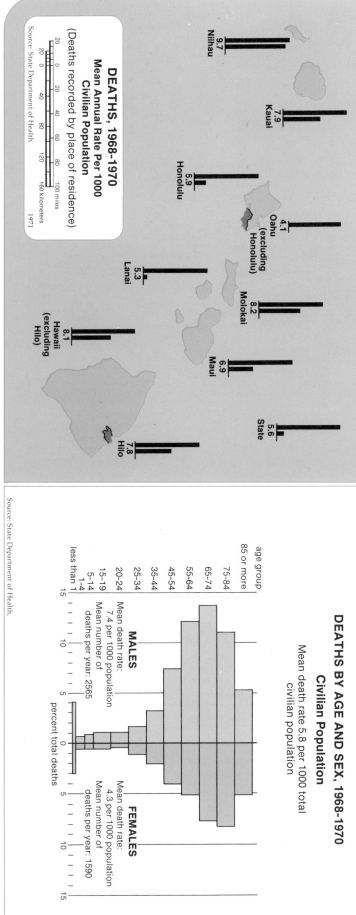

DEATHS, 1968-1970
Mean Annual Rate Per 1000
Civilian Population
(Deaths recorded by place of residence)

Niihau 9.7
Kauai 7.9
Honolulu 5.9
Oahu (excluding Honolulu) 4.1
Lanai 5.3
Molokai 8.2
Hawaii (excluding Hilo) 8.1
Maui 6.9
Hilo 7.8
State 5.6

Source: State Department of Health

1971

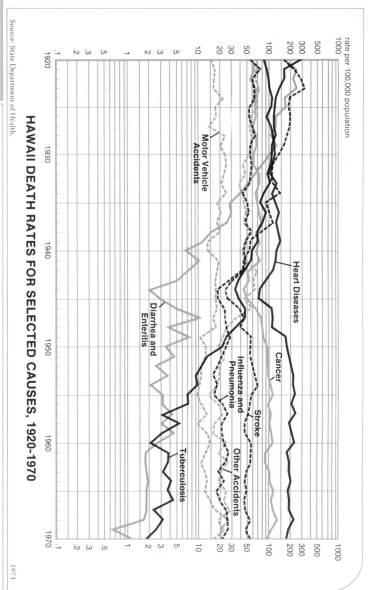

HAWAII DEATH RATES FOR SELECTED CAUSES, 1920-1970

rate per 100,000 population

Heart Diseases
Cancer
Stroke
Motor Vehicle Accidents
Diarrhea and Enteritis
Influenza and Pneumonia
Other Accidents
Tuberculosis

1920 1930 1940 1950 1960 1970

Source: State Department of Health.

1971

DEATHS BY AGE AND SEX, 1968-1970
Civilian Population

Mean death rate 5.8 per 1000 total civilian population

age group
85 or more
75-84
65-74
55-64
45-54
35-44
25-34
20-24
15-19
5-14
1-4
less than 1

MALES
Mean death rate:
7.4 per 1000 population
Mean number of
deaths per year: 2565

FEMALES
Mean death rate:
4.3 per 1000 population
Mean number of
deaths per year: 1590

percent total deaths

Source: State Department of Health.

1971

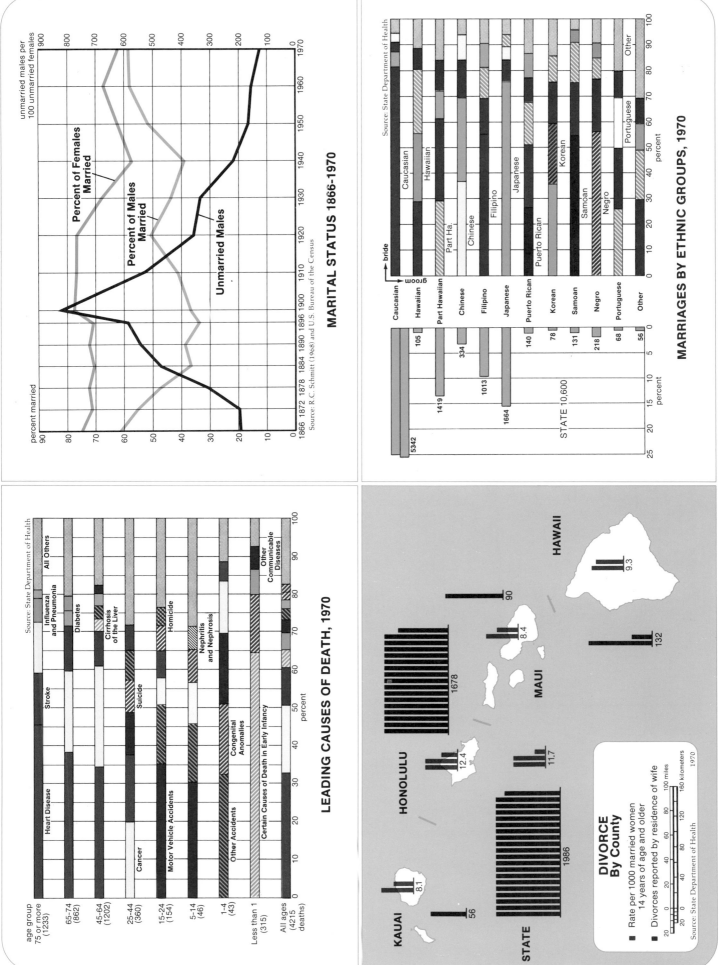

MARITAL STATUS 1866-1970

Source: R.C. Schmitt (1968) and U.S. Bureau of the Census

unmarried males per
100 unmarried females

Percent of Females
Married

Percent of Males
Married

Unmarried Males

percent married

MARRIAGES BY ETHNIC GROUPS, 1970

Source: State Department of Health

bride

groom

Caucasian
Hawaiian
Part Hawaiian
Chinese
Filipino
Japanese
Puerto Rican
Korean
Samoan
Negro
Portuguese
Other

percent

Caucasian 5342
Hawaiian 1419
Part Ha. 105
Chinese 334
Filipino 1013
Japanese 1664
Puerto Rican 140
Korean 78
Samoan 131
Negro 218
Portuguese 68
Other 56

STATE 10,600

percent

LEADING CAUSES OF DEATH, 1970

Source: State Department of Health

age group

75 or more (1233) — Heart Disease — Stroke — Influenza and Pneumonia — Diabetes — All Others

65-74 (862)

45-64 (1202) — Cancer — Cirrhosis of the Liver

25-44 (360) — Suicide

15-24 (154) — Motor Vehicle Accidents — Homicide

5-14 (46)

1-4 (43) — Other Accidents — Nephritis and Nephrosis — Congenital Anomalies

Less than 1 (315) — Certain Causes of Death in Early Infancy — Other Communicable Diseases

All ages (4215 deaths)

percent

DIVORCE By County

■ Rate per 1000 married women 14 years of age and older
■ Divorces reported by residence of wife

Source: State Department of Health

1970

HAWAII 9.3 / 132
MAUI 8.4 / 90
HONOLULU 12.4 / 1678
11.7
KAUAI 8.1 / 56
STATE 1986

100 miles
160 kilometers

115

MIGRATION

For more than a century migration has been a major factor in population growth and redistribution in Hawaii. As noted earlier, large numbers of workers were brought to Hawaii from China, Japan, Portugal, the Philippines, and other areas between 1852 and the 1930s as plantation laborers. After 1930 the mainland United States became the chief source of new residents, as well as the major destination of Hawaii's out-migrants.

In the decade between the 1960 and 1970 censuses, an estimated 192,541 persons (other than military personnel and their dependents) moved to Hawaii, while an estimated 140,095 civilians other than military dependents moved out of the State. Approximately 156,025 of the in-migrants came to Hawaii from the mainland, while 36,516 were immigrants from abroad, chiefly the Philippines. Net in-migration thus averaged 5,245 annually. Some 470,000 military personnel and dependents moved to Hawaii during the decade, but they stayed on the average only 2.5 years. On leaving, they took with them most of the 4,400 babies born to military couples every year in the islands—about 27 percent of all babies born in Hawaii. Including military personnel and dependents, net in-migration averaged only 1,136 annually during the decade. Net in-migration thus accounted for 8.5 percent of overall growth for the decade when the armed forces and their dependents are included, but 39.7 percent when the analysis is limited to the rest of the population.

Most of the civilians moving to Hawaii during the post-World War II period have been relatively young persons, usually less than 30 years of age; only a small number of retired and older persons have migrated to Hawaii, possibly because of high transportation and living costs, and many older persons already living in the islands have moved away upon reaching retirement age. The new residents have usually come from California and other western states, and many of them have been professional and technical workers. The out-migrants, in contrast, have included sizeable numbers of unskilled and semiskilled persons, along with young island-born persons who have left to attend school, enter the armed forces, or seek work on the mainland. The number of Hawaii-born persons living on the mainland increased from 588 in 1850 to 1,307 in 1900, 19,437 in 1930, 115,070 in 1960, and an estimated 200,000 in 1970.

R. C. S.

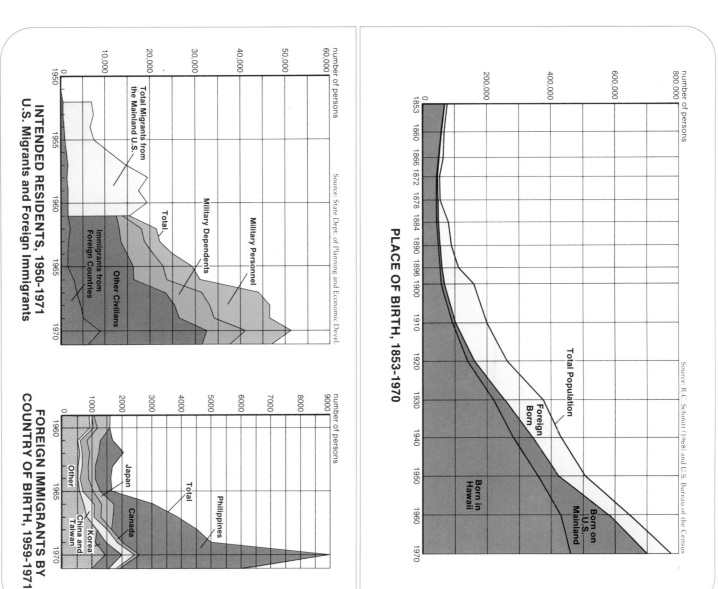

PLACE OF BIRTH, 1853–1970

Source: R.C. Schmitt (1968) and U.S. Bureau of the Census

INTENDED RESIDENTS, 1950–1971
U.S. Migrants and Foreign Immigrants

Source: State Dept. of Planning and Economic Devel.

FOREIGN IMMIGRANTS BY
COUNTRY OF BIRTH, 1959–1971

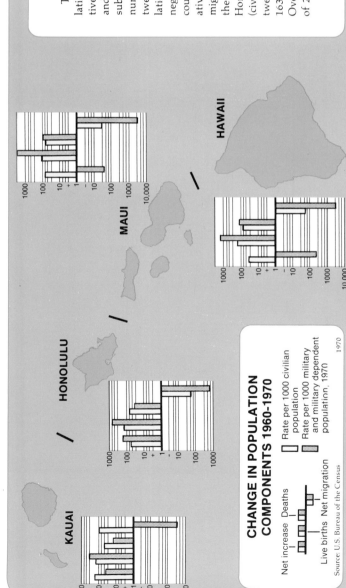

The graphs to the left show the rate of change for the civilian population and for the military and military-dependent population, respectively, in the major components of population change: births, deaths, and net migration. Births are additions to the population, deaths are subtractions. Net migration represents the difference between the number of people entering and leaving the State and counties. Between 1960 and 1970 net migration was positive for the civilian population of the City and County of Honolulu, representing a gain, but negative—or a loss of population—in all military-status groups and counties. The "net change" is a demographer's term which can be negative as well as positive. It is the combined effect of births, deaths, and migration. In all counties the civilian net change was positive, but for the military population it was positive only in the City and County of Honolulu and in Kauai County. For the total population of the State (civilian and military combined), there was a positive net change between 1960 and 1970 of 137,141 persons. This was comprised of 163,762 live births, 38,243 deaths, and a net in-migration of 11,622. Over the decade this represents a growth in the population of the State of 22 percent.

KAUAI

HONOLULU

MAUI

HAWAII

CHANGE IN POPULATION COMPONENTS 1960-1970

Net increase   Deaths

Live births   Net migration

Rate per 1000 civilian population

Rate per 1000 military and military dependent population, 1970

Source: U.S. Bureau of the Census

1970

STATE TOTAL 697,790

46% Resident in the Same House

6% Not Reported

25% Resident in Other Locations (see bar graph at left)

23% Resident in Same County but Different House

Population More Than Five Years of Age, 1970

RESIDENCE MOVING OF THE STATE POPULATION

percent

1969-70   234,125

1965-68   230,270

1960-64   117,414

1950-59   98,777

1949 or earlier   35,439

Always lived in same house   52,534

State Total: 769,913

KAUAI 27,135

HONOLULU 570,530

MAUI 42,124

HAWAII 58,001

LOCATION OF RESIDENTS, 1965

Source: U.S. Bureau of the Census

1970

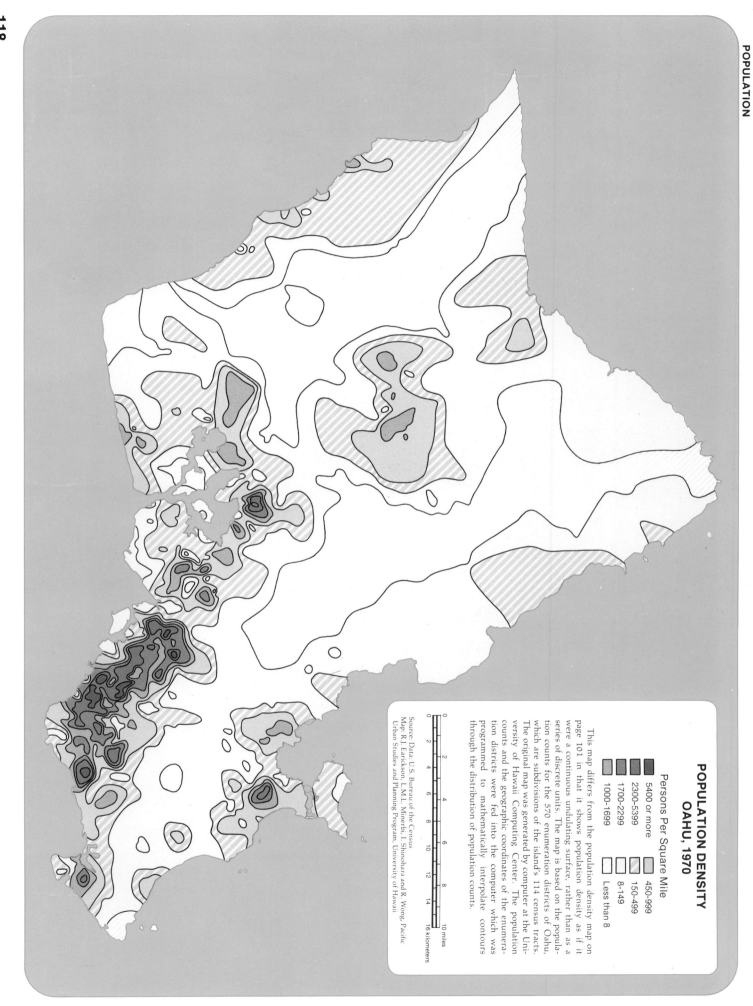

POPULATION DENSITY
OAHU, 1970

Persons Per Square Mile

5400 or more
2300-5399
1700-2299
1000-1699
450-999
150-499
8-149
Less than 8

This map differs from the population density map on page 101 in that it shows population density as if it were a continuous undulating surface, rather than as a series of discrete units. The map is based on the population counts for the 570 enumeration districts of Oahu, which are subdivisions of the island's 114 census tracts. The original map was generated by computer at the University of Hawaii Computing Center. The population counts and the geographic coordinates of the enumeration districts were fed into the computer which was programmed to mathematically interpolate contours through the distribution of population counts.

Source: Data: U.S. Bureau of the Census
Map: R.I. Earickson, L.M.L. Minerbi, I. Shinohara and R. Wong, Pacific Urban Studies and Planning Program, University of Hawaii

0 2 4 6 8 10 miles
0 2 4 6 8 10 12 14 16 kilometers

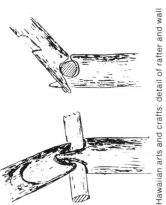

Hawaiian arts and crafts: detail of rafter and wall post in house construction.
Bishop Museum drawing from Te Rangi Hiroa (1964:87).

URBAN CENTERS

The 1970 census reveals that the State of Hawaii has nine places with populations of over 10,000, and that, of these, all but one—the city of Hilo on the Big Island—are within the county of Honolulu which covers the island of Oahu. Two other cities, Wailuku on the island of Maui with nearly 8,000 and adjacent Kahului with more than 8,000 (having almost doubled its population since 1960) approach this size, but otherwise Honolulu and its satellites on Oahu dominate the urban life of the State. Their combined populations in 1970 made up 62 percent of the total, compared with only 26 percent in 1900. Honolulu alone contains more than half of the urban population of the State.

Population pressure on Oahu is intensified by physical and human conditions which severely limit the available living and working space. In area, the island has less than 10 percent of the State's total of 6,425 square miles, and, since the surface configuration is extremely varied (46 percent of the area is mountainous with slopes exceeding 20 percent), most of the residents and their works have been crowded into a series of narrow, low valleys and sloping lands at the southeastern end of the island from which there is easiest access to Pearl Harbor, Keehi Lagoon, Honolulu Harbor, and Honolulu International Airport. The city center is directly northeast of Honolulu Harbor, and wherever expansion has not been blocked by physical features or zoning restrictions, the growing pace of construction has promoted the spread of the built-up area in both directions along the southeastern coast and up the slender valleys etched into the face of the Koolau Range, the city's dramatic backdrop. Within the past decade, thanks to new highways and especially to two tunnels through the mountain barrier, suburban communities on the low-lying lands and slopes of the opposite, or "windward," side of the southern Koolaus have become increasingly tied in with the capital. Such places as Kaneohe, Kailua, and Waimanalo have thus grown into extensive exurban agglomerations, most of whose working populations commute daily to Honolulu, but whose residents are generally served by shopping centers and other local facilities. Several splendid beaches in this area are shared with other residents of the island. Oahu is otherwise amply provided with recreational facilities oriented to the sea, even on the "leeward" coast, within the city limits of Honolulu.

Agriculture is another activity which helps to check the expansion of the city, although this situation is rapidly changing. Although it is the most urbanized island of the Hawaiian chain, Oahu has over half the State's acreage deemed suitable for intensive agriculture (page 135). But between 1954 and 1965 an estimated 6,184 acres of agricultural land were shifted to non-agricultural use.

Housing and transportation are among the most pressing urban problems, as the demand, again at an accelerating pace, has tended to outrun the supply. Housing on Oahu is generally considered inadequate, especially for lower income groups, the elderly, students, and some military personnel and their dependents. Housing problems, notably on Oahu, are somewhat unusual by the standards of the nation as a whole. For example, the cost of renting, and especially of owning, a home in Hawaii is exceeded only in Alaska. This is due to a number of factors in addition to the expense of building materials, most of which are imported. Residential land is scarce, expensive, and often unpurchasable, since much desirable property is owned by corporations, trusts, and individuals who lease it for "development" and occupancy, both commercial and residential. The owner-occupancy rate on Oahu is thus a meager 45 percent, much "developed" property apparently being used for speculative purposes, and the usual processes of "filtration" (high-cost land becoming less costly in time) is virtually reversed. Public housing is also considered inadequate, and though there has been sizable effort to remedy this situation through legislation and project construction, effective implementation is hindered by various factors, especially excessive costs.

Some of the above conditions are also responsible for Oahu's problems of transportation (page 170). The linear structure of the city, the cramping of habitable areas by physical features, the ownership of centrally located lands by government and private interests, all serve to inhibit traffic flow by denying alternative routes and confining vehicles to a few overburdened thoroughfares. Conventional work schedules cause heavy congestion at peak hours, particularly as most workers use private cars for the journey to work.

D. H. K.

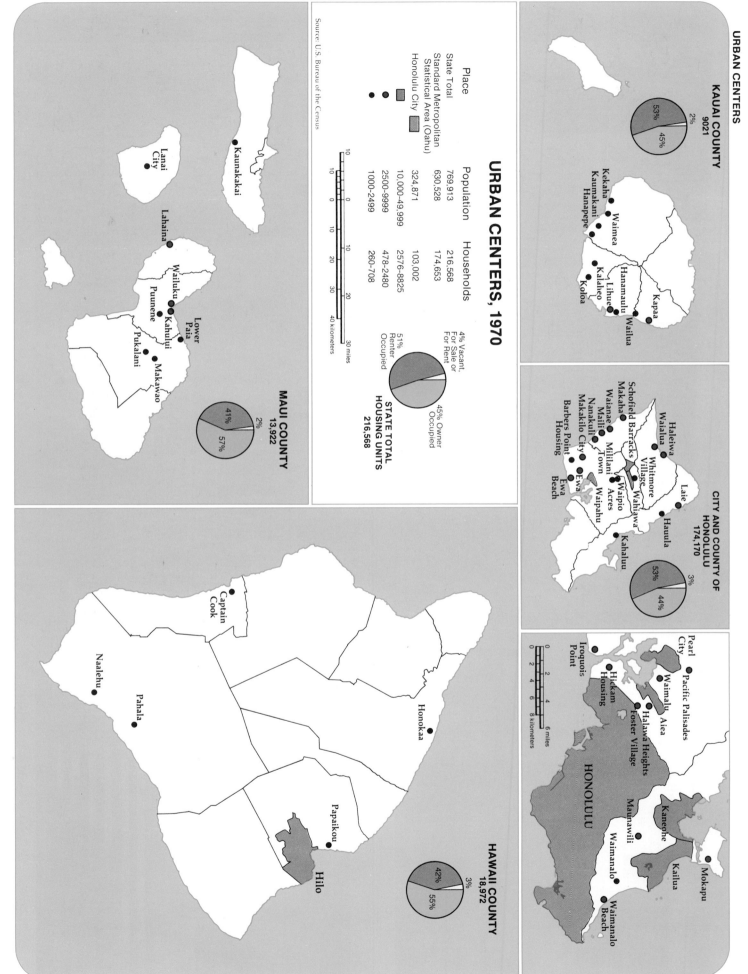

URBAN CENTERS, 1970

KAUAI COUNTY
9021

Kekaha
Kaumakani
Hanapepe
Waimea
Hanamaulu
Lihue
Kalaheo
Koloa
Wailua
Kapaa

2%
53%
45%

CITY AND COUNTY OF HONOLULU
174,170

Haleiwa
Waialua
Schofield Barracks
Makaha
Waianae
Maili
Nanakuli
Makakilo City
Barbers Point Housing
Ewa Beach
Whitmore Village
Mililani Town
Waipio Acres
Wahiawa
Waipahu
Laie
Hauula
Kahaluu

3%
53%
44%

Pearl City
Pacific Palisades
Waimalu
Aiea
Hickam Housing
Halawa Heights
Foster Village
Iroquois Point
Kaneohe
Maunawili
Waimanalo
Kailua
Mokapu
Waimanalo Beach

HONOLULU

0 2 4 6 8 kilometers
0 2 4 6 miles

Place | Population | Households
State Total | 769,913 | 216,568
Standard Metropolitan Statistical Area (Oahu) | 630,528 | 174,653
Honolulu City | 324,871 | 103,002

● 10,000-49,999 | 2576-8825
● 2500-9999 | 478-2480
• 1000-2499 | 260-708

10 10
0 0
10 10
20 20
30 20
40 kilometers 30 miles

4% Vacant, For Sale or For Rent
51% Renter Occupied
45% Owner Occupied

STATE TOTAL HOUSING UNITS
216,568

Source: U.S. Bureau of the Census

Lanai City
Kaunakakai
Lahaina
Wailuku
Puunene
Kahului
Lower Paia
Pukalani
Makawao

MAUI COUNTY
13,922

2%
41%
57%

Captain Cook
Naalehu
Pahala
Honokaa
Papaikou
Hilo

HAWAII COUNTY
18,972

3%
42%
55%

120

Honolulu, Oahu. Looking east across Sand Island and the downtown business district, with Waikiki and Diamond Head at the right and Koko Head in the distance. The island of Molokai is in the far distance.

Photograph by R. M. Towill Corporation, Honolulu.

Kahului (foreground) and Wailuku, Maui. Looking west across the two towns toward the West Maui mountains. In the far distance is the island of Lanai.

Photograph by R. M. Towill Corporation, Honolulu.

Hilo, Hawaii. View south across Hilo Bay. The downtown area is in the right foreground, a shopping center and government buildings in the center, and hotel, airport, and light industrial areas to the left.

Photograph by R. M. Towill Corporation, Honolulu.

121

Hawaiian arts and crafts: detail of plaiting of a makaloa mat.
Bishop Museum drawing from Te Rangi Hiroa (1964:120)

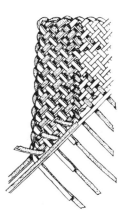

LANGUAGES

Not every resident of Hawaii is multilingual, but many different languages and dialects are spoken in Hawaii. We single out for comment several languages, each of which has been the mother tongue of one of the ethnic groups who have resided in Hawaii since Captain Cook's arrival, at which time, of course, Hawaiian was the language of the islands.

English is the first language of the majority of residents and its use is widespread. It has been in competition with a variety of languages, among which are those of immigrants from several countries. Contacts between speakers of these languages became numerous in the last half of the nineteenth century and early decades of the present and inevitably influenced the English spoken in the islands. Many factors favored the dominance of English, although this dominance has been checked to some degree by the recent liberalization of immigration laws, a marked increase in visitors from Japan, and a continuing awareness by many people in Hawaii of the values of a multicultural and multilingual society.

English in Hawaii assumes a variety of styles. Mainland English is a major influence, but many people speak a recognizably regional form of the language. Some speakers of this Hawaiian English shift from one to another of its various subtypes, which have been viewed as a continuum, encompassing utterances characteristic of an English-based Hawaiian pidgin, an English-based Hawaiian creole, nonstandard Hawaiian English, or standard Hawaiian English. Each of these subtypes has characteristic features, but individual speakers do not necessarily restrict themselves in range.

Tsuzaki (1971) illustrates varying ways of expressing a single

idea. To the standard (Hawaiian) English "I am eating," correspond the possible equivalents in pidgin: "Me kaukau," "Me eat," "I kaukau," or "I eat"; in creole: "I stay eat," "I stay kaukau"; and in nonstandard: "I stay eating," or "I eating." *Kaukau* is said to be a Hawaiianization of the Chinese pidgin English *chowchow*; thus the example illustrates both grammatical and vocabulary features. For differences in pronunciation, ready examples are at hand in such words as "ship" (rhyming with "sheep") or "pet" (rhyming with "pat").

Hawaiian is the home language of all residents of the island of Niihau and of individual families on the other islands. It is studied by other residents, and many outsiders learn at least a few words and display interest in Hawaiian songs, church services, and other aspects of the culture. Hawaiian is a member of the Polynesian branch of the Malayo-Polynesian family of languages. Exemplifying the influence of languages with which it has been in contact are such Hawaiian loanwords as *Kalikimaka*, from English "Christmas"; *Pake*, "Chinese," attributed to Cantonese; *pakaliao*, "codfish," from Portuguese; *paniolo*, "cowboy," probably from Spanish; *popoki*, "cat," said to be from English "poor pussy."

Samoan, another Polynesian language, has been introduced in this century. The language is used actively in homes and churches, even though most Samoans who come to Hawaii are familiar with English. The language is taught at the Church College of Hawaii at Laie and is heard on the radio (page 178). Speakers of Samoan were recently the largest single group of non-English native speakers in Hawaii's public schools.

Related to Hawaiian are the different Malayo-Polynesian Philippine languages. The Filipinos comprise about one-tenth of the State's present population. They do not all share the same mother tongue. At the time of the first large migration (1907-1931), English had acquired official status, gradually supplanting Spanish. For the majority of the earlier immigrants, Ilocano, used in northern Luzon, was the mother tongue, though some immigrants spoke Visayan (Bisayan) or other Philippine languages. Today, Ilocano, heard on radio and television programs, is the dominant language of the local Filipinos. In recent decades, however, Tagalog, on which the national language of the Philippines is based, is ever more prevalent in Hawaii; perhaps one-third of the Ilocano speakers in the islands know Tagalog, reinforced by movies and other recent contacts.

Chinese were among the earliest immigrants to Hawaii; in 1876 there were already more than 2,000 in the islands, but the main migration took place between 1877 and 1898. Almost all

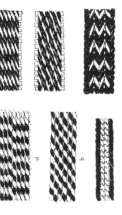

Hawaiian arts and crafts: basket decoration. Bishop Museum drawing from Te Rangi Hiroa (1964:163)

were from Kwangtung province and spoke forms of Chinese used there: Hakka (a type of speech akin to northern Chinese) by perhaps 25 percent of the group; types of Cantonese by the vast majority of the rest. Mandarin, or Kuo Yü (the national language), based largely on the prestigious language of Peking, is taught at the University of Hawaii, and it is the language of Chinese films. Cantonese, however, has been the language usually taught in the local Chinese language schools. No matter what type of Chinese they speak, literate Chinese share the ability to read material written in Chinese characters. The Chinese language newspaper is evidence of the high regard for literacy held by Hawaii's Chinese (page 177).

Hawaii's Japanese population stems from periods of immigration which began in 1868 and were most active from 1885 to 1924. Not all the immigrants spoke standard Japanese, but churches, language schools, travel, radio, television, movies, and newspapers make it a familiar language in Hawaii. Stores and hotels in Waikiki have recently begun to use Japanese in dealing with increasing numbers of guests from Japan. The usual way of writing Japanese employs Chinese characters (*kanji*) together with *hiragana* or *katakana*, syllabic symbols to represent elements not provided by the characters: verb endings, prepositions, and the like, as well as foreign words.

Approximately two-thirds of Hawaii's Japanese population originated in the prefectures of Yamaguchi, Hiroshima, Kumamoto, and Okinawa. Representatives of the last-named prefecture first reached Hawaii in 1900, and their regional form of speech is not readily understood by speakers from the Naichi or main island prefectures, where regional languages are less divergent. Okinawans may account for about one-fifth of the total Japanese population, but their language is now rarely used except among the older members of the group. English is replacing Japanese for the younger generations; Hawaii's regional Japanese tends to resemble the dialects of western Japan, rather than Tokyo standard, and shows the influence of languages with which it has been in contact—English, Hawaiian, and others.

Koreans arrived chiefly in 1904 and 1905, speaking a language grammatically similar to Japanese. Like the latter, Korean has many words composed of Chinese elements. It has its own alphabet. Korean script, like the Japanese, may make use of Chinese characters together with the Korean letters, combined so as to indicate syllable division. Regional variations of Korean do not present a great problem. The language is taught at the university, and in a language school. The Korean Christian churches have helped preserve the identity of the language, though English is gradually replacing it.

Most of the Portuguese immigrants to Hawaii arrived between 1878 and 1913 and acquired English with relative speed. Dialect variations between the speakers from Madeira and the Azores (including São Miguel) were leveled. At present the language is largely limited to occasional use by older members of the group. The language has been offered consistently at the university since 1964 and recently has been taught at the Hilo campus.

Spanish, closely related to Portuguese, was the language of the Puerto Rican immigrants, who arrived chiefly in 1901. Migrants from Spain came between 1907 and 1913. Some older Puerto Ricans still use Spanish at home and in connection with church and other organized activities. The word *borinki*, derived from Borinquén, the indigenous name of Puerto Rico, is sometimes applied to them locally.

In Hawaii, students have the opportunity to learn, besides those discussed above, a wide variety of languages: French, Latin, German, Russian, Hindi, Indonesian, Greek, Italian, Vietnamese, Hebrew, Sanskrit, Cambodian, Thai, Lao, Burmese, Bengali, Tamil, Marathi, Polish, Pali, Old Persian, Dutch, and others.

In the table below are given the first five cardinal numbers as they occur in each of the major languages used in Hawaii. This may make clear cultural and linguistic similarities and differences between these competing forms of speech.

E. C. K.

The two sets of numerals in Ilocano, Tagalog, Japanese, and Korean show the retention of indigenous numerals as well as the use of borrowed ones. The second set for Ilocano and Tagalog reflect Spanish influence; that for Japanese and Korean reflect Chinese forms, which are represented directly by Cantonese and Hakka.

English	Hawaiian	Samoan	Cantonese	Hakka	Japanese	Korean	Spanish	Portuguese	Ilocano	Tagalog
one	'ekahi	tasi	yat,	yit	hitotsu; ichi 一	hana; il 一 (하나; 일)	uno	um	maysá; uno	isá; uno
two	'elua	lua	í	nyì i	futatsu; ni 二	tul; i 二 (둘; 이)	dos	dous	duwá; dos	dalawá; dos
three	'ekolu	tolu	,sám	sam	mittsu; san 三	set; sam 三 (셋; 삼)	tres	três	talló; tres	tatló; tres
four	'ehā	fa	sz'	sì	yottsu; shi or yon 四	net; sa 四 (넷; 사)	cuatro	quatro	uppát; kuwatro	ápat; kuwatro
five	'elima	lima	³ng	ňg	itsutsu; go 五	tasot; o 五 (다섯; 오)	cinco	cinco	limá; singko	limá; singko

MAJOR HAWAII RELIGIONS

Indigenous Hawaiian

Shinto

Taoist

Buddhism

Christian

Judaism

RELIGIONS

The religious environment of Hawaii is unique on the American scene. While our statistics are not precise, they do demonstrate the remarkable variety of religious backgrounds and affiliations. Buddhism and Shinto are present as major religious communities. The "new religious movements" referred to in the tables are often combinations of Buddhist, Shinto, and Christian elements. These groups originated in Japan, some as early as the late 1800s, and several came to Hawaii in the 1920s. Their great growth, however, has taken place since 1945. Traditional Hawaiian faith and practices have influenced the development of Christianity in the islands, and ancient customs linger on. Hawaii is one of those cosmopolitan centers where one can become aware of the faith of other men.

However, a study of religious history reveals that geographical proximity does not assure understanding or harmony. Differences in faith may lead to intolerance and conflict. Religious bigotry may be more difficult to analyze and remedy than racial prejudice. For instance, the first Roman Catholic priests who arrived in Hawaii in 1827 were expelled by Protestant-influenced rulers. Catholics returned only after French authorities threatened the local government. The wartime experience of Buddhists in Hawaii is not reassuring: Buddhist temples and schools were closed; most priests were interned, and Buddhists were threatened with internment for persisting in holding "alien creeds."

Some aspects of religious expression in Hawaii show evidence that newcomers wanted to do things the "way they were done back home." The New England missionaries transplanted New England steeples and Protestant church music and theology. Most Buddhist churches use the Japanese language and art imported from Japan. These religious and cultural expressions can provide a creative base for exploration and for establishing identity, or they may be walls to defend one faith against others.

Perhaps it is no longer the American expectation that ethnic and religious distinctions need to be put into a "melting pot." We are increasingly aware that some distinctiveness of faith and

identity is of value. Christians are uneasy in the knowledge that "Christianization" has often meant "Westernization," that Western clothes often went with the Christian religion. Christians are troubled because, though they may use Hawaiian traditions in worship, such as singing Queen Liliuokalani's prayer and giving leis to new members, Hawaiians have become a minority group whose identity is uncertain in an increasingly dominant "haole society." Buddhists are both hopeful and uncertain as to what "becoming Americanized" means. More recent immigrants— Samoan, Filipino, and Tongan—bring their own cultural and religious experiences.

The proportion of Protestants in the population is somewhat lower than the national average, but informal reports indicate that some Protestant and Pentecostal groups have grown more rapidly than any other religious denominations in Hawaii in the last ten years. Among Buddhist groups Nichiren Sho-shu has increased most rapidly in size. The traditional Buddhist denominations have generally increased in membership, but proportionally not as rapidly as the general population. The Christian churches came to the islands with varying experiences and philosophies of national or ethnic missionization. The Methodist church, for example, organized churches that served chiefly Korean or Japanese or Filipino persons. "Language" pastors were common. The United Church of Christ, the chief traditional Protestant denomination, on the other hand, did not organize congregations along ethnic or language lines. Ethnically, Buddhist congregations in Hawaii are almost entirely homogeneous. "English departments" have been organized in some temples, but they have not flourished. The socioreligious indigenization of Buddhism is undergoing a test in the present generation of young laymen and clergy.

Since Vatican II and other recent ecumenical events, we have hope that a new world of religious awareness is being discovered. Denominations and church councils are showing new openness and cooperation. Increasing numbers of university students throughout the country as well as in Hawaii are enrolling in courses in world religion. Our attitude toward religious and ethnic differences is more significant than the fact that such distinctions exist. The different faiths and traditions in Hawaii may be viewed on several levels: as an opportunity for personal and community enrichment, as a challenge to convert others, or, less seriously, as quaint customs which are interesting tourist attractions.

R. T. B.

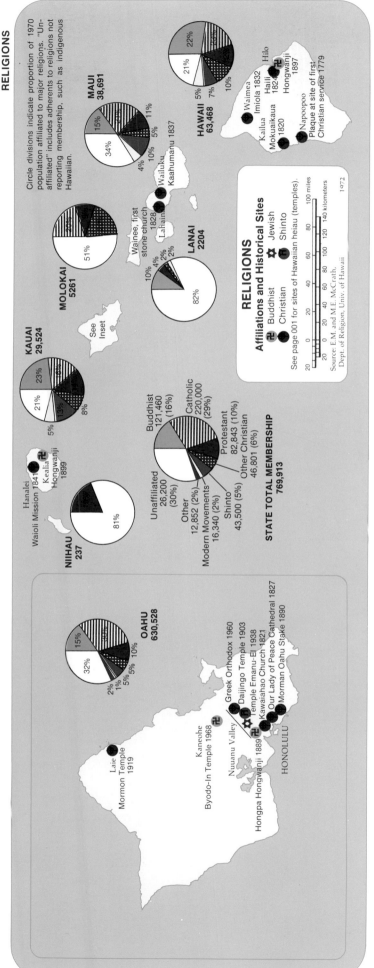

Circle divisions indicate proportion of 1970 population affiliated to major religions. "Unaffiliated" includes adherents to religions not reporting membership, such as indigenous Hawaiian.

NIIHAU 237 — 81%

KAUAI 29,524 — 5%, 8%, 13%, 21%, 23%

OAHU 630,528 — 2%, 1%, 5%, 5%, 10%, 15%, 32%

MOLOKAI 5261 — 51%

MAUI 38,691 — 34%, 15%, 11%, 5%, 10%, 22%

LANAI 2204 — 82%, 10%, 4%, 2%, 2%

HAWAII 63,468 — 5%, 7%, 10%, 21%, 22%, 34%

State total pie:
- Buddhist 121,460 (16%)
- Catholic 220,000 (29%)
- Protestant 82,843 (10%)
- Other Christian 46,801 (6%)
- Shinto 43,500 (5%)
- Modern Movements 16,340 (2%)
- Other 12,852 (2%)
- Unaffiliated 26,200 (30%)

STATE TOTAL MEMBERSHIP 769,913

Historical sites — OAHU: Laie Mormon Temple 1919; Byodo-In Temple 1968; Kaneohe; Nuuanu Valley; Honpa Hongwanji 1889; HONOLULU; Greek Orthodox 1960; Daijingo Temple 1903; Temple Emanu-El 1938; Kawaiahao Church 1821; Our Lady of Peace Cathedral 1827; Mormon Oahu Stake 1890

KAUAI: Hanalei Waioli Mission 1841; Kealia Hongwanji 1899

MAUI: Wainee, first stone church 1828; Lahaina; Wailuku, Kaahumanu 1837

HAWAII: Waimea, Imiola 1832; Kailua 1824; Hilo, Haili 1824; Hongwanji 1897; Mokuaikaua 1820; Napoopoo, Plaque at site of first Christian service 1779

RELIGIONS
Affiliations and Historical Sites
卍 Buddhist   ✡ Jewish
☆ Christian   卍 Shinto
See page 001 for sites of Hawaiian heiau (temples).
20 0 20 40 60 80 100 miles
20 0 20 40 60 80 100 120 140 kilometers
Source: E.M. and M.E. McCrath, Dept. of Religion, Univ. of Hawaii
1972

CHURCHES AND CHURCH MEMBERSHIP, 1972

Denomination	Membership*	Churches
BUDDHIST		
Bodaiji	200	1
Chinese Buddhist Assembly	2,000	1
Diamond Sangha	30	2
Hawaii Chinese Buddhist Society	450	2
Higashi Hongwanji	6,000	6
Honpa Hongwanji	30,000	38
Jodo Mission	2,900	15
Koboji Shingon	200	NA
Koon Yum Temple (Kwan Yin) (includes Confucianists and Taoists)	2,000	1
Myohoji Mission	280	1
Nichiren Mission	2,400	4
Nichiren Shoshu	28,800	NA
Shingon Mission	10,000	14
Shinshu Kyokai Mission	200	1
Soto Mission	6,000	10
Todaiji Mission	30,000	NA
CHRISTIAN		
Catholic	220,000	69
Protestant (with membership of 500 or more)		
American Baptist	750	4
Assembly of God	2,370	33
Church of Christ	2,605	9
Church of God	500	10
Church of the Living God	1,000	13

Denomination	Membership*	Churches
Church of the Nazarene	719	11
Conservative/International Baptist	700	1
Disciples of Christ	1,289	4
Episcopal	13,384	41
Hoomana Naavao	5,000	NA
Hoomana oke Akua ole	10,000	NA
Korean Christian	665	3
Lutheran	4,355	19
Missionary	900	7
Presbyterian	1,000	3
Salvation Army	1,368	11
Southern Baptist	9,500	45
United Church of Christ	17,997	110
United Methodist	7,000	30
Protestant (with membership of less than 500) total	1,741	22
Holiness Faiths	200	5
Apostolic Faith		
Calvary United Pentecostal	225	2
Church of the Latter Day Rain	NA	NA
Door of Faith (Pentecostal)	3,500	38
Hawaiian Pentecostal Full Gospel Assembly	100	1
Honolulu Holiness	150	NA
Lamb of God (Pentecostal)	300	2

Denomination	Membership*	Churches
Peaceful Church of God in Christ (Pentecostal)	400	6
Pentecostal Holiness	150	1
Trinity Apostolic	50	1
Metaphysical Christian		
Christian Science	500	4
Hawaii Church of Religious Science	84	1
Unity Church of Hawaii	250	1
Other Christian		
Church of the Latter Day Saints	30,000	53
Church of the Latter Day Saints Reorganized	1,050	4
Greek Orthodox	500	1
Jehovah's Witnesses	6,500	41
Religious Society of Friends (Quakers)	61	1
Seventh Day Adventists	2,781	20
Tenshin-Shi	NA	1
JEWISH		
Congregation Sof Ma'arav	100	1
Temple Emanu-El	972	1
SHINTO		
Daijingu Temple of Hawaii	40,000	4
Inari jinjya	NA	NA
Ishizuchi Shrine	NA	NA
Izumo Taishakyo Mission	3,000	1

Denomination	Membership*	Churches
Kotohira Jinsha Mission	500	1
NEW RELIGIOUS MOVEMENTS (primarily Japanese derivation)		
Church of the Messianity	1,800	4
Konko Kyo Mission	1,000	6
Perfect Liberty Church	220	1
Rissho Kosei Kai Church	1,200	4
Seicho no Ie, Hawaii	2,000	5
Tensho Kotai Jingu Kyo (Dancing Goddess)	7,120	15
Tenri Kyo Hawaii Dendocho	3,000	21
OTHER RELIGIOUS FAITHS		
Baha'i	1,267	28
Church of Scientology	9,000	1
Hare Krishna	1,200	1
Holy Order of Mans	24	2
Indigenous Hawaiian	NA	NA
International Meditation Society	NA	NA
Ramakrishna Vedanta	20	1
Subud	34	1
Unitarian	235	1

*Membership as estimated by church central offices on Oahu. NA indicates not available.

Source: E.M. and M.E. McCrath, Department of Religion, University of Hawaii 1972

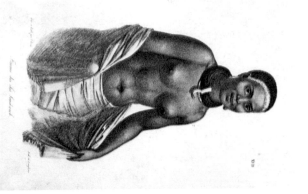

Hawaiian arts and crafts: stamp designs for clothing.
Bishop Museum drawing from Te Rangi Hiroa (1964:195)

Louis Choris: *Woman of the Sandwich Islands.*
Honolulu Academy of Arts

THE ARTS

A sense of beauty permeated the lives of the ancient Hawaiians, a beautiful people in a beautiful land. The esthetic impulse was not limited to the current category "Fine Arts," but informed all creations from fishhooks to warfare. Dance, chant, love, cult, and sport, in all of which beauty and efficacy were judged one, were prime occupations of a people living easily in a subsistence economy.

Even in the context of Polynesia, the arts of Hawaii display extraordinary subtlety and finesse. The designs are simple and elegant, the handling of surface texture, particularly sensitive. The Hawaiian did not seek to impose himself on his material, but to recognize its peculiar mana and, by a few discreet touches, to release it to the perception of all. He did not try to rival or reproduce nature, but to distill its human and spiritual significance (page 85).

After Cook, certain areas of Hawaiian artistic activity were abandoned, but for sociological and religious reasons rather than from a general sense of cultural inferiority. Not only did Hawaiian culture survive, it became the foundation and inspiration for the most important subsequent achievements. Among the periodic re-emphases of Hawaiian culture should be mentioned Kalakaua's reign and the work of mid-twentieth century artists.

Other cultures were introduced from the Pacific, the Orient, and the West, giving Hawaii its unique richness. The process of mutual influence and accommodation is an important area for future study.

Visual Arts. Ancient Hawaiian visual arts and crafts were closely connected to religion. The overthrow of the social and religious kapus led to the systematic destruction of temple and family cult images. Although some stone images are made even today, Hawaiian art was channeled into Western forms or genres less obviously religious. Native woods were used for chairs and tables as well as calabashes. Feathers were used for fans and holokus, and, by the last of the great Hawaiian featherworkers, Johanna Cluney, for formal hatbands and ties, as well as leis.

The first Western artists to visit Hawaii were members of ships' companies charged with making an accurate visual record of the landscapes, fauna, peoples, and artifacts encountered. Among these artists were John Webber (visited 1778), Louis Choris (1816), Jacques Arago (1819), and Robert Dampier (1825). Choris was an authentic genius with great insight into the personalities, life styles, and arts of the Hawaiians.

Missionaries used the visual arts for education and propaganda. Lorrin Andrews directed the production of the important and varied Lahainaluna Engravings (approximate dates 1833–1846) by Hawaiians such as Kepohoni. Island newspaper illustrations were artistic and pioneering. As Honolulu grew, it spawned a school of urban topography, exemplified by the Paul Emmert-George Burgess lithographs (1854).

Artists came to reside in the islands, such as the Bostonian Charles Furneaux (arrived 1879) and the Frenchman Jules Tavernier (1884). D. Howard Hitchcock, whose career spans the late nineteenth and early twentieth centuries, was the first island-born haole artist. These and others concentrated on the esthetic assimilation of the Hawaiian landscape, with its strange sights, uneven lighting, and jumble of abundance. Attempts at portraying the place of man in that landscape evolved into a composition common to several artists: the bottom section is an area of water; above it, a very thin strip of houses; beyond them, the mountains and sky. The human community is depicted living in and from the island elements without disturbing them.

A tradition of Christian folk art and architecture came to Hawaii with the painted churches of the Belgian Sacred Hearts Fathers, John Berchmans Velghe (especially St. Benedict's, Honaunau, completed 1902) and his disciple Matthias Evarist Gielen (especially Star of the Sea, Kalapana, ca. 1930).

In the twentieth century an unusually large number of good and even great artists have worked in Hawaii. Numerous art societies attest to a wide popular interest. Huc M. Luquiens and John Kelly were master printers, the former specializing in land-

scapes, the latter in sensuous studies of Polynesian women. Luquiens wrote an early appreciation of ancient Hawaiian art.

The kamaaina Juliette May Fraser was stimulated by visitor Padraic Colum's literary work to pioneer in the representation of ancient Hawaiian life and mythology on a mural scale. English-born, much-traveled, Madge Tennent arrived in 1923 after studying in Paris. Her paintings of large, rhythmic Hawaiian women explored the special esthetic of the race and provided an inspiring image for later artists. The Tennent Art Foundation Gallery is devoted to her work. Isami Doi combined local influences and Japanese tradition in works which move from charming, spiritual depictions of Kauai life to intensely purified and imaginative icons of Buddhist mysticism. The Maui artist Tadashi Sato paints limpid oils reminiscent of the sea.

Internationally known, Jean Charlot arrived in 1949. His murals, sculpture, writings, and teaching helped stimulate an interest in monumental public art, which has blessed Hawaii with more works per capita than perhaps any other state. His scholarly researches and reviews helped direct attention to ancient Hawaiian art forms such as petroglyphs, to the history of local art, and to the fruitful contemporary art scene.

Tseng Yu-ho arrived from China in 1949, already a finely trained artist, and developed an original, modern style of great radiance. Her scholarship is equally famous. Edward Stasack has based a bas-relief mural on petroglyphs. Ron Kowalke's prints combine mysticism and geometry in a deep human concern. Stasack and Kowalke have had a great influence.

Of the many photographers attracted to Hawaii, Theodore Kelsey and Ray Jerome Baker offer haunting images of the Hawaiian people. Robert Wenkam combines his work with conservationism, while Francis Haar and Philip Spalding are predominantly art photographers.

Sculpture, especially monumental work, is currently being revived by, among others, Satoru Abe, Eli Marozzi, Bumpei Akaji, Edward M. Brownlee, Fred H. Roster, and Mirella Belshe.

Erica Karawina has done significant work in stained glass. Hester Robinson and Ruthadell Anderson are leaders in the practice of weaving as an art form. Local potters included the great Shugen Inouye, a Zen priest, who died in 1964 at the age of 29. He felt that his work combined the four elements, but it did not exclude violence and tragedy.

The Bishop Museum, founded in 1889 and devoted to ethnology and natural history, has the largest collection of Hawaiiana in the world. The Honolulu Academy of Arts (opened 1927) and

Madge Tennent: Ukelele Player

Dept. of Art, University of Hawaii

Kepohoni: Lahainaluna.

Honolulu Academy of Arts

Tseng Yu-ho: Impressions.

Jean Charlot Collection

Isami Doi: Occult.

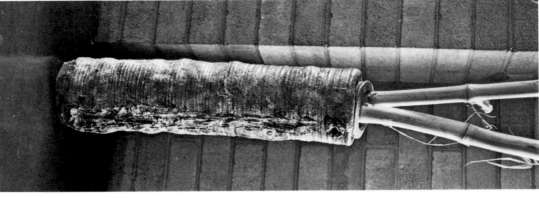

Shugen Inouye: Vase.

Photograph by E.A. Wingert

its annex contain an important Oriental collection as well as Western and local art. Some homes of the *alii* have been maintained with memorabilia. The State Department of Education operates an artmobile. The State Foundation on Culture and the Arts (established 1965) uses one percent of all public building funds for art commissions and projects.

Architecture. The Hawaiian did not seek to dominate his environment, but to live organically within it. The hut was as modest as the functions it performed for this outdoor people. Even the most imposing structures, the great heiau, followed the forms of their sites, evoking contemporary earth sculpture. The unobtrusiveness of man in a paradisical land remains an ideal.

The first Western settlers imported architects and even prefabricated buildings. But subtle accommodations were introduced. Native materials such as island woods, coral blocks, and, later, volcanic stone were found attractive. The Victorian Iolani Palace (1882) luxuriated in vegetal decoration. Ralph Adams Cram opened the sides of his Georgian Central Union Church (1924) onto an expanse of lawn. Kamaainas reacted to unadapted buildings in a Hawaiian way, appreciating discretion, spaciousness, free-flowing air, and garden settings.

Some see the emergence of a genuine regional style in such buildings as the Waioli Mission (1841), the Honolulu Academy of Arts (finished by Hardie Phillips, 1926), the 1924-1942 work of Charles W. Dickey, and buildings by Hart Wood, especially the First Church of Christ Scientist (1923). A long, horizontal, high-peaked roof, sloping down until it nears the ground, recalls Polynesian long houses. Houses open onto lanais which open onto gardens. Regardless of its sources, this style was felt to be appropriate to Hawaii.

The Chinese and Japanese communities confined their traditional architecture mainly to temples, although some elements and materials, such as tiles, were employed in public buildings. Oriental architecture was, however, a powerful influence on garden buildings, on such key works as the Academy of Arts, and especially on domestic architecture. The Japanese-style house is now a fixture.

Unfortunately, too many new buildings have a massive, heavy concrete style ill-suited to their locale. The general aspect of Honolulu now differs little from any mainland city.

Haphazard city planning produced earlier some colorful neighborhoods, now in danger of destruction, but uncoordinated planning has become a definite liability. Some plantation towns, have been planned with care, and certain architects, such as Alfred Preis, have designed suburban complexes with attention to the special character of the environment.

Music. Ancient Hawaiian music consisted of chants, often accompanied by percussive instruments, which were composed on all sorts of occasions and for many purposes. Critical judgment was acute, and skill, highly prized. Chant was inseparable from the Hawaiians' terse, liquid, and elliptical poetry. Rhythms shifted in subtle and dramatic ways. Tone intervals were smaller than in the Western scale. Scales were developed at will.

Many of these characteristics can be found today, despite assimilation of outside influences. The Hawaiians were intrigued by the melodic aspect of the hymns introduced by the first missionaries, but priority was still accorded to the words.

Throughout the nineteenth century, *alii* such as Likelike, Leleiohoku, and Kalakaua were composers. The greatest and most prolific was Liliuokalani, whose "Aloha 'Oe" is the best-known Hawaiian composition. Her protest songs are being revived by the contemporary ethnic movement.

Variously named through its history, the Royal Hawaiian Band was perhaps a continuation of the traditional court musicians. Its most famous director, the Potsdamer Henry Berger (tenure 1872-1915) composed songs with a Germanic cast, notably "Hawai'i Pono'i" to the words of Kalakaua.

In the first part of the twentieth century, Charles E. King compiled Hawaiian songs and composed in a lilting style. Mary Kawena Pukui, Ka'upena Wong, and Noelani Mahoe are among the many who continue traditional music. Kui Lee wrote authentically Hawaiian songs in a modern idiom. Others have adopted more popular commercial styles, such as Harry Owens, Alfred Apaka, Jack DeMello, and Don Ho. An interesting combination with serious rock has been achieved by the group Sunday Manoa.

Of the many organizations for the cultivation of Western classical music, the most important is the Honolulu Symphony Orchestra. Founded in 1900, its first professional conductor was the estimable Australian composer Fritz Hart (tenure 1932-1949). Georges Barati (1950-1967) maintained a serious program, enlarged the orchestra's activities, and was instrumental in the building of the present concert hall. He was succeeded by Robert LaMarchina.

Language schools, radio and television programs, festivals, and family practices have made Oriental music a part of everyday life. Visiting troupes draw large and varied crowds. Filipino music and dance, long emphasized by the consulate, are beginning to take their rightful place in local media.

Dance. The ancient Hawaiian hula, of which there were diverse types, was a highly religious act, requiring long training; stylized gestures were used for description and narration in con-

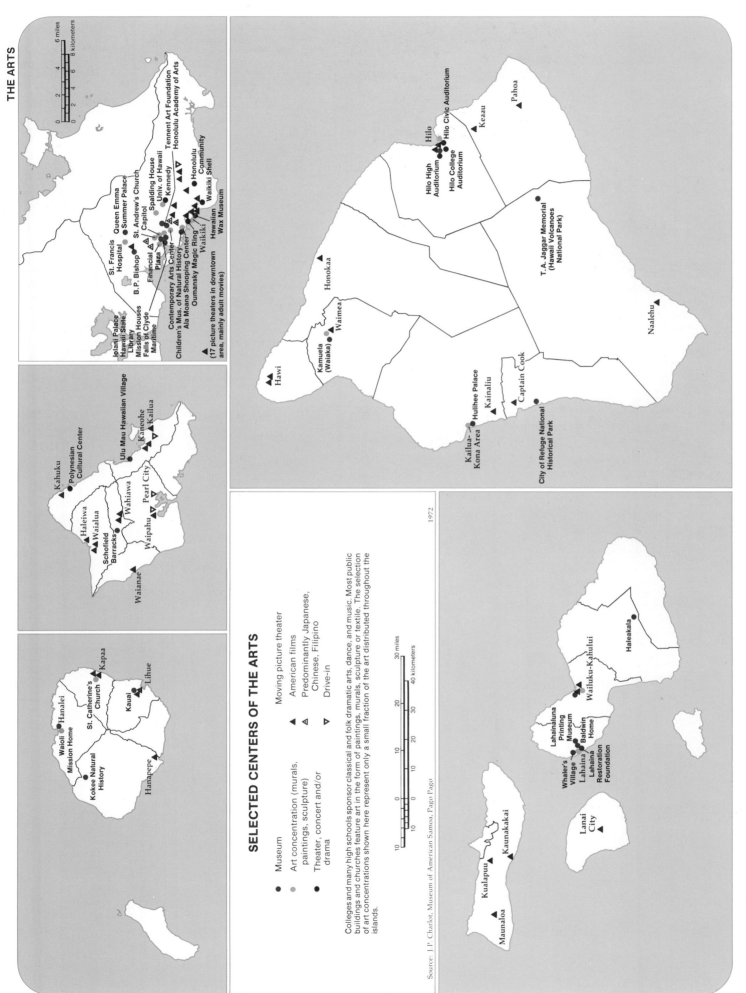

SELECTED CENTERS OF THE ARTS

- ● Museum
- ● Art concentration (murals, paintings, sculpture)
- ● Theater, concert and/or drama

- ▲ Moving picture theater
- ▲ American films
- ◮ Predominantly Japanese, Chinese, Filipino
- ▽ Drive-in

Colleges and many high schools sponsor classical and folk dramatic arts, dance, and music. Most public buildings and churches feature art in the form of paintings, murals, sculpture or textile. The selection of art concentrations shown here represent only a small fraction of the art distributed throughout the islands.

1972

Source: J.P. Charlot, Museum of American Samoa, Pago Pago

Oahu (Honolulu) map labels:
Iolani Palace
Hawaii State Library
Mission Houses
Falls of Clyde
Maritime
St. Francis Hospital
B.P. Bishop
St. Andrew's Church
Queen Emma Summer Palace
Capitol
Financial Plaza
Contemporary Arts Center
Children's Mus. of Natural History
Ala Moana Shopping Center
Oumansky Magic Ring
Spalding House
Univ. of Hawaii
Kennedy
Tennent Art Foundation
Honolulu Academy of Arts
Honolulu Community
Waikiki
Waikiki Shell
Hawaiian Wax Museum
(17 picture theaters in downtown area, mainly adult movies)

Kauai map labels:
Kapaa
Lihue
Kauai
St. Catherine's Church
Hanalei
Waioli Mission Home
Kokee Natural History
Hanapepe

Central Oahu map labels:
Kahuku
Polynesian Cultural Center
Ulu Mau Hawaiian Village
Kaneohe
Kailua
Haleiwa
Waialua
Wahiawa
Pearl City
Schofield Barracks
Waipahu
Waianae

Hawaii (Big Island) map labels:
Pahoa
Keaau
Hilo
Hilo Civic Auditorium
Hilo High Auditorium
Hilo College Auditorium
T. A. Jaggar Memorial (Hawaii Volcanoes National Park)
Honokaa
Waimea
Kamuela (Waiaka)
Hawi
Hulihee Palace
Kailua-Kona Area
Kainaliu
Captain Cook
City of Refuge National Historical Park
Naalehu

Maui / Molokai / Lanai map labels:
Haleakala
Wailuku-Kahului
Lahainaluna Printing Museum
Whaler's Village
Baldwin Home
Lahaina Restoration Foundation
Kualapuu
Kaunakakai
Maunaloa
Lanai City

6 miles
8 kilometers

10   20   30 miles
40 kilometers

Jean Charlot: illustration for Act 2, Scene 4 of his play *Naauao*.

Jean Charlot Collection

Iolani Luahine.

Photograph by F. Haar.

First Church of Christ Scientist, Honolulu; Hart Wood, architect.

Hawaii State Archives

junction with chant. Christian missionaries campaigned against the hula because of its pagan connections and alleged indecencies. Kalakaua patronized the hula with great perseverance despite criticisms. The dancing master Ioanne Ukeke and members of the royal troupe continued to teach after the king's death. The growing interest of outsiders—scholars, literati, and tourists —gradually removed the missionary-inspired prejudice. Iolani Luahine is the foremost contemporary exponent of the traditional hula as a religious act.

Recently Tahitian, Samoan, Tongan, and Fijian dances have been introduced to the islands, partly through the efforts of the Polynesian Cultural Center at Laie.

Oriental dances are a regular feature of traditional festivals, such as the widely attended Bon dances.

Programs of Western classical and modern dance are offered occasionally at the University of Hawaii and other institutions.

Dramatic Arts. The hula kii, in which a story was enacted by puppets in an esoteric language, was the most theatrical of ancient Hawaiian arts. As early as the reign of Kamehameha II, pageants and parades are mentioned, perhaps attempts at replacing ancient festivals. Pageants, usually on historical themes, continue to be presented by churches, schools, and other groups. The Kamehameha Day and Aloha Week parades, organized entirely by Hawaiians, are annual events.

Of Hawaii's many theatrical organizations, the Honolulu Community Theatre presents mostly popular works; the University of Hawaii Theatre, serious modern and classical drama; the Honolulu Theatre for Youth, original, participatory works for children and adolescents.

Oriental drama—especially Peking Opera, Noh, and Kabuki— is presented frequently by local and visiting groups. Earle Ernst of the University of Hawaii has stimulated much interest in Kabuki through his writings and stage productions.

Aldyth Morris, Jean Charlot, and John Dominis Holt, among others, have written original plays on Hawaiian themes. But movies and television have barely begun to exploit the visual and thematic possibilities of Hawaii. A talented group of local film-makers offers hope for the future.

J.P.C.

THE ECONOMY

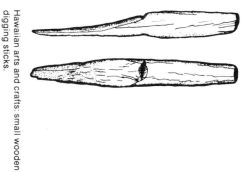

Hawaiian arts and crafts: small wooden digging sticks.

Drawing by T. Stell Newman

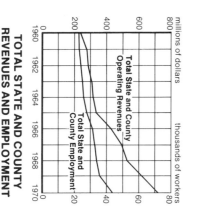

millions of dollars

thousands of workers

Total State and County Operating Revenues

Total State and County Employment

TOTAL STATE AND COUNTY REVENUES AND EMPLOYMENT

THE ECONOMY

With more than 80 percent of the State's economic activity located on Oahu, the Hawaiian economy is geographically concentrated and centralized. But as is true in other states it has become increasingly diversified. The pre-World War II economy was essentially agricultural, centered on the sugar and pineapple industries. Since the war, a number of economic activities have been added or expanded: the Pacific Defense Headquarters, manufacturing, construction, the visitor industry, and the production of livestock and a wide variety of agricultural commodities. In addition, major educational and cultural institutions have become a part of Hawaii's growing community resources. The expanding population supports a vigorous retail and wholesale trade market, statewide and intercontinental surface and air transportation systems, as well as an extensive communications network. Scientific and specialized fields including astronomy, oceanography, and fish farming are expected to provide additional diversification. The rapid growth of the Hawaiian economy is supported by investments of Hawaii-based financial institutions augmented by mainland and foreign capital.

During the last 20 years the visitor industry has emerged as the most vigorously growing segment of Hawaii's economy. In 1970 approximately 1.8 million visitors spent an estimated $570 million in the islands. The industry is expanding more rapidly on the neighbor islands where it is the principal growth stimulant (page 164). Manufacturing has also gained a significant position. Processed agricultural products and high-fashion garments are the principal exports, while more than 90 percent of all other manufactured products are consumed in Hawaii. The majority of manufacturing facilities are still located on Oahu, but additional facilities are being constructed on the neighbor islands (page 156).

Sugarcane and pineapple continue to occupy the prime positions among Hawaiian agricultural products, but diversified agricultural products other than sugar and pineapple are becoming economically significant (page 144). The construction industry has also become highly diversified, and utilization of advanced techniques, such as prestressed concrete and factory-manufactured houses and components, is now well established. The high level of construction activity during the decade of the 1960s, both for expansion and replacement of industrial and residential buildings, is another barometer of recent growth in the economy.

The federal government makes a major contribution to the State's economy largely because the defense headquarters of the Pacific is located here (page 166). Federal expenditures in Hawaii totaled nearly $1.1 billion during 1970. Of the total, $683.4 million, or 63.4 percent, were military expenditures and $395.3 million were civilian outlays. During the past decade, military expenditures in Hawaii rose at an average annual rate of 6.2 percent although the number of personnel stationed in Hawaii has remained fairly constant (page 166). Nonmilitary federal expenditures, including grants-in-aid, transfer payments, and budgets for civilian agencies such as the Federal Aviation Administration, increased during the decade 1960-1970 at an average annual rate of 13.3 percent.

Hawaii's local governmental structure is the most highly centralized of all 50 states. It has only five administrative units—the State of Hawaii, the counties of Hawaii, Maui, and Kauai, and the City and County of Honolulu—and a public education system that operates under a single, statewide school board. Total state and local government revenues have increased at an average annual rate of 11.6 percent since 1960, reaching $720.4 million in 1970. The State of Hawaii accounted for $577.7 million, or more than 80 percent, of the total revenues collected in 1970. In tax structure, Hawaii is best described as a sales-income tax state, with more than 75 percent of all taxes collected originating from these sources.

State operating expenditures reached $570.2 million, including $65.4 million in cash for capital projects, during fiscal 1970. Expenditures have increased at an average annual rate of 13.5 percent during the last decade. Outlays for education totaled $217.9 million, or 43.2 percent, of net operating expenditures; for health, safety, and welfare functions, $109.2 million, or 21.6 percent. Other outlays included: general government administration and staff, $64.1 million; debt service, $28.2 million; highways, $11.9 million for operating expenses; and all other, $73.5 million.

County operating expenditures have increased at an average of 7.0 percent annually since 1960, reaching $136.2 million in fiscal 1970. Of this total almost 80 percent is generated by the City and County of Honolulu. Major county outlays include general government administration and staff, public safety, highways, and public schools.

B.O.H.

TEN-YEAR CHANGE IN EMPLOYMENT

	change	
Government	+49%	
Retail Trade	+71%	
Wholesale Trade	+34%	
Hotels	+208%	
Other Services	+74%	
Transportation, Communication, Utilities	+61%	
Construction	+43%	
Finance	+95%	
Diversified Manufacturing	+29%	
Sugar	−26%	
Pineapple	−27%	
Diversified Agriculture	+112%	
Non-Agricultural Self-Employment	+32%	

☐ 1970
☐ 1960

thousands of persons

Source: Bank of Hawaii, Dept. of Business Research

CHANGING PROFILE OF INDUSTRIES

Federal Government Expenditures	32.6%	36.4%	33.2%
Visitor Industry	3.9%	9.8%	17.6%
Diversified Manufacturing	11.5%	11.1%	12.9%
Construction	10.9%	20.6%	24.1%
Sugar	20.0%	9.5%	6.1%
Pineapple	16.5%	9.0%	4.2%
Diversified Agriculture	4.6%	3.6%	1.9%

☐ 1950, Total $620,700,000
☐ 1960, Total $1,334,000,000
☐ 1970, Total $3,246,800,800

millions of dollars

Source: Bank of Hawaii, Dept. of Business Research

ECONOMIC PATTERN FOR THE STATE

TOTAL RESIDENT POPULATION AS OF JULY 1	1970	773,667	CONSTRUCTION COMPLETED	1970	$784 million	
	1960	641,520		1960	$275 million	
EMPLOYMENT	1970	335,450	RETAIL SALES	1970	$2.0 billion	
	1960	228,050		1960	$948 million	
PERSONAL INCOME	1970	$3.4 billion	BANK DEBITS	1970	$23.3 billion	
	1960	$1.5 billion		1960	$6.3 billion	
FEDERAL EXPENDITURES	1970	$1.1 billion	REAL PROPERTY TAX BASE	1970	$7.7 billion	
	1960	$486 million		1960	$3.2 billion	
HOUSING INVENTORY	1970	245,620	SUGAR PRODUCTION	1970	$197 million	
	1960	165,506		1960	$127 million	
VISITOR ARRIVALS	1970	1,798,591	PINEAPPLE PRODUCTION	1970	$135 million	
	1960	296,517		1960	$119 million	
HOTEL ROOM INVENTORY	1970	30,323	DIVERSIFIED AGRICULTURE	1970	$63 million	
	1960	9,522		1960	$47 million	

Source: Bank of Hawaii, Dept. of Business Research

TAXES COLLECTED IN HAWAII

millions of dollars

Source: Bank of Hawaii, Dept. of Business Research

state and country taxes

federal taxes

1960 · 1962 · 1964 · 1966 · 1968 · 1970

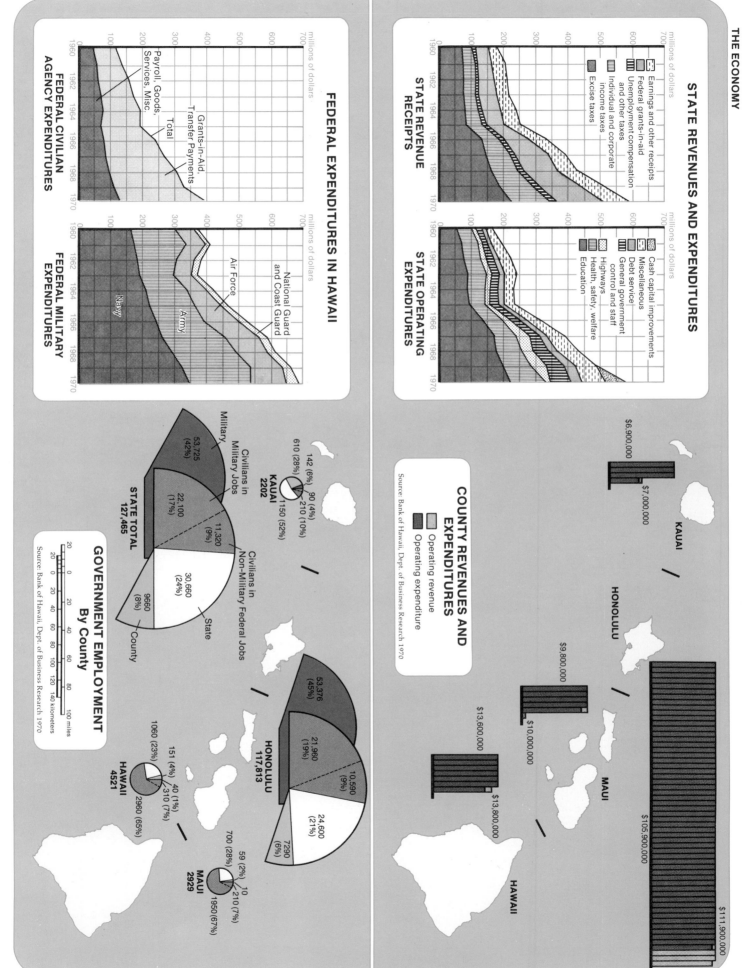

STATE REVENUES AND EXPENDITURES

STATE REVENUE RECEIPTS

millions of dollars

Earnings and other receipts
Federal grants-in-aid
Unemployment compensation and other taxes
Individual and corporate income taxes
Excise taxes

STATE OPERATING EXPENDITURES

Cash capital improvements
Miscellaneous
Debt service
General government control and staff
Highways
Health, safety, welfare
Education

Source: Bank of Hawaii, Dept. of Business Research 1970

COUNTY REVENUES AND EXPENDITURES

Operating revenue
Operating expenditure

KAUAI $6,900,000
$7,000,000

HONOLULU $9,800,000
$10,000,000
$105,900,000
$111,900,000

MAUI $13,600,000
$13,800,000

HAWAII

FEDERAL EXPENDITURES IN HAWAII

FEDERAL CIVILIAN AGENCY EXPENDITURES

millions of dollars

Payroll, Goods, Services, Misc.
Grants-in-Aid
Transfer Payments
Total

FEDERAL MILITARY EXPENDITURES

millions of dollars

National Guard and Coast Guard
Air Force
Army
Navy

GOVERNMENT EMPLOYMENT By County

Source: Bank of Hawaii, Dept. of Business Research 1970

0 20 40 60 80 100 120 140 kilometers
0 20 40 60 80 100 miles

KAUAI 2202
142 (6%)
610 (28%)
90 (4%)
210 (10%)
1150 (52%)

STATE TOTAL 127,465
Military 53,725 (42%)
Civilians in Military Jobs 22,100 (17%)
Civilians in Non-Military Federal Jobs 11,320 (9%)
State 30,660 (24%)
County 9660 (8%)

HONOLULU 117,813
53,376 (45%)
21,960 (19%)
10,590 (9%)
24,600 (21%)
7290 (6%)

HAWAII 4521
151 (4%)
1060 (23%)
40 (1%)
310 (7%)
2960 (65%)

MAUI 2929
59 (2%)
700 (28%)
10
210 (7%)
1950 (67%)

LAND TENURE

Hawaii is a state of limited total land area with a very limited supply of prime agricultural land and beautiful beach land—most of it under enormous pressure for residential and resort development. The need to identify the highest and best use of Hawaii's lands grows more urgent as the population continues to increase. And the process of land-use decision making becomes increasingly complex.

All uses for land have grown more competitive. Of increasing importance is the demand for living space. To meet this need, land will probably be taken from the areas having irreplaceable, highly productive soils. Such land-use decisions are essentially irreversible and therefore should be made only with a full awareness of the physical characteristics of the land involved, as well as the environmental and socioeconomic consequences of the decision.

As larger segments of land are given over to urban pursuits, the danger and likelihood of costly mistakes in locating urban structures on soils ill suited to the purpose, or on lands needed for open space, will similarly grow. To minimize such mistakes, increasing attention must be given to matching the physical environment to the requirements for specific uses; this is equally true for rural land uses.

Hawaii consists of eight major islands and 124 minor islands having a combined total land area of 6,425 square miles. Ninety-eight percent, 4,050,176 acres, is on the six largest islands—Kauai, Oahu, Molokai, Lanai, Maui, and Hawaii. A seventh island (Niihau) is owned in entirety by a private family, and the eighth (Kahoolawe) is now uninhabitable, primarily because of lack of water.

Not all the land area of the six largest islands is usable; 12 percent of the total is too steep for development or lacks productive capacity. Barren and steep land found within the national parks, game management areas, forest reserves, and military reservations throughout the State are incorporated in these use acreages.

Ownership of the usable land is highly concentrated. The state, county, and federal governments together are the largest landowners, controlling about 48 percent of the total land area. About four-fifths of these public lands (including Hawaiian Home lands) belong to the State of Hawaii. These state lands constitute the bulk of the forest reserves or the conservation district. About one-fourth is under lease, principally for pasture and sugarcane. The Department of Land and Natural Resources is the State's land management agency for state lands. Most of the federal acreage is in national parks on Hawaii and Maui and in military holdings on Oahu and Kauai.

Private ownership of land (52 percent of the total land area) is also highly concentrated; seven-eighths of this private land is in the hands of fewer than 40 owners, each with 5,000 acres or more. In addition to Lanai and Niihau, which are in effect 100 percent privately owned, large private landholders own 60 percent of the land on Molokai and 40 to 50 percent on Oahu, Hawaii, Kauai, and Maui. Ownership of areas of less than 5,000 acres is most extensive on Oahu. Agricultural uses, particularly for grazing and sugarcane, constitute the major application of the large private landholdings. A substantial acreage is unproductive and classified as conservation land. Only a small acreage, about one percent of the total area of large landholdings, is in urban uses.

H. L. B.

Hawaiian arts and crafts: stone weight for an octopus lure.

Drawing by T. Stell Newman

LAND USE ACREAGES, 1968

Land Use	Kauai	Oahu	Molokai	Lanai	Maui	Hawaii	Total Acres
Plantation Agriculture	**61,626**	**59,839**	**17,280**	**16,236**	**61,897**	**114,775**	**331,653**
Pineapple	2,699	18,987	17,276	16,236	14,078	—	69,276
Sugar Cane	58,927	40,852	4	—	47,819	114,775	262,377
Nonplantation Agriculture	**55,311**	**51,741**	**90,072**	**—**	**180,511**	**820,053**	**1,197,688**
Vegetable	339	2,102	845	—	1,506	1,916	6,708
Orchard	455	1,670	104	—	536	21,529	24,294
Water Crop	305	237	—	—	202	230	974
Forage	229	167	—	—	14	13	423
Grazing	53,637	38,608	86,850	—	176,810	794,629	1,150,534
Dairy	8	618	1	—	108	3	738
Poultry	5	255	1	—	7	7	275
Swine	—	103	—	—	—	—	103
Feed Lot	—	38	—	—	—	—	38
Salt Bed	—	16	—	—	—	—	16
Idle Agricultural Land	333	7,927	2,271	—	1,328	1,726	13,585
Forest & Forest Reserve	**196,271**	**148,799**	**50,375**	**5,926**	**170,539**	**908,083**	**1,479,993**
Forest	38,716	30,033	2,037	5,926	14,504	197,823	289,039
Forest Reserve	157,555	118,766	48,338	—	156,035	710,260	1,190,954
Recreation	**11,244**	**5,184**	**415**	**66,683**	**18,980**	**231,750**	**334,256**
Recreation	9,524	5,184	415	106	1,225	794	17,248
Game Management	1,720	—	—	66,577	—	19,288	87,585
National Park	—	—	—	—	17,755	211,668	229,423
Military	**1,886**	**35,055**	**316**	**—**	**—**	**791**	**38,048**
Urban	**4,550**	**56,850**	**1,091**	**435**	**6,204**	**86,575**	**155,705**
Underdeveloped Subdivision	—	2,385	—	—	—	74,429	76,814
Military	150	17,508	—	—	—	—	17,658
Civilian	4,400	36,957	1,091	435	6,204	12,146	61,233
Pali & Barren Land	**22,235**	**23,799**	**7,477**	**—**	**27,852**	**421,945**	**503,308**
Quarry	**23**	**1,077**	**30**	**—**	**85**	**247**	**1,462**
Military	—	142	—	—	—	—	142
Civilian	23	935	30	—	85	247	1,320
Water	**966**	**6,584**	**48**	**—**	**364**	**101**	**8,063**
Grand Total	**354,112**	**388,928**	**167,104**	**89,280**	**466,432**	**2,584,320**	**4,050,176**

Source: Land Study Bureau, University of Hawaii 1969

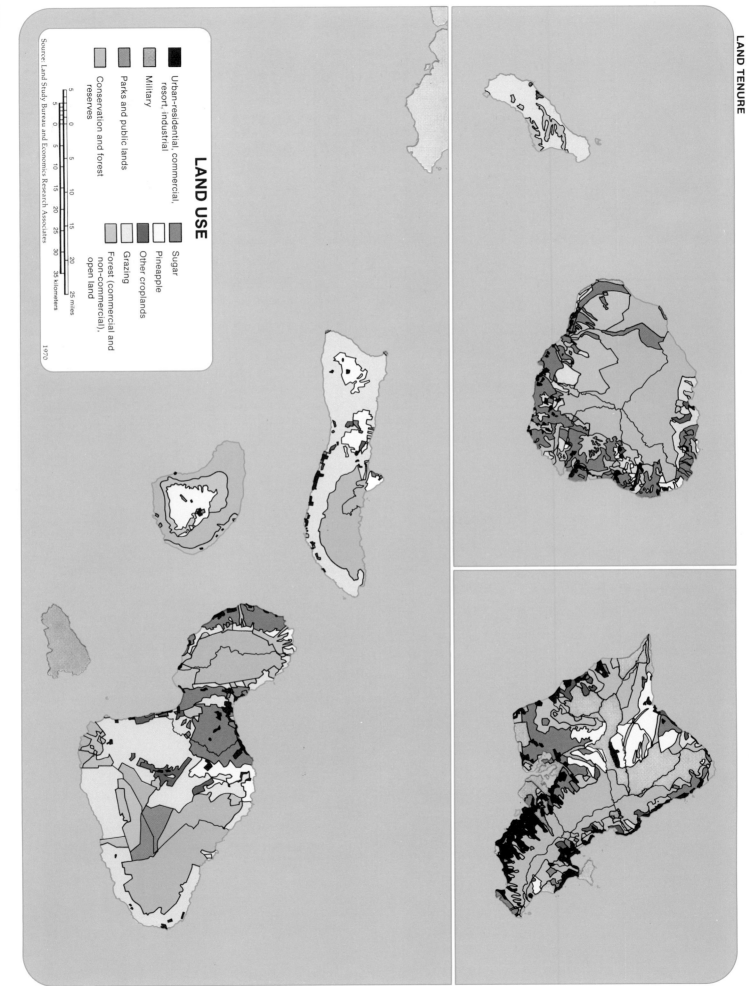

LAND USE

- ■ Urban-residential, commercial, resort, industrial
- ▨ Military
- ▨ Parks and public lands
- ▨ Conservation and forest reserves

- ▨ Sugar
- ▨ Pineapple
- ▨ Other croplands
- ☐ Grazing
- ▨ Forest (commercial and non-commercial), open land

5
5
0
0 5 10 15 20 25 30 35 kilometers
0 5 10 15 20 25 miles

Source: Land Study Bureau and Economics Research Associates

1970

Agriculture is the predominant land use in the Fiftieth State. Almost three-fourths of the total land area is used for forestry and grazing and for plantations and diversified crops. Forest and forest reserves account for 50 percent of the area in this broad use category and embrace primarily those lands of importance for watershed protection. Grazing lands comprise 38 percent and generally include areas rated poor in overall agricultural productivity. Plantations use 11 percent of the total agricultural area and more than three-fourths of the State's "prime" agricultural land. Diversified crops, consisting primarily of orchard crops and vegetables, are produced on only one percent of the land area. Eighty-nine percent of the 24,294 acres in orchards are found on the island of Hawaii. Oahu has the largest acreage of vegetables as well as the largest area devoted to dairy, poultry, and swine enterprises.

Lands classified as urban comprise about 4 percent of the total area of the State. The urban land acreage was not differentiated as to residential, commercial, and industrial uses. Lands zoned for urban use but remaining undeveloped were placed in a separate category as were also built-up military areas. A major portion of this land use acreage is found on the island of Hawaii, where 74,429 acres of land are subdivided but as yet undeveloped. Military use occupies only one percent of the total area, but this figure does not include the 17,658 acres in military housing and other urbanlike uses included under urban lands. Ninety-two percent of the military acreage is located on Oahu.

Pali and barren lands, that is, lands incapable of use because of steepness or lack of productive capacity, occupy about 12 percent of the total area. Essentially all the remaining land is in national parks, game management reserves, and other recreational areas.

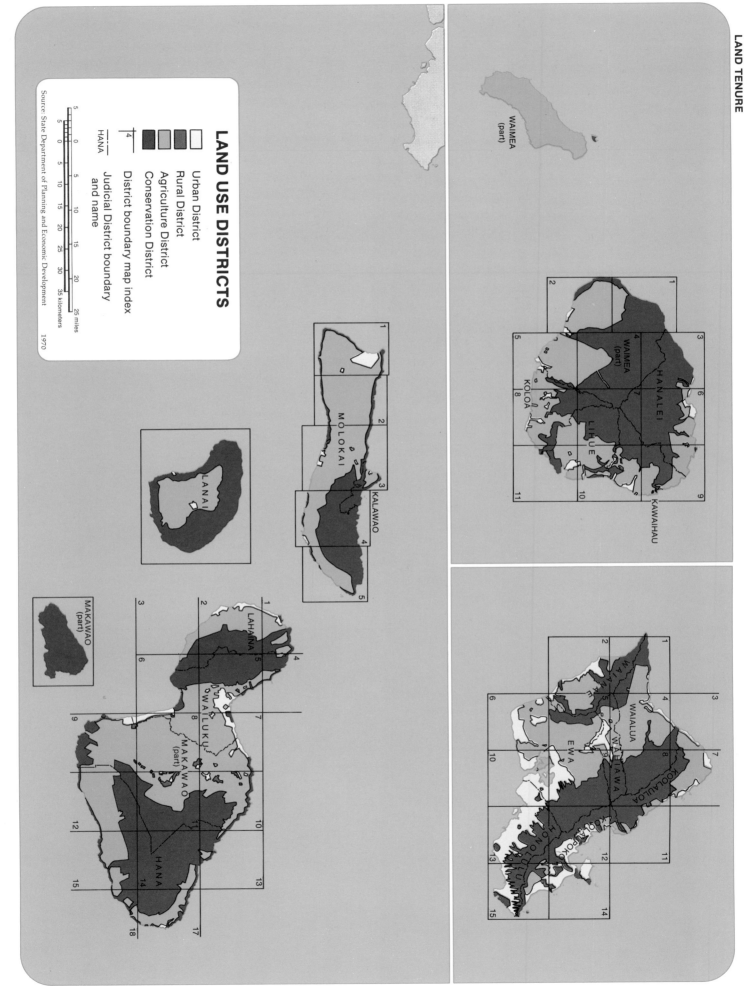

138

LAND USE DISTRICTS

Urban District
Rural District
Agriculture District
Conservation District

District boundary map index

Judicial District boundary
and name

HĀNA

Source: State Department of Planning and Economic Development   1970

5   0   5   10   15   20   25   30   35 kilometers
5   0   5   10   15   20   25 miles

WAIMEA
(part)

1   2
5   3
4   WAIMEA
(part)
KOLOA   8   HANALEI   6
7
11   LIHUE   9
10   KAWAIHAU

MOLOKAI
1
2
3
KALAWAO
4
5

LANAI

2   1
WAI...
3   WAIALUA   4
5
6   EWA   WAHIAWA   7
10   8
9
KOOLAULOA
13   HONO...   12   11
...LUA   KOOLAU...
14
15

MAKAWAO
(part)

3   2   LAHAINA   1
5
6   4
WAILUKU   7
8
9   MAKAWAO
(part)
12   10   13
HANA
15   14
18   17

Hawaii was the first state to adopt a general plan and a land use law. This law, passed in 1961, established the State Land Use Commission whose task it is to classify and regulate the use of all lands in the State. Particular attention is given to encouraging orderly and efficient development of land for urban use, with least possible encroachment on prime agricultural land, and giving maximum economy and efficiency in public services and utilities. The law and its amendments of 1963 and 1965 provide for four districts: urban, agriculture, conservation, and rural. Urban districts are generally defined as lands already in urban use, with a reserve to accommodate foreseeable growth. Agriculture districts include lands with a high capacity for intensive cultivation; minimum lot size is one acre. Conservation districts are lands in the existing forest and water reserves, lands in national or state parks, lands with a general slope of 20 percent or more, and marine waters and offshore islands. Rural districts are lands primarily in small farms mixed with low-density residential lots; for residences, the minimum lot size for one house is one-half acre. Public facilities may be placed in rural districts. In addition to the Land Use Commission, administration of the Land Use Law is the concern of the state departments of Planning and Economic Development, Land and Natural Resources, and Taxation; the counties of Kauai, Maui, and Hawaii; the City and County of Honolulu; and the Land Study Bureau of the University of Hawaii. Land uses within urban districts are administered solely by the counties. For agriculture and rural districts the commission establishes regulations, and the counties are responsible for their administration. The counties may choose to adopt more stringent controls than those imposed by the State. In the conservation districts, land uses are administered solely by the State Department of Land and Natural Resources. District boundaries may be changed by the commission through a petition and public hearing process.

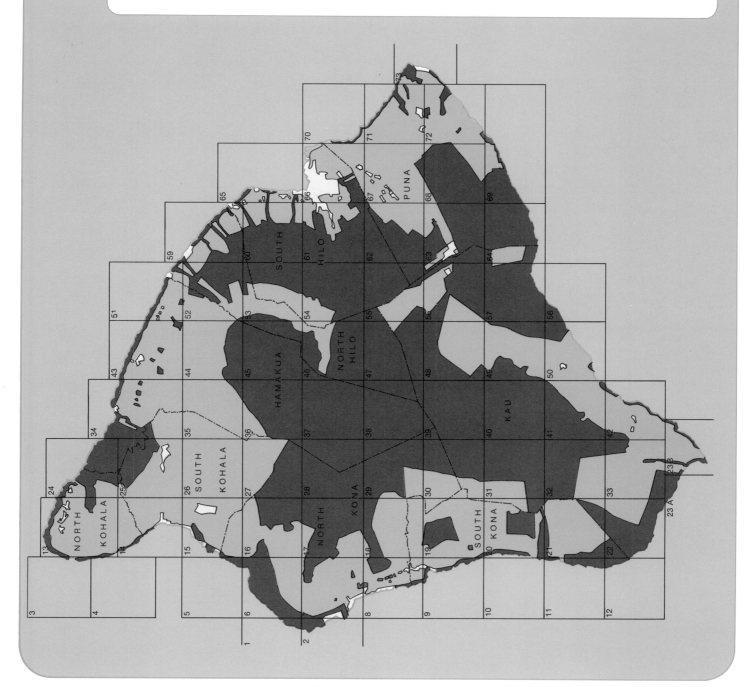

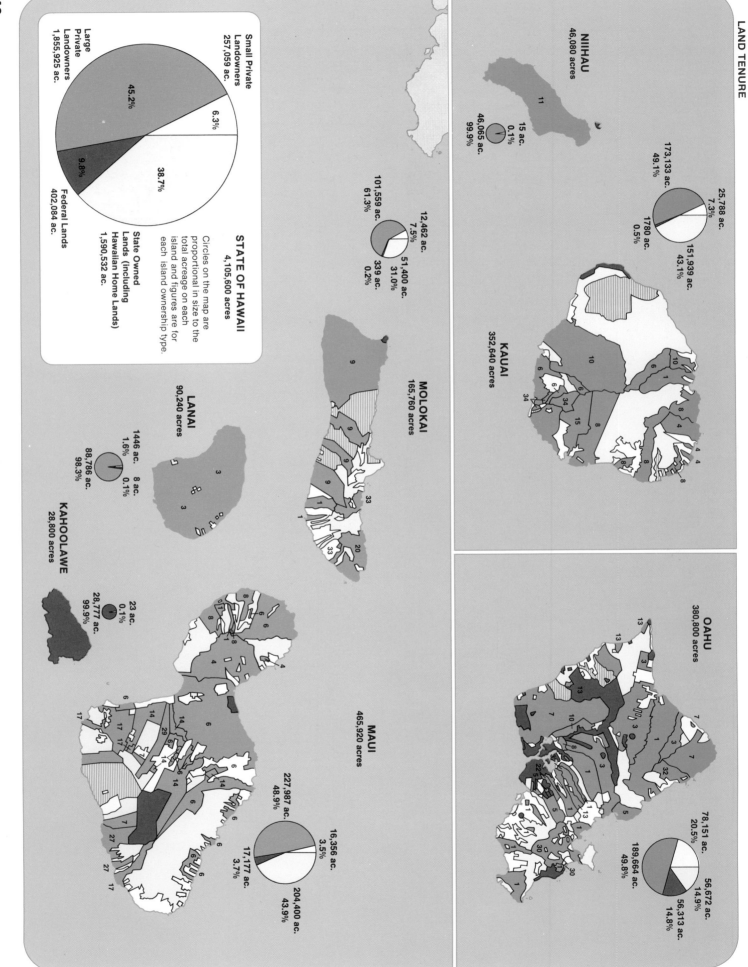

140

NIIHAU
46,080 acres

11

15 ac.
0.1%
46,065 ac.
99.9%

KAUAI
352,640 acres

25,788 ac.
7.3%

173,133 ac.
49.1%

1780 ac.
0.5%

151,939 ac.
43.1%

10

6

6

34

1

10

15

8

8

8

4

4

4

8

8

OAHU
380,800 acres

13

13

3

13

7

10

1

3

7

1

3

5

13

1

1

32

7

5

30

30

1

22.5

5

78,151 ac.
20.5%

56,672 ac.
14.9%

189,664 ac.
49.8%

56,313 ac.
14.8%

MOLOKAI
165,760 acres

12,462 ac.
7.5%

101,559 ac.
61.3%

339 ac.
0.2%

51,400 ac.
31.0%

9

9

9

9

9

1

33

33

20

1

STATE OF HAWAII
4,105,600 acres

Circles on the map are
proportional in size to the
total acreage on each
island and figures are for
each island ownership type.

Small Private
Landowners
257,059 ac.

6.3%

45.2%

38.7%

9.8%

Large
Private
Landowners
1,855,925 ac.

Federal Lands
402,084 ac.

State Owned
Lands (including
Hawaiian Home Lands)
1,590,532 ac.

LANAI
90,240 acres

1446 ac.
1.6%

88,786 ac.
98.3%

8 ac.
0.1%

3

3

3

KAHOOLAWE
28,800 acres

23 ac.
0.1%

28,777 ac.
99.9%

MAUI
465,920 acres

8

6

8

1

4

4

6

6

17

17

17

17

14

29

14

14

14

6

6

6

6

7

27

27

6

6

6

17

227,987 ac.
48.9%

17,177 ac.
3.7%

16,356 ac.
3.5%

204,400 ac.
43.9%

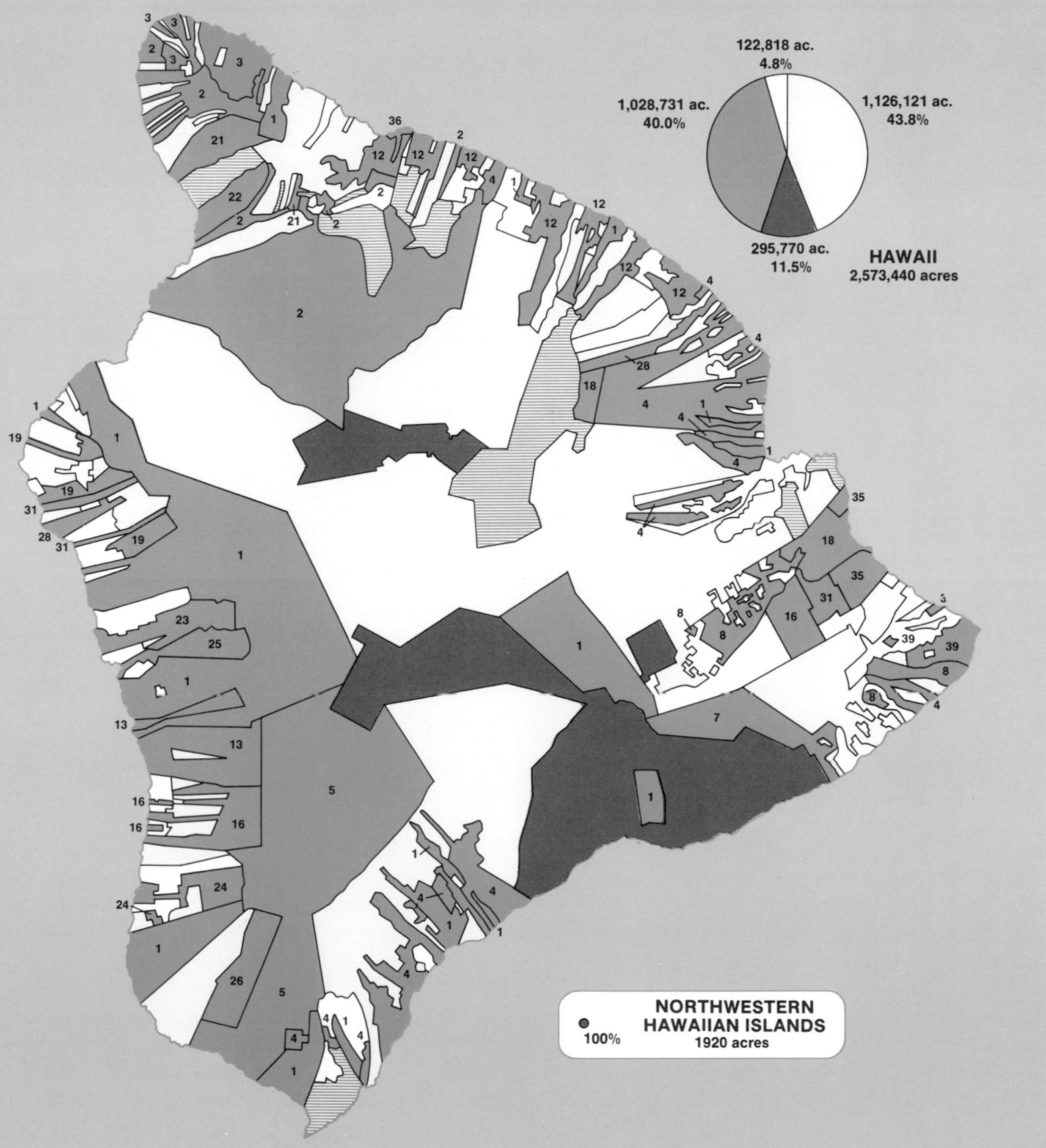

LAND OWNERSHIP

		acreage	1,590,532
	State of Hawaii		
	Hawaiian Home Lands		402,084
	Federal Government		
	Major Private Landowners		
1	Bernice P. Bishop Estate		369,462
2	Richard S. Smart (Parker Ranch)		185,940
3	Castle and Cooke, Inc.		153,912
4	C. Brewer and Co., Ltd.		145,147
5	Samuel M. Damon Estate		143,842
6	Alexander and Baldwin, Inc.		126,790
7	James Campbell Estate		81,549
8	Amfac, Inc.		81,417
9	Molokai Ranch, Ltd.		73,975
10	Gay and Robinson		55,800
11	Niihau Ranch		46,065
12	Theo H. Davies and Co., Ltd.		43,490
13	McCandless Heirs		37,622
14	Haleakala Ranch Co.		33,041
15	Grove Farm Co., Inc.		22,616
16	Yee Hop, Ltd.		21,830
17	Ulupala Kua Ranch, Inc.		21,557
18	W. H. Shipman, Ltd.		20,599
19	Thelma K. Stillman Trust (Huehue Ranch)		15,438
20	Puu-O-Hoku Ranch (G. W. Murphy)		14,262
21	Kahua Ranch, Ltd.		14,013
22	Queen's Hospital		13,065
23	W. H. Greenwell, Ltd.		12,149
24	Dillingham Investment Corp.		11,471
25	Kealakekua Ranch (S. Greenwell)		11,136
26	Hawaiian Ocean View Estate		10,642
27	Kaupo Ranch, Ltd.		10,037
28	Queen Liliuokalani Trust		9,794
29	Kaonoulu Ranch Co., Ltd.		8,813
30	Estate of H. K. L. Castle (Kaneohe Ranch)		8,606
31	Frank R. Greenwell (Palani Ranch)		6,917
32	Zion Securities Corp.		6,514
33	Francis H. Ii Brown, et al		6,164
34	Eric A. and August F. Knudsen Trust		5,879
35	Hawaiian Paradise Park Corp.		5,503
36	Bernice P. Bishop Museum		5,257
37	Austin Heirs		5,255
38	Capital Investment Co., Ltd.		5,182
39	Kapoho Land & Development Co., Ltd.		5,174
	Small private landowners (less than 5000 acres)		257,059

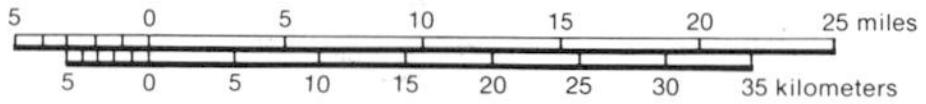

Source: Land Study Bureau, University of Hawaii
Economics Research Associates

1969

5   0   5   10   15   20   25 miles

5 0 5 10 15 20 25 30 35 kilometers

122,818 ac.
4.8%

1,126,121 ac.
43.8%

HAWAII
2,573,440 acres

1,028,731 ac.
40.0%

295,770 ac.
11.5%

**NORTHWESTERN
HAWAIIAN ISLANDS**
1920 acres

● 100%

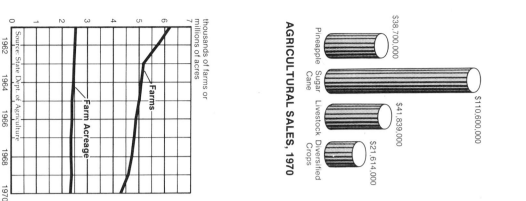

AGRICULTURAL SALES, 1970

Pineapple $38,700,000
Sugar Cane $110,600,000
Livestock $41,839,000
Diversified Crops $21,614,000

NUMBER AND SIZE OF FARMS

thousands of farms or millions of acres

Farms

Farm Acreage

1962 1964 1966 1968 1970

Source: State Dept. of Agriculture

AGRICULTURE

The pace of change in Hawaiian agriculture has been increasing during the past decade. Acreages, production volumes, and market values of agricultural products are going through a period of modification in all categories: plantation farming of sugar and pineapple, cattle ranching, fruit and nut farming, and diversified farming of small units by single farmer-operators. Evidence of this change is the general reduction in the number of farms, the overall increase in agricultural output, and the tendency toward an increase in the size of farms. Both geographic and economic factors have been at work in bringing about these alterations. In many areas prime agricultural land is being priced out of the market by land-use changes from agricultural to urban. Climate, soil, water supply, topographic conditions, and availability of land have been factors involved in closing down marginal operations, particularly in the plantation industries. Increasing foreign competition for mainland markets is also leading to unprofitable operations. In the past, agriculture in Hawaii has been dominated by the sugar and pineapple industries. Although these are still the major single crops, there has been a slow but steady growth of diversified agriculture. In 1970 the total value of diversified agriculture was $63,500,000 as compared with $110,600,000 for the sugar industry and $38,700,000 for the pineapple industry (page 142).

From the first decade of this century the production of sugarcane has increased from about 5 tons per acre to over 11 tons per acre, giving the four sugar-producing islands (Hawaii, Maui, Oahu, and Kauai) the highest yield per acre in the world. The total land in cane has fluctuated during the same period, but has slowly risen since a postwar low in 1948 of 206,550 acres to a 1968 high of 242,476 acres. Since then, cane acreage has begun to decrease owing primarily to the shutting down of two of Hawaii's 23 plantations (page 143). The loss of these lands to cane growing amounts to 9.6 percent of the total acreage under cultivation, but some of this land is being used to produce grain sorghum for cattle feed and, during 1970, blight-resistant seed corn. The highly mechanized sugar plantations are located on

coastal mountain slopes where rainfall can vary from 15 to 212 inches per year, depending on exposure and elevation. About half the total cane land is supplied by complex irrigation systems.

Pineapple is grown on all the major islands of the State except the Big Island. In 1970 there were 59 farms producing pineapple, but only three companies accounted for about 90 percent of the total agricultural value of pineapple sales (page 143). Acreage in pineapple has diminished over the past decade, but production has shown no great change.

The production of livestock has contributed greatly to the diversification of agriculture in the State. In 1970 some two-thirds of all diversified agriculture sales were of livestock products including cattle, hogs, milk, eggs, broilers, and chickens. Of these activities, cattle raising is the most important; grazing lands cover some 52 percent of the State's lands, with 80 percent on Hawaii, 9 percent on Maui, 5 percent on Molokai, 3 percent on Kauai, and 3 percent on Oahu.

Before 1956, Oahu was the principal production area of papaya in the State. The shift of major production to the Puna area of the island of Hawaii is attributed to urbanization and virus disease on Oahu, favorable growing conditions and low-cost land on the Big Island, and the inauguration of direct jet flights from Hilo to the mainland. During the decade 1960-1970, papaya planting increased from 500 to 1,700 acres, with 1,600 acres on the Big Island. At the same time yields have increased from 24,000 to 33,000 pounds per acre.

Besides pineapple and papaya, major fruits are banana, passion fruit, orange, tangerine, avocado, and guava. The most important of these is the banana, although this crop is decreasing in acreage harvested, with only 760 acres in 1970. Oahu produced most of the banana crop. Of lesser importance are lichee and mango.

Over half the vegetable and melon production of the State is in tomatoes, lettuce, head cabbages, and cucumbers. The number of vegetable farms has decreased from 762 in 1961 to 488 in 1970, but vegetable marketing volumes have been relatively stable. More than 54,000,000 pounds were produced in 1970.

Other crops, such as macadamia nuts and ornamental plants and flowers, are increasing in acreage and in production. In 1970 nut production became the second most significant of all the diversified crops. The 760 coffee farms in the Kona district of the island of Hawaii have suffered badly during the past decade owing to low world coffee prices and high labor costs.

J. R. H.

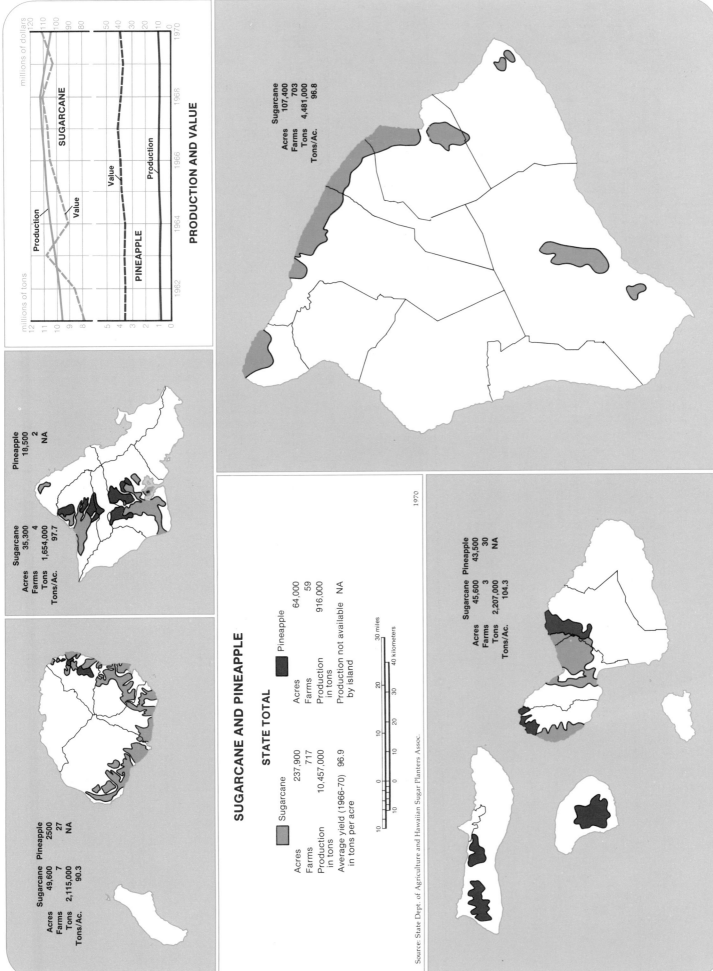

PRODUCTION AND VALUE

millions of dollars

SUGARCANE

PINEAPPLE

Value

Value

Production

Production

millions of tons

1962 1964 1966 1968 1970

SUGARCANE AND PINEAPPLE

STATE TOTAL

	Sugarcane	Pineapple
Acres	237,900	64,000
Farms	717	59
Production in tons	10,457,000	916,000
Average yield (1966–70) in tons per acre	96.9	Production not available NA by island

	Sugarcane	Pineapple
Acres	107,400	18,500
Farms	703	2
Tons	4,481,000	NA
Tons/Ac.	96.8	

	Sugarcane	Pineapple
Acres	35,300	2500
Farms	4	27
Tons	1,654,000	NA
Tons/Ac.	97.7	

	Sugarcane	Pineapple
Acres	49,600	2500
Farms	7	27
Tons	2,115,000	NA
Tons/Ac.	90.3	

	Sugarcane	Pineapple
Acres	45,600	43,500
Farms	3	30
Tons	2,207,000	NA
Tons/Ac.	104.3	

1970

30 miles

40 kilometers

Source: State Dept. of Agriculture and Hawaiian Sugar Planters Assoc.

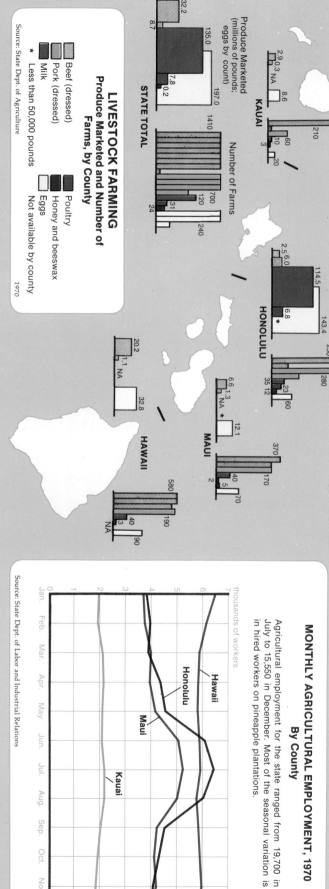

DIVERSIFIED CROPS
Produce Marketed and Number of Farms, by County

- Vegetables and melons
- Fruits (excluding pineapple)
- Coffee
- * Less than 50,000 pounds
- Macadamia nuts
- Taro
- Flowers and horticulture
- NA Not applicable

Produce Marketed (millions of pounds)

Number of Farms

STATE TOTAL
54.1 / 36.0 / 11.5 / 8.5 / 4.9 / NA
488 / 409 / 760 / 250 / 459 / 118

KAUAI
2.3 / 1.6 / 4.5 / * / * / NA
58 / 49 / 6 / 40 / 17

HONOLULU
16.4 / 4.5 / 0.2 / * / NA
234 / 126 / 154 / 1.8

MAUI
15.9 / 1.1 / 1.5 / * / NA
89 / 44 / 40 / 2 / 57

HAWAII
19.4 / 25.7 / 11.4 / 4.7 / 2.3 / NA
107 / 190 / 760 / 241 / 231 / 30

Source: State Department of Agriculture

STATE VALUE OF CROP SALES

millions of dollars

Macadamia Nuts (in shell)
Other Crops
Vegetables and Melons
Coffee (parchment)
Fruit (excluding pineapple)

1962 1964 1966 1968 1970

Cattle
Milk
Hogs
Poultry
Eggs

millions of dollars

1962 1964 1966 1968 1970

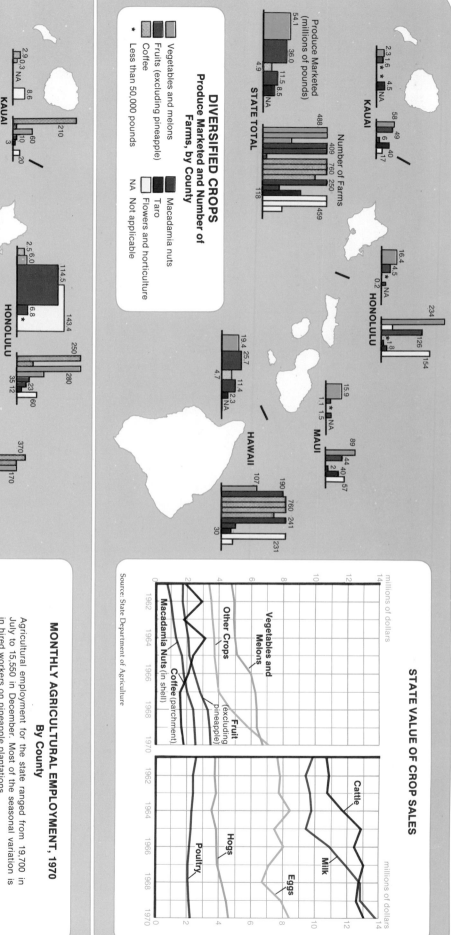

LIVESTOCK FARMING
Produce Marketed and Number of Farms, by County

- Beef (dressed)
- Pork (dressed)
- Milk
- * Less than 50,000 pounds
- Poultry
- Honey and beeswax
- Eggs
- NA Not available by county

Produce Marketed (millions of pounds; eggs by count)

Number of Farms

STATE TOTAL
32.2 / 8.7 / 135.0 / 7.8 / 0.2 / 197.0
1410 / 700 / 120 / 240 / 31 / 24

KAUAI
2.9 / 0.3 / NA
210 / 60 / 10 / 20 / 3

HONOLULU
2.5 / 6.0 / 114.5 / 6.8 / * / 143.4
250 / 280 / 23 / 60 / 35 / 12

MAUI
6.6 / 1.3 / NA / * / 12.1
370 / 170 / 40 / 70 / 5 / 2

HAWAII
20.2 / 1.1 / NA / 32.8
580 / 190 / 40 / 90 / 3 / NA

Source: State Dept. of Agriculture

1970

MONTHLY AGRICULTURAL EMPLOYMENT, 1970
By County

Agricultural employment for the state ranged from 19,700 in July to 15,550 in December. Most of the seasonal variation is in hired workers on pineapple plantations.

thousands of workers

Hawaii
Honolulu
Maui
Kauai

Jan. Feb. Mar. Apr. May Jun. Jul. Aug. Sep. Oct. Nov. Dec.

Source: State Dept. of Labor and Industrial Relations

PASTURE AND DIVERSIFIED CROPS

☐ Range and Pasture   ▲ Dairy

• Diversified crop; significant area of production:

B Bananas	**M** Macadamia nuts
C Coffee	**O** Oranges; other citrus
E Eggs and poultry	**P** Papayas
F Flowers and	**S** Seed corn
horticulture	**Sor** Sorghum
H Hogs	**T** Taro
L Liikoi (passion fruit)	**V** Vegetables

1970

Source: State Department of Agriculture

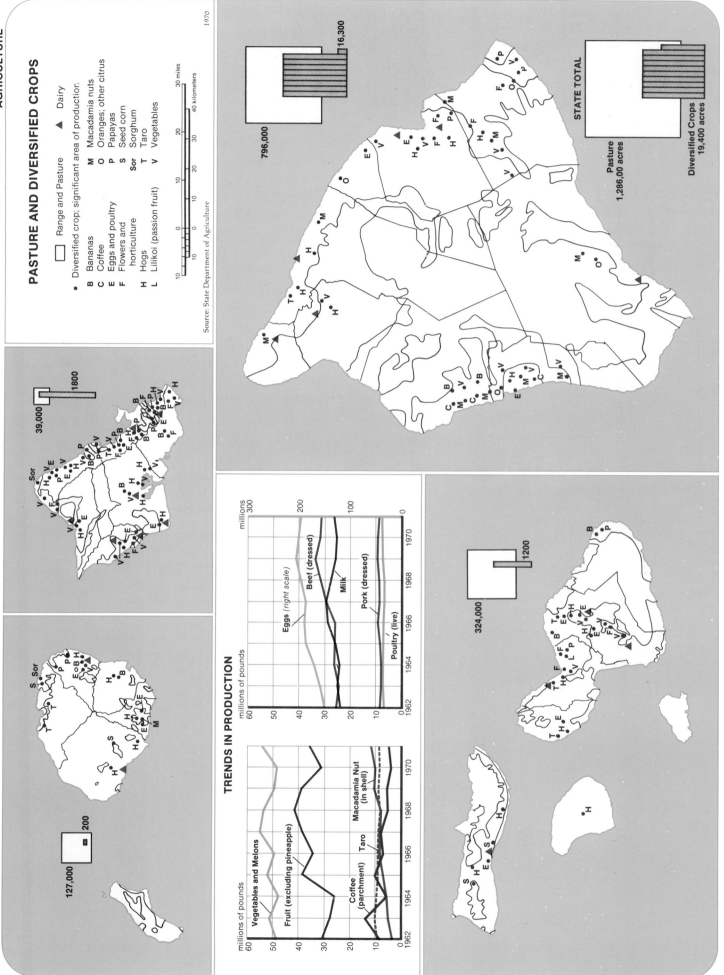

STATE TOTAL

Pasture
1,286,00 acres

Diversified Crops
19,400 acres

796,000

16,300

39,000

1800

127,000

200

324,000

1200

TRENDS IN PRODUCTION

millions of pounds

Vegetables and Melons

Fruit (excluding pineapple)

Macadamia Nut
(in shell)

Coffee
(parchment)

Taro

millions

300

200

100

0

Eggs *(right scale)*

Beef (dressed)

Milk

Pork (dressed)

Poultry (live)

60

50

40

30

20

10

0

1962   1964   1966   1968   1970

30 miles

40 kilometers

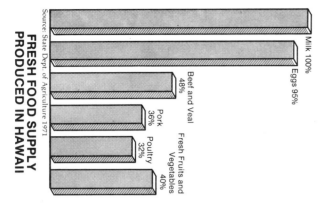

**FRESH FOOD SUPPLY
PRODUCED IN HAWAII**

Milk 100%

Eggs 95%

Beef and Veal 48%

Pork 36%

Poultry 32%

Fresh Fruits and Vegetables 40%

Source: State Dept. of Agriculture 1971

Hawaiian arts and crafts: stone poi pounder base.

Drawing by T. Stell Newman

FOOD SOURCES

Perhaps nowhere else in the world is there a resident population with as many different eating habits as Hawaii. Polynesian, American, Chinese, Japanese, Filipino, and other Asian cuisines are all present. Many families take advantage of this great diversity of local foods and enjoy them all, but there are just as many who adhere strictly to one traditional eating style.

A survey of restaurants is one indication of this diversity of eating habits. American-style restaurants predominate on all islands, in a wide variety of types from the most exclusive and unhurried to the practical, quick-service drive-in, with a full range of moderate-cost restaurants, coffee shops, and special food shops in between. Japanese and Chinese restaurants are also common, and these cuisines are represented by a similar range of high-, moderate-, and low-cost establishments. In Honolulu and other towns on Oahu there are several Hawaiian, Samoan, Korean, Mexican, Italian, German, and French restaurants. Not counted in the accompanying table (page 147) are the many formal and informal Hawaiian luaus offering their own special foods to residents and visitors.

A casual observer might think that Hawaii produces most of its own foodstuffs, considering the extent of agricultural land use in the State. But this is far from correct. Hawaii is highly dependent on shipping and the importation of food items for the maintenance of an adequate and smooth flow of food supplies to the population. The two major agricultural crops, sugar and pineapple, contribute little in the way of edible food products. The most important foods produced in Hawaii are dairy products, eggs, meat, fresh vegetables, fruit (see table on this page), and fish (page 148).

The major source of all other food is the mainland United States. Millions of pounds of fresh produce and packaged and frozen foods are shipped to Hawaii each year. A larger proportion than the current 40 percent of fresh produce demands might be met by local producers, but cost factors in labor, production, and manufacturing, and inefficiencies in production and transport work against this partial self-sufficiency. Interisland transport by barge normally takes a minimum of two days compared with a one-day air-freight service for fresh produce from the mainland. Substantial imports of food are also received in Hawaii from other countries: beef from Australia, New Zealand, and Japan; butter from New Zealand; fresh fruits and vegetables from Canada, New Zealand, and Japan; and canned food items from Japan, Taiwan, and Europe. These shipments from mainland and foreign ports constitute Hawaii's food lifeline. The total value of food imports in 1971 from the U.S. mainland was about $147 million, and from foreign countries, $25 million.

Despite Hawaii's dependence on outside sources for food, an increasing quantity of locally grown fresh produce and meat products are being sent to island markets each year (page 147). Each of the main islands produces a variety of vegetable crops, including cabbage, lettuce, cucumbers, tomatoes, celery, and onions. Oahu has the largest acreage in vegetables, as well as the largest area devoted to dairying, poultry raising, and pig farming. Local commercial fruits include watermelons, bananas, oranges, papayas, and pineapples. Almost 90 percent of the commercial orchards are found on the island of Hawaii.

A number of factors, such as the current interest in capital investment in diversified agriculture, the availability of additional agricultural lands for diversified crop use, the development of cooperative shipping and handling arrangements among producers, and the creation of larger and more efficient meat processing facilities, are all helping to make Hawaii's food products more competitive with imported food items in local markets.

In the past, hunting, fishing, gardening, and collection of wild fruits provided for all of Hawaii's food needs. Today, only a minority of the population, mostly residents of rural areas, depend in any large measure on these activities for food. Nevertheless, at times these sources of foods are of major importance for some families. But expanding urban settlement and the high cost of land tend to discourage individual efforts in food production. Fishing grounds and shellfish and crab grounds near shore are threatened by new land developments and by water pollution, while game reserves for pigs, sheep, goats, deer, and edible birds are declining in area and are being managed for sport and for trophy hunters rather than for food gatherers.

J. L. E.

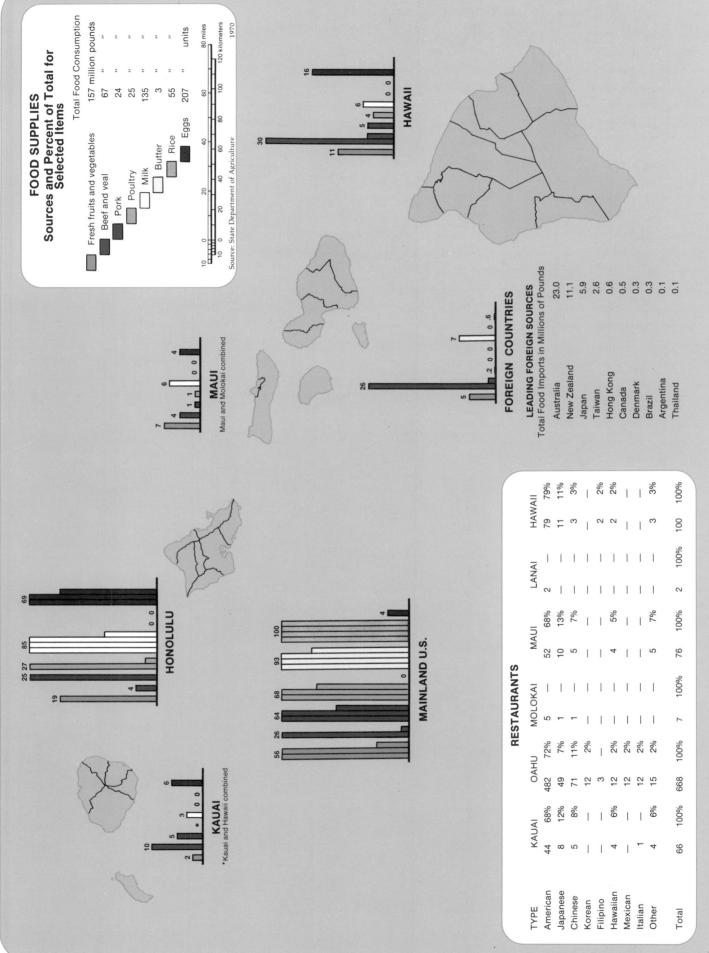

148

COMMERCIAL FISHING

Fish has always been an important item in the Hawaiian diet. Beginning with the earliest reports of Captain Cook and other explorers, Hawaii was described as having a "fish and poi" economy. The sea was the major source of animal protein at that time.

Today, the commercial fishing industry is a small segment of the State's economy. The annual value of the commercial catch accounts for less than one percent of the value of the gross state product. This very low figure has resulted, not from an absolute decline in the volume of commercial catch over the years, but to the very rapid growth of other sectors of the economy.

In 1970 there were 1,264 licensed commercial fishermen in Hawaii operating out of about 70 ports (page 149). Three ports account for 85 percent of the catch: Kewalo Basin (Oahu), 77

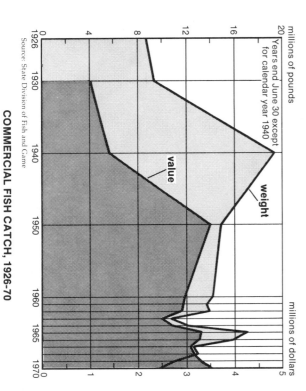

millions of pounds

20

16

12

8

4

0

1926 1930 1940 1950 1960 1965 1970

Years end June 30 except
for calendar year 1940

value

weight

millions of dollars

5

4

3

2

1

0

Source: State Division of Fish and Game

COMMERCIAL FISH CATCH, 1926-70

percent; Maalaea (Maui), 5 percent; and Hilo (Hawaii), 3 percent. In 1970 the fishing fleet was made up of 670 relatively small, old vessels. Thirty-eight of these, the larger ones, were equipped for high-sea fishing—14 tuna (aku) and 24 flagline vessels.

Hawaiian fishery can be divided into three types: high-sea or pelagic, inshore, and pond (aquaculture). The high-sea fishery is concerned principally with tuna, the most important species being skipjack tuna (aku). The average annual landing is approximately 5,000 metric tons, which accounts for about 75 percent by weight of the State's total marine catch. Fishing trips are usually made within 90 miles of the coast. The primary fishing gear consists of a bamboo pole to which is attached a length of line bearing a hook. Live bait, a small anchovy, is used exclusively. This technique is called pole-line and live-bait fishing. Skipjack tuna is the most important underexploited species in the Pacific Ocean, with a potential catch many times the level of the present catch. Skipjack fishery could be an important industry in Hawaii if the fishing technique were improved.

Yellowfin and bigeye tuna (ahi) are other important species for high-sea fishing. These fish usually live in deep water and are caught with flagline (longline) techniques. The flagline is made up of a number of units of gear called baskets. Each basket of gear is composed of a main line from which branch lines are supported. Each branch line bears a single hook. The flagline is supported at the surface by glass or metal floats. All of the flagline catches in Hawaii are consumed locally as sashimi (raw fish).

Inshore fisheries are of modest potential and therefore do not afford the basis for a major commercial fishing industry. For some of the species, an increasing portion of the catchable stock is taken by sport fishermen.

Aquaculture formed an integral part of the Hawaiian culture in the past. In 1901 there were more than 100 ponds used for the commercial production of fish. Today only six fishponds are being operated commercially (page 149). The decline in this activity has been due primarily to low yields of fish per acre and the increasing demands on coastal areas for other uses, such as housing development and recreation. However, in recent years, the accumulated scientific knowledge and the need for a substantial increase in the world supply of protein have stimulated new interest in aquatic farming. With Hawaii's warm weather and rich natural resources, aquaculture could again become an important industry.

Y. C. S.

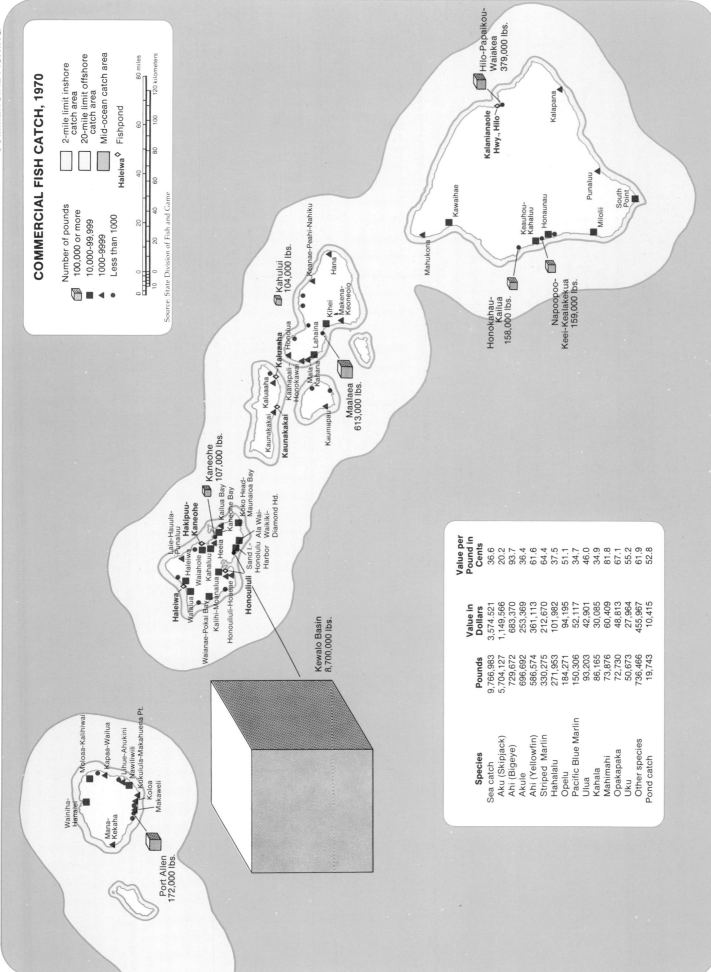

COMMERCIAL FISH CATCH, 1970

Number of pounds

▥ / ■	100,000 or more
▲	10,000-99,999
•	1000-9999
	Less than 1000

Haleiwa ◇ Fishpond

▢	2-mile limit inshore catch area
▢	20-mile limit offshore catch area
▨	Mid-ocean catch area

Source: State Division of Fish and Game

0 10 20 40 60 80 miles
0 10 20 40 60 80 100 120 kilometers

Hilo-Papaikou-Waiakea 379,000 lbs.
Kalanianaole Hwy., Hilo
Kalapana
Punaluu
South Point
Miloiii
Honaunau
Keauhou-Kahaluu
Napoopoo-Keei-Kealakekua 159,000 lbs.
Honokohau-Kailua 158,000 lbs.
Mahukona
Kawaihae

Kahului 104,000 lbs.
Keanae-Peahi-Nahiku
Hana
Kihei
Makena-Keoneoio
Kaluaaha
Honolua
Lahaina
Kaanapali
Honokawai
Mala
Kahana
Maalaea 613,000 lbs.
Kaunapau
Kaunakakai
Kaluaaha

Kaneohe 107,000 lbs.
Hakipuu-Kaneohe
Late-Hauula-Punaluu
Waiahole
Haleiwa
Wailua
Kailua Bay
Kahaluu
Kaneohe Bay
Heeia
Koko Head-Maunaloa Bay
Waianae-Pokai Bay
Kalihi-Moanalua
Honouliuli-Honouliuli
Sand I.-Honolulu Harbor
Ala Wai-Waikiki-Diamond Hd.
Haleiwa
Honouliuli

Kewalo Basin 8,700,000 lbs.

Wainiha-Hanalei
Moloaa-Kalihiwai
Kapaa-Wailua
Lihue-Ahukini
Nawiliwili
Kukuiula-Makahuena Pt.
Koloa
Makaweli
Mana-Kekaha
Port Allen 172,000 lbs.

Species	Pounds	Value in Dollars	Value per Pound in Cents
Sea catch			
Aku (Skipjack)	9,766,983	3,574,521	36.6
Ahi (Bigeye)	5,704,127	1,149,566	20.2
Akule	729,672	683,370	93.7
Ahi (Yellowfin)	696,692	253,369	36.4
Striped Marlin	586,574	361,113	61.6
Hahalalu	330,275	212,670	64.4
Opelu	271,953	101,982	37.5
Pacific Blue Marlin	184,271	94,195	51.1
Ulua	150,306	52,117	34.7
Kahala	93,203	42,901	46.0
Mahimahi	86,165	30,085	34.9
Opakapaka	73,876	60,409	81.8
Uku	72,730	48,813	67.1
Other species	50,673	27,964	55.2
Pond catch	736,466	455,967	61.9
	19,743	10,415	52.8

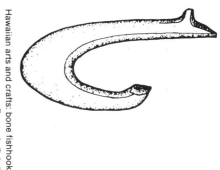

FORESTRY

Forestry is concerned with understanding and managing the forest resources that help to make Hawaii an attractive place in which to live. Forests give visual pleasure; they release oxygen into the air; they bind the soil to prevent erosion that clogs streams and beaches; they facilitate filtration of rainwater into the soil and thus help to recharge the groundwater supply; they give shelter and food to wildlife; they provide attractive recreation settings for hikes and picnicking; and they supply wood, fruits, and other products for the economy. In short, the diverse forest ecosystems help maintain environmental conditions desirable for human and other animal life.

The early Hawaiians with their primitive tools made minimal use of forest resources for current necessities, although they did derive from the forests a wide variety of products, such as logs, bird feathers for ceremonial dress, and plant dyes. Not long after the first contact with Europeans in 1778, however, economic exploitation of forests became a prime concern. Sandalwood was the first important commercial export. Although commercial supplies of sandalwood were exhausted in the 1830s, forests became increasingly important for supplies of fuel wood for household and industrial use, and for posts, poles and railroad ties, as well as lumber. Modification of the vegetation and landscape begun by the Hawaiians for cultivation of food crops and by burning was accelerated by Europeans who introduced many new plants and cleared more land for crops and grazing. Introduced cattle, sheep, goats, and pigs ran wild in great numbers. The result was degeneration of large previously wooded areas to bare, eroded land. Reforestation began in 1874, and the first forest reserves were established in 1904 on Oahu and Hawaii to protect watersheds. Watershed protection and rehabilitation remained essentially the only concern of government forestry until the mid-1950s. Since then the concerns of forestry have become more diversified.

Hawaii has nearly 2 million acres of forest land—almost half the area of the State. About 1.2 million acres are held in 68 forest reserves, to protect forest and watershed from man and livestock. Most of the forest lies on mountain slopes between elevations of 2,000 and 6,000 feet, where rainfall is generally more than 50 inches a year.

Forest lands are classified as commercial, those capable of producing industrial wood, and noncommercial, lands where

soil, climate, slope, or drainage do not permit growing sawtimber crops. Native trees, principally ohia and koa, dominate on about 750,000 acres of commercial forest land and on nearly 250,000 acres of noncommercial forest land. More than nine-tenths of the commercial ohia and koa forests are on the island of Hawaii. Introduced trees, principally eucalyptus, have been planted on less than 4 percent of the commercial forest land but comprise about 40 percent of the sawtimber volume in the islands. Young stands of exotic, planted trees average 8,000 board feet per acre; mature native stands, barely 500. Dominant in the noncommercial forests are tree associations such as kiawe, kukui, scrub ohia, and koa, and shrub associations such as mamani, pukiawe, and koa haole. The commercial forest land lies almost equally within and outside the forest reserves. Two-thirds of the forests are privately owned and concentrated in a few large holdings.

Harvesting of Hawaii's timber resources in recent years has been sporadic and small in scale. The bulk of the timber cut, primarily robusta eucalyptus, ohia, and koa, is used locally for buildings, furniture, pallets, and craftwood articles. Recent annual production of lumber in the islands has been less than 3 million board feet, while more than 100 million board feet are imported.

Hawaii's forests are important in many other ways than as a source of lumber. They help maintain biogeochemical cycles of oxygen, nitrogen, carbon, and other elements essential to all forms of life. They slow natural erosion, thus reducing the deposits of sediment that kill coral polyps in the surrounding sea. They provide many minor but useful products—maile for leis, hapuu fiber, honey, perfume. The forest ecosystems are presently in a state of accelerated evolution brought on by modern man's extensive introductions of foreign plants and animals. Many rare native plants, birds, mollusks, and insects are disappearing largely as a result of man's interference. Preserving some part of these unique ecosystems is a major goal of forestry. Forested mountains serve as a verdant backdrop to beaches, towns, and residential areas, creating a panorama that is often taken for granted by resident and visitor alike. More people each year look to forest lands for recreation and a refreshing change from their usual surroundings. Careful management of Hawaii's forests contributes to the biological, social, and economic well-being of the State and must be vigorously pursued in the future in the face of increasing competition for land for other purposes.

R. E. N.

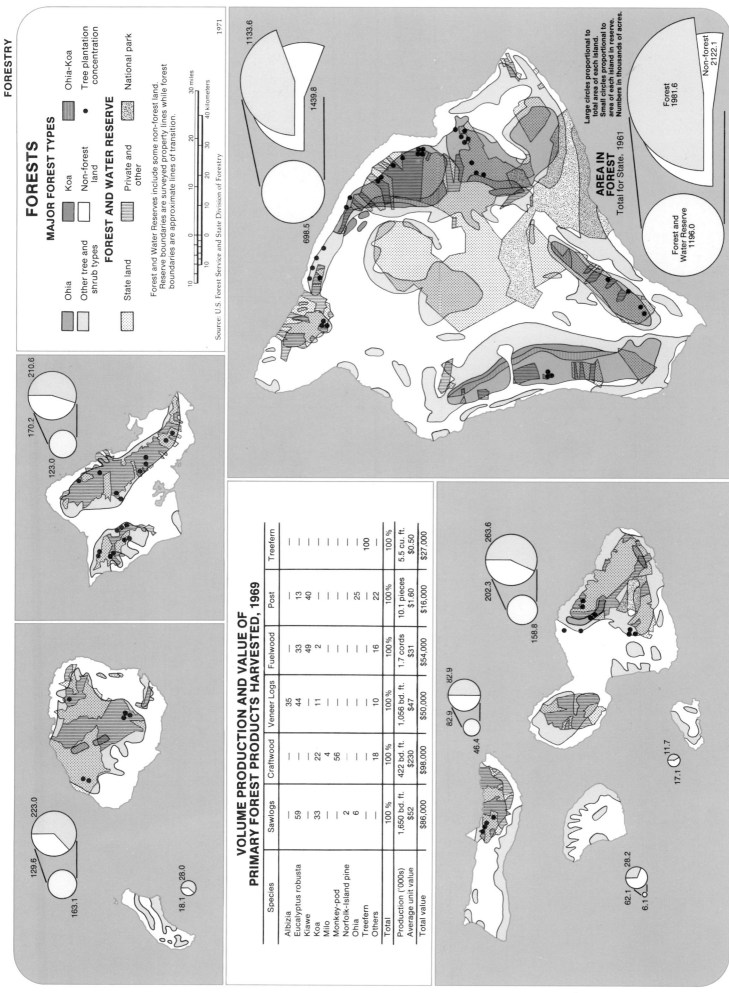

FORESTS

MAJOR FOREST TYPES

▨ Ohia		▨ Ohia-Koa	
▨ Other tree and shrub types	□ Koa	□ Non-forest land	• Tree plantation concentration

FOREST AND WATER RESERVE

▨ State land	▨ Private and other	▒ National park

Forest and Water Reserves include some non-forest land. Reserve boundaries are surveyed property lines while forest boundaries are approximate lines of transition.

1971

Source: U.S. Forest Service and State Division of Forestry

AREA IN FOREST
Total for State, 1961

Large circles proportional to total area of each island. Small circles proportional to area of each island in reserve. Numbers in thousands of acres.

Forest 1981.6
Non-forest 2122.1

Forest and Water Reserve 1196.0

VOLUME PRODUCTION AND VALUE OF PRIMARY FOREST PRODUCTS HARVESTED, 1969

Species	Sawlogs	Craftwood	Veneer Logs	Fuelwood	Post	Treefern
Albizia	–	–	35	–	–	–
Eucalyptus robusta	59	–	44	33	13	–
Kiawe	33	22	11	49	40	–
Milo	–	4	–	2	–	–
Monkey-pod	–	56	–	–	–	–
Norfolk-Island pine	2	–	–	–	–	–
Ohia	6	–	–	–	25	–
Treefern	–	–	–	–	–	100
Others	–	18	10	16	22	–
Total	100 %	100 %	100 %	100 %	100 %	100 %
Production ('000s)	1,650 bd. ft.	422 bd. ft.	1,056 bd. ft.	1.7 cords	10.1 pieces	5.5 cu. ft.
Average unit value	$52	$230	$47	$31	$1.60	$0.50
Total value	$86,000	$98,000	$50,000	$54,000	$16,000	$27,000

151

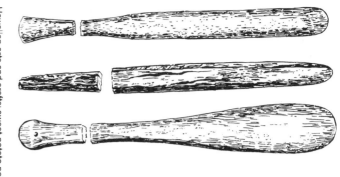

Hawaiian arts and crafts: sweet potato poi mixers.
Bishop Museum drawing from Te Rangi Hiroa (1964:25)

ENERGY

In its evolution from a Stone-Age monoculture of simple material needs to the complex multicultural community it now sustains, Hawaii has depended upon and used many of the same resources in meeting its energy requirements as have other cultures of the world. Before the arrival of Captain James Cook in 1778, the traditional energy sources were wind, water, and wood; after 1778 came draft animals, coal, petroleum, and manufactured gas, all as introduced resources. The interest shown by the Western powers in the Pacific region in the nineteenth century resulted in many profound changes, one of which was the development of Hawaii by 1900 as an acknowledged center of trade, commerce, agriculture, and industry. In this development the introduction of Western technology was inevitable, and reliance upon its productivity and the conveniences it brought has continued unabated to the present time. All of this created a growing demand for energy. The traditional sources of energy and those introduced in the early days were gradually replaced by more efficient, more reliable, and more economical resources needed for the increased use of Western technology. The complex society Hawaii now sustains requires substantial amounts of energy to maintain the quality of living most of its residents consider desirable. This requirement for energy is now met almost entirely by petroleum, electricity, and manufactured gas. Of these, petroleum is the most important today in Hawaii, because it is the basic resource used in the production of electricity and manufactured gas.

Petroleum. Inasmuch as Hawaii has no natural ground oil resources, it must import sufficient amounts of petroleum in various forms, from crude to refined, to provide fuel for about 400,000 motor vehicles, to generate electricity, to produce manufactured gas, and to meet other power needs. The nearest sources are on the west coast of the United States, more than 2,000 miles from Hawaii, but some oil is imported from other areas, in particular the Middle East. From these sources, the major American oil companies which supply the Western markets deliver the precious commodity to Hawaii in large ocean tankers. According to records compiled by the Hawaii civil defense agency, a total of 1,959,000 tons of petroleum were delivered to Hawaii in 1960, 405,000 tons of which were crude oil. In 1970 the total delivered had increased to 4,091,000 tons, of which 1,772,000 tons were crude oil.

In 1960 Standard Oil Company of California, Western Operations, built Hawaiian Refinery, an oil refinery of 35,000 barrels per day capacity, at Barbers Point, Oahu, the first such facility in the State. The crude oil refined at this facility produces ten products, all of which are marketed in Hawaii. Its presence and operation does not alter the State's complete dependence on outside sources for petroleum, however, for all the crude oil processed has to be imported. Hawaiian Refinery's success as a manufacturing industry stimulated the construction of another refinery at Barbers Point by other interests (Hawaiian Independent Refinery). The target date for the construction of this second refinery is mid-1972.

Manufactured Gas. Gas is mainly a residential-use energy source in Hawaii, although moderate commercial and industrial demands do exist. The natural gas ordinarily marketed as a fuel in other areas is not available in Hawaii, and so a comparable gas is produced to meet the demand by vaporizing low-sulphur fuel oil to force the separation of raw gas, which is then processed to obtain manufactured gas. Honolulu Gas Company is the only producer and distributor of this commodity in Hawaii. Today it services customers on the islands of Oahu, Maui, and Hawaii, and it will begin service on Kauai in 1972. This specific activity of Honolulu Gas Company is a public utility operation, and as such it comes under the purview of the Hawaii Public Utilities Commission.

One of Hawaiian Refinery's products is liquified petroleum gas. Honolulu Gas Company took over the marketing of this "bottled gas" as a nonutility operation. Available in moveable tanks which may be used in any locality without the need for a transmission system, bottled gas is currently popular in Hawaii, particularly in newly opened settlement areas which have no conventional public utility power and fuel systems.

Electricity. In Hawaii today electricity is produced on each populated island except Niihau, where there is no sophisticated

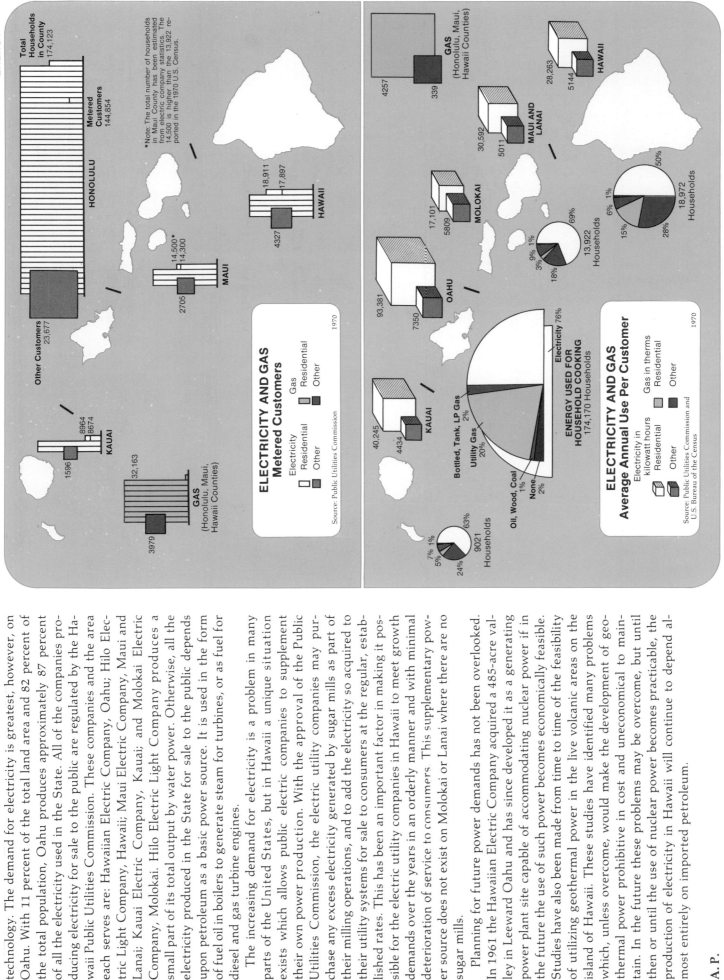

ELECTRICITY AND GAS
Metered Customers

Electricity   Gas
☐ Residential
☐ Other   ■ Residential   ■ Other

Source: Public Utilities Commission   1970

*Note: The total number of households in Maui County has been estimated from electric company statistics. The 14,500 is higher than the 13,922 reported in the 1970 U.S. Census.

Total Households in County
174,123

Metered Customers
144,854

HONOLULU

Other Customers
23,677

KAUAI
1596   8964   8674

GAS
(Honolulu, Maui, Hawaii Counties)
32,163
3979

MAUI
14,500*
14,300
2705

HAWAII
18,911
17,897
4327

ELECTRICITY AND GAS
Average Annual Use Per Customer

Electricity in kilowatt hours
☐ Residential
☐ Other

Gas in therms
■ Residential
■ Other

Source: Public Utilities Commission and U.S. Bureau of the Census   1970

GAS
(Honolulu, Maui, Hawaii Counties)
4257
339

HAWAII
28,263
5144

MAUI AND LANAI
30,592
5011

MOLOKAI
17,101
5809

OAHU
93,381
7350

KAUAI
40,245
4434

ENERGY USED FOR HOUSEHOLD COOKING
174,170 Households

Electricity 76%
Utility Gas 20%
Bottled, Tank, LP Gas 2%
Oil, Wood, Coal 1%
None 2%

18,972 Households
50% 28% 15% 6% 1%

13,922 Households
69% 18% 3% 9% 1%

9021 Households
63% 24% 5% 7% 1%

153

technology. The demand for electricity is greatest, however, on Oahu. With 11 percent of the total land area and 82 percent of the total population, Oahu produces approximately 87 percent of all the electricity used in the State. All of the companies producing electricity for sale to the public are regulated by the Hawaii Public Utilities Commission. These companies and the area each serves are: Hawaiian Electric Company, Oahu; Hilo Electric Light Company, Hawaii; Maui Electric Company, Maui and Lanai; Kauai Electric Company, Kauai; and Molokai Electric Company, Molokai. Hilo Electric Light Company produces a small part of its total output by water power. Otherwise, all the electricity produced in the State for sale to the public depends upon petroleum as a basic power source. It is used in the form of fuel oil in boilers to generate steam for turbines, or as fuel for diesel and gas turbine engines.

The increasing demand for electricity is a problem in many parts of the United States, but in Hawaii a unique situation exists which allows public electric companies to supplement their own power production. With the approval of the Public Utilities Commission, the electric utility companies may purchase any excess electricity generated by sugar mills as part of their milling operations, and to add the electricity so acquired to their utility systems for sale to consumers at the regular, established rates. This has been an important factor in making it possible for the electric utility companies in Hawaii to meet growth demands over the years in an orderly manner and with minimal deterioration of service to consumers. This supplementary power source does not exist on Molokai or Lanai where there are no sugar mills.

Planning for future power demands has not been overlooked. In 1961 the Hawaiian Electric Company acquired a 485-acre valley in Leeward Oahu and has since developed it as a generating power plant site capable of accommodating nuclear power if in the future the use of such power becomes economically feasible. Studies have also been made from time to time of the feasibility of utilizing geothermal power in the live volcanic areas on the island of Hawaii. These studies have identified many problems which, unless overcome, would make the development of geothermal power prohibitive in cost and uneconomical to maintain. In the future these problems may be overcome, but until then or until the use of nuclear power becomes practicable, the production of electricity in Hawaii will continue to depend almost entirely on imported petroleum.

A. P.

Note: Sugar company power houses on Kauai, Maui and Hawaii supply important amounts of electrical energy from time to time to community systems

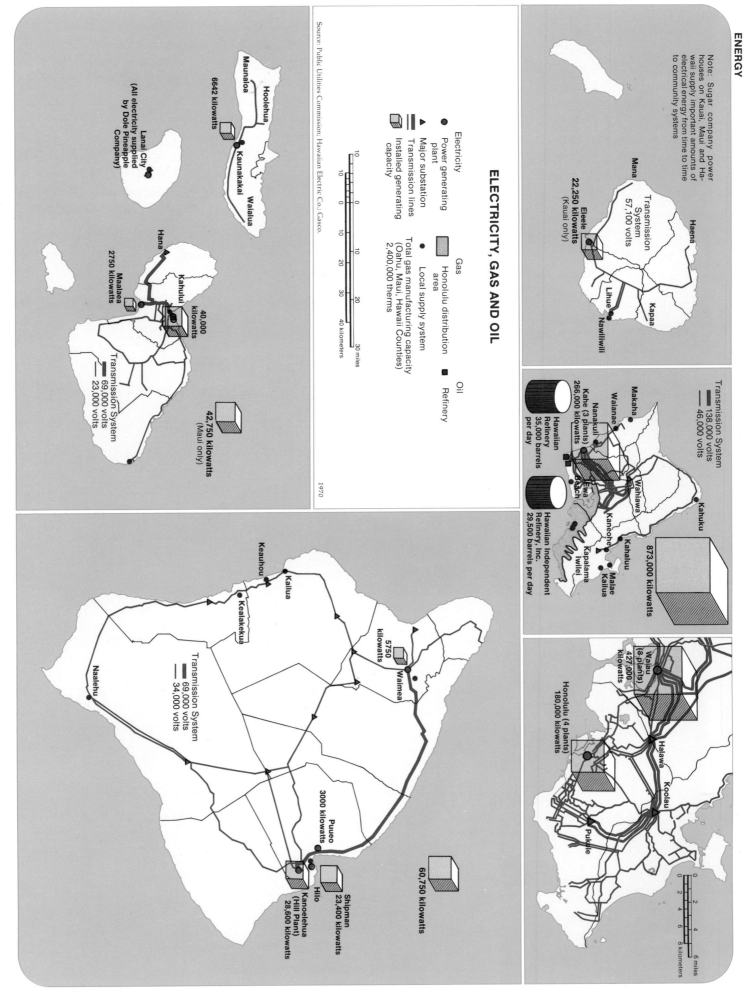

ELECTRICITY, GAS AND OIL

Electricity

- ● Power generating plant
- ▲ Major substation
- ‖ Transmission lines
- ⬛ Installed generating capacity

Gas

- ▨ Honolulu distribution area
- ● Local supply system
- ▨ Total gas manufacturing capacity (Oahu, Maui, Hawaii Counties) 2,400,000 therms

Oil

- ■ Refinery

Source: Public Utilities Commission; Hawaiian Electric Co.; Gasco.

1970

Kauai
Transmission System 57,100 volts
Eleele 22,250 kilowatts (Kauai only)
Mana
Haena
Lihue
Nawiliwili
Kapaa

Oahu
Transmission System
138,000 volts
46,000 volts
873,000 kilowatts
Hawaiian Refinery 35,000 barrels per day
Hawaiian Independent Refinery, Inc. 29,500 barrels per day
Kahe (3 plants) 266,000 kilowatts
Makaha
Waianae
Nanakuli
Ewa Beach
Ewa
Kapalama
Iwilei
Malae
Kailua
Kaneohe
Kahaluu
Wahiawa
Kahuku

Oahu (detail)
Waiau (8 plants) 427,000 kilowatts
Honolulu (4 plants) 180,000 kilowatts
Halawa
Koolau
Pukele

Molokai / Lanai / Maui
Maunaloa
Hoolehua 6642 kilowatts
Kaunakakai
Waialua
Lanai City (All electricity supplied by Dole Pineapple Company)
Hana
Maalaea 2750 kilowatts
Kahului 40,000 kilowatts
Transmission System 69,000 volts 23,000 volts
42,750 kilowatts (Maui only)

Hawaii
Keauhou
Kailua
Kealakekua
Naalehu
Waimea 5750 kilowatts
Puueo 3000 kilowatts
Kanoelehua (Hill Plant) 28,600 kilowatts
Hilo
Shipman 23,400 kilowatts
60,750 kilowatts
Transmission System 69,000 volts 34,000 volts

10 0 10 20 30 40 kilometers
10 0 10 20 30 miles

0 2 4 6 8 kilometers
0 2 4 6 miles

MANUFACTURING

In 1970 total manufacturing sales in Hawaii amounted to $751.7 million, ranking manufacturing as one of the State's leading industries. The key to the growth of manufacturing has been its ability to diversify and to concentrate production on selected activities in the absence of many of the natural resources and other components required for a major manufacturing area. Industrial areas in the State are concentrated principally in the area surrounding Honolulu Harbor where some ten major industrial areas cover a combined total of about 2,000 acres. Employment in manufacturing averaged 25,330 during 1970, making it one of the major categories of employment in the State.

"Diversified" manufacturing sales (a term used to designate all such sales other than processed sugarcane and pineapple) reached $420 million, or 55.9 percent of the total in 1970. During the last 10 years, diversified manufacturing expanded at an average rate of 11 percent annually, and by 1968 it surpassed the value of sugar and pineapple combined. Major diversified products in Hawaii include chemicals and petroleum, building materials, garment wear, lumber and wood products, and printing and publishing materials.

Raw sugar processing was valued at $196.7 million during 1970, following an average growth rate of 4.4 percent annually since 1960, and a record of $200 million set in 1968. Recently, some marginal sugar lands on Kauai and the Big Island have been closed down, consolidated, or converted to other uses in response to a sharp rise in production costs. Consequently, the tonnage of sugar produced was somewhat lower in 1970 following a number of years of expanding production.

Pineapple canning contributed an all-time record of $135 million to total manufacturing sales in Hawaii in 1970, while production of pineapples reached 28.8 million cases. The pineapple industry has been expanding its interests in foreign operations as a result of increasing production costs in Hawaii.

Following its organization in 1962, the Hawaii Manufacturers Association instituted a "Ten Most Wanted Industries" program. To date, 9 of the 19 industries appearing on the annual lists have been successfully established in Hawaii. The current

"Most Wanted" list includes the following industries: (1) bagasse wallboard for island and Pacific requirements; (2) quality gift goods; (3) various types of industrial maintenance; (4) machinery works, such as a tool and die shop, steel heat treating, and metal pretreatment and production; (5) oceanic and maritime support facilities; (6) recreational equipment; (7) recycling of waste products; (8) food and industrial repacking facilities; (9) secondary forest products; and (10) tropical fruit (other than pineapple) processing.

B. O. H.

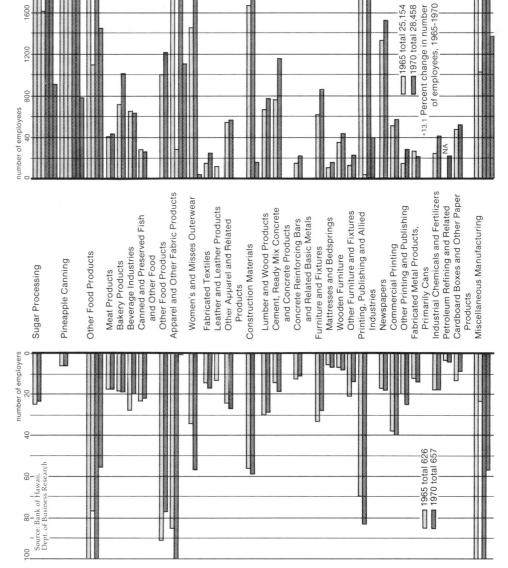

MANUFACTURERS AND EMPLOYMENT

155

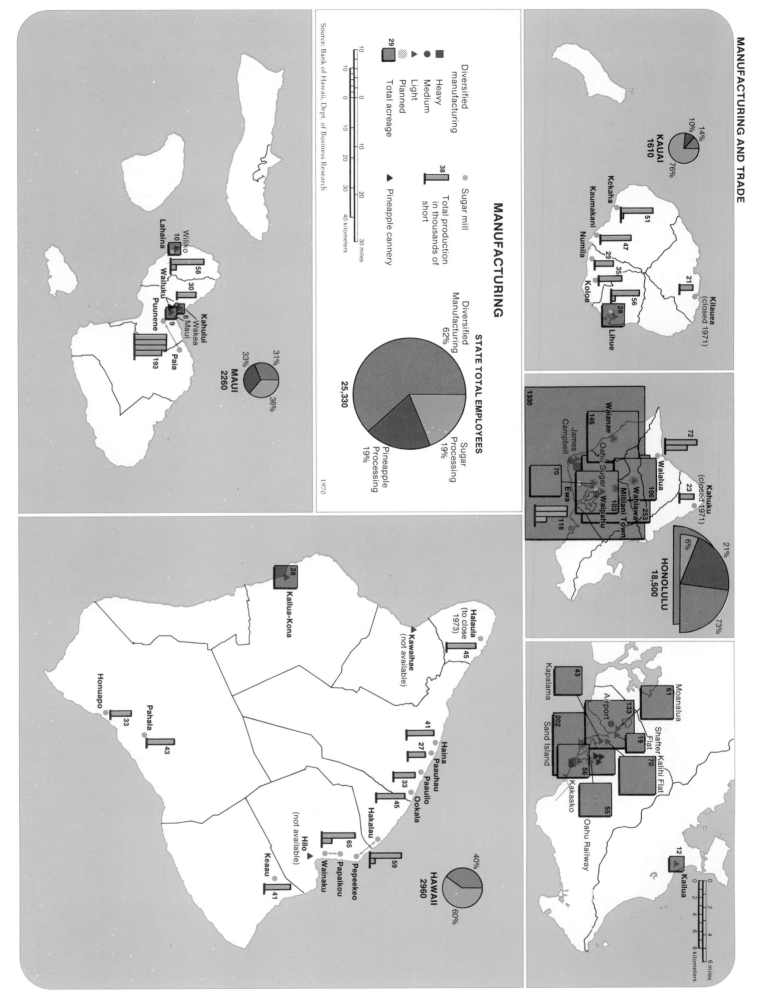

MANUFACTURING

STATE TOTAL EMPLOYEES

Diversified
Manufacturing
62%

25,330

Sugar
Processing
19%

Pineapple
Processing
19%

1970

Diversified
manufacturing

Heavy
Medium
Light
Planned
Total acreage

29

Sugar mill

Total production
in thousands of
short

38

Pineapple cannery

Source: Bank of Hawaii, Dept. of Business Research

KAUAI
1610

14%
10%
76%

Kekaha
Kaumakani
Numila
Koloa
Lihue

Kilauea
(closed 1971)

51
47
29
35
56
28
21

MAUI
2260

31%
33%
36%

Wiliko
Lahaina
Wailuku
Puunene
Kahului
Wakea
Maui
Paia

10
58
30
9
6
193

HONOLULU
18,500

21%
6%
73%

Waianae
James Campbell
Oahu Sugar
Waialua
Mililani Town
Wahiawa
Waipahu
Ewa

1330
146
103
106
253
72
23
70
118

Kahuku
(closed 1971)

Moanalua
Kapalama
Airport
Shafter Kalihi Flat
Sand Island
Kakaako
Oahu Railway
Kailua

43
61
133
19
202
70
56
55
12

HAWAII
2960

40%
60%

Kailua-Kona
Halaula
(to close 1973)
Kawaihae
(not available)
Honuapo
Pahala
Haina
Paauhau
Paauilo
Ookala
Hakalau
Hilo
(not available)
Wainaku
Papaikou
Pepeekeo
Keaau

28
45
33
43
41
27
33
45
65
59
41

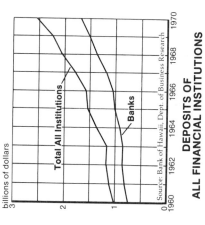

billions of dollars

Total All Institutions

Banks

Source: Bank of Hawaii, Dept. of Business Research

**DEPOSITS OF
ALL FINANCIAL INSTITUTIONS**

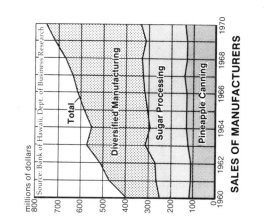

millions of dollars

Source: Bank of Hawaii, Dept. of Business Research

Total

Diversified Manufacturing

Sugar Processing

Pineapple Canning

SALES OF MANUFACTURERS

FINANCE AND TRADE

Financial activity in Hawaii comprises a diversity of organizations, including commercial banks, trust companies, savings and loan associations, federal credit unions, industrial loan companies, small loan companies, and local and overseas-based insurance companies. Each is important to the Hawaiian economy by facilitating the flow of credit and investments.

Total deposits in all financial institutions in Hawaii reached $2.6 billion in 1970, for an average annual increase of 9.9 percent since 1960. About two-thirds of the 1970 total, or $1.7 billion, consisted of bank-held deposits.

Total loans outstanding by all financial institutions in Hawaii at the end of 1970 amounted to $2.3 billion, following an average annual growth rate of 12.1 percent since 1960. Bank loans accounted for $1.2 billion or 51.3 percent of the loan total in 1970.

Reflecting the substantial volume of construction during the last decade, total mortgage loans outstanding reached $1.8 billion in 1970, more than three times the amount of mortgage loans outstanding in 1960. With a combined total of $716 million, savings and loan associations and industrial loan companies held 40 percent of all mortgage loans outstanding in 1970.

Financial institutions in Hawaii issued an estimated total of $667.7 million in consumer loans in 1970, following a 12.2 percent average annual increase during the decade of the sixties. Banks accounted for 44.7 percent of the total, providing an estimated $298.2 million in 1970.

Reflecting expanding economic activity in Hawaii, bank demand deposits reached $608.8 million in 1970, for an average annual increase of 8.3 percent since 1960. Debits to bank demand deposits totaled $23.3 billion in 1970, having exhibited an average annual increase of 14.0 percent during the decade.

Total life insurance in force reached $7,441.1 million in 1970. Growth of insurance has averaged 11.3 percent annually since 1960. Investments of mainland and foreign insurance companies in Hawaii totaled $828.8 million in 1970, having increased by an annual average of 13.1 percent between 1960 and 1970. Hawaii is a favored investment area, and insurance company invest-

ments in Hawaii annually exceed the volume of premium payments. Consistently, mortgage loans constitute the largest share of insurance company investments; in 1960 they amounted to $599.7 million.

Over the years, Hawaii's expanding population and urbanization have caused a marked increase in the demand for goods and services. Although Hawaii's industries continue to expand and diversify, local production is far short of the needs of the market, and the level of imports has been advancing steadily. Accordingly, much attention has been given to expanding the production of export commodities to alleviate the imbalance in Hawaii's mainland and foreign trade.

Hawaii's mid-Pacific location makes it dependent on fast, efficient transportation with the mainland United States and foreign countries. Consequently, Hawaiian shipping firms have pioneered in developing surface and air containerized facilities which are among the most modern in the world. In 1969 Hawaii's imports amounted to 7.4 million tons, valued at more than $1.2 billion and consisting largely of crude oil, petroleum products, manufactured goods, and construction materials. The U.S. mainland accounts for about 56 percent of all surface shipments to Hawaii and is the source of 90 percent of all food and beverage imports, valued at more than $147 million annually.

Retail sales in Hawaii passed the $2 billion mark during 1970, more than double the $948 million recorded in 1960. With certain exceptions, sales of brand-name items and the proportionate share of categories of retail commodities generally conform to mainland market patterns.

Corresponding to trends on the mainland, traditional central business districts in Hawaii are undergoing transformation from predominately retail to financial centers, while older retail districts are accommodating changes in market characteristics. Planned unit shopping centers are growing in numbers and are capturing an increasing share of the $2 billion retail market. Starting in 1950 with 93,000 square feet, the total gross leasable area of planned unit shopping centers on Oahu had increased to 1.4 million square feet by 1960. The combined total reached 3.8 million square feet by 1970. The Ala Moana Regional Shopping Center in Honolulu has only recently been surpassed as the largest regional center in the United States.

B. O. H.

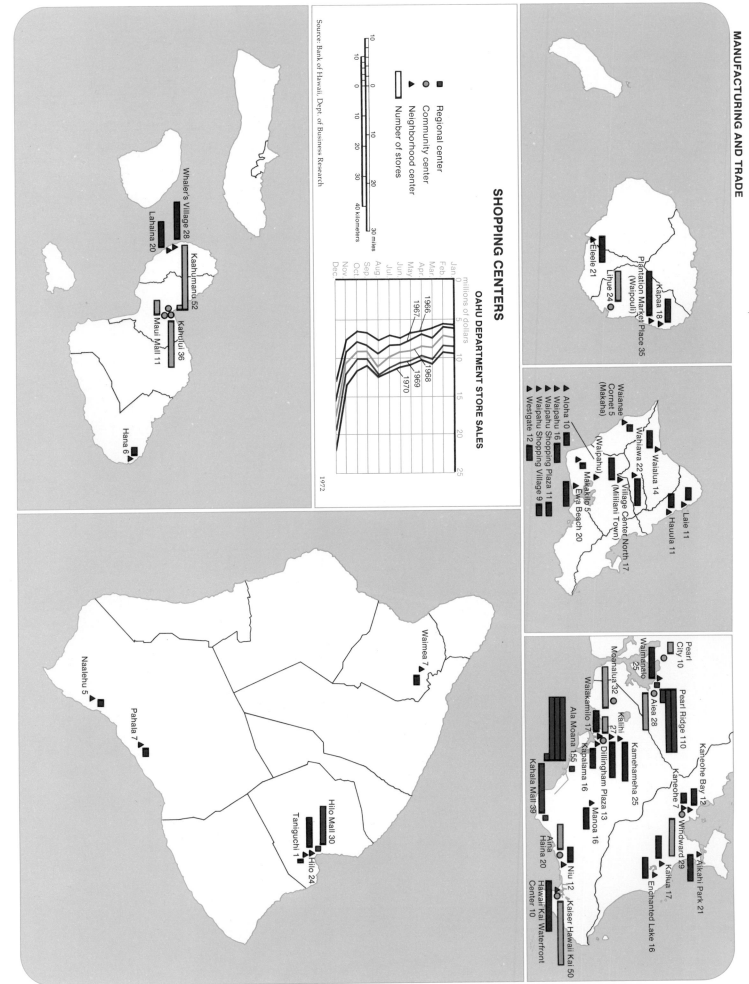

SHOPPING CENTERS

Regional center ■
Community center ●
Neighborhood center ▲

Number of stores

10
10
0   0
10
20   10
30
20
40 kilometers
30 miles

Source: Bank of Hawaii, Dept. of Business Research

OAHU DEPARTMENT STORE SALES

millions of dollars

0   5   10   15   20   25

Jan
Feb
Mar
Apr
May
Jun
Jul
Aug
Sep
Oct
Nov
Dec

1966
1967
1968
1969
1970

1972

Kauai

Plantation Market Place (Waipouli) 35
Lihue 24
Kapaa 18
Eleele 21

Oahu (west)

Aloha 10
Waipahu 16
Waipahu Shopping Plaza 11
Waipahu Shopping Village 9
Westgate 12
Waianae Cornet 5 (Makaha)
Village Center North 17 (Mililani Town)
Makakilo 5
Ewa Beach 20
Wahiawa 22
Waialua 14
Laie 11
Haula 11

Oahu (east)

Pearl City 10
Waimanalo 25
Moanalua 32
Aiea 28
Pearl Ridge 110
Kaneohe Bay 12
Waiakamilo 17
Kalihi 27
Dillingham Plaza 13
Kamehameha 25
Kaneohe 7
Windward 29
Ala Moana 155
Kapalama 16
Manoa 16
Alakahi Park 21
Kahala Mall 39
Aina Haina 20
Niu 12
Kahala 17
Enchanted Lake 16
Hawaii Kai Waterfront Center 10
Kaiser Hawaii Kai 50

Maui

Whaler's Village 28
Lahaina 20
Kaahumanu 52
Maui Mall 11
Kahului 36
Hana 6

Hawaii

Waimea 7
Naalehu 5
Pahala 7
Hilo Mall 30
Taniguchi 1
Hilo 24

STATE BALANCE OF TRADE, 1969

	RECEIPTS (millions of dollars)	PAYMENTS (millions of dollars)	NET RECEIPTS (millions of dollars)
Commodity Exports			
Sugar	182		
Pineapple	120		
Canned Tuna, Coffee, Tropical Fruits, Nuts and Other Agricultural Products	13		
Garments, Scrap Metal, Petroleum, Flowers and Other Products	53		
Total Commodity Exports	$368		
Commodity Imports			
Domestic			
Fruits and Vegetables		10	
Meat, Fish, Poultry and Dairy		47	
Canned and Other Processed Food		63	
Total Food Imports			120
Vehicles, Tires and Parts		124	
Fuel		70	
Construction Materials		96	
Fertilizer, Insecticides and Industrial Chemicals		7	
Machinery and Appliances		62	
Iron and Steel Products		19	
Clothing, Drugs, Tobacco, Newsprint, Feed and Grain and Other Products		531	
Total Non-Food Imports			909
Foreign			
Fuel		61	
Miscellaneous Products		106	
Total Direct Foreign Imports			167
Total Commodity Imports		$1,196	−$828
Federal Government Expenditures			
Civilian Payrolls and Purchases	56		
Grants-in-Aid	109		
Transfer Payments	111		
Tax Refunds and Miscellaneous	50		
Total Civilian			326
Military Payrolls	455		
Military Purchases	205		
Total Military			660
Total Federal Expenditures	$986		
Payments to Federal Civilian Agencies			
Postal Payments		20	
Customs		13	
Civil Service Retirement		14	
Tax Payments		572	
Other Federal Payments		15	
Total Federal Payments		$634	+$352
Goods and Services Sold			
Expenditures of Visitors and Transients, including Crews of Commercial Carriers	585		
Shipping and Airlines Services	74		
Advertising, Communications and Other Business Services	61		
Total Services	$720		
Purchased Services from Mainland and Foreign Countries			
Travel Expenditures of Hawaiian Residents, including Students in Mainland Schools		138	
Surface and Air Freight		102	
Net Cost of Insurance, Entertainment, Communications and Miscellaneous Business Expenses		78	
Total Services Purchased		$318	+$402
Return on Investments	124		
Interest, Dividends and Profits Paid to Overseas Investors		155	−31
Remittances, Gifts, Immigrants' Funds	15	23	−8
Total Receipts	$2,213		
Total Payments		$2,326	−$113

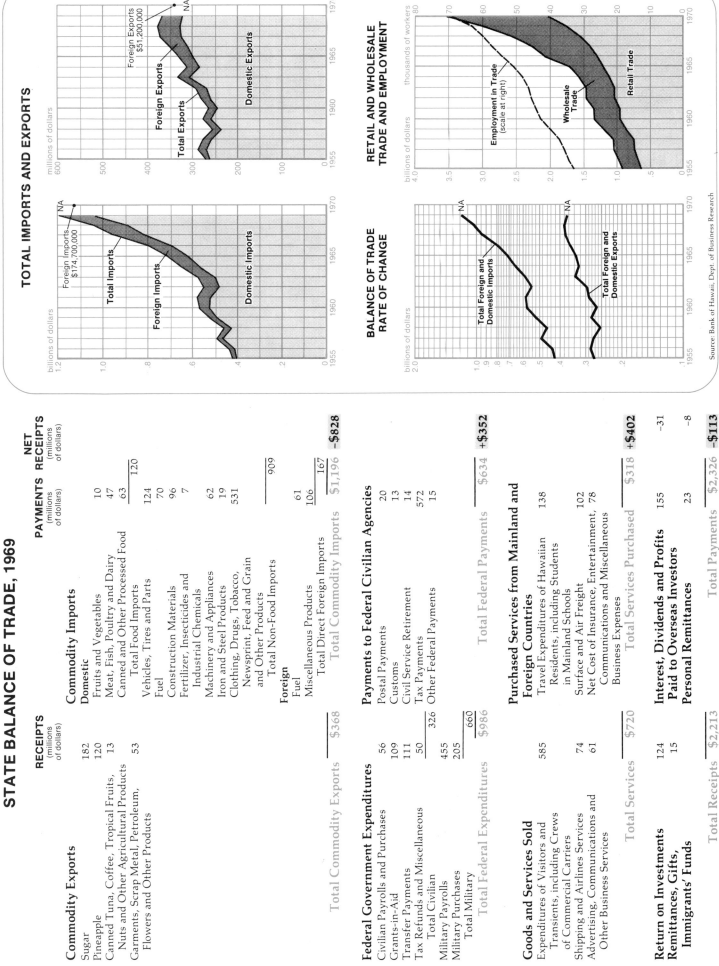

MANUFACTURING AND TRADE

TOTAL IMPORTS AND EXPORTS

millions of dollars — 600, 500, 400, 300, 200, 100, 0 (1955, 1960, 1965, 1970)

Foreign Exports $51,200,000 — NA
Foreign Exports
Total Exports
Domestic Exports

billions of dollars — 1.2, 1.0, .8, .6, .4, .2, 0 (1955, 1960, 1965, 1970)

Foreign Imports $174,700,000 — NA
Total Imports
Foreign Imports
Domestic Imports

RETAIL AND WHOLESALE TRADE AND EMPLOYMENT

thousands of workers — 80, 70, 60, 50, 40, 30, 20, 10, 0
billions of dollars — 4.0, 3.5, 3.0, 2.5, 2.0, 1.5, 1.0, .5, 0 (1955, 1960, 1965, 1970)

Employment in Trade (scale at right)
Wholesale Trade
Retail Trade

BALANCE OF TRADE RATE OF CHANGE

billions of dollars — 2.0, 1.0, .9, .8, .7, .6, .5, .4, .3, .2, .1 (1955, 1960, 1965, 1970)

Total Foreign and Domestic Imports — NA
Total Foreign and Domestic Exports — NA

Source: Bank of Hawaii, Dept. of Business Research

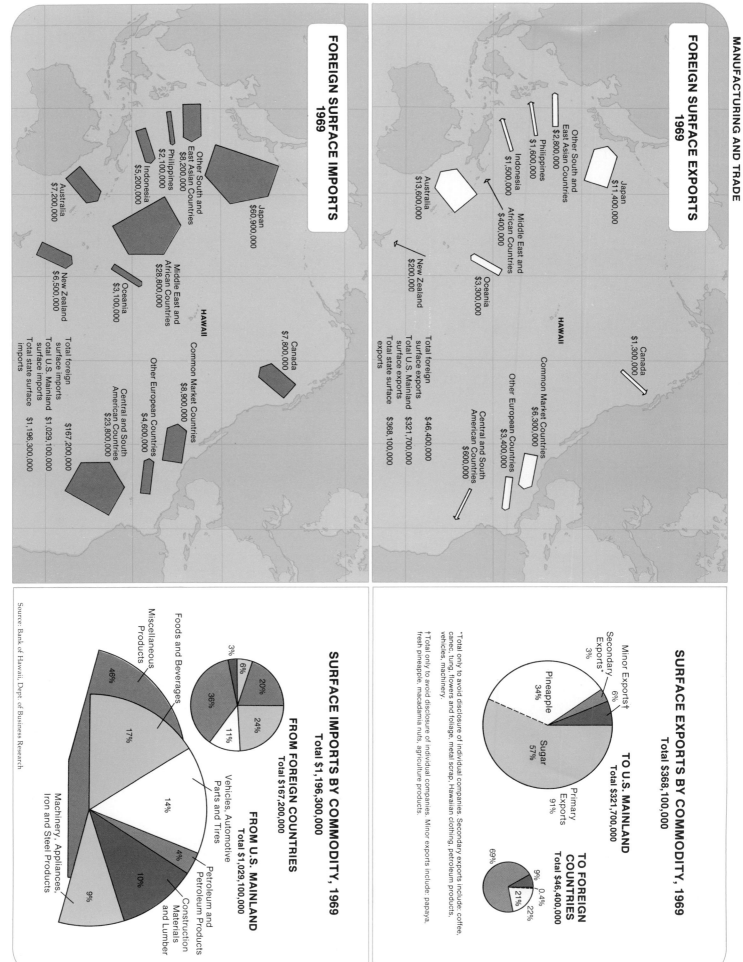

**FOREIGN SURFACE EXPORTS
1969**

Japan
$11,400,000

Other South and
East Asian Countries
$2,800,000

Philippines
$1,600,000

Indonesia
$1,500,000

Middle East and
African Countries
$400,000

Australia
$13,600,000

New Zealand
$200,000

Oceania
$3,300,000

Canada
$1,300,000

HAWAII

Common Market Countries
$6,300,000

Other European Countries
$3,400,000

Central and South
American Countries
$600,000

Total foreign
surface exports $46,400,000
Total U.S. Mainland
surface exports $321,700,000
Total state surface
exports $368,100,000

**FOREIGN SURFACE IMPORTS
1969**

Other South and
East Asian Countries
$8,200,000

Philippines
$2,100,000

Indonesia
$5,200,000

Australia
$7,200,000

Japan
$60,900,000

New Zealand
$6,500,000

Middle East and
African Countries
$28,800,000

Oceania
$3,100,000

HAWAII

Canada
$7,800,000

Common Market Countries
$8,900,000

Other European Countries
$4,600,000

Central and South
American Countries
$23,800,000

Total foreign
surface imports $167,200,000
Total U.S. Mainland
surface imports $1,029,100,000
Total state surface
imports $1,196,300,000

SURFACE EXPORTS BY COMMODITY, 1969
Total $368,100,000

Minor Exports†
6%

Secondary
Exports*
3%

Pineapple
34%

Sugar
57%

TO U.S. MAINLAND
Total $321,700,000

Primary
Exports
91%

**TO FOREIGN
COUNTRIES**
Total $46,400,000

69%

9%

0.4%

22%

21%

*Total only to avoid disclosure of individual companies. Secondary exports include: coffee, canec, tung, flowers and foliage, metal scrap, Hawaiian clothing, petroleum products, vehicles, machinery.

†Total only to avoid disclosure of individual companies. Minor exports include: papaya, fresh pineapple, macadamia nuts, agriculture products.

SURFACE IMPORTS BY COMMODITY, 1969
Total $1,196,300,000

FROM FOREIGN COUNTRIES
Total $167,200,000

20%

24%

11%

36%

6%

3%

FROM U.S. MAINLAND
Total $1,029,100,000

Foods and Beverages

Miscellaneous
Products

14%

4%

10%

9%

Vehicles, Automotive
Parts and Tires

Petroleum and
Petroleum Products

Construction
Materials
and Lumber

Machinery, Appliances,
Iron and Steel Products

46%

17%

Source: Bank of Hawaii, Dept. of Business Research

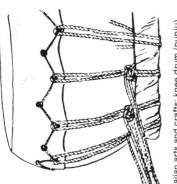

Hawaiian arts and crafts: knee drum (puniu).
Bishop Museum drawing from Te Rangi Hiroa (1964-404).

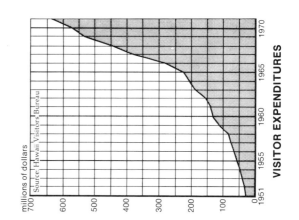

millions of dollars

Source Hawaii Visitors Bureau

VISITOR EXPENDITURES

TOURISM

Tourism in Hawaii has grown rapidly since its modest nineteenth-century origins. In part this growth has resulted from continual improvements in transportation: the first regular steamship service from the mainland in 1867, interisland air service in 1929, a transpacific airline in 1936, and sharp reductions in air fares in 1952 and 1963. Another factor has been the stimulus provided by government and business through the Hawaii Visitors Bureau, first established as the Hawaiian Promotion Committee in 1903. Constantly improving accommodations have likewise contributed, with such notable developments as the first luxury hotel in Honolulu, the Hawaiian, in 1872; the earliest large Waikiki hotel, the Seaside Annex, in 1894; the Royal Hawaiian Hotel, in 1927; and, on the neighbor islands, the Volcano House in 1866 and Kona Inn in 1928. State and county governments have made significant efforts in recent years to plan for and guide this growth.

Expansion has been especially rapid since World War II. Annual visitor arrivals increased from 2,040 in 1886 to 9,700 in 1922, 32,000 in 1941, 52,000 in 1951, 320,000 in 1961, and 1,819,000 in 1971. The average number of visitors present at any one time rose from 2,100 in 1941 to 41,000 in 1971, and their annual expenditures (excluding transpacific travel) increased from $16.4 million to $645 million during the same 30-year period (page 161). Hotel rooms numbered 1,572 at the end of 1946, 6,825 in 1960, and 36,000 in 1972.

Most of the visitors to Hawaii come from the western United States and other parts of the mainland, but a growing number are residents of Japan, Australia, and other countries of the Far East and South Pacific. In 1971, 79 percent of all visitors staying overnight or longer came on westbound flights or sailings while 21 percent arrived on eastbound or northbound carriers. Among westbound visitors destined for Hawaii, half were residents of either the Pacific or Mountain states, and over a third were Californians. About 12 percent of the eastbound visitors were members of the American armed forces on Rest and Recuperation leave from Southeast Asia; half of the rest were tourists from Japan. By census division, visitor rates per 100,000 population ranged from 155 in the East South Central states to 1,841 in the Pacific states.

Hawaii Visitors' Bureau surveys reveal the typical island visitor to be a relatively affluent person of middle years. Median age in 1971 was 43 years, and there were only 74 males for every 100 females. Fifty-four percent of all party heads reported themselves to be professional or technical workers or businessmen, managers, or officials. Median annual family income before taxes was $20,800, approximately double the national level.

Most visitors came by air, stayed in hotels, and saw at least one neighbor island. Only 0.3 percent arrived by ship in 1971, compared with 43.6 percent in 1951. Thirty percent arrived in either June, July, or August, while only 23 percent came in the winter months. More than a third had made at least one earlier visit to Hawaii. Three-fourths were on pleasure trips. The average intended length of stay in 1971 was 11.1 days, compared with 17.2 in 1961 and 25.0 in 1951. Eighty-five percent planned to stay in a hotel rather than in a rented apartment or with friends or relatives, and three out of five planned to see at least one of the neighbor islands. An earlier survey, limited to Oahu visitors, estimated their average expenditure at $37.23 per visitor-day, chiefly for lodging ($10.84) and food ($9.28).

An inventory of accommodations available in the islands as of February 1972 reported 281 hotels, apartment hotels, motels, and similar facilities, with a total of 35,797 rentable units: 24,742 on Oahu, 4,241 on the Big Island, 3,979 on Maui, 2,719 on Kauai, 105 on Molokai, and 11 on Lanai. Major concentrations existed in Waikiki and the adjacent Ala Moana area on Oahu, the Lahaina district on Maui, Hilo and Kailua-Keauhou on Hawaii, and Wailua-Kapaa on Kauai.

Although most of the interest in Hawaiian tourism centers on the mainlanders and foreigners visiting the islands, it should not be forgotten that the islanders themselves are frequent travelers. A 1971 sample survey indicated that 34 percent of Oahu households had members who had visited a neighbor island during the preceding 12 months, 24 percent had members who had traveled to the mainland, and almost 10 percent, to a foreign country.

R. C. S.

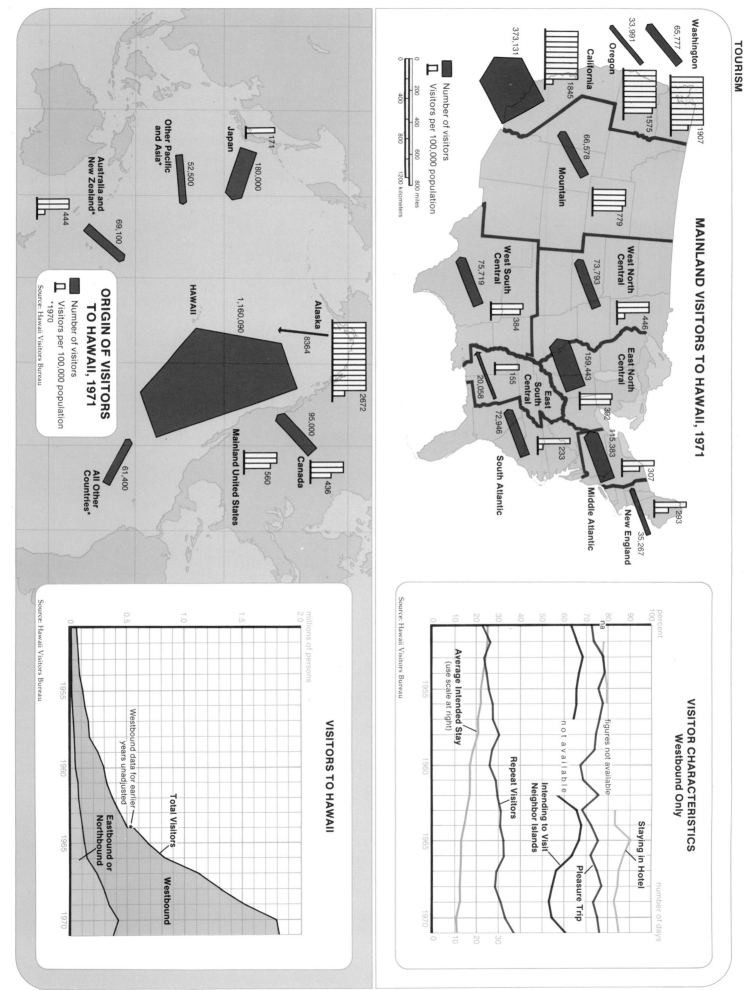

MAINLAND VISITORS TO HAWAII, 1971

Number of visitors

Visitors per 100,000 population

0   200   400   600   800   1200 kilometers
0   200   400   600   800 miles

Washington   65,777   1907
Oregon   33,991
California   373,131   1845   1575
Mountain   66,578   779
West North Central   73,793
West South Central   75,719   384
East North Central   159,443   446   392   115,383
East South Central   72,946   20,058   155   233
South Atlantic   115,383
Middle Atlantic   307
New England   35,267   293

Source: Hawaii Visitors Bureau

ORIGIN OF VISITORS TO HAWAII, 1971

Number of visitors

Visitors per 100,000 population

*1970

Source: Hawaii Visitors Bureau

Japan   180,000   171
Other Pacific and Asia*   52,500
Australia and New Zealand*   444
69,100
HAWAII   1,160,090
Alaska   8364   2672
Canada   95,000   436
Mainland United States   560
All Other Countries*   61,400

VISITOR CHARACTERISTICS
Westbound Only

percent
100
90
80   na
70
60
50
40
30
20
10
0

1955   1960   1965   1970

number of days
30
20
10
0

figures not available

not available

Average Intended Stay (use scale at right)

Repeat Visitors

Intending to Visit Neighbor Islands

Pleasure Trip

Staying in Hotel

Source: Hawaii Visitors Bureau

VISITORS TO HAWAII

millions of persons
2.0
1.5
1.0
0.5
0

1955   1960   1965   1970

Total Visitors

Westbound

Eastbound or Northbound

Westbound data for earlier years unadjusted   *

Source: Hawaii Visitors Bureau

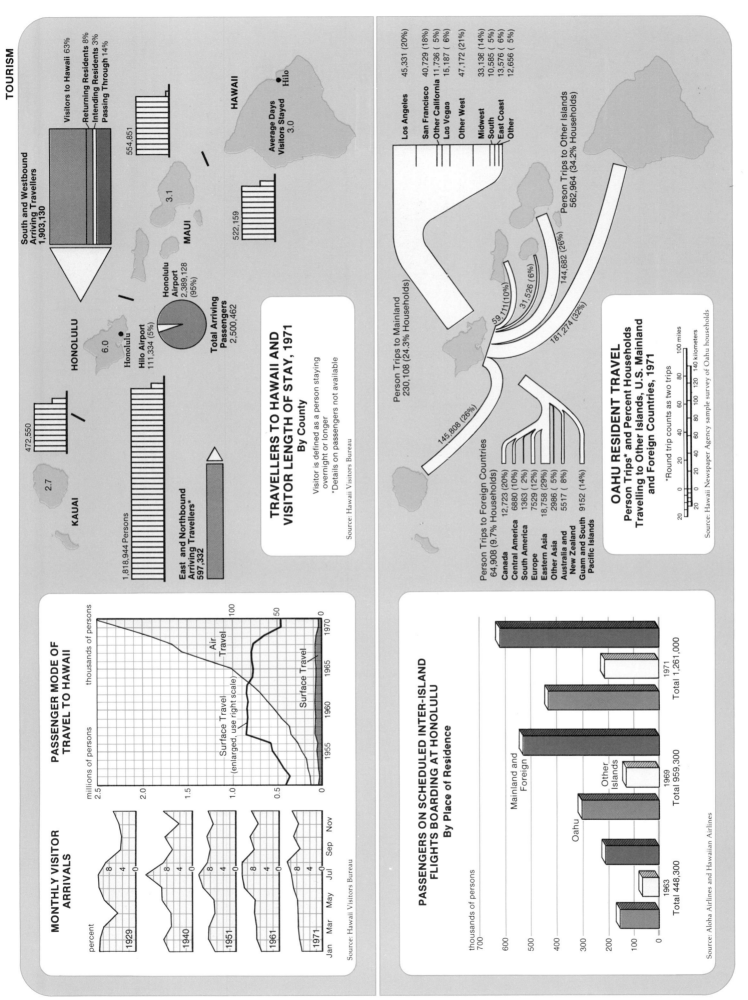

MONTHLY VISITOR ARRIVALS

percent

1929
1940
1951
1961
1971

Jan Mar May Jul Sep Nov

Source: Hawaii Visitors Bureau

PASSENGER MODE OF TRAVEL TO HAWAII

thousands of persons

millions of persons

Air Travel

Surface Travel

Surface Travel (enlarged, use right scale)

Surface Travel

1955 1960 1965 1970

Source: Hawaii Visitors Bureau

South and Westbound Arriving Travellers 1,903,130

Visitors to Hawaii 63%
Returning Residents 8%
Intending Residents 3%
Passing Through 14%

KAUAI 2.7
472,550

HONOLULU 6.0

Honolulu Airport 2,389,128 (95%)
Hilo Airport 111,334 (5%)

Total Arriving Passengers 2,500,462

MAUI 3.1
554,851
522,159

HAWAII
Average Days Visitors Stayed 3.0
Hilo

1,818,944 Persons

East and Northbound Arriving Travellers* 597,332

TRAVELLERS TO HAWAII AND VISITOR LENGTH OF STAY, 1971
By County

Visitor is defined as a person staying overnight or longer
*Details on passengers not available

Source: Hawaii Visitors Bureau

PASSENGERS ON SCHEDULED INTER-ISLAND FLIGHTS BOARDING AT HONOLULU
By Place of Residence

thousands of persons

Mainland and Foreign

Oahu

Other Islands

1963 Total 448,300
1969 Total 959,300
1971 Total 1,261,000

Source: Aloha Airlines and Hawaiian Airlines

Person Trips to Mainland
230,108 (24.3% Households)

Los Angeles 45,331 (20%)
San Francisco 40,729 (18%)
Other California 11,736 (5%)
Las Vegas 15,187 (6%)
Other West 47,172 (21%)
Midwest 33,136 (14%)
South 10,585 (5%)
East Coast 13,576 (6%)
Other 12,656 (5%)

Person Trips to Other Islands
562,964 (34.2% Households)

59,111 (10%)
31,526 (6%)
144,682 (26%)
181,274 (32%)
145,808 (26%)

Person Trips to Foreign Countries
64,908 (9.7% Households)

Canada 12,723 (20%)
Central America 6880 (10%)
South America 1363 (2%)
Europe 7529 (12%)
Eastern Asia 18,758 (29%)
Other Asia 2986 (5%)
Australia and New Zealand 5517 (8%)
Guam and South Pacific Islands 9152 (14%)

OAHU RESIDENT TRAVEL
Person Trips* and Percent Households Travelling to Other Islands, U.S. Mainland and Foreign Countries, 1971

*Round trip counts as two trips

0 20 40 60 80 100 miles
20 40 60 80 100 120 140 kilometers

Source: Hawaii Newspaper Agency sample survey of Oahu households

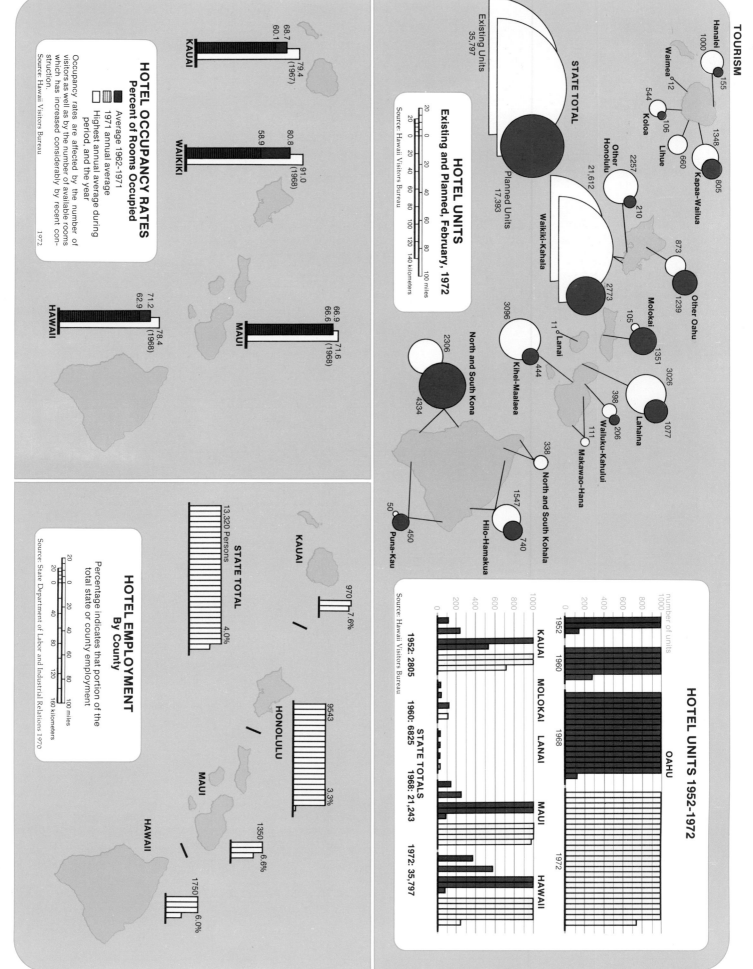

HOTEL UNITS
Existing and Planned, February, 1972

STATE TOTAL
Existing Units 35,797
Planned Units 17,393

Hanalei 1000 / 155
Waimea 712
Koloa 544 / 106
Lihue 660
Kapaa-Wailua 1348 / 805
Other Honolulu 2257 / 210
Waikiki-Kahala 21,612
Other Oahu 1239
873 / 2773
Molokai 105
Lanai 11
North and South Kona 3096 / 2306
4334
Kihei-Maalaea 444 / 1351
Lahaina 3026 / 1077
Wailuku-Kahului 398 / 206
Makawao-Hana 111
North and South Kohala 1547 / 740
Hilo-Hamakua 338
Puna-Kau 50 / 450

Source: Hawaii Visitors Bureau

Scale: 20 0 20 40 60 80 100 miles / 20 0 20 40 60 80 100 120 140 kilometers

HOTEL UNITS 1952-1972

number of units: 0 200 400 600 800 1000

1952, 1960, 1968, 1972

OAHU, KAUAI, MOLOKAI, LANAI, MAUI, HAWAII

STATE TOTALS
1952: 2805   1960: 6825   1968: 21,243   1972: 35,797

Source: Hawaii Visitors Bureau

HOTEL OCCUPANCY RATES
Percent of Rooms Occupied

KAUAI 68.7 / 60.1 / 79.4 (1967)
WAIKIKI 80.8 / 58.9 / 91.0 (1968)
MAUI 66.9 / 66.6 / 71.6 (1968)
HAWAII 71.2 / 62.9 / 78.4 (1968)

☐ Average 1962-1971
■ 1971 annual average
☐ Highest annual average during period, and the year

Occupancy rates are affected by the number of visitors as well as by the number of available rooms which has increased considerably by recent construction.

Source: Hawaii Visitors Bureau

1972

HOTEL EMPLOYMENT
By County

STATE TOTAL
13,320 Persons

KAUAI 970 / 7.6% / 4.0%
HONOLULU 9543 / 3.3%
MAUI 1350 / 6.6%
HAWAII 1750 / 6.0%

Percentage indicates that portion of the total state or county employment

Source: State Department of Labor and Industrial Relations 1970

Scale: 20 0 20 40 60 80 100 miles / 20 0 20 40 60 80 100 120 140 160 kilometers

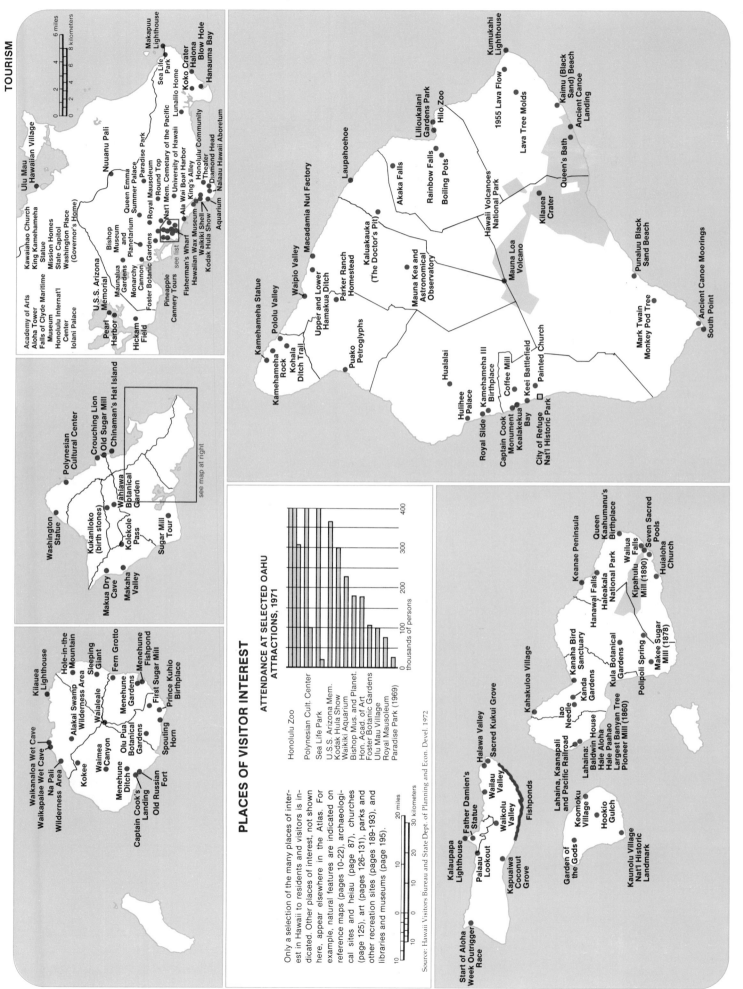

PLACES OF VISITOR INTEREST

Only a selection of the many places of interest to residents and visitors is indicated. Other places of interest, not shown here, appear elsewhere in the Atlas. For example, natural features are indicated on reference maps (pages 10–22), archaeological sites and heiau (page 87), churches (page 125), art (pages 126–131), parks and other recreation sites (pages 189–193), and libraries and museums (page 195).

ATTENDANCE AT SELECTED OAHU ATTRACTIONS, 1971

Honolulu Zoo
Polynesian Cult. Center
Sea Life Park
U.S.S. Arizona Mem.
Kodak Hula Show
Waikiki Aquarium
Bishop Mus. and Planet.
Hon. Acad. of Art
Foster Botanic Gardens
Ulu Mau Village
Royal Mausoleum
Paradise Park (1969)

thousands of persons

Source: Hawaii Visitors Bureau and State Dept. of Planning and Econ. Devel. 1972

Oahu (main map)

Academy of Arts
Aloha Tower
Falls of Clyde Maritime Museum
Honolulu Internat'l Center
Iolani Palace
Kawaiahao Church
King Kamehameha Statue
Mission Homes
State Capitol
Washington Place (Governor's Home)
U.S.S. Arizona
Pearl Harbor
Hickam Field
Pineapple Cannery Tours
Maunalua Gardens
Bishop Museum and Planetarium
Monarchy Cannon
Foster Botanic Gardens
Queen Emma Summer Palace
Paradise Park
Royal Mausoleum
Round Top
Nuuanu Pali
Ulu Mau Hawaiian Village
Makapuu Lighthouse
Sea Life Park
Lunalilo Home
Koko Crater
Halona Blow Hole
Hanauma Bay
Diamond Head
Aquarium
Nalaau Hawaii Arboretum
Kodak Hula Show
Waikiki Shell
Hawaiian Wax Museum
King's Alley
Honolulu Community Theater
Nat'l Mem. Cemetary of the Pacific
University of Hawaii
Ala Wai Boat Harbor
Fisherman's Wharf

Oahu (inset)

Polynesian Cultural Center
Crouching Lion
Old Sugar Mill
Chinaman's Hat Island
Washington Statue
Kukaniloko (birth stones)
Wahiawa Botanical Garden
Kolekole Pass
Makua Dry Cave
Makaha Valley
Sugar Mill Tour
see map at right

Kauai

Waikanaloa Wet Cave
Waikapalae Wet Cave
Na Pali Wilderness Area
Kilauea Lighthouse
Hole-in-the Mountain
Alakai Swamp Wilderness Area
Waialeale
Sleeping Giant
Fern Grotto
Kokee
Waimea Canyon
Menehune Ditch
Menehune Gardens
Olu Pua Botanical Gardens
Menehune Fishpond
First Sugar Mill
Prince Kuhio Birthplace
Spouting Horn
Captain Cook's Landing
Old Russian Fort

Hawaii (island)

Kamehameha Statue
Kamehameha Rock
Kohala Ditch Trail
Pololu Valley
Waipio Valley
Macadamia Nut Factory
Upper and Lower Hamakua Ditch
Parker Ranch Homestead
Puako Petroglyphs
Kaluakauka (The Doctor's Pit)
Laupahoehoe
Liliuokalani Gardens Park
Hilo Zoo
Kumukahi Lighthouse
Kaimu (Black Sand) Beach
Ancient Canoe Landing
1955 Lava Flow
Lava Tree Molds
Akaka Falls
Rainbow Falls
Boiling Pots
Hawaii Volcanoes National Park
Queen's Bath
Kilauea Crater
Mauna Kea and Astronomical Observatory
Mauna Loa Volcano
Punaluu Black Sand Beach
Mark Twain Monkey Pod Tree
Ancient Canoe Moorings
South Point
Hualalai
Hulihee Palace
Royal Slide
Captain Cook Monument
Kealakekua Bay
Kamehameha III Birthplace
Coffee Mill
Keei Battlefield
Painted Church
City of Refuge Nat'l Historic Park

Maui, Molokai, Lanai

Start of Aloha Week Outrigger Race
Kalaupapa Lighthouse
Palaau Lookout
Father Damien's Statue
Halawa Valley
Wailau Valley
Waikolu Valley
Kapuaiwa Coconut Grove
Fishponds
Sacred Kukui Grove
Keomoku Village
Hookio Gulch
Garden of the Gods
Kaunolu Village Nat'l Historic Landmark
Kahakuloa Village
Iao Needle
Kanda Gardens
Baldwin House
Lahaina: Hale Aloha Hale Paahao Largest Banyan Tree Pioneer Mill (1860)
Lahaina, Kaanapali and Pacific Railroad
Keanae Peninsula
Hanawai Falls
Kanaha Bird Sanctuary
Kula Botanical Gardens
Haleakala National Park
Polipoli Spring
Makee Sugar Mill (1878)
Kipahulu Mill (1890)
Queen Kaahumanu's Birthplace
Seven Sacred Pools
Wailua Falls
Huialoha Church

Scale bars

6 miles
8 kilometers
20 miles
30 kilometers

THE MILITARY

The military constitutes a major presence in Hawaii in terms of personnel, physical facilities and landholdings, contribution to the economy, and political and social relations. The Navy has been the dominant service ever since 1887, when the Hawaiian Kingdom first conceded the use of Pearl Harbor to the U.S. Navy. Today, in terms of personnel, the Air Force, Army, and Coast Guard are first in numbers, with the Air Force, Army, and Coast Guard following in that order. In 1971 there were 112,943 military personnel and dependents in the islands—a highly mobile and relatively young population (page 104).

Not included in this total are personnel of the Hawaii National Guard, under the State Department of Defense. In 1971 the personnel strength of the Hawaii Army National Guard was 2,941 and of the Hawaii Air National Guard, 1,569.

The military is a major owner and user of land in Hawaii (page 135). Twenty-six percent of the land area of Oahu is owned or leased by the military, 4 percent of the island of Hawaii, all of Kahoolawe, but less than one percent of the other islands. Most of these lands are used by the Army (71 percent) and Navy (25 percent).

Military expenditures make the largest single contribution to the State's economy (page 132). For the first half of 1971, appropriated fund expenditures amounted to $340.8 million. By service, the total spending for the first half of 1971 was as follows: Navy and Marine Corps, $166.8 million; Army, $105.9 million; Air Force, $60.6 million; Coast Guard, $6.5 million; and National Guard and Reserve Officer Training Corps, $1 million. About 37 percent of the total expended is for military payrolls, 37 percent of the total expended is for military payrolls, 37 percent for civilian payrolls, and 26 percent for local purchases.

Some 22,000 civilians are employed by the military in various technical trade, secretarial, and support jobs. The military is thus one of the largest single employers in the State and accounts for 66 percent of the civilians employed by the federal government in Hawaii (page 134).

As headquarters for all military operations in the Pacific, Hawaii retains considerable strategic importance. Its location on the western frontier of the United States and in the central Pacific remains a key factor in Hawaii's maintenance as a major base of operations.

Staff

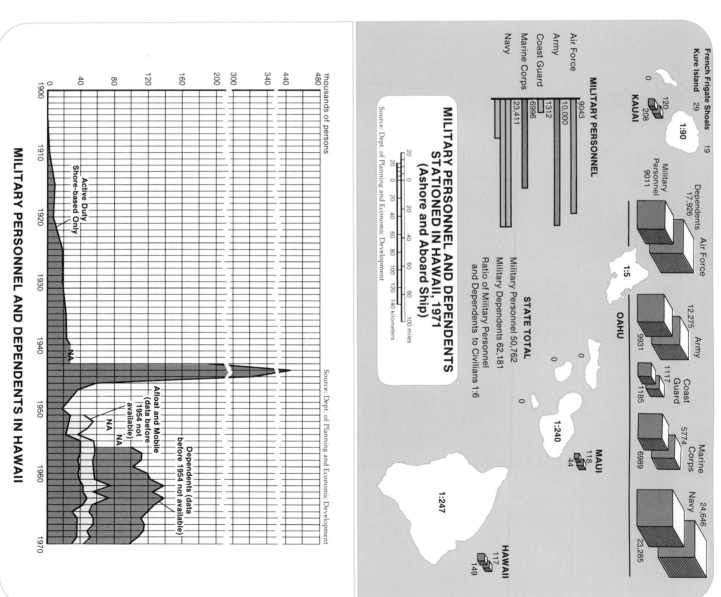

MILITARY PERSONNEL AND DEPENDENTS STATIONED IN HAWAII, 1971 (Ashore and Aboard Ship)

MILITARY PERSONNEL

	Military Personnel	Dependents
Air Force	9043	9011
Army	10,000	17,926
Coast Guard	1312	
Marine Corps	6996	
Navy	23,411	

French Frigate Shoals 29
Kure Island 19

KAUAI
120 / 208 — 1:90

OAHU
Air Force 9931 / 12,275
Army 9931 / 1185
Coast Guard 1117
1:5

MAUI 118 / 44 — 1:240

HAWAII 117 / 149 — 1:247

Marine Corps 5774 / 6989 — 1:247
Navy 24,646 / 23,285

STATE TOTAL
Military Personnel 50,762
Military Dependents 62,181
Ratio of Military Personnel and Dependents to Civilians 1:6

0 20 40 60 80 100 120 140 kilometers
0 20 40 60 80 100 miles

Source: Dept. of Planning and Economic Development

MILITARY PERSONNEL AND DEPENDENTS IN HAWAII

thousands of persons

0 40 80 120 160 200 300 340 440 480

Active Duty Shore-based Only

Afloat and Mobile (data before 1954 not available)

Dependents (data before 1954 not available)

NA

1900 1910 1920 1930 1940 1950 1960 1970

Source: Dept. of Planning and Economic Development

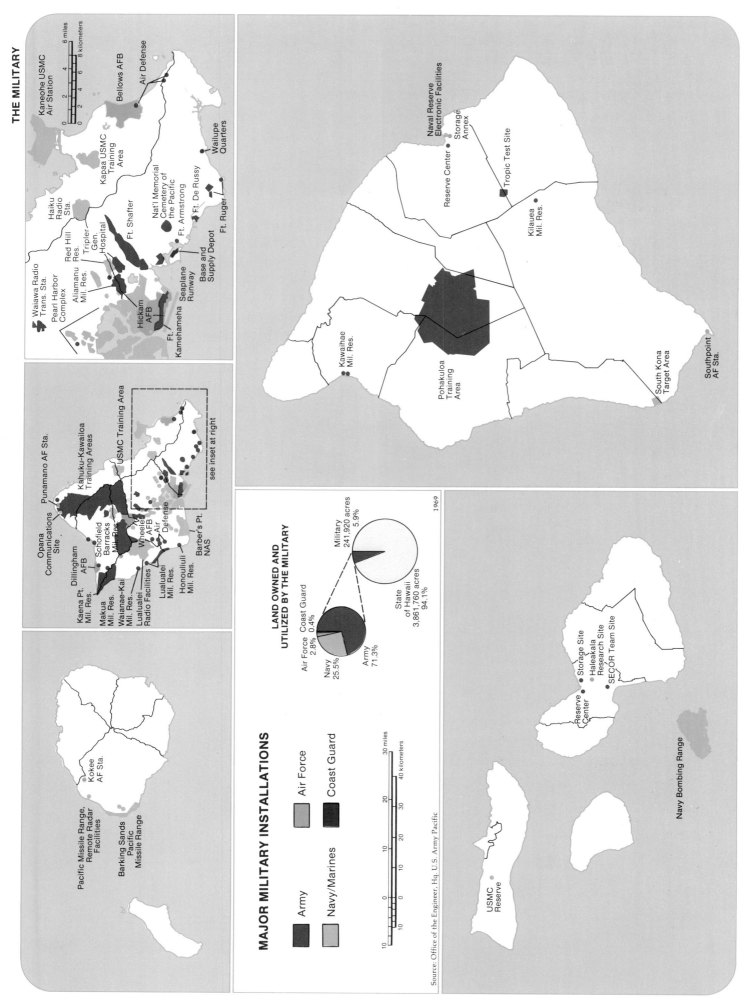

Kaneohe USMC Air Station

Bellows AFB

Air Defense

6 miles
8 kilometers

Kapaa USMC Training Area

Haiku Radio Sta.

Wailupe Quarters

Waiawa Radio Trans. Sta.

Pearl Harbor Complex

Red Hill Res.

Tripler Gen. Hospital

Ft. Shafter

Nat'l Memorial Cemetery of the Pacific

Ft. Armstrong

Ft. De Russy

Ft. Ruger

Aliamanu Mil. Res.

Hickam AFB

Ft. Kamehameha

Seaplane Runway

Base and Supply Depot

Naval Reserve Electronic Facilities

Reserve Center

Storage Annex

Tropic Test Site

Kilauea Mil. Res.

Kawaihae Mil. Res.

Pohakuloa Training Area

South Kona Target Area

Southpoint AF Sta.

Punamano AF Sta.

Opana Communications Site

Kahuku-Kawailoa Training Areas

USMC Training Area

see inset at right

Kaena Pt. Mil. Res.

Dillingham AFB

Schofield Barracks

Wheeler AFB

Air Defense

Makua Mil. Res.

Waianae-Kai Mil. Res.

Lualualei Mil. Res.

Lualualei Radio Facilities

Honouliuli Mil. Res.

Barber's Pt. NAS

Kokee AF Sta.

Pacific Missile Range, Remote Radar Facilities

Barking Sands Pacific Missile Range

MAJOR MILITARY INSTALLATIONS

- Army
- Navy/Marines
- Air Force
- Coast Guard

0   10   20   30 miles

10   0   10   20   30   40 kilometers

LAND OWNED AND UTILIZED BY THE MILITARY

Military 241,920 acres 5.9%

Air Force 2.8%   Coast Guard 0.4%

Navy 25.5%

Army 71.3%

State of Hawaii 3,861,760 acres 94.1%

1969

Source: Office of the Engineer, Hq. U.S. Army Pacific

Reserve Center

Storage Site

Haleakala Research Site

SECOR Team Site

USMC Reserve

Navy Bombing Range

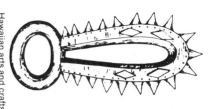

Hawaiian arts and crafts: open frame shark-tooth club.
Bishop Museum drawing from Te Rangi Hiroa (1964:452)

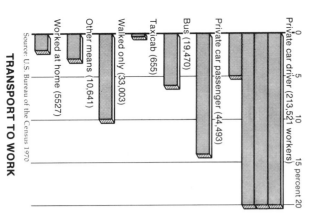

TRANSPORT TO WORK

Private car driver (213,521 workers)

Private car passenger (44,493)

Bus (19,470)

Taxicab (655)

Walked only (33,003)

Other means (10,641)

Worked at home (5527)

0   5   10   15   20 percent

Source: U.S. Bureau of the Census 1970

TRANSPORT

Hawaii's transportation network differs from that of the other 49 states in several ways. Most obviously, Hawaii is the only state that must rely almost entirely upon air and sea transport for exports and imports. The insular nature of the State also rules out any form of statewide land transportation. Hawaii's inability to be self-sufficient as an agricultural and/or industrial state creates an imbalance between westward and eastward trade, creating a major backhaul problem for both air and sea transport. This imbalance is reflected in freight rates and adds to the cost of living in the State; Honolulu ranks second among major American metropolitan areas with respect to cost of living.

The major cities in Hawaii are located near or on the water; as a result, streets are often not laid out in the north-south, east-west grid systems common on the mainland. Normally, streets are said to run *mauka* (toward the mountains) or *makai* (toward the sea), and between major physical and/or geographical areas (such as Diamond Head and Ewa in Honolulu). The major traffic corridor in Honolulu is parallel to the coast, with feeder lines running up into the valleys and hills. Honolulu is the only city in the State with a major mass transit system. This system has evolved from the horse-drawn cart of 1868 to the present diesel bus system. In 1971 the City bought its own fleet of buses and contracted with a private firm to run them. Up until that time the system was privately owned and operated. The fleet consists of 108 buses; it is expected that the number will increase to about 250. In addition, there are three other bus systems serving outlying areas from Honolulu.

Several plans for future transportation developments are under study or being implemented. These include a fixed-rail mass transit system running between Pearl City and Hawaii Kai in Honolulu, with buses serving on feeder routes, and a system

using hydrofoils and other watercraft on the ocean, streams, and canals to supplement and/or replace the proposed fixed-rail system. At the same time, it is expected that a ferry system will be operating to the other islands by 1973. This system, along with interisland transportation by air-cushion vehicles, hydrofoils, short and/or vertical take-off and landing craft (STOL, VTOL), and even surface-effect vehicles, is looked upon as a possible means of allowing people to live on neighbor islands and work on Oahu, thereby making unnecessary the further development of mass transit on Oahu.

Hawaii also differs from other states in the organization it has set up to deal with the development of transportation. When Hawaii became a state in 1959, the Department of Transportation was established to replace existing divisions and commissions in administering all major ports, airports, and highways. All major ports and all airports are owned and operated by the State through the Harbors and Airports division of the Department of Transportation, and the highways are under its control through the Highways Division. Through this organizational arrangement, Hawaii is better able to coordinate the financing and development of transportation facilities and services, and it has set a model to be emulated by other states.

Hawaii has had a total of seven railroads that have gained common carrier status—two each on Oahu, Hawaii, and Kauai, and one on Maui. The last of these went out of business in 1947, and today Hawaii is the only state in the Union without a common carrier railroad, although Hawaii does have some private freight transportation railroads which move bulk sugarcane and pineapple. In 1970 an amusement railroad connecting Lahaina and Kaanapali on the island of Maui was put into operation on abandoned tracks from an old sugarcane train. The train has six miles of track; it carried 114,000 passengers in 1970 and forecasts 145,000 for 1972. With these minor exceptions, all passengers and freight carried on land in Hawaii are served by some form of motor transport. Private cars are the major form of transportation for journeys to work and for general household activities.

In 1970 Hawaii had a total of 45,089 trucks registered to carry freight. The typical truck fleet is small: 35 percent of the fleets have only one truck, 48 percent have one to five, and only 24 percent have 20 trucks or more. The State Constitution of 1959 placed common and contract carriers under the economic regulatory control of the Public Utilities Commission. There were also, in 1970, 1,119 privately owned passenger buses distributed throughout Hawaii, most of them used as tour buses for visitors.

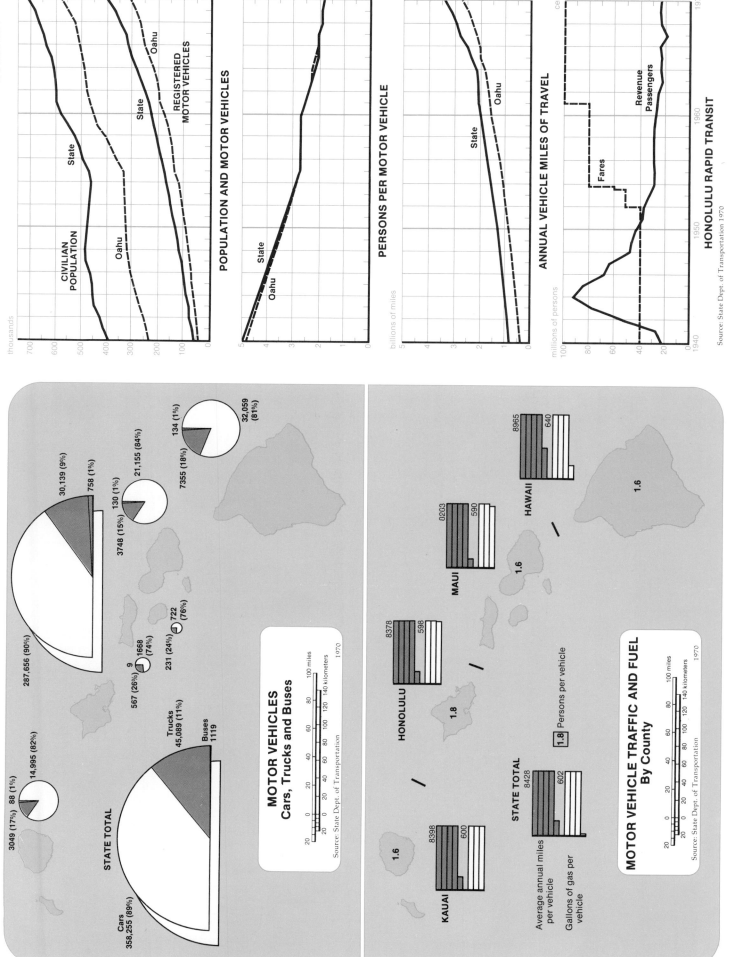

POPULATION AND MOTOR VEHICLES

CIVILIAN POPULATION — State, Oahu

REGISTERED MOTOR VEHICLES — State, Oahu

thousands

PERSONS PER MOTOR VEHICLE — State, Oahu

billions of miles

ANNUAL VEHICLE MILES OF TRAVEL — State, Oahu

HONOLULU RAPID TRANSIT

Fares — Revenue Passengers

cents

millions of persons

1940 1950 1960 1970

Source: State Dept. of Transportation 1970

MOTOR VEHICLES
Cars, Trucks and Buses

STATE TOTAL

Cars 358,255 (89%)
Trucks 45,089 (11%)
Buses 1119

3049 (17%) 88 (1%)
14,995 (82%)

567 (26%) 9
1668 (74%)

231 (24%) 722 (76%)

3748 (15%) 130 (1%)
21,155 (84%)

30,139 (9%) 758 (1%)
287,656 (90%)

7355 (18%) 134 (1%)
32,059 (81%)

Source: State Dept. of Transportation

MOTOR VEHICLE TRAFFIC AND FUEL
By County

STATE TOTAL
8428 602

KAUAI 8398 600 1.6

HONOLULU 8378 598 1.8

MAUI 9203 590 1.6

HAWAII 8965 640 1.6

Average annual miles per vehicle

Gallons of gas per vehicle

1.8 Persons per vehicle

Source: State Dept. of Transportation

Source: State Dept. of Transportation 1970

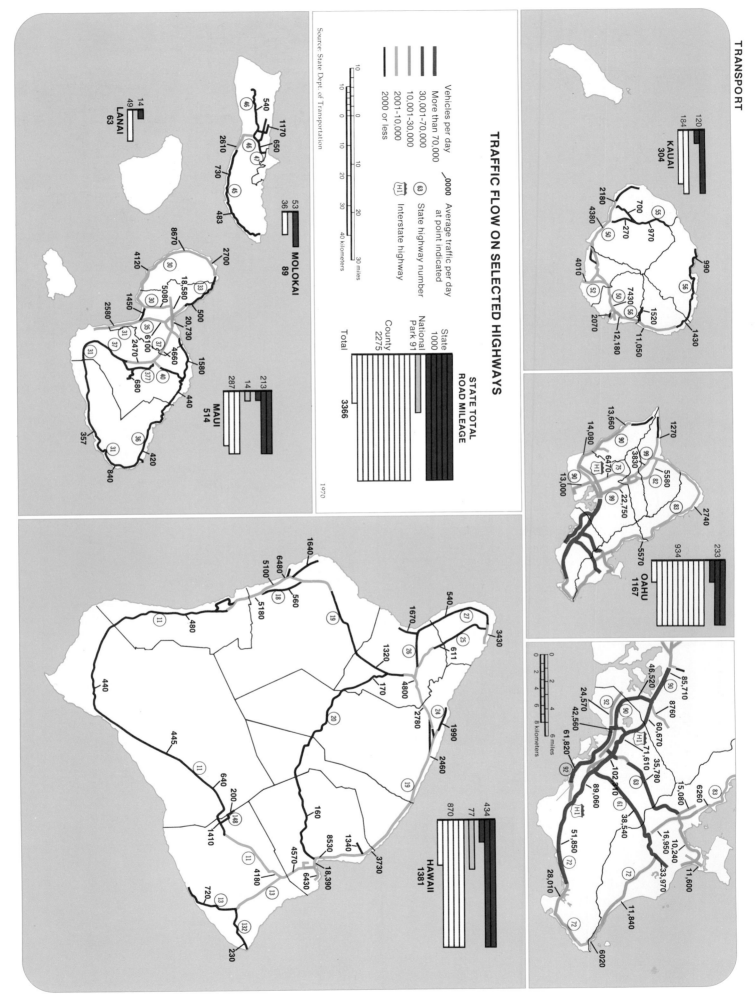

TRAFFIC FLOW ON SELECTED HIGHWAYS

Vehicles per day

More than 70,000
30,001–70,000
10,001–30,000
2001–10,000
2000 or less

_0000_ Average traffic per day
at point indicated

(63) State highway number

H1 Interstate highway

STATE TOTAL
ROAD MILEAGE

State 1000
National Park 91
County 2275
Total 3366

Source: State Dept. of Transportation

1970

KAUAI 304

MOLOKAI 89

LANAI 63

MAUI 514

OAHU 1167

HAWAII 1381

Hawaiian arts and crafts: stone club (pikoi).
Bishop Museum drawing from Te Rangi Hiroa (1964:458)

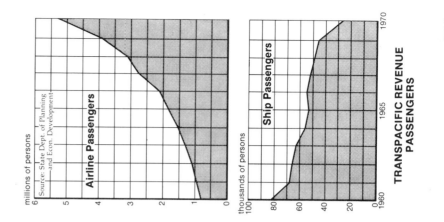

millions of persons

Source: State Dept. of Planning
and Econ. Development

Airline Passengers

6
5
4
3
2
1
0

thousands of persons

Ship Passengers

100
80
60
40
20
0

1960   1965   1970

TRANSPACIFIC REVENUE PASSENGERS

Overseas Shipping

The history of Hawaii and the development of shipping are inevitably connected. The arrival of the first people by canoe, the discovery of Hawaii by Captain Cook in 1778, the birth of today's dominant domestic carrier, Matson Lines, in 1882 all attest to this relationship. Today Hawaii is served by six scheduled ship operators, four of them American (American President Lines, Matson Lines, Pacific Far East Lines, and Seatrain Lines). While ships carried only 26,966 of the 5,270,242 passengers to and from Hawaii in 1970, shipping accounted for 7.8 million tons of freight. It is interesting to note that while the United States has only four passenger liners in service, all of them serve Hawaii on a regular basis. These vessels are the S.S. *President Wilson* and S.S. *President Cleveland* of American President Lines, and the S.S. *Mariposa* and S.S. *Monterey* of Pacific Far East Lines. The only other scheduled passenger line serving Hawaii is the British Pacific and Orient Lines. Two of P & O's vessels, the *Canberra* and the *Oriana*, each carry over 2,000 passengers while the combined capacity of the four American vessels is just over 1,600. In addition to these scheduled carriers, there are several nonscheduled carriers and five tug and barge services, three of which are based in Hawaii.

Interisland Shipping

Although there were many small operators providing interisland service, the first major carrier to provide such services was the Inter-Island Steam Navigation Company, which commenced operations in 1883. After this firm merged with the Wilder Steamship Company in 1905 it was the only interisland operator until 1935 when Young Brothers began its tug and barge service. Inter-Island was forced to cease operations in 1950, and, except for a two-year operation (1950-1952) by the Hilo Navigation Company using an old Inter-Island vessel, Young Brothers has been the only exclusively interisland water common carrier. Young Brothers provides a minimum of three round trips a week between Honolulu and Nawiliwili, Kaunakakai, Kahului, and Hilo, each round trip taking approximately two days. The only other significant carriers in the interisland trade are Matson Lines, carrying mainly transshipment cargo, and a tug and barge subsidiary of Dole Pineapple Company that mainly transports pineapple from Lanai to the cannery on Oahu. There has been no interisland water passenger service since 1949. In 1970 the water carriers accounted for 4.8 million tons of interisland cargo, compared with only 33,000 tons for air carriers.

Overseas Air Carriers

The first scheduled air carrier operations to Hawaii commenced in 1936, and until 1969 the Hawaii-Mainland trade was plied by a maximum of three scheduled carriers—Pan American World Airways, United Airlines, and Northwest Orient Airlines. The Pacific air route awards of 1969 added Western Airlines, Continental Airlines, Braniff Airlines, American Airlines, and Trans World Airlines to this list. In addition, Hawaii is served by ten foreign scheduled carriers and eight domestic nonscheduled carriers. For the first nine months of 1971 the scheduled domestic airlines had an average load factor of 45.8 percent on the Hawaiian run, with United and Pan American being the dominant carriers, accounting for almost 60 percent of the passengers carried (36.2 and 21.7 percent, respectively).

Interisland Air Transportation

Scheduled air carrier service between the islands of Hawaii was inaugurated in 1929 by Hawaiian Airlines, which continued as the only approved scheduled carrier until Trans-Pacific Airlines (now Aloha Airlines) was granted permission to serve in this capacity in 1949. Today these two airlines remain the only scheduled common carriers, although there are air taxi, air tour, and commuter air carriers that provide supplemental service. Due to the nature of these latter operations there is much movement into and out of business, and no meaningful statistics are available. In the 12-month period ending October 31, 1971, Hawaiian Airlines carried 57.3 percent of the passengers on scheduled flights and 85.7 percent of the air freight, while Aloha accounted for the remainder. All overseas and interisland traffic is under the regulatory control of the Federal Aviation Agency (FAA) and Civil Aeronautics Board (CAB).

H. D. B.

There are seven deep-water ports in Hawaii: the Navy's Pearl Harbor on Oahu, and six State-owned commercial ports (Honolulu on Oahu, Hilo and Kawaihae on Hawaii, Kahului on Maui, and Nawiliwili and Port Allen on Kauai). There are also six commercial barge harbors: Kailua on Hawaii, Hana on Maui, Kamalapau (Lanai's only port), and Kaunakakai (Molokai's major port), Haleolono (source of bulk sand and cinders), and Kalaupapa on Molokai. All deep-water ports have a basin depth of 35 feet, heavy lift capacities, and transit shed facilities, but only Honolulu and Hilo have facilities for containerized cargo. Honolulu is by far the most important commercial port, accounting for over 50 percent of the overseas and interisland cargo tonnage. In addition it has the most extensive facilities for providing supplies, heavy lift, containerized cargo, and repairs. For repairs, there is a commercial floating drydock with a deadweight capacity of 2,800 tons and a marine railway with a capacity of 1,450 tons. The Navy facilities at Pearl Harbor have been used by commercial vessels in exceptional circumstances. Barbers Point is a privately owned anchorage and barge landing used primarily by oil tankers servicing the nearby refinery.

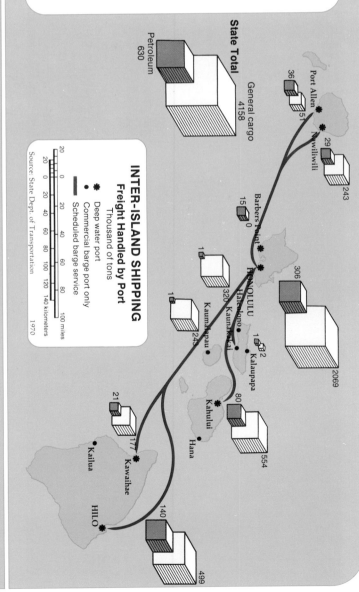

INTER-ISLAND SHIPPING
Freight Handled by Port
Thousand of tons

* Deep water port
● Commercial barge port only
— Scheduled barge service

Source: State Dept. of Transportation

State Total
Petroleum 630
General cargo 4158

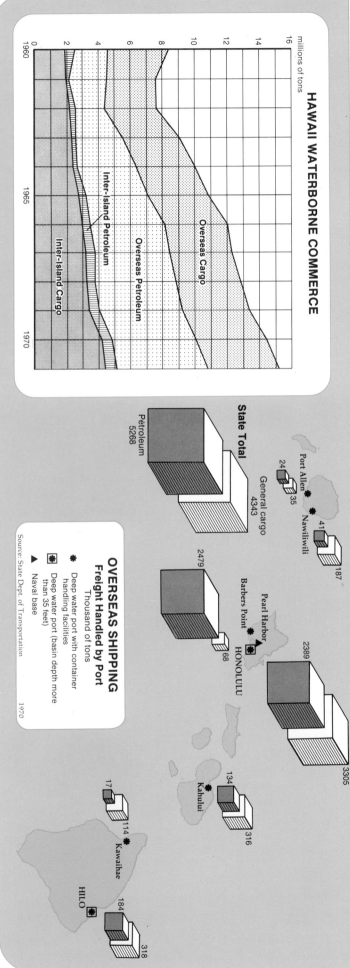

HAWAII WATERBORNE COMMERCE

millions of tons

Inter-island Cargo
Inter-island Petroleum
Overseas Petroleum
Overseas Cargo

Source: State Dept. of Transportation

State Total
Petroleum 5268
General cargo 4343

OVERSEAS SHIPPING
Freight Handled by Port
Thousand of tons

* Deep water port with container handling facilities
✴ Deep water port (basin depth more than 35 feet)
▲ Naval base

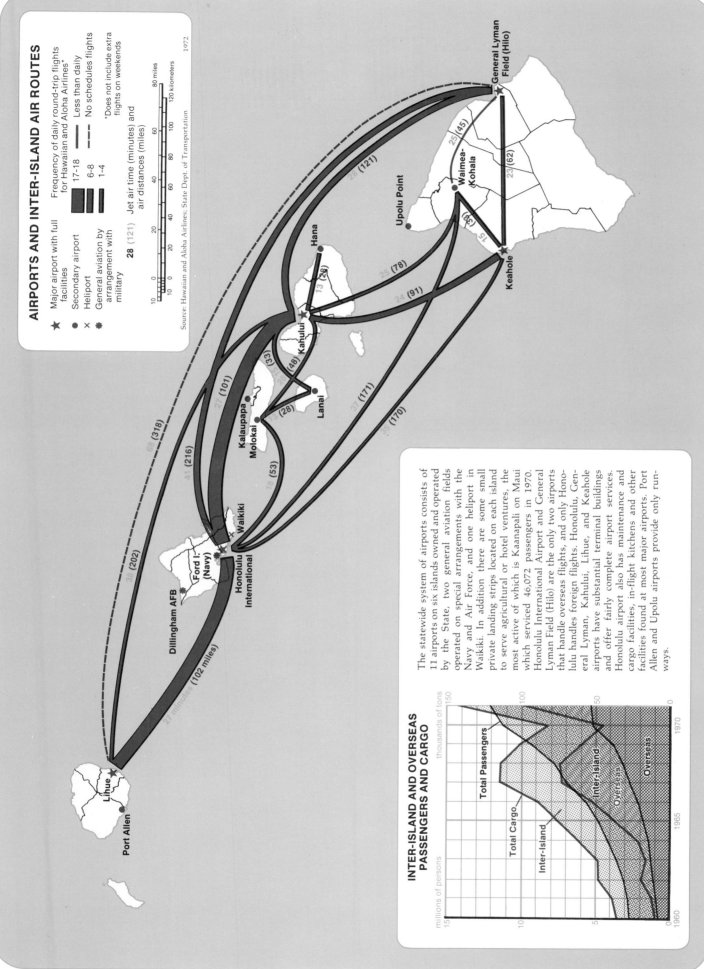

AIRPORTS AND INTER-ISLAND AIR ROUTES

Frequency of daily round-trip flights
for Hawaiian and Aloha Airlines*

17-18		Less than daily
6-8		No schedules flights
1-4		*Does not include extra flights on weekends

★ Major airport with full facilities
● Secondary airport
× Heliport
✳ General aviation by arrangement with military

28 (121) Jet air time (minutes) and air distances (miles)

Source: Hawaiian and Aloha Airlines; State Dept. of Transportation

1972

Port Allen

Lihue

38 (202)

68 (318)

21 minutes (102 miles)

41 (216)

Dillingham AFB

Ford I. (Navy)

Honolulu International

Waikiki

19 (53)

27 (101)

Kalaupapa
Molokai

13 (28)

Lanai

Kahului

13 (29)

Hana

(48)

35 (33)

24 (91)

25 (78)

37 (171)

35 (170)

Upolu Point

28 (121)

Waimea-Kohala

25 (45)

15 (?)

General Lyman Field (Hilo)

23 (62)

Keahole

Scale:
0 10 20 40 60 80 miles
0 10 20 40 60 80 100 120 kilometers

INTER-ISLAND AND OVERSEAS PASSENGERS AND CARGO

The statewide system of airports consists of 11 airports on six islands owned and operated by the State, two general aviation fields operated on special arrangements with the Navy and Air Force, and one heliport in Waikiki. In addition there are some small private landing strips located on each island to serve agricultural or hotel ventures, the most active of which is Kaanapali on Maui which serviced 46,072 passengers in 1970. Honolulu International Airport and General Lyman Field (Hilo) are the only two airports that handle overseas flights, and only Honolulu handles foreign flights. Honolulu, General Lyman, Kahului, Lihue, and Keahole airports have substantial terminal buildings and offer fairly complete airport services. Honolulu airport also has maintenance and cargo facilities, in-flight kitchens and other facilities found at most major airports. Port Allen and Upolu airports provide only runways.

thousands of tons
150
100
50
0

millions of persons
15
10
5
0

1960   1965   1970

Total Passengers

Total Cargo

Inter-Island

Overseas

Inter-Island

Overseas

173

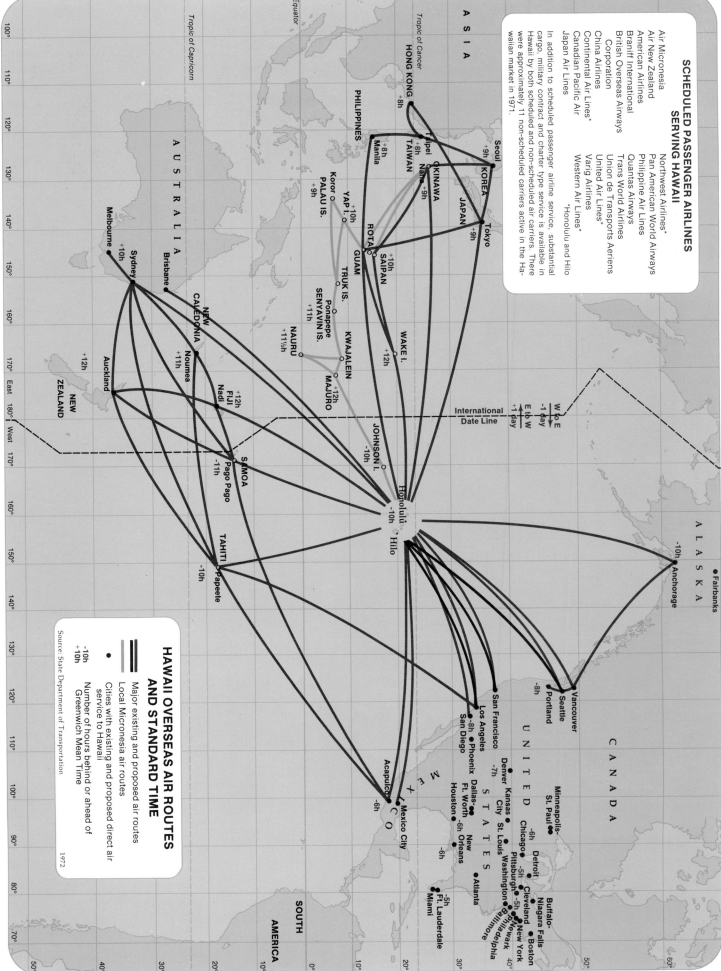

SCHEDULED PASSENGER AIRLINES
SERVING HAWAII

Air Micronesia	Northwest Airlines*
Air New Zealand	Pan American World Airways
American Airlines	Philippine Air Lines
Braniff International	Quantas Airways
British Overseas Airways	Trans World Airlines
Corporation	Union de Transports Aeriens
China Airlines	United Air Lines
Continental Air Lines*	Varig Airlines
Canadian Pacific Air	Western Air Lines*
Japan Air Lines	*Honolulu and Hilo

In addition to scheduled passenger airline service, substantial cargo, military contract and charter type service is available in Hawaii by both scheduled and non-scheduled air carriers. There were approximately 11 non-scheduled carriers active in the Hawaiian market in 1971.

HAWAII OVERSEAS AIR ROUTES
AND STANDARD TIME

Major existing and proposed air routes

Local Micronesia air routes

● Cities with existing and proposed direct air service to Hawaii

-10h Number of hours behind or ahead of
+10h Greenwich Mean Time

Source: State Department of Transportation

1972

Drawing by T. Stell Newman

Hawaiian arts and crafts: sennit (cooking fiber cordage).

COMMUNICATIONS

This discussion of communications is limited to the technological methods of transmitting information by mechanical or electronic means. Hawaii's isolated position in the Pacific Ocean and its insular nature give special importance to communications. The multi-ethnic composition of the population and the use of several languages give a distinctive character to local newspapers, books, and radio and television programs. Some special emergency communications systems are dealt with on page 196.

Because Hawaii is a group of separate islands more than 2,000 miles from any continent, postal services in and to the State face some unique problems. All mail between the islands is carried by air, and within each island by road. First-class mail from the U.S. mainland is airlifted on a space-available basis from major gateway cities, while second, third, and fourth class mail—"surface mail"—is carried by ship. Fifty-two percent of the mail originating in Honolulu is destined for delivery in the city itself, 38 percent for the U.S. mainland, 9 percent for post offices in the rest of Hawaii, and less than one percent for American Samoa, Guam, and foreign countries. Seventy percent of the incoming mail is addressed to Honolulu and 30 percent to the rest of the State.

The graph shows the weight of first-class and airmail passing annually through the State airport system. All overseas airmail passed through Honolulu International Airport until 1967, when direct flights to the U.S. mainland began from Hilo Airport. Hilo handled almost 228,000 pounds of mail in 1971 as compared with Honolulu's 42,569,000. A marked increase in overseas mail occurred between 1966 and 1969 while Honolulu served as transshipment point for Asian mails. Tokyo is now the transshipment point.

In 1971 Oahu had 22 radio stations, Hawaii 5, Kauai 2, and Maui 2 (page 178). Several new stations are expected to commence operation between 1972 and 1975. Nine radio stations carry programs for ethnic groups other than Caucasian (page 178).

Hawaii's first live television show was broadcast on December 2, 1952, by station KGMB. By 1955 all three major national networks were established in Hawaii—KGMB (CBS), KHON (NBC), and KHVH (ABC) (page 178). KHET, Hawaii's educational TV network station, made its debut in 1966 (page 178). KIKU, an independent station broadcasting 90 percent in Japanese, appeared in 1967. Most of its programs come from NET, Tokyo.

Television has become one of the chief communications media in the islands for news, educational and entertainment programs, and local and national commercial advertising. The 1970 census estimated that 94 percent, or 190,000 homes, had one or more television receivers. The proportions by county were as follows:

TV Receivers	Hawaii	Honolulu	Kauai	Maui
one	75%	70%	77%	74%
two or more	14	25	10	15
none	11	5	13	11

Educational and informational films in 16mm are distributed in Hawaii by three major film libraries. The State Department of Education library contains more than 12,500 films; the State Public Library, 1,150; and the University of Hawaii Library, 1,400 films. The Hawaii Visitors' Bureau, the State Department of Health, and some major airlines, tourist agencies, and local companies have small film collections relating directly to their own special activities. Military films are available at the audiovisual centers of the Army, Navy, Air Force, Tripler Army Medical Center, and Civil Defense. Since 1945, Hawaii has been the scene of an increasing number of commercial and independent motion picture productions. The Manoa Film Board, which represents the independent film-maker in Hawaii, held its first annual Hawaii Film Festival in January 1972, with entries from around the world.

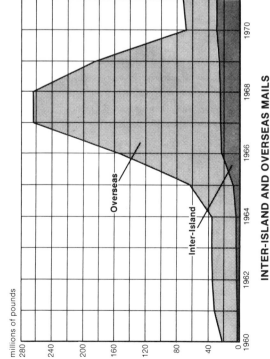

INTER-ISLAND AND OVERSEAS MAILS STATEWIDE AIRPORT SYSTEM

(Graph showing millions of pounds, years 1960–1970, with areas labeled "Overseas" and "Inter-Island")

PAID OVERSEAS TELEPHONE (VOICE) CALLS, 1971

Hawaii to/from Locality	Number of Calls
Mainland United States	4,306,400
Japan	64,300
Canada	60,000
Philippines	19,300
Guam	15,500
Alaska	14,000
Australia	8,000
Europe	6,500
Hong Kong	6,000
American Samoa	5,000
Korea	4,000
Other South Pacific Islands	3,700
Midway/Wake	3,400
New Zealand	3,100
Carribean	3,100
South Vietnam	2,000
Taiwan	2,000
Mexico	2,000
Southeast Asia	1,700
Fiji	900
Thailand	700
Tahiti	700
South America	600
Central America	300
Africa	120

Source: Hawaiian Telephone Company

Communications from the world's telecommunications systems are fed into a satellite earth station at Paumalu, Oahu, by way of the worldwide satellite communication system operated under INTELSAT, the International Telecommunications Satellite Consortium. This station complex, connected by microwave links to conventional networks serving Hawaii, has three antennas; it is one of the largest systems of its kind in the world. All forms of overseas commercial communications are processed through this station—telephone calls, telegraph messages, data, facsimile, and television.

The University of Hawaii is undertaking a demonstration program using satellite communication for education which it calls PEACESAT (Pan Pacific Education and Communication Experiments Using Satellites). The purpose of PEACESAT is to demonstrate the benefits of currently available telecommunication technology when applied specifically to the needs of sparsely populated, less industrialized areas. The project uses part of the ATS-1 satellite of the National Aeronautics and Space Administration whose coverage area includes most of the Pacific Basin. In April 1971, the first ground stations were successfully tested and utilized. The satellite network includes ground stations in Hawaii at the university's Manoa campus (Honolulu), Hawaii Community College (Hilo), and Maui Community College (Kahului). In the Pacific Basin there are ground stations at Wellington, New Zealand; Suva, Fiji; American Samoa; the Kingdom of Tonga; Papua and New Guinea; and Saipan, Trust Territory of the Pacific Islands. There is regular two-way exchange between these points by voice, facsimile, and slow-scan TV.

Another university project utilizing the satellite complex is an international educational computer system developed under a United States-Japan pact which will tie in with ALOHA, an educational computer system on the University of Hawaii Manoa campus designed to serve as an information retrieval center for the community colleges and interested institutions. The United States-Japan system design will include information stored in a central computer that will be available immediately and simultaneously to approximately 500 remote sites in developing countries around the Pacific.

S.E.S.

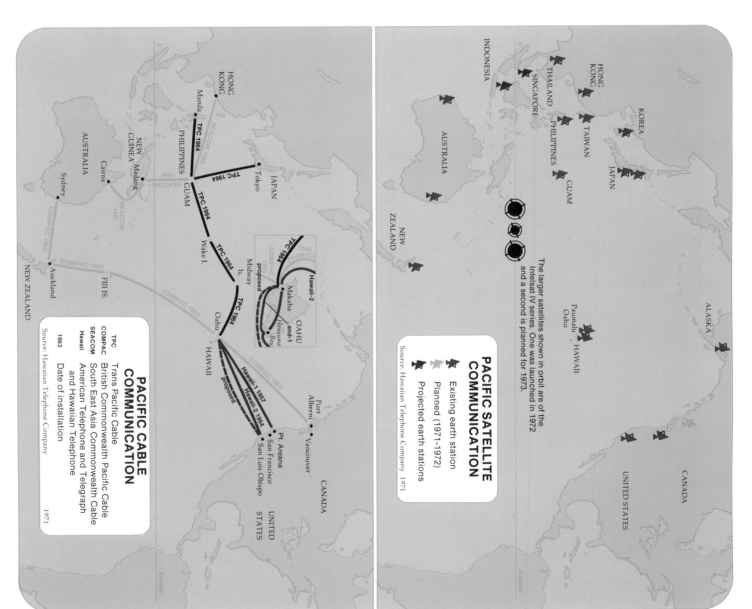

PACIFIC SATELLITE COMMUNICATION

The larger satellites shown in orbit are of the Intelsat IV series. One was launched in 1972 and a second is planned for 1973.

▲ Existing earth station
▲ Planned (1971–1972)
▲ Projected earth stations

Source: Hawaiian Telephone Company 1971

PACIFIC CABLE COMMUNICATION

TPC	Trans Pacific Cable
COMPAC	British Commonwealth Pacific Cable
SEACOM	South East Asia Commonwealth Cable
Hawaii	American Telephone and Telegraph and Hawaiian Telephone
1963	Date of installation

Source: Hawaiian Telephone Company 1971

There are three English-language daily newspapers in Hawaii and four foreign-language or bilingual dailies. Nine weekly newspapers are published in the State, including one each on Kauai, Maui, and Hawaii, and a group of six newspapers published by one firm for local communities on Oahu. There are also many specialized publications, among them a Catholic weekly, the university student newspaper which appears three times weekly, and a biweekly Japanese paper. Hawaii has three major book publishers—The University Press of Hawaii, Bishop Museum Press, and Island Heritage. In addition, twelve printing and distributing companies publish guidebooks and brochures for the local market. Some 13 mainland book publishers maintain sales offices in Honolulu. Twenty magazines are published locally, most of them trade or tourist oriented. The more general periodicals are *Honolulu*, *Hawaii Business and Industry*, and *Beacon Magazine*. *Sunset*, *TV Guide*, and the *Army Times* maintain editorial field offices in Honolulu. Scholarly journals with international circulations that are edited and published in Hawaii include *Journal of Medical Entomology*, *Pacific Science*, *Asian Perspectives*, *Oceanic Linguistics*, and *Philosophy East and West*; the *International Journal of Leprosy* is edited in Hawaii.

In 1880 Hawaii businessmen, frustrated by the slow communications systems of the time, invested in one of the first permanent telephone installations. By the end of 1881 the number of subscribers had tripled to 119, and by the end of 1882 there were 179. In 1972 there were 445,995 telephones installed in 91 percent of the residential dwellings in Hawaii. The first electronic switching went into service in 1972 as part of a program to replace obsolete equipment. Nearly twice as many telephones can be serviced with electronic switching; and twice as many telephones have been projected for 1980—813,000 in 96 percent of residences. Telephone communications within Hawaii are carried via the interisland microwave system, and outside the State by the Pacific cable system and the satellite system (page 176). Although the first Atlantic telegraph cable was laid in 1866, the first transoceanic voice link was not completed until 80 years later (Scotland to Newfoundland). The first Pacific voice cable to link North America with Asia went into service in 1964. The 6,200-mile voice bridge was from Tokyo to Honolulu to Oakland, California. Direct dialing between islands and to the U.S. mainland, Canada, and Mexico became effective in 1972.

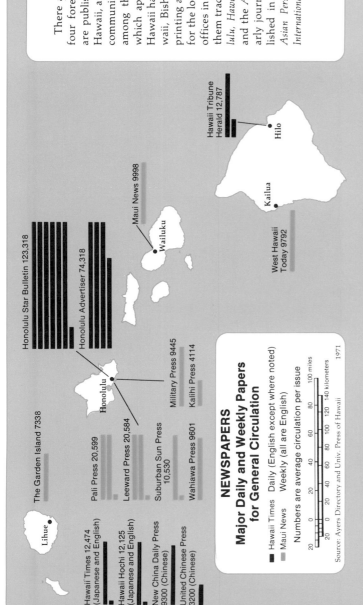

Lihue

Honolulu Star Bulletin 123,318

The Garden Island 7338

Honolulu Advertiser 74,318

Pali Press 20,599

Leeward Press 20,584

Suburban Sun Press 10,530

Military Press 9445

Kalihi Press 4114

Wahiawa Press 9601

Hawaii Times 12,474 (Japanese and English)

Hawaii Hochi 12,125 (Japanese and English)

New China Daily Press 9300 (Chinese)

United Chinese Press 3200 (Chinese)

Honolulu

Wailuku

Maui News 9998

Hilo

Kailua

Hawaii Tribune Herald 12,787

West Hawaii Today 9792

NEWSPAPERS
Major Daily and Weekly Papers
for General Circulation

Hawaii Times Daily (English except where noted)

Maui News Weekly (all are English)

Numbers are average circulation per issue

20 0 20 40 60 80 100 miles

20 0 20 40 60 80 100 120 140 kilometers

1971

Source: Ayers Directory and Univ. Press of Hawaii

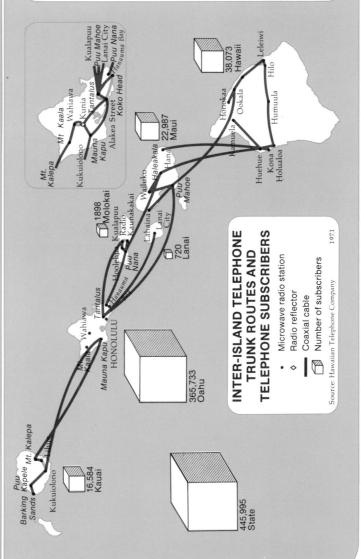

445,995 State

365,733 Oahu

16,584 Kauai

38,073 Hawaii

22,987 Maui

1898 Molokai

720 Lanai

HONOLULU

Puu Kapele Mt. Kalepa

Barking Sands

Kukuiolono

Lihue

Mauna Kapu

Mt. Kaala

Wahiawa

Tantalus

Kualapuu Molokai

Hoolehua

Puu Nana Radio

Hanauma Kaunakakai

Lahaina Lanai City

Wailuku Haleakala

Hana Puu Mahoe

Kona Huehue Holualoa

Kamuela Homokaa Ookala

Humuula Hilo Leleiwi

Hilo

Mt. Kalepa

Mt. Kaala Wahiawa

Kunia Tantalus

Kukuiolono Mauna Kapu

Alakea Street Koko Head

Kualapuu Puu Mahoe

Lanai City Puu Nana Hanauma Bay

Haleakala

Homokaa Kamuela Ookala

Huehue Kona Holualoa

Hilo Humuula Leleiwi

INTER-ISLAND TELEPHONE
TRUNK ROUTES AND
TELEPHONE SUBSCRIBERS

Microwave radio station

Radio reflector

Coaxial cable

Number of subscribers

1971

Source: Hawaiian Telephone Company

Programing for the three commercial television and three radio networks in Hawaii originates from network stations in Honolulu. Broadcasts are normally transmitted via commercial telephone circuits to network affiliate stations on the islands of Kauai, Maui, and Hawaii. Television programs from national networks are transmitted directly to Hawaii via satellite, or indirectly via videotape and film carried by commercial airlines. National radio hookups are made through commercial telephone channels. An exception is KIKU-TV in Honolulu whose main source of programing is NET, Tokyo, Japan. Ninety percent of its programs are Japanese, the remainder being Hawaiian, Filipino, Korean, and English. KIKU-TV programs are carried by telephone circuits to Kauai and Maui but with limited coverage. Special ethnic radio programs are broadcast weekly as shown in the following table (time given in hours per week).

Station	Japanese	Korean	Tagalog	Ilocano	German	Samoan
KUAI (Kauai)	–	–	6	–	–	–
KAIM (Oahu)	–	–	36	–	–	–
KCCN (Oahu)	–	–	–	10.5	1	–
KNDI (Oahu)	19	17	1	–	–	–
KORL (Oahu)	–	–	10.5	–	–	–
KZOO (Oahu)	133	–	–	–	–	–
KAHU (Oahu)	–	–	15	–	–	–
KHLO (Hawaii)	6	–	3	–	–	0.5
KKON (Hawaii)	7	–	1	–	–	–
Total Hours	165	17	72.5	10.5	1	0.5

RADIO AND TELEVISION

KMVI	Network television or radio station
KAIM	Independent radio station
550(5)	AM frequency in kilohertz and transmitter size in kilowatts
94.7(30)	FM frequency in megahertz and transmitter size in kilowatts
KAII 7TV (30,16)	TV channel and transmitter size in kilowatts (video, audio)

*University of Hawaii non-commercial station broadcasting popular music, drama and educational programs.
†Japanese language station.

Source: G. A. Bond, Univ. of Hawaii Dept. of Communications.

1972

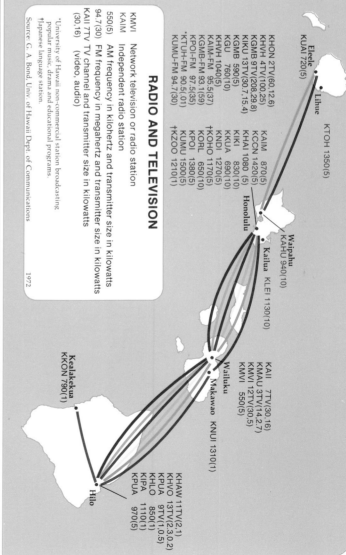

The Hawaii ETV network comprises two standard broadcast transmitters and eight translators—low-power "transmitters" which receive a broadcast signal, translate it to another channel, and transmit it to the immediate area. They also serve to relay the signal to subsequent translators. As established, the system is not capable of quality transmission, particularly at its extremities. As the signal is relayed, there is deterioration of signal strength. This is especially apparent on Kauai because of the long overwater path and the number of successive relays. However, the system was relatively inexpensive to install and to operate and maintain. It covers a wide area and under normal conditions gives a satisfactory black-and-white signal. Broadcasting time is approximately 75 hours per week and is devoted to three general program areas—in-school instruction, in-service teacher training, and public television. Instructional programs are broadcast from 8:30 A.M. to 4:30 P.M. Monday to Friday. The programs from 4:30 until 10:00 P.M. weekdays and from 3:00 to 10:00 P.M. Sundays are designed to instruct, enlighten, and entertain the general public. Most of the public television broadcasts are in color.

EDUCATIONAL TELEVISION TRANSMISSION NETWORK

●   Standard transmitter
∘   Translator
(5,25)   Transmitter wattage (audio, video)

Source: A. O. Peck, Hawaii ETV

1972

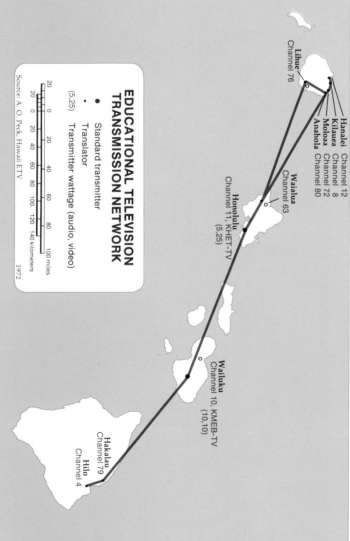

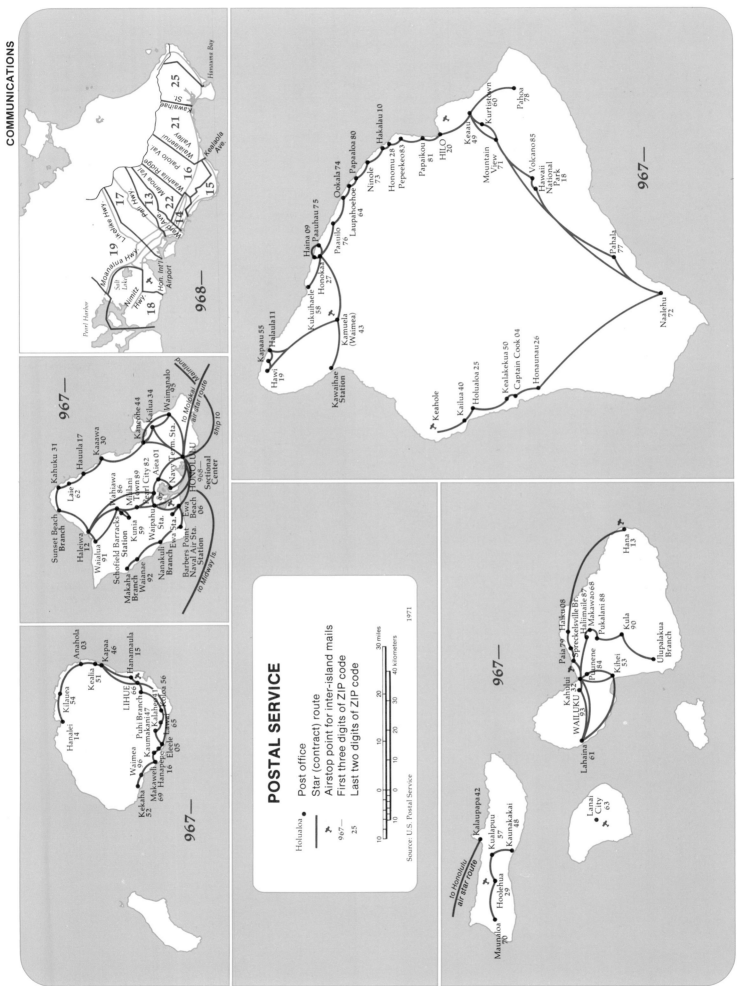

POSTAL SERVICE

Holualoa •	Post office
967—	Star (contract) route
⌁	Airstop point for inter-island mails
967—	First three digits of ZIP code
25	Last two digits of ZIP code

Source: U.S. Postal Service

1971

Hawaii (island):
Captain Cook 04 · Haina 09 · Hakalau 10 · Halaula 11 · Hawaii National Park 18 · Hawi 19 · HILO 20 · Holualoa 25 · Honaunau 26 · Honokaa 27 · Honomu 28 · Kailua 40 · Kamuela (Waimea) 43 · Keaau 49 · Kealakekua 50 · Kapaau 55 · Kukuihaele 58 · Kurtistown 60 · Laupahoehoe 64 · Mountain View 71 · Naalehu 72 · Ninole 73 · Ookala 74 · Paauilo 76 · Paauhau 75 · Pahala 77 · Pahoa 78 · Papaaloa 80 · Papaikou 81 · Pepeekeo 83 · Volcano 85 · Keahole · Kawaihae Station

Oahu:
Aiea 01 · Haleiwa 12 · Hauula 17 · Kaaawa 30 · Kahuku 31 · Kailua 34 · Kaneohe 44 · Kunia 59 · Laie 62 · Mililani Town 89 · Pearl City 82 · Sunset Beach Branch · Wahiawa 86 · Waialua 91 · Waianae 92 · Waimanalo 95 · Waipahu Sta. 97 · Ewa Beach 06 · HONOLULU Sectional Center 968 · Makaha Branch · Schofield Barracks Station · Navy Term. Sta. · Ewa Sta. · Barbers Point Naval Air Sta. · Nanakuli Branch

Kauai:
Anahola 03 · Eleele 16 · Hanalei 14 · Hanamaula 15 · Hanapepe 16 · Kalaheo 41 · Kapaa 46 · Kaumakani 47 · Kealia 51 · Kekaha 52 · Kilauea 54 · Koloa 56 · LIHUE 66 · Lawai 65 · Makaweli 69 · Puhi Branch · Waimea 96

Maui:
Haiku 08 · Haliimaile 87 · Hana 13 · Kahului 32 · Kihei 53 · Kula 90 · Lahaina 61 · Makawao 68 · Paia 79 · Puunene 84 · Pukalani 88 · Spreckelsville Br. · Ulupalakua Branch · WAILUKU 93

Molokai:
Hoolehua 29 · Kalaupapa 42 · Kaunakakai 48 · Kualapuu 57 · Maunaloa 70

Lanai:
Lanai City 63

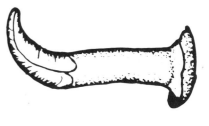

Bronze nail (A.D. 1550–1850) used in copper-sheathed boat hulls.

Drawing by T. Stell Newman

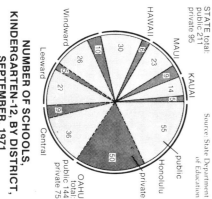

NUMBER OF SCHOOLS, KINDERGARTEN-12, BY DISTRICT, SEPTEMBER, 1971

Source: State Department of Education

STATE total: public 211 private 95

MAUI

KAUAI

HAWAII

Windward

Leeward

Central

OAHU total: public 144 private 75

Honolulu

public

private

30 18 23 9 14 5 26 5 9 27 36 50 55 10

EDUCATION

Hawaii's public schools are administered by the State Department of Education as a single educational unit. No other state in the Union has this feature. The principal executive body of the department is the Board of Education. Eight members are elected by the qualified voters of their respective school districts, and the other three are chosen at-large in the City and County of Honolulu. All serve for a term of four years. The board appoints a superintendent who supervises the seven school districts and their respective district superintendents. For each school district there is a School Advisory Council whose members are appointed by the governor.

The State Legislature exercises fiscal control over all public education. The school board has no taxing power, as do local school districts on the mainland. For the 1971-1972 school year, the department's operating budget was $161 million. Of this amount $16 million came from federal funds, $10 million from special monies, and the balance from state general funds. Capital improvement projects received $26 million.

Teachers' salary and classification schedules are established by law and are uniform throughout the State. One significant development in education is the collective bargaining law passed in 1970. For the first time, teachers in Hawaii have the means to negotiate directly in policy formation and decision making relative to pay increases, working conditions, and professional improvement. Grass-roots teacher involvement has become a reality.

In addition to elementary, intermediate, and high schools (page 181), the public system includes special schools to care for physically disabled and mentally retarded children. Illiteracy among native-born citizens is almost nonexistent. State law requires that all children between the ages of 6 and 18 must attend either a public or a private school.

Private schools are more prominent in Hawaii than in most states. From a few mission schools in the 1820s, the number has grown to the present 93 private schools, operated by both religious and nonreligious organizations. Most are small in enrollment, but a few are among the largest schools in Hawaii (page 181).

The University of Hawaii (page 182) was founded in 1907 as a federal land-grant institution specializing in agriculture and mechanic arts; it is tax supported by the State. Governance of the university is vested in a Board of Regents appointed by the governor, and its chief executive officer is the president, responsible for education and management.

The distinctive geographical setting of Hawaii has helped the university to achieve excellence in such sciences as geophysics, oceanography, marine biology, and astronomy. Hawaii's multiracial community and its ties with Asia and the Pacific have given added significance to the study of linguistics, genetics, philosophy, education, and ethnic relations.

In recent years the university has become increasingly responsive to the needs of students. Greater student participation with the university faculty and administration in judgments on major issues and policy recommendations is a generally accepted goal; students are already involved in curriculum building to achieve contemporary relevance and quality in teaching and research.

The university's role in helping to control environmental quality began to take shape in 1970 with the creation of the Environmental Center, and participation in programs concerning the future of the Pacific Basin has become more conspicuous today than ever before.

In 1964 the community colleges came under the jurisdiction of the University of Hawaii. They prepare high school graduates and others for employment in technical, vocational, and semi-professional occupations. The colleges also offer lower-division and preprofessional courses which are generally honored by the Manoa and Hilo campuses of the university. The 1970s are seen as the era of universal post-secondary education, and the community colleges offer increased opportunity to the citizens of Hawaii.

The East-West Center was established by Congress in 1960; it is a joint project of the U.S. Department of State and the University of Hawaii. Its goal is to promote better understanding and relations among the peoples of Asia, the Pacific, and the United States through open interchange of ideas in cultural and technological fields. The center's five institutes focus on problem-oriented programs covering East-West communications, culture learning, food, population, and technology.

Five private colleges offer university preparatory, liberal arts, and vocational programs leading toward associate and degree diplomas.

D.S.N.

PUBLIC AND PRIVATE SCHOOLS

Heeia Public school
Aloha Private school

Enrollment

• ▲	5-100	
• ▲	101-300	
● ▲	301-500	
■	501-1000	
■	1001-2000	
★	2001-3582	

● Elementary (kindergarten-6)

● Elementary and intermediate (kindergarten-7, 8 or 9)

● Intermediate (7-9)

● Intermediate and high school (7-12)

○ High school (10-12 or 9-12)

● Elementary through high school (kindergarten-12)

Source: State Department of Education

1971

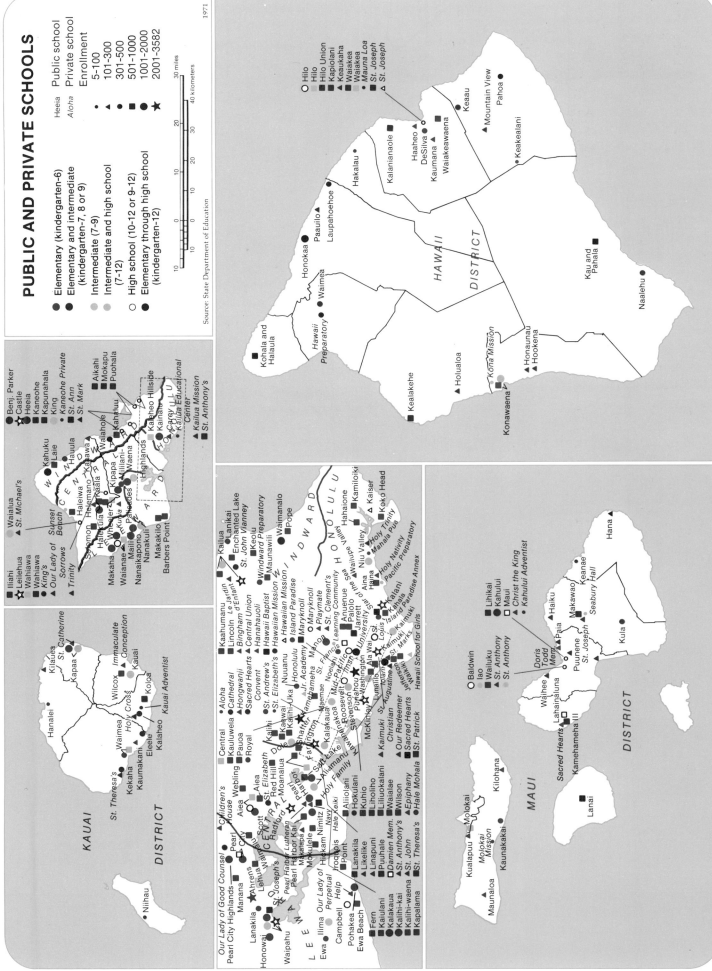

KAUAI DISTRICT

Hanalei
Kilauea • *St. Catherine*
Kapaa *Immaculate*
Kauai *Conception*
Wilcox
Waimea • *Holy Cross*
Kekaha *Koloa*
Kaumakani Kalaheo • *Kauai Adventist*
Eleele
St. Theresa's

Niihau

HAWAII DISTRICT

○ Hilo
● Hilo Union ▲ Hilo
■ Kapiolani ▲ Keaukaha
■ Waiakea ▲ Waiakea
▲ St. Joseph *Mauna Loa*
★ St. Joseph

Honokaa ▲
Waimea ● Laupahoehoe ■
Kalanianaole ●
Haaheo ▲
Hawaii ● Kaumana ▲ DeSilva ■
Preparatory Waiakeawaena ▲
Kohala and Halaula ■
Hakalau ▲
Mountain View ▲ Keaau ■
Pahoa ●
Keakealani ▲

Kona Mission Honaunau ▲
Holualoa ▲ Hookena ▲
Kealakehe ■
Konawaena ■
Naalehu •
Kau and Pahala ■

MAUI DISTRICT

○ Baldwin
Iao ■ Wailuku ● Lihikai ■
▲ St. Anthony ● Kahului
▲ St. Anthony □ Maui
Christ the King
Kahului Adventist

Waihee ▲
Lahainaluna ● *Doris Todd Mem.*
Sacred Hearts ▲ Puunene •
Kamehameha III ■ *St. Joseph*

Haiku ▲
Makawao ▲ Keanae ▲
Paia ● *Seabury Hall*
Kula •
Hana ▲

Molokai
Kualapuu ▲
Molokai Mission ▲
Kaunakakai ■
Kilohana ■

Maunaloa ▲
Lanai ■

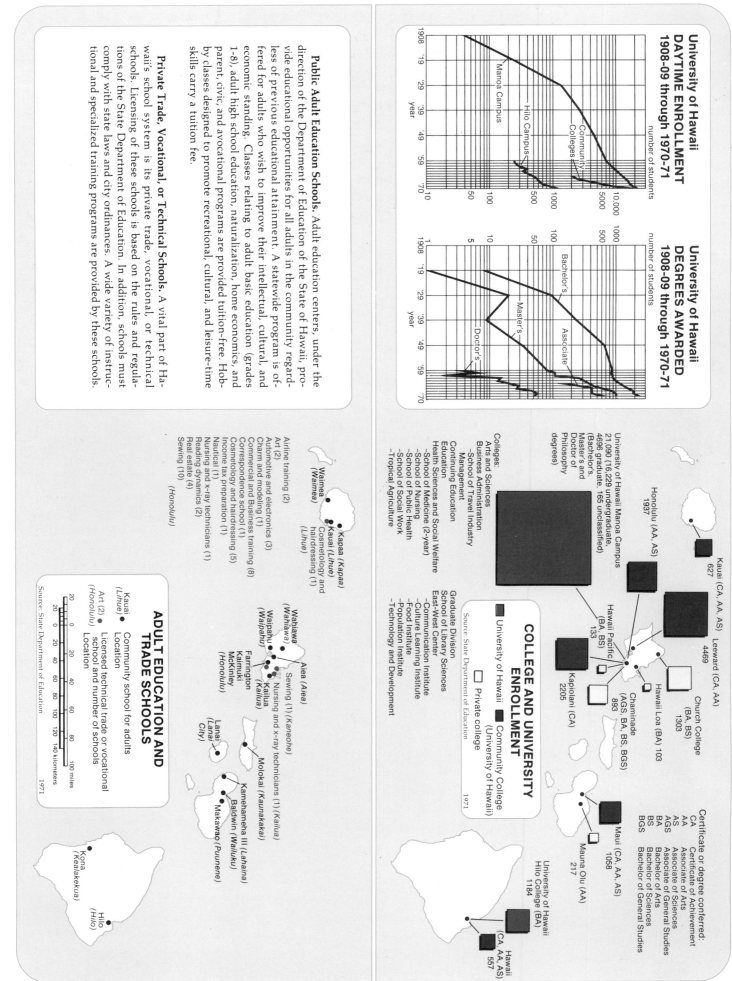

University of Hawaii
DAYTIME ENROLLMENT
1908-09 through 1970-71

number of students

Manoa Campus

Community Colleges

Hilo Campus

year

University of Hawaii
DEGREES AWARDED
1908-09 through 1970-71

number of students

Bachelor's

Master's

Associate

Doctor's

year

Public Adult Education Schools.
Adult education centers, under the direction of the Department of Education of the State of Hawaii, provide educational opportunities for all adults in the community regardless of previous educational attainment. A statewide program is offered for adults who wish to improve their intellectual, cultural, and economic standing. Classes relating to adult basic education (grades 1-8), adult high school education, naturalization, home economics, and parent, civic, and avocational programs are provided tuition-free. Hobby classes designed to promote recreational, cultural, and leisure-time skills carry a tuition fee.

Private Trade, Vocational, or Technical Schools.
A vital part of Hawaii's school system is its private trade, vocational, or technical schools. Licensing of these schools is based on the rules and regulations of the State Department of Education. In addition, schools must comply with state laws and city ordinances. A wide variety of instructional and specialized training programs are provided by these schools.

Waimea
(Waimea)

Kapaa *(Kapaa)*

Kauai *(Lihue)*
Cosmetology and hairdressing (1)
(Lihue)

Airline training (2)
Art (2)
Automotive and electronics (3)
Charm and modeling (1)
Commercial and Business training (8)
Correspondence school (1)
Cosmetology and hairdressing (5)
Income tax preparation (1)
Nautical (1)
Nursing and x-ray technicians (2)
Real estate (4)
Reading dynamics (2)
Sewing (10)

(Honolulu)

Wahiawa
(Wahiawa)

Waipahu
(Waipahu)

Farrington
Kaimuki
McKinley
(Honolulu)

Aiea *(Aiea)*

Kailua
(Kailua)

Sewing (1) *(Kaneohe)*

Nursing and x-ray technicians (1) *(Kailua)*

Lanai
(Lanai City)

Molokai *(Kaunakakai)*

Kamehameha III *(Lahaina)*

Baldwin *(Wailuku)*

Makawao *(Puunene)*

Kona
(Kealakekua)

Hilo
(Hilo)

ADULT EDUCATION AND
TRADE SCHOOLS

Kauai
(Lihue) ●

Art (2) ●
(Honolulu)

● Community school for adults Location

■ Licensed technical trade or vocational school and number of schools Location

Source: State Department of Education 1971

20 0 20 40 60 80 100 120 140 kilometers
20 0 20 40 60 80 100 miles

University of Hawaii Manoa Campus
21,090 (16,229 undergraduate, 4696 graduate, 165 unclassified)

Honolulu (AA, AS) 1937

Colleges:
Arts and Sciences
Business Administration
Management
-School of Travel Industry
Continuing Education
Education
Health Sciences and Social Welfare
-School of Medicine
-School of Nursing
-School of Public Health
-School of Social Work
-Tropical Agriculture

Graduate Division
School of Library Sciences
East-West Center
-Communication Institute
-Culture Learning Institute
-Food Institute
-Population Institute
-Technology and Development

Source: State Department of Education 1971

COLLEGE AND UNIVERSITY
ENROLLMENT

■ University of Hawaii
(University of Hawaii)

■ Community College
(University of Hawaii)

□ Private college

Certificate or degree conferred:
CA Certificate of Achievement
AA Associate of Arts
AS Associate of Sciences
AGS Associate of General Studies
BA Bachelor of Arts
BS Bachelor of Sciences
BGS Bachelor of General Studies

Kauai (CA, AA, AS) 627

Leeward (CA, AA, AS) 4469

Church College (BA, BS) 1303

Hawaii Loa (BA) 103

Hawaii Pacific (BA, BS) 133

Chaminade (AGS, BA, BS, BGS) 893

Kapiolani (CA) 2205

Maui (CA, AA, AS) 1058

Mauna Olu (AA) 217

University of Hawaii Hilo College (BA) 1184

Hawaii (CA, AA, AS) 557

Scientific Resources

Hawaii has been fortunate in its share of that most valuable scientific resource—capable and experienced people. The social and economic attainments of the last hundred years owe much to the work of scientists in fields such as agriculture, geology, medicine, education, and engineering. Successful sugar and pineapple cultivation, for example, depend in part on ingenious irrigation systems, hybrid plants, and locally adapted field techniques developed through scientific experiments.

Many of Hawaii's key scientific organizations are of long standing: today's Medical Services Division and the Statistics Office of the State Department of Health began, respectively, in 1850 and 1895; Queen's Medical Center Laboratory in 1859; the Bernice P. Bishop Museum in 1889; the entomology branch of the State Department of Agriculture in 1893; and the Hawaiian Sugar Planters' Association Experiment Station in 1895. The University of Hawaii was founded in 1907. The first of several university research institutes were the Hawaii Institute of Marine Biology, established in 1922, and the Hawaii Agricultural Experiment Station in 1929.

Most of the present scientific organizations date from the 1950s and 1960s, with the greatest growth occurring since 1965. In 1971 there were 5,593 people directly employed in professional and technical jobs in 303 organizations. Almost half of this work is in private industry, and one-third in government agencies such as the local federal offices of the National Aeronautics and Space Administration, Bureau of Commercial Fisheries, Soil Conservation Service, and National Weather Bureau, and in agencies of the State and Counties. Of special significance are the growth of companies in computer science and in research and development which have contributed toward modernization and expansion of the tourist industry, urban planning, social services, communications, and many other activities.

Hawaii has a role in space exploration through the Kokee Tracking Station on Kauai, and in space communications research with projects on Oahu, Maui, and Hawaii. Astronomy has become an important science in Hawaii, partly because of the latitude of the islands and the availability of sites for delicate instruments in clear mountain air. The University of Hawaii observatories atop Haleakala and Mauna Kea are to be joined by another observatory on Mauna Kea, a project of the French government.

Hawaii affords special opportunities for the study of island and ocean environments. Ecological projects sponsored by the U.S. National Committee for the International Biological Program, and oceanographic studies by the Oceanic Institute and the Hawaii Institute of Geophysics are current examples.

Among social scientists, Hawaii holds special interest for research in ethnology, archaeology, sociology, languages, religions, and the arts.

Local science also benefits each year from visiting scientists who come as participants to professional meetings, as consultants to industry and government, or as visiting faculty to the University of Hawaii. Professional associations in Hawaii, of which there were 45 in 1971, cater to a wide range of scientific interests. Approximately half of these associations are local branches of national societies. Other important scientific resources are the scientific collections of libraries, data banks maintained by research agencies, and special laboratories and equipment. Twenty-four public, university, and special libraries have specialized scientific collections (page 195).

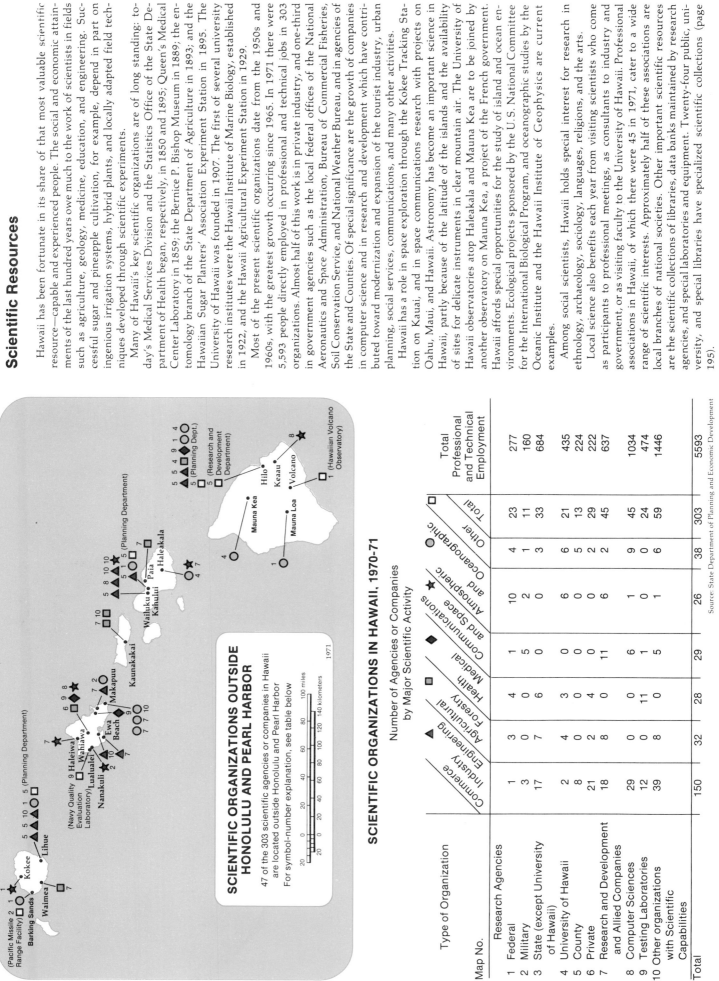

SCIENTIFIC ORGANIZATIONS OUTSIDE HONOLULU AND PEARL HARBOR

47 of the 303 scientific agencies or companies in Hawaii are located outside Honolulu and Pearl Harbor

For symbol-number explanation, see table below

1971

SCIENTIFIC ORGANIZATIONS IN HAWAII, 1970-71

Number of Agencies or Companies by Major Scientific Activity

Type of Organization / Map No.	Commerce Industry	Engineering	Agricultural Forestry	Health Medical	Communications	Atmospheric and Space	Oceanographic	Other	Total	Total Professional and Technical Employment
Research Agencies										
1 Federal	1	3	4	1		10	4		23	277
2 Military	3	0	0	5		2	1		11	160
3 State (except University of Hawaii)	17	7	6	0		0	3		33	684
4 University of Hawaii	2	4	3	0		6	6		21	435
5 County	8	0	0	0		0	5		13	224
6 Private	21	2	4	0		0	2		29	222
7 Research and Development and Allied Companies	18	8	0	11		6	2		45	637
8 Computer Sciences	29	0	0	6		1	9		45	1034
9 Testing Laboratories	12	0	11	1		0	0		24	474
10 Other organizations with Scientific Capabilities	39	8	0	5		1	6		59	1446
Total	150	32	28	29		26	38		303	5593

Source: State Department of Planning and Economic Development

HEALTH

By modern standards, the people of Hawaii are healthy. The health of the community compares favorably with the rest of the United States, as judged from both vital statistics (page 184) and from sickness and injury statistics (page 184). Life expectancy at birth in Hawaii averages slightly above the national figures of 74 years for women and 66.6 for men. Hawaii probably enjoys the most advanced health conditions in the tropical world and among the best in the Pacific. One measure is provided by the international comparison of infant mortality rates (page 184).

The current situation has been achieved over a long period of time through improvements in diet, income, housing, hygiene, education, medical technology and services, and many other factors. For instance, strict animal quarantine rules have helped Hawaii remain one of the few places in the world that is free of rabies. Community immunization programs keep diphtheria, smallpox, pertussis, tetanus, poliomyelitis, and measles in check. Once a serious concern, leprosy averaged only 15 new cases per year from 1965 to 1970, but an increase to 30 new cases was noted in 1971. An average of 77 percent of these new cases were among foreign-born immigrants. Some communicable diseases have been more persistent. Each year more than 300 persons in the islands are known to develop active tuberculosis, but 70 percent of them are foreign-born immigrants. Gonorrhea is increasing rapidly: 569 cases were reported in 1965 and 1,976 in 1970. The most prevalent chronic disease in Hawaii is dental decay, and the attack rate is among the highest in the nation. Children 14 years of age in Hawaii have an average of 11.4 teeth attacked by decay, while the average for the nation among children of this age is estimated as 8.

The chief risks to health in Hawaii today stem largely from the culturally modified environment and from various forms of behavior that expose people to potential health dangers. Motor vehicle accidents are the chief cause of death and injury to those under 35. Increasing alcohol and drug addiction, venereal disease, and mental illness involve complex interactions among people, their life-styles, and the environment. The living conditions in some parts of the State are better than in others (page 185). In many rural areas on all islands, poor housing, unsafe water and inadequate sewage and garbage disposal (page 198) add to the risk of tuberculosis, scarlet fever, hepatitis, and dysentery. In Honolulu people are beginning to experience the health risks associated with modern cities—excessive noise, air pollution (page 61), and congested and otherwise inadequate living space.

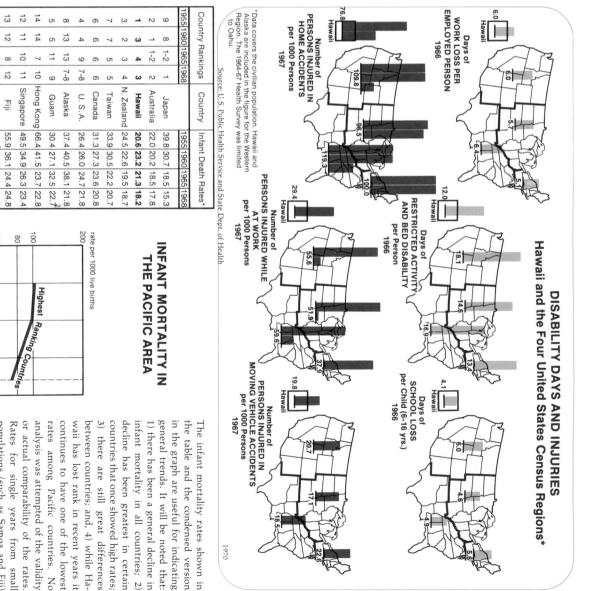

DISABILITY DAYS AND INJURIES
Hawaii and the Four United States Census Regions*

Days of WORK LOSS PER EMPLOYED PERSON 1966 — 6.0 Hawaii; 6.0; 5.7; 6.4; 5.1

Number of PERSONS INJURED IN HOME ACCIDENTS per 1000 Persons 1967 — 76.8 Hawaii; 109.8; 96.5; 119.3; 100.0

Days of RESTRICTED ACTIVITY AND BED DISABILITY per Person 1966 — 12.0 Hawaii; 18.1; 14.6; 16.9; 13.4

Number of PERSONS INJURED AT WORK per 1000 Persons 1967 — 29.4 Hawaii; 55.6; 51.9; 59.6; 37.9

Days of SCHOOL LOSS per Child (6–16 yrs.) 1966 — 4.1 Hawaii; 6.0; 4.6; 4.9; 5.6

Number of PERSONS INJURED IN MOVING VEHICLE ACCIDENTS per 1000 Persons 1967 — 19.8 Hawaii; 20.7; 17.1; 22.6; 18.5

1970

*Data covers the civilian population. Hawaii and Alaska are included in the figure for the Western Region. The 1964-67 Health Survey was limited to Oahu.

Source: U.S. Public Health Service and State Dept. of Health

Country Rankings				Country	Infant Death Rates*			
1955	1960	1965	1968		1955	1960	1965	1968
9	8	1-2	1	Japan	39.8	30.7	18.5	15.3
2	1	1-2	2	Australia	22.0	20.2	18.5	17.8
1	3	4	3	Hawaii	20.6	23.2	21.3	18.2
3	2	3	4	N. Zealand	24.5	22.6	19.5	18.7
7	7	5	5	Taiwan	33.9	30.5	22.2	20.7
6	6	6	6	Canada	31.3	27.3	23.6	20.8
4	4	9	7-8	U.S.A.	26.4	26.0	24.7	21.8
8	13	13	7-8	Alaska	37.4	40.5	38.1	21.8
5	5	11	9	Guam	30.4	27.1	32.5	22.7
14	14	7	10	Hong Kong	66.4	41.5	23.7	22.8
12	11	10	11	Singapore	49.5	34.9	26.3	23.4
13	12	8	12	Fiji	55.9	36.1	24.4	24.8
10	—	15	13	W. Samoa	41.3	—	42.5	26.3
11	9	12	14	Am. Samoa	44.5	31.5	33.6	28.6
—	10	14	15	Trust Terr. Pacific Is.	—	32.4	43.5	32.6
15	15	16	16	Malaysia	78.4	68.9	50.0	42.2
16	17	17	17	Mexico	83.3	74.2	60.7	64.2
17	16	18	18	Philippines	84.3	73.1	72.9	70.1
18	18	19	19	Colombia	104.2	99.8	82.4	74.9

* Rate of infant deaths under one year per 1000 live births
1 1956   2 1967

INFANT MORTALITY IN THE PACIFIC AREA

rate per 1000 live births

Highest Ranking Countries

Medium Ranking Countries

Hawaii

Lowest Ranking Countries

1950 1955 1960 1965 1968

The infant mortality rates shown in the table and the condensed version in the graph are useful for indicating general trends. It will be noted that: 1) there has been a general decline in infant mortality in all countries; 2) decline has been greatest in certain countries that once showed high rates; 3) there are still great differences between countries; and, 4) while Hawaii has lost rank in recent years it continues to have one of the lowest rates among Pacific countries. No analysis was attempted of the validity or actual comparability of the rates. Rates for single years from small populations (such as Samoa and Fiji) tend to be less reliable as indicators of average conditions than rates from large populations (such as the United States and Japan). Rate reliability is also influenced by such things as the completeness of reporting of infant deaths. Comparability of rates between countries may be affected, for example, by differences in the definition of an infant death versus a fetal death.

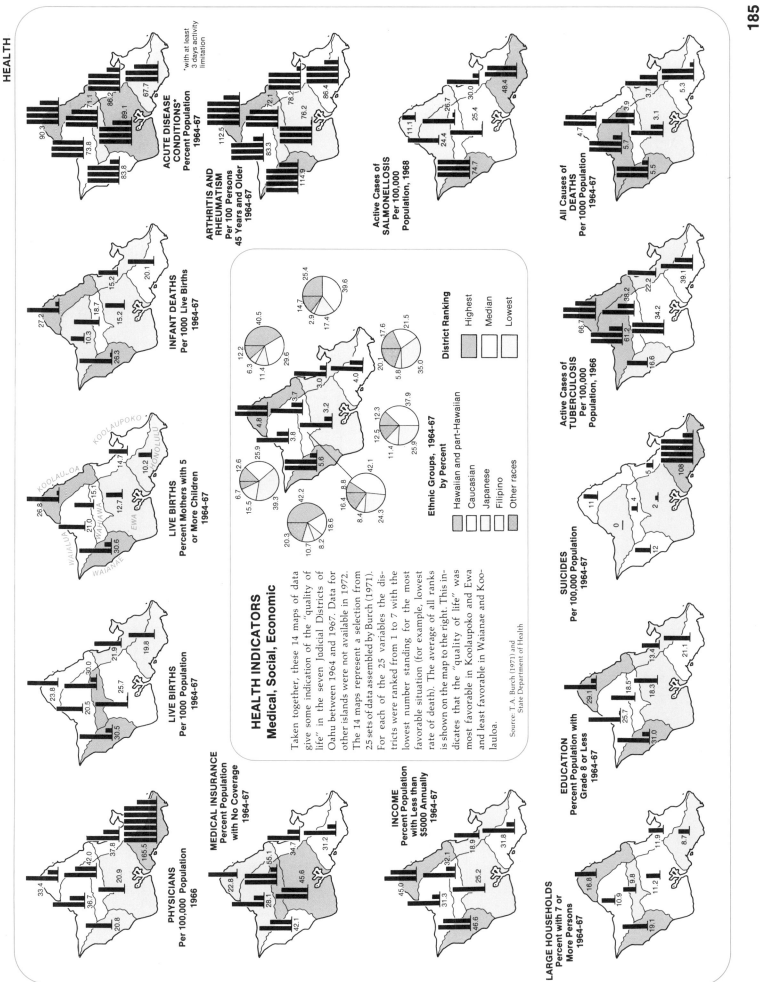

*with at least 3 days activity limitation

ACUTE DISEASE CONDITIONS*
Percent Population
1964-67

90.3 73.8 83.8 71.1 86.2 89.1 67.7

ARTHRITIS AND RHEUMATISM
Per 100 Persons
45 Years and Older
1964-67

112.5 83.3 114.9 72.1 78.2 76.2 86.4

Active Cases of SALMONELLOSIS
Per 100,000
Population, 1968

11.1 24.4 74.7 26.7 30.0 25.4 48.4

All Causes of DEATHS
Per 1000 Population
1964-67

4.7 5.7 5.5 3.9 3.7 3.1 5.3

INFANT DEATHS
Per 1000 Live Births
1964-67

27.2 10.3 26.3 18.7 15.2 15.2 20.1

KOOLAUPOKO
KOOLAU-OA
HONOLULU
WAIALUA
WAHIAWA
EWA
WAIANAE

LIVE BIRTHS
Percent Mothers with 5
or More Children
1964-67

26.8 21.0 30.6 15.1 14.7 12.7 10.2

**HEALTH INDICATORS
Medical, Social, Economic**

Taken together, these 14 maps of data give some indication of the "quality of life" in the seven Judicial Districts of Oahu between 1964 and 1967. Data for other islands were not available in 1972. The 14 maps represent a selection from 25 sets of data assembled by Burch (1971). For each of the 25 variables the districts were ranked from 1 to 7 with the lowest number standing for the most favorable situation (for example, lowest rate of death). The average of all ranks is shown on the map to the right. This indicates that the "quality of life" was most favorable in Koolaupoko and Ewa and least favorable in Waianae and Koolauloa.

Source: T.A. Burch (1971) and
State Department of Health

**Ethnic Groups, 1964-67
by Percent**

15.5 12.6 25.9 39.3 6.7
20.3 10.7 8.2 18.6 42.2 16.4
24.3 8.4 16.4 8.8 42.1
11.4 12.5 12.3 37.9 25.9 35.0
20.1 5.8 17.6 21.5
4.8 3.7 3.0 3.2 4.0
3.8 5.6
12.2 6.3 11.4 29.6 40.5
14.7 2.9 17.4 25.4 39.6

District Ranking

Highest
Median
Lowest

Hawaiian and part-Hawaiian
Caucasian
Japanese
Filipino
Other races

Active Cases of TUBERCULOSIS
Per 100,000
Population, 1966

66.7 61.2 16.6 38.2 22.2 34.2 39.1

PHYSICIANS
Per 100,000 Population
1966

33.4 36.7 20.8 42.0 37.8 165.5 20.9

MEDICAL INSURANCE
Percent Population
with No Coverage
1964-67

22.8 28.1 42.1 55.1 34.7 45.6 31.2

INCOME
Percent Population
with Less than
$5000 Annually
1964-67

45.0 31.3 46.6 32.1 18.9 25.2 31.8

SUICIDES
Per 100,000 Population
1964-67

11 0 12 4 2

EDUCATION
Percent Population with
Grade 8 or Less
1964-67

29.1 25.7 31.0 18.5 18.3 21.1 13.4

LARGE HOUSEHOLDS
Percent with 7 or
More Persons
1964-67

16.8 10.9 19.1 9.8 11.2 11.2 11.9 8.7

185

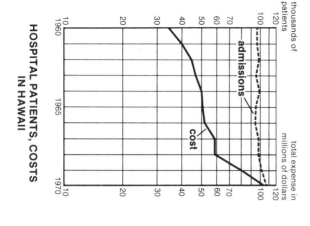

Hawaiian arts and crafts: stamp design for clothing.

HOSPITAL PATIENTS, COSTS IN HAWAII

thousands of patients

total expense in millions of dollars

admissions

cost

HEALTH SERVICES

Hawaii's system for health promotion and medical service is a complex blending of four major factors—people, facilities and institutions, organizations, and money.

The People. More than 12,000 professional health and medical practitioners, technicians, and technologists, and a host of administrative, clerical, and vocational workers combine their skills to deliver needed health and medical care services to Hawaii's citizens. As an industry, the medical care system accounts for about 4 percent of the employed civilian labor force. The doctors, dentists, nurses, and others concerned with health service are generally concentrated according to the concentration of the population, with Oahu enjoying immediate contact with the greatest number of sophisticated and specialized practitioners. While this proportional distribution of health manpower provides the full range of medical services for sparse populations on outer islands, these skills and services are available to residents of semi-isolated areas through the visits of physician-specialists from Oahu and the transport of patients to Honolulu. Even on Oahu, however, the great majority of health workers are found in Honolulu, where most of the hospitals and physicians' offices are located. Because most health workers are employed by hospitals and other organizations and institutions, their distribution is controlled by the location of these employers. Physicians and dentists, however, being mainly in private practice, decide the location of their own offices. A large number of physicians in Hawaii, about 30 or 40 percent, belong to group medical practices. This trend, which tends even more to concentrate physicians and their allied workers in large groupings, is more fully developed in Hawaii than anywhere else in the world.

Although medical and health services are concentrated disproportionately in Honolulu, Hawaii has available the full range of professional and technical skills to be found anywhere, including even the skills and knowledge of the few remaining native healers, numbering fewer than 100.

The Facilities. Hospitals, including many institutions that provide bed care for acutely ill and long-term chronically ill or rehabilitating patients, though tending to be centrally located in Honolulu, are generally available to Hawaii's people wherever they live. Indeed, the ratio of hospital and skilled nursing care beds to the population is greater on the outer islands than it is on Oahu. Hawaii's facilities for in-patient medical care include 33 hospitals of various types, 27 skilled nursing care institutions including nursing homes and extended-care facilities, and 148 care homes.

The services offered through these institutions range from the most sophisticated organ transplant capabilities to the least complicated custodial services. The more elaborate surgical procedures and therapeutic facilities, including the two specialized rehabilitation hospitals, are located in metropolitan Honolulu; these serve not only the dispersed outer island populations of Hawaii, but the more remote populations of outlying Pacific islands as well.

Seventeen hospitals are operated directly by the state government and one by the federal government; fifteen are nonprofit community hospitals. Private ownership is predominant for the remainder of medical institutions—the nursing homes, extended-care facilities, and care homes. In all, they provide nearly 8,000 beds, or a ratio of more than 10 beds per 1,000 people. Hospital beds are available at a rate of 7.1 beds per 1,000 population, ranking Hawaii somewhat lower than the national rate of 7.8 per 1,000. Similarly, lower rates also exist with respect to long-term and nursing care beds.

Two organized home nursing and care services are provided on Oahu by a hospital and by a private group medical clinic. On each outer island, these services are offered by staff members of the Department of Health.

Eighty-three drug stores and 25 hospital and clinic pharmacies provide a well-developed and generally well distributed system for dispensing drugs and medical appliances.

The laboratory needs of the system are met through hospital-based and free-standing clinical medical and dental laboratories. As is true of manpower and facilities, both laboratory and pharmacy services tend to be centralized in Honolulu.

The Organizations. A wide array of health and medical services are provided directly by government, and these fall almost entirely under state domain. From the highly centralized Kinau

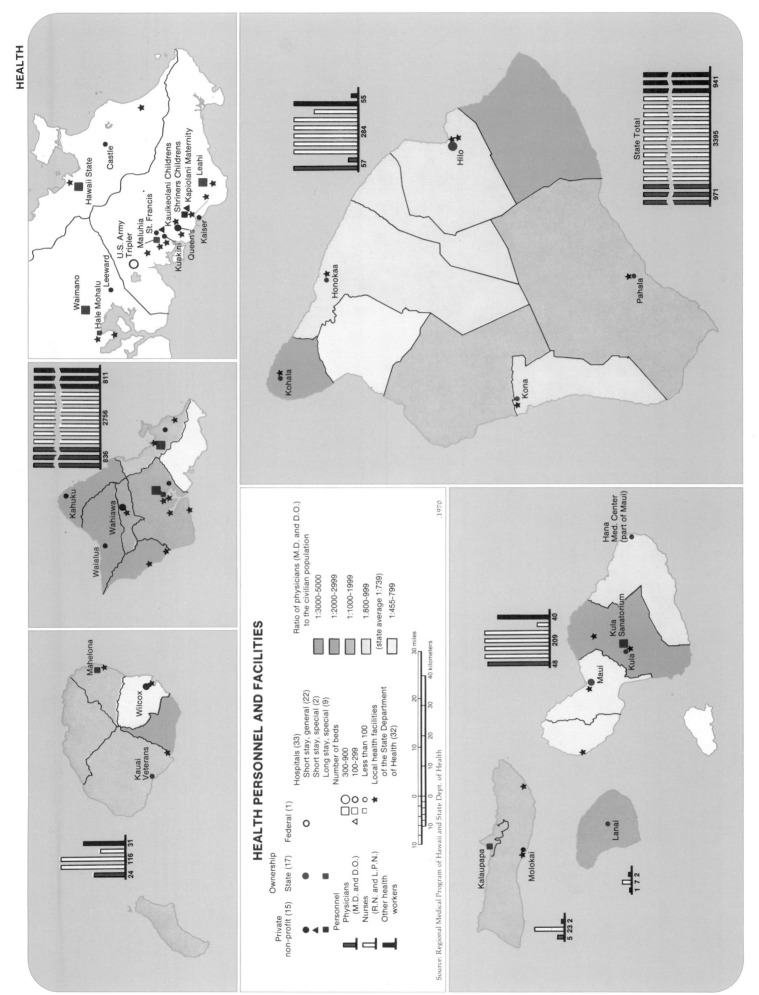

HEALTH PERSONNEL AND FACILITIES

Private
non-profit (15)   Ownership   State (17)   Federal (1)

Personnel

Physicians
(M.D. and D.O.)

Nurses
(R.N. and L.P.N.)

Other health
workers

Hospitals (33)

Short stay, general (22)
Short stay, special (2)
Long stay, special (9)

Number of beds
300-900
100-299
Less than 100

Local health facilities
of the State Department
of Health (32)

Ratio of physicians (M.D. and D.O.)
to the civilian population

1:3000-5000
1:2000-2999
1:1000-1999
1:800-999
(state average 1:739)
1:455-799

Source: Regional Medical Program of Hawaii and State Dept. of Health

1970

0   10   20   30 miles

10   0   10   20   30   40 kilometers

State Total

941   3395   971

811   836   2756

31   24   116

55   57   284

40   48   209

5   23   2

1   7   2

Castle
Hawaii State
U.S. Army Tripler
Maluhia
St. Francis
Kuakini
Queen's
Kaiser
Kauikeolani Childrens
Shriners Childrens
Kapiolani Maternity
Leahi
Waimano
Hale Mohalu
Leeward

Mahelona
Wilcox
Kauai Veterans

Kahuku
Wahiawa
Waialua

Hilo
Honokaa
Kohala
Kona
Pahala

Maui
Kula
Kula Sanatorium
Hana Med. Center (part of Maui)

Kalaupapa
Molokai
Lanai

187

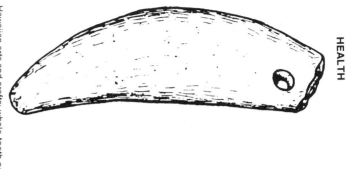

Hawaiian arts and crafts: whale-tooth pendant.
Bishop Museum drawing from Te Rangi Hiroa (1964:535)

Hale and its branch offices in each county come the provision and coordination of 17 hospitals; 32 health centers, mental health clinics, and other clinics of various types; and a large number of inspectorial, regulatory, and advisory activities—all of which are designed to preserve, promote, and improve the health of Hawaii's citizens. The State Department of Health is responsible for (1) insuring purity of foods and drugs; (2) measurement and control of air, water, and noise pollution; (3) management of acute and specialized hospitals (including those for the treatment of leprosy, tuberculosis, mental illness, and mental retardation); (4) provision of the major part of emergency ambulance services on islands other than Oahu (page 197); (5) education of the public on health matters; (6) prevention and control of infectious and chronic diseases; (7) maintaining records of births, deaths, marriages, and other vital data.

Closely akin in their intent and purpose are the rich variety of nongovernmental health organizations that have as their focus either education or service in prevention or treatment of illness, or rehabilitation. Included are voluntary, nonprofit service agencies which deal specifically with cancer, heart disease, respiratory ailments, crippled children, birth control and family planning, mental health, alcoholism, and many other human afflictions and problems. Most are state or regional affiliates of parent national organizations and rely heavily on contributions from the public for the funds that make possible the services they provide. For the most part, the voluntary health organizations are represented in branch or local offices throughout the State.

Another set of organizations is important to the control and design of Hawaii's health care system—the professional socie-

ties. Fifty-three different professions and occupations in the health field are represented by individual professional associations, ranging from the full-time offices of the state medical, dental, and nursing associations to part-time activities of many others. Each outer island has its local counterpart of every major association. Most have the single function of representing and regulating the practices of their members and maintaining high standards of professional practice in their special fields. Some offer additional services such as medical and dental insurance programs.

Professional and technical education and training needs are met largely through the University of Hawaii. Here, and through its system of community colleges, education is offered in medicine, nursing, public health, social work, medical technology, speech pathology and audiology, dental hygiene, dental assistance, and nutrition. Specialized programs for various technicians and assistants are conducted by many hospitals and medical clinics as well.

The Money. Through governmental and private channels, Hawaii's citizens spend an estimated 210 million dollars each year for health and medical services. Nearly one-third of this amount is accounted for by state expenditures of federal and state monies for the services provided by the Department of Health and for the medical assistance programs administered by the Department of Social Services and Housing. The remaining two-thirds is paid directly by the consumers of health service, in the form of insurance prepayments, charitable contributions, and cash.

Both commercial and nonprofit health and medical insurance plans are offered in Hawaii, with the preponderance of prepaid care being handled by the Hawaii Medical Service Association and the Kaiser Foundation Health Plan. An additional 107 local, national, and foreign companies account for the balance of health insurance.

R. E. M.

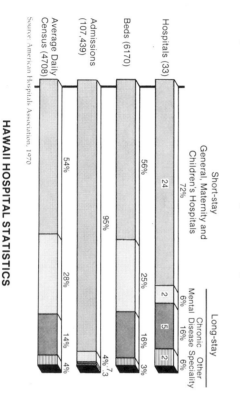

HAWAII HOSPITAL STATISTICS

	Short-stay General, Maternity and Children's Hospitals		Long-stay Chronic Disease	Other Mental Specialty	
Hospitals (33)	24 72%		2 6%	5 16%	2 6%
Beds (6170)	56%	25%	16%		3%
Admissions (107,439)	95%		4%	7%	.3%
Average Daily Census (4708)	54%	28%	14%		4%

Source: American Hospitals Association, 1970

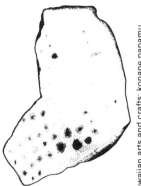

Hawaiian arts and crafts: konane papamu (stone "checkers" game board).

Drawing by T. Stell Newman

PERCENT OF TOTAL POPULATION PARTICIPATING IN MAJOR OUTDOOR RECREATION, 1970,71

Activity	Percent
Beachgoing, sunbathing	33%
Swimming, ocean	31
Driving for pleasure, sightseeing	20
Picnicking	20
Walking for pleasure	18
Fishing from shore, pier, net fishing, clamming	15
Bicycling	13
Swimming, pool	11
Attending outdoor sports events	11
Attending cultural and educational events and exhibits	11
Basketball	7
Golf	7
Baseball	7
Beach camping	6
Nature walks, enjoying natural areas	6
Surfing	6
Attending outdoor concerts, plays	5
Jogging	5
Hiking	5
Fishing from boat, deep sea fishing	5
Skindiving	4
Hunting	2

Source: State Dept. of Planning and Economic Devel.

RECREATION

Hawaii offers diverse and complex recreational opportunities. As might be expected, beach- and water-oriented activities are the overwhelming recreational favorites. In a recent survey (State of Hawaii, 1971), beachgoing and swimming ranked as the two most popular forms of outdoor recreation. While most of Hawaii's state and county recreation facilities are located on the beach, inland sites add important variety. The facilities serve a wide range of needs: intensively used urban parks are filled with the shouts of children at play as parents relax over a picnic, while remote state park lands, such as those on Kauai's Na Pali coast, offer a wilderness experience.

The accompanying maps show areas for recreational opportunity, including national parks, state parks, county beach parks, campgrounds, golf courses, boat-launching facilities, selected diving and surfing sites, and areas for hunting and freshwater fishing. There are some popular forms of recreation which are not shown because they do not lend themselves to mapping. For example, "driving for pleasure" and "walking for pleasure" are, respectively, the third and fifth most popular forms of outdoor recreation (see accompanying table), but they can be referred to only indirectly on the reference maps (pages 10-22) that show trails and roads.

All of the surfing, swimming, diving, and sunbathing, and much of the camping, walking, driving for pleasure, and picnicking take place on or near the shoreline. The State has 934 miles of tidal shoreline on the islands of Kauai, Oahu, Molokai, Lanai, Maui, and Hawaii. About 185 miles are classified as sandy beach, but only 13 percent of this mileage is considered best suited for beach recreation use. Most of the State's sandy shoreline is undesirable for recreation because of such features as steeply sloping beach, dangerous currents and surf, difficult access, and insufficient land for parking and other support facilities. Not all prime sandy beach frontage is available for public use, although the State has title to nearly all beach land seaward of the high-water mark. The usual deciding factor in determining access to beaches is the ownership of the adjoining land. Privately owned land frequently cuts off access to a publicly owned beach unless rights-of-way are established. In the case of the State-owned prime beach frontage, adjoining land use is currently as follows: 19 percent urban, 4 percent resort, 12 percent military, 28 percent public park, 3 percent quasi-public park, 33 percent agriculture, conservation, and open land.

Fishing from shore or pier, net fishing, and clamming—taken as a whole—comprise the sixth most popular form of recreation in Hawaii. Shore-based saltwater fishing accounts for most of the fishing activity, but offshore boat fishing for marlin, tunas, mahimahi, ahi, bonefish, and ono is also popular. Charter boats operate from Kauai, Oahu, Maui, and Hawaii. Freshwater fishing in the State is limited to some reservoirs and to a few streams on Kauai. Unmapped, but certainly not unimportant, are the multitude of other types of sport fishing, such as spear fishing, crabbing, and opihi picking.

Approximately 75 percent of the State's pleasure-boat owners use public or privately owned boat-launching ramps. More than 182,000 launchings were recorded in 1970, predominantly on weekends.

Organized sports are popular on all islands. The Pacific Coast League's "Hawaii Islanders" attracted an attendance of 375,957 baseball fans in 1971. High school and league baseball and football games hold strong interest. Approximately 4,500 adults are active in league baseball on Oahu, and about 6,500 young players are members of Little Leagues. Leagues on all islands tend to be based on age, sex, ethnic group, and place of employment; examples, respectively, are Little Leagues, women's softball, Americans of Samoan Ancestry, and the Restaurant League. Numerous informal games are played in public parks and elsewhere.

The City and County of Honolulu and the counties of Hawaii, Kauai, and Maui operate recreation programs in conjunction with county playing fields. On Oahu about 50,000 tennis players participated in league play in 1971, but organized games account for only a small part of the tennis played on the city's 72 courts.

Other important recreational activities are attending movies (page 129) and boxing and wrestling matches. Attendance at boxing events in 1971 was over 100,000. Cockfighting is a popular (though currently illegal) entertainment, especially in rural districts. Educational and cultural events are also important as recreation (page 165).

A. S.

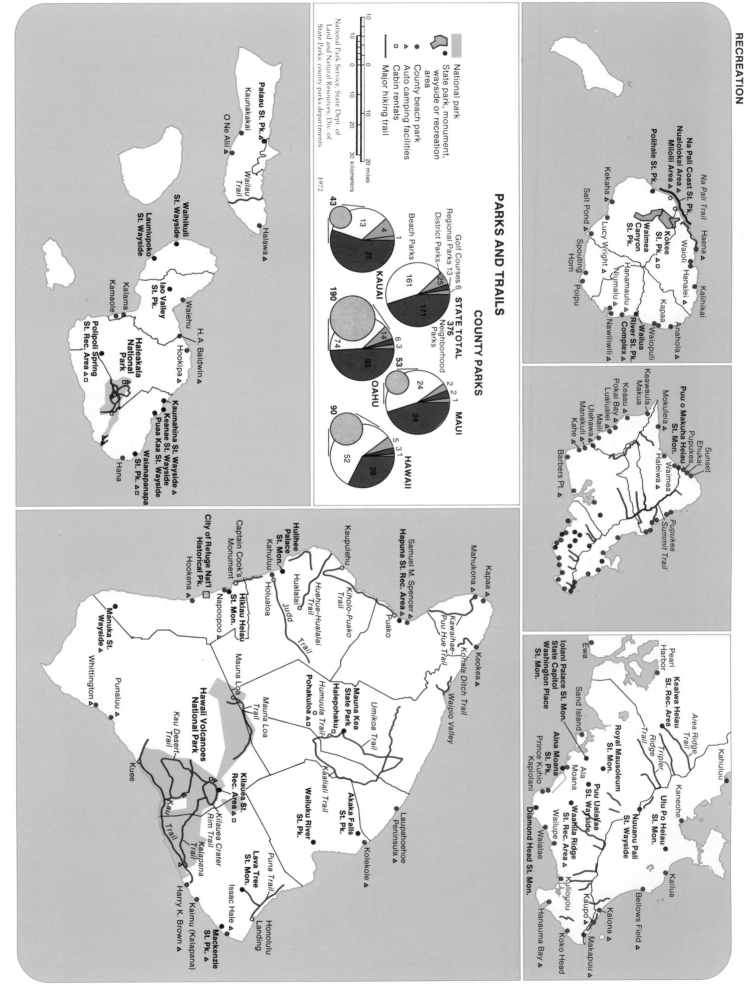

PARKS AND TRAILS

Hawaii has three kinds of public parks: national parks, which are designed to preserve natural and historic areas of outstanding national significance; state parks, which include areas recognized by the State as worthy of preservation; and county parks, which are primarily for local community recreation. There are three units of the national parks system in the State: Hawaii Volcanoes National Park and City of Refuge National Historic Park on Hawaii, and Haleakala National Park on Maui. In 1971 the national parks recorded a total of 1,478,900 visits. The 41 units of the state park system comprise 14 state parks, 8 state recreation areas, 8 state waysides, 10 state monuments, and the State Capitol. During the year ending June 30, 1971, these units recorded a total of 13,007,000 visits. The county parks are by far the most heavily patronized. In 1972 there were 376 parks in the Kauai, Hawaii, Maui, and Honolulu county systems. These parks tend to be located in and near population centers. County beach parks are shown on page 190.

Parks in Hawaii are used all year round. While there is an increase in use during the summer months, 70 percent of respondents in the state survey cited above (State of Hawaii, 1971) indicated that they use parks and other outdoor recreation facilities with the same frequency throughout the year. The survey also indicated that there is little difference among ethnic or income groups in time spent in outdoor recreation, but that young people between 5 and 18 years of age spend about twice as much time as adults. Those between 5 and 18 years spend on the average four hours a day on weekends in outdoor recreation, and two hours a day on weekdays. The most popular sites for family outings on Oahu, in terms of frequency of visits, are the beach parks at Ala Moana, Waikiki, Kailua, and Kaneohe; on Maui, the beach parks in the Kihei and Lahaina areas; and on the Big Island, the beaches near Hilo and at Hapuna and Kawaihae.

Besides playing fields and other game areas, many parks have facilities for family and large-group picnics and camping. Camping areas are usually designated within parks, and campers use the general facilities rather than special campground services. Most campers use tents or vehicle "campers." In most parks camping is by permit for limited time periods. Cabins for family and group recreation are also available in some state parks (see map).

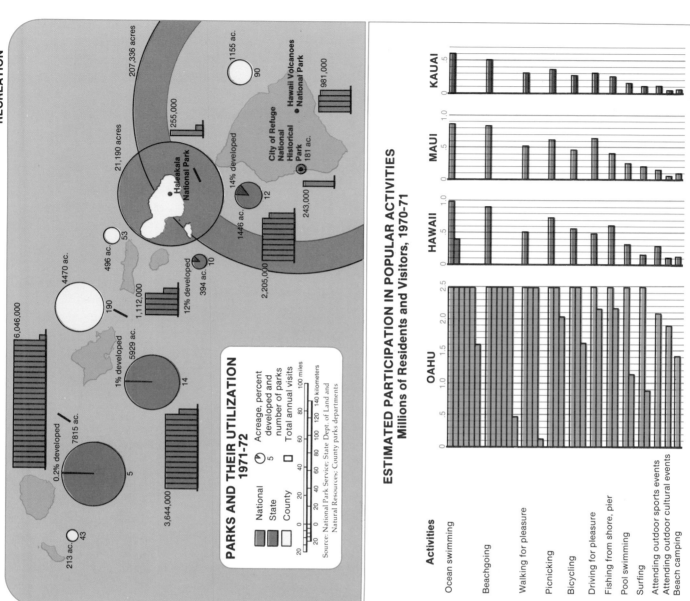

PARKS AND THEIR UTILIZATION 1971-72

National	⊕ Acreage, percent developed and	
State	5 number of parks	
County	☐ Total annual visits	

Source: National Park Service; State Dept. of Land and Natural Resources; County parks departments

ESTIMATED PARTICIPATION IN POPULAR ACTIVITIES
Millions of Residents and Visitors, 1970-71

Activities

Ocean swimming
Beachgoing
Walking for pleasure
Picnicking
Bicycling
Driving for pleasure
Fishing from shore, pier
Pool swimming
Surfing
Attending outdoor sports events
Attending outdoor cultural events
Beach camping

OAHU HAWAII MAUI KAUAI

Source: State Department of Planning and Economic Development

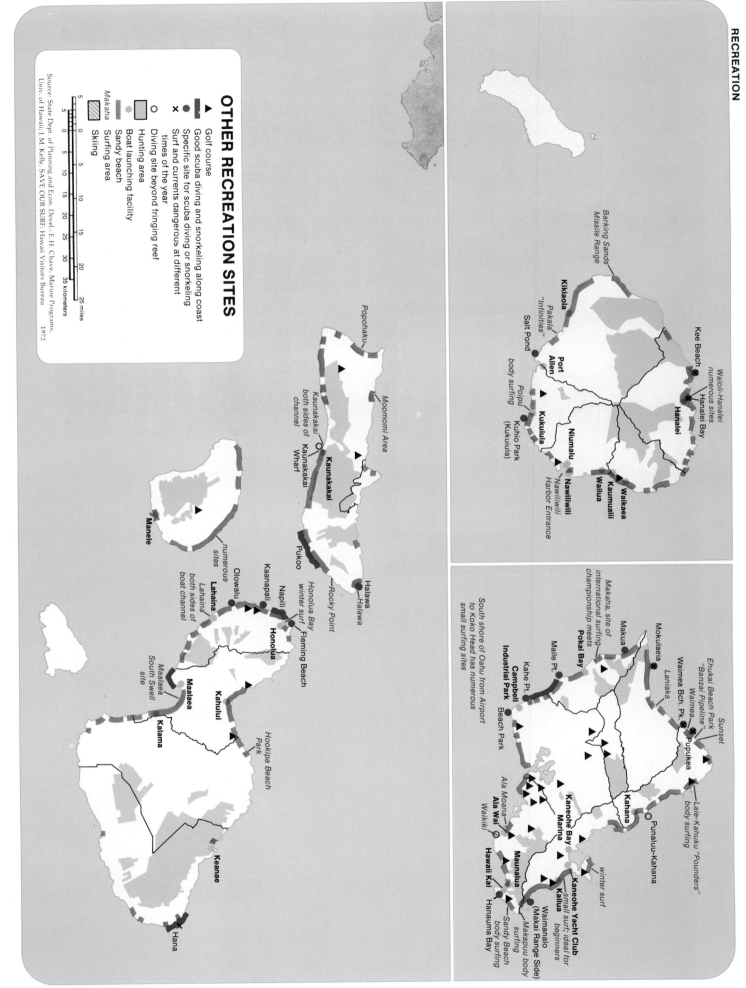

OTHER RECREATION SITES

▲ Golf course

▼ Good scuba diving and snorkeling along coast

○ Specific site for scuba diving or snorkeling

✕ Surf and currents dangerous at different times of the year

● Diving site beyond fringing reef

━ Hunting area

▮ Boat launching facility

✚ Sandy beach

▨ Surfing area

▨ Skiing

Makaha

Source: State Dept. of Planning and Econ. Devel.: E. H. Chave, Marine Programs, Univ. of Hawaii; J. M. Kelly, SAVE OUR SURF; Hawaii Visitors Bureau, 1972

5   0   5   10   15   20   25   30   35 kilometers
5   0   5   10   15   20   25 miles

Kauai

Barking Sands Missile Range
Kikiaola
Pakala "Infinities"
Port Allen
Salt Pond
Poipu body surfing
Kuhio Park (Kukuiula)
Kukuiula
Niumalu
Nawiliwili
Nawiliwili Harbor Entrance
Wailua
Kaumualii
Waikaea
Hanalei
Hanalei Bay
Waioli-Hanalei numerous sites
Kee Beach

Molokai
Popohaku
Moomomi Area
Kaunakakai
Kaunakakai Wharf
Kaunakakai channel/ both sides of Kaunakakai channel
Pukoo
Honolua Bay winter surf/ Fleming Beach
Halawa
Halawa
Rocky Point

Lanai
Manele

Maui
Olowalu
Lahaina
Lahaina both sides of boat channel
Kaanapali
Napili
Honolua
numerous sites
Maalaea
Maalaea South Swell site
Kahului
Kalama
Keanae
Hookipa Beach Park
Hana

Oahu
Makaha, site of international surfing championship meets
Pokai Bay
Makua
Mokuleia
Maile Pt.
Kahe Pt.
Campbell Industrial Park
Beach Park
Ehukai Beach Park "Banzai Pipeline"
Waimea Bch. Pk.
Waimea
Laniaka
Pupukea
Sunset
Laie-Kahuku "Pounders" body surfing
Kahana
Punaluu-Kahana
winter surf
Kaneohe Bay
Marina
Kaneohe Yacht Club
Kailua
Waimanalo (Makai Range Side) small surf; ideal for beginners
Makapuu body surfing
Ala Moana-Ala Wai
Waikiki
Maunalua
Hawaii Kai
Hanauma Bay
Sandy Beach body surfing
South shore of Oahu from Airport to Koko Head has numerous small surfing sites

Hawaii is internationally famous for surfing. Board surfing, paipo boarding, and body surfing are all popular, particularly among those under 26 years of age, who account for more than 85 percent of Hawaii's estimated 75,000 surfers. There are hundreds of surfing sites along the coasts of the islands, but only a few of the best known are shown on the map. Judging the quality of a surfing site is a complex matter. Wind and wave conditions, pollution, access problems, crowding, competition with other recreational uses, and distance from home are all factors that enter into the evaluation of a particular site. There is also the important variable of experience: the conditions eagerly sought by experienced big-wave adherents may bring nothing but bleak disaster to beginners.

Diving areas are good throughout the islands, but those selected for the map are easily accessible from public roads without trespassing on private lands. The diving areas themselves feature outstanding displays of coral and other marine life. Hanauma Bay on Oahu has been set aside especially for diving because of its outstanding natural fauna of fishes, corals, and other marine life (page 80).

Hunting activity in the State is directed toward the taking of deer, feral sheep, goats, and pigs, as well as doves and other game birds. The map indicates the approximately one million acres on which hunting is possible. Not all these lands may be open for hunting at any one time. In 1971, 10,302 hunting licenses were purchased by residents and nonresidents.

Hawaii had 40 golf courses in 1972. Of these, six 18-hole courses and two 9-hole courses were publicly owned; ten 18-hole courses and seven 9-hole courses were privately owned but open to the public; five 18-hole courses and one 9-hole course were for private use only; and six 18-hole courses and three 9-hole courses were maintained by the military. The well-known Hawaiian Open golf championship is held each year at the Waialae Country Club on Oahu.

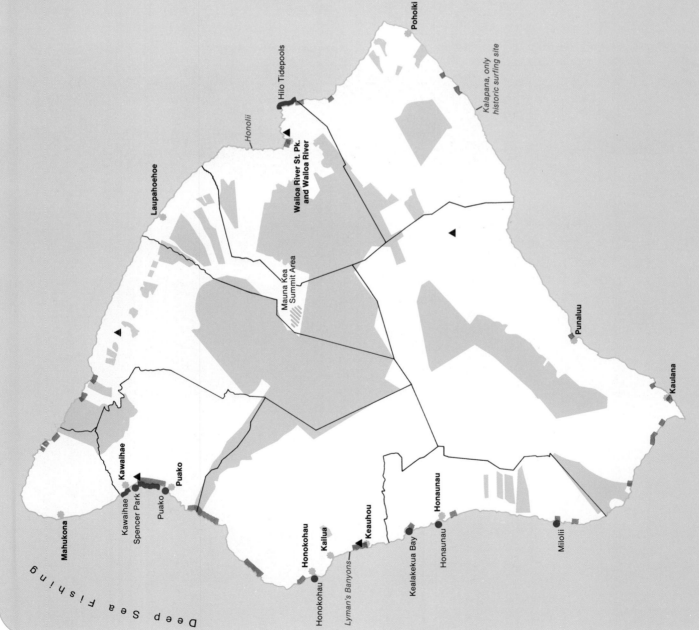

Deep Sea Fishing

Mahukona

Kawaihae
Kawaihae Spencer Park
Puako
Puako

Honokohau
Honokohau
Kailua

Lyman's Banyons

Keauhou
Keauhou

Kealakekua Bay

Honaunau
Honaunau

Milolii

Laupahoehoe

Honolii

Hilo Tidepools

Wailoa River St. Pk. and Wailoa River

Mauna Kea Summit Area

Kalapana, only historic surfing site

Pohoiki

Punaluu

Kaulana

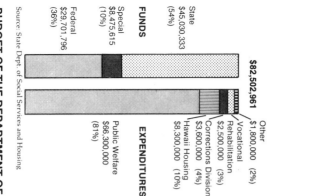

Source: State Dept. of Social Services and Housing

BUDGET OF THE DEPARTMENT OF SOCIAL SERVICES AND HOUSING 1970-71

$82,502,961

FUNDS
- State $45,030,333 (54%)
- Special $8,475,615 (10%)
- Federal $29,701,796 (36%)

EXPENDITURES
- Other $1,800,000 (2%)
- Vocational Rehabilitation $2,500,000 (3%)
- Corrections Division $3,600,000 (4%)
- Hawaii Housing $8,300,000 (10%)
- Public Welfare $66,300,000 (81%)

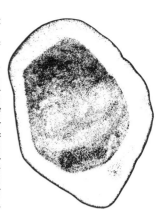

Hawaiian arts and crafts: hollowed stone bowl or basin.

Drawing by T. Stell Newman

SERVICES

Libraries. The University of Hawaii libraries at the Manoa campus and the Hawaii State Library in Honolulu with 700,000 and 230,000 items, respectively, are the largest in the State. Most libraries in Hawaii are small, but many, for example, the State Archives and the libraries of the Bishop Museum and the Hawaiian Sugar Planters' Association, contain rare or special collections. All high schools and community colleges, most government agencies and military units, and many private companies and organizations have their own libraries. The map on page 195 locates all public, university, and college libraries in the State, and a selection of the large number of special ones, most of which are on Oahu, mainly in Honolulu. The Hawaii State Library system includes a central library in the main town in each county with branch libraries in most districts. An inter-library loan system makes the larger collections of the central libraries available to their branches, and bookmobiles operate on Oahu, Maui, and Hawaii to serve rural communities.

Municipal Services. Ambulance services (page 197) are provided by the State Department of Health on all islands except Oahu, where the City and County of Honolulu and three private companies have charge. Fire departments are maintained by county governments, and services include special rescue facilities. On Oahu a helicopter is maintained for fire fighting and for ocean and mountain rescue operations. Police in Hawaii are organized by county, and unlike most states there is no state police force. The Honolulu Police Department staff numbered 1,395 in 1971, that of Kauai 90, Maui 157, and Hawaii 166. (See page 196 for civil defense.)

Water supplies are currently adequate on all populated islands (page 45). In 1970, fewer than one percent of households in the counties of Kauai, Honolulu, and Maui were not served by a public or private community water system (page 198). Twelve percent of households in Hawaii County were not connected to a community water system but relied on individual sources such as wells, streams, and rain catchment tanks. Extension of public sewerage systems has not been as rapid as water service, especially in rural areas. In 1972 the largest systems, serving the cities of Honolulu, Hilo, Wailuku, and Kahului, discharged raw sewage without treatment into the ocean, but treatment plants are planned. Most other public systems, while much smaller,

carry treatment to either primary or secondary stages. In many towns and in most rural areas, private septic tanks, cesspools, or lava tubes are used for sewage disposal.

Social Services. The provision of social services is undertaken by a large number of government, trade, and voluntary organizations. Federal agencies, such as the Social Security Administration and the Bureau of Employees Compensation, provide direct services, but federal funds also support state agencies such as the departments of Health and Social Services and Housing, and county agencies such as the City Demonstration Agency (Model Cities) and the Office of Human Resources. (For a review of health services see page 186.)

The major responsibility for providing social services is borne by the State Department of Social Services and Housing. Demands on the department have increased sharply since 1968. Between 1970 and 1971 economic assistance for welfare recipients increased 48 percent, owing in part to a rise in unemployment, an increase in population (especially in-migrants), and rising costs. Public welfare expenditures by the department in 1970-1971 amounted to $66.3 million, or 80 percent of its total budget of $82.5 million. Social welfare services include care of children in foster homes, arranging adoptions, licensing day-care centers, and family counseling. The Hawaii Housing Authority, a division of the department, maintained 6,196 living units in 1971 for elderly and low-income families. It was estimated in 1971 that an additional 22,000 public housing units would be needed in Hawaii by 1976. The department also provides vocational rehabilitation services, supervision of paroles, pardons, and criminal injuries compensation, and the maintenance of the State's correction facilities.

More than 400 voluntary, church, and other nonprofit organizations provide a wide range of social services in such areas as child care, safety, legal aid, labor relations, physical handicaps, care of the aged, drug abuse, suicide, and animal care. Financial support comes primarily from community donations, membership subscriptions, and government and philanthropic grants. Federated community funding for social services in Honolulu began in 1919 with the United Welfare Fund, reorganized as the Honolulu Community Chest in 1944, and as the Aloha United Fund in 1967. The fund distributed $4.2 million among 49 member organizations in 1971, chief recipients being the American Red Cross, the American Cancer Society, the Council on Social Work Education, and the YWCA, and the YMCA.

Staff

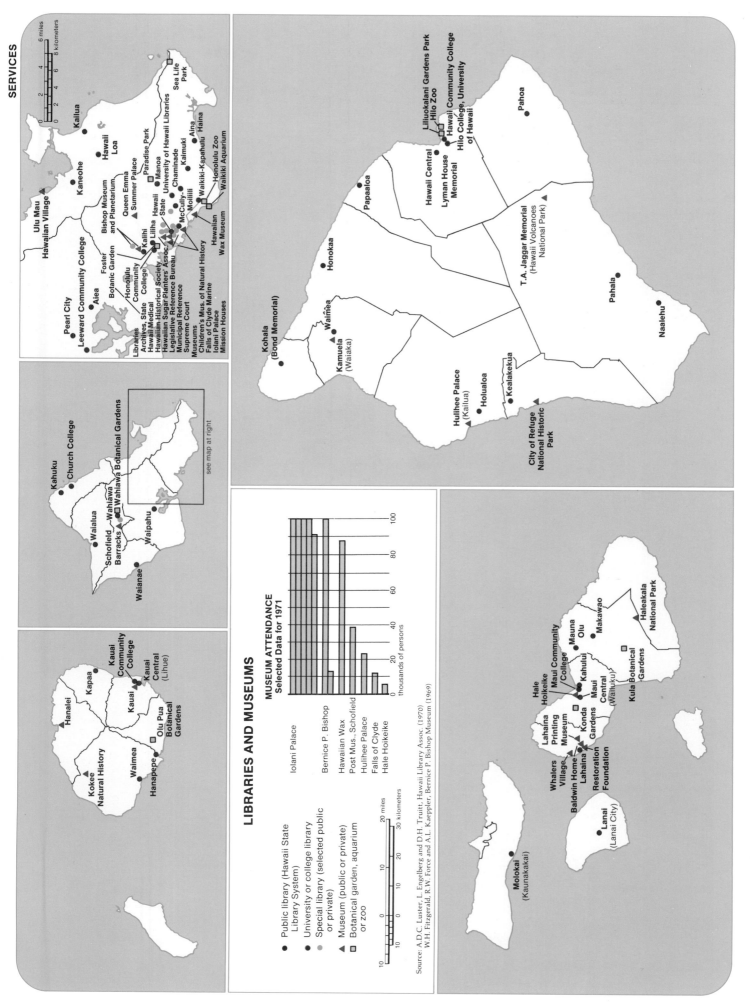

LIBRARIES AND MUSEUMS

Source: A.D.C. Luster, L. Engelberg and D.H. Truitt, Hawaii Library Assoc. (1970)
W.H. Fitzgerald, R.W. Force and A.L. Kaeppler, Bernice P. Bishop Museum (1969)

Civil defense in Hawaii is organized first at the county level of government to serve each island. The Civil Defense Division, State Department of Defense, coordinates plans, programs, and operations for the State and is responsible for dealing with major emergencies of disaster proportions. State civil defense also works with the Defense Civil Preparedness Agency of the federal government as part of the national defense system and with the Office of Emergency Preparedness, Executive Office of the President, on emergency preparedness programs.

The objective of civil defense is to minimize casualties, reduce property damage, and restore essential public services in the event of natural disaster. It also has the task of insuring maximum survival of the population in the event of nuclear war. Civil defense is government in time of emergency, but to be effective it must depend on considerable support from leaders in industry, agriculture, labor, finance, and from the community at large.

Most civil defense actions are initiated at the county level for local emergencies such as flood, drought, fire, earthquake, and volcanic eruption. In turn the state and federal governments assume responsibility for funding and/or aid as the situation demands. State civil defense provides the organization, facilities, and equipment to meet emergencies both natural and man-made, such as tsunamis, severe weather, aircraft accidents, major fires, major marine pollution, and other catastrophes beyond the resources of the local jurisdictions. Two primary sources of warning are the National Weather Service for tsunamis, floods, and storms, and the 326th Air Division, USAF, for enemy attack. Other kinds of warnings could originate from a variety of community agencies or facilities.

Warnings are transmitted over the Hawaii Warning System (HAWAS) simultaneously to State Warning Point and to County Warning Points located in county police headquarters. These warning points alert the public through siren signals and radio broadcast over Civ-Alert, the State's emergency broadcast system. Emergency Operating Centers (EOCs) are activated at state and county level. The diagram at the right shows the telecommunications network capable of use in an emergency. It includes the routine communications systems of county, state, and federal agencies, with links to the civil defense system on the mainland. Much of the system operates by cooperative agreement; for instance, the network can incorporate, when appropriate, the communications systems of commercial and public television, private industry, and amateur "ham" radio operators.

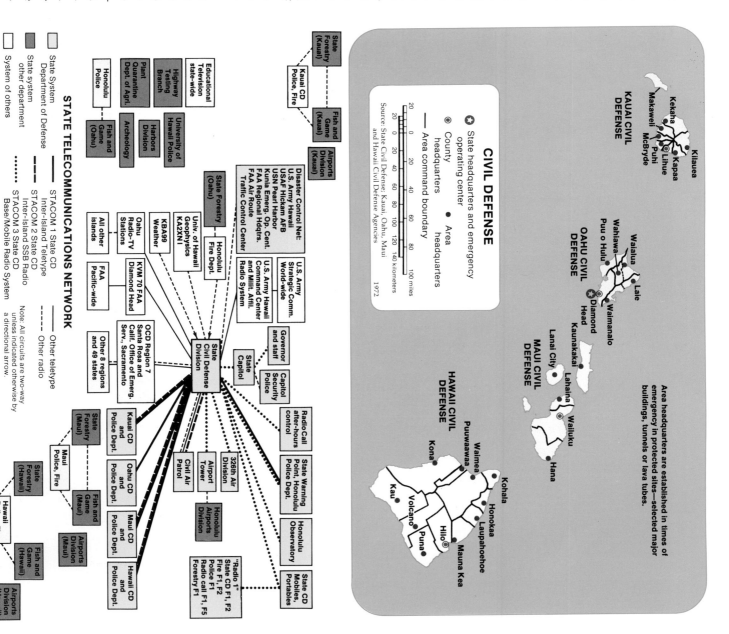

CIVIL DEFENSE

KAUAI CIVIL DEFENSE
Kilauea
Kekaha
Kapaa
Makaweli
Lihue
Puhi
McBryde

OAHU CIVIL DEFENSE
Waialua
Wahiawa
Laie
Puu o Hulu
Waimanalo
Diamond Head
Kaunakakai
Lanai City
Lahaina
Wailuku
Hana
MAUI CIVIL DEFENSE

HAWAII CIVIL DEFENSE
Puuwaawaa
Waimea
Kohala
Honokaa
Laupahoehoe
Mauna Kea
Kona
Kau
Volcano
Puna
Hilo

✪ State headquarters and emergency operating center
◉ County headquarters ● Area headquarters
— Area command boundary

1972

Source: State Civil Defense; Kauai, Oahu, Maui and Hawaii Civil Defense Agencies

20 0 20 40 60 80 100 120 140 kilometers
20 0 20 40 60 80 100 miles

Area headquarters are established in times of emergency in protected sites—selected major buildings, tunnels or lava tubes.

STATE TELECOMMUNICATIONS NETWORK

— STACOM 1 State CD Inter-Island Teletype
—— STACOM 2 State CD Inter-Island SSB Radio
······ STACOM 3 State CD Base/Mobile Radio System

——— Other teletype
----- Other radio

Note: All circuits are two-way unless indicated otherwise by a directional arrow.

■ State System
■ State system other department
□ System of others

State System Department of Defense

State Forestry (Kauai)
Kauai CD Police, Fire
Fish and Game (Kauai)
Airports Division (Kauai)

Honolulu Police
Educational Television state-wide
Highway Testing Branch
University of Hawaii Police
Plant Quarantine Dept. of Agri.
Harbors Division
Fish and Game (Oahu)
Archeology

State Forestry (Oahu)
Honolulu Fire Dept.
Univ. of Hawaii Geophysics KA2XNI
KBA99 Weather
Oahu Radio-TV Stations
KVM 70 FAA Diamond Head
All other islands

Disaster Control Net:
U.S. Army Hawaii
USAF Hickam AFB
USN Pearl Harbor
Kunia Emerg. Op. Cent.
FAA Regional Hdqtrs.
FAA Air Route Traffic Control Center

U.S. Army Strategic Comm. World-wide
U.S. Army Hawaii Command Center and Milit. Affil. Radio System

OCD Region 7 Santa Rosa and Calif. Office of Emerg. Serv., Sacramento

FAA Pacific-wide
Other 8 regions and 49 states

State Civil Defense Division

Governor and staff
State Capitol
Capitol Security Police
Radio Call after-hours control

Kauai CD and Police Dept.
Oahu CD and Police Dept.
Civil Air Patrol
326th Air Division
Honolulu Airports Division

Maui CD and Police Dept.
Hawaii CD and Police Dept.
Airport Tower

State Warning Point, Honolulu Police Dept.
Honolulu Observatory
State CD Mobiles, Portables
"Radio 1" State CD F1, F2 Fire F1 Police F1 Radio call F1, F5 Forestry F1

State Forestry (Maui)
Maui Police, Fire
State Forestry (Hawaii)
Hawaii Police, Fire

Fish and Game (Maui)
Airports Division (Maui)
Fish and Game (Hawaii)
Airports Division (Hawaii)

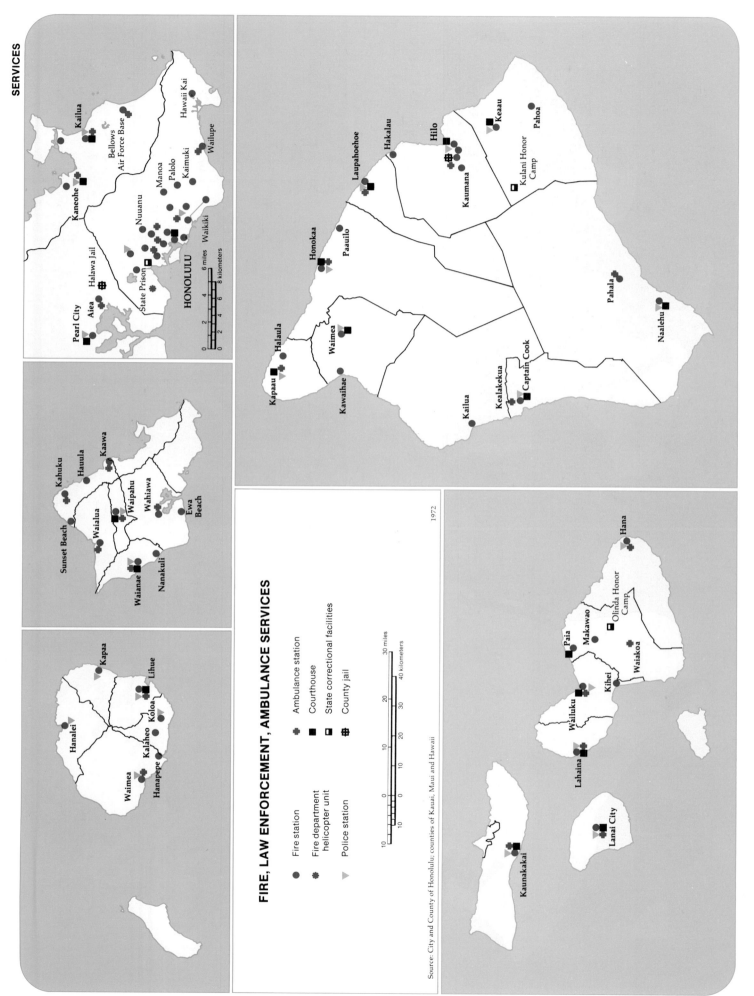

HONOLULU

Pearl City
Aiea
Halawa Jail
State Prison

Kailua
Bellows
Air Force Base
Kaneohe
Nuuanu
Manoa
Palolo
Kaimuki
Wailupe
Hawaii Kai
Waikiki

6 miles
8 kilometers

Kahuku
Hauula
Kaawa
Sunset Beach
Waialua
Waipahu
Wahiawa
Waianae
Nanakuli
Ewa Beach

Kapaa
Lihue
Koloa
Kalaheo
Hanapepe
Waimea
Hanalei

Laupahoehoe
Hakalau
Hilo
Keaau
Pahoa
Kulani Honor Camp
Kaumana
Honokaa
Paauilo
Halaula
Waimea
Kawaihae
Kapaau
Kailua
Kealakekua
Captain Cook
Pahala
Naalehu

Paia
Makawao
Olinda Honor Camp
Hana
Wailuku
Kihei
Waiakoa
Lahaina
Kaunakakai
Lanai City

FIRE, LAW ENFORCEMENT, AMBULANCE SERVICES

Fire station

Fire department helicopter unit

Police station

Ambulance station

Courthouse

State correctional facilities

County jail

1972

30 miles

40 kilometers

Source: City and County of Honolulu; counties of Kauai, Maui and Hawaii

SERVICES

WATER AND SEWERAGE SERVICES

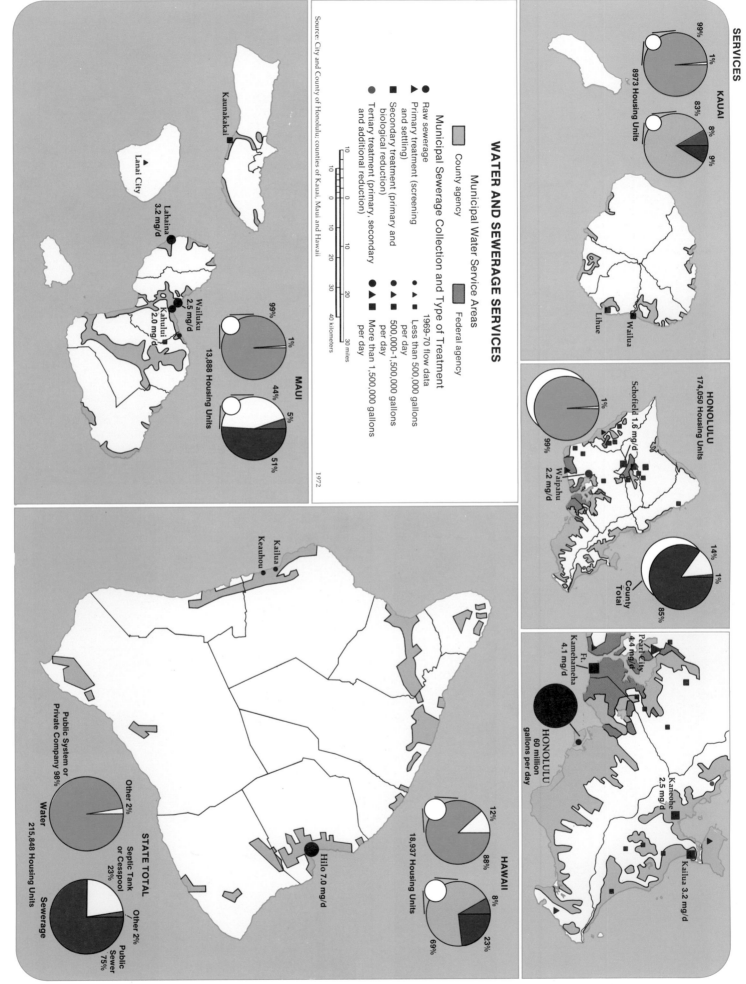

Municipal Sewerage Collection and Type of Treatment

1969-70 flow data

	Less than 500,000 gallons per day	500,000-1,500,000 gallons per day	More than 1,500,000 gallons per day
● Raw sewerage	●	●	●
▲ Primary treatment (screening and settling)	▲	▲	▲
■ Secondary treatment (primary and biological reduction)	■	■	■
● Tertiary treatment (primary, secondary and additional reduction)	●	●	●

Municipal Water Service Areas

County agency

Federal agency

10
0   10   20   30   40 kilometers
0   10   20   30 miles

Source: City and County of Honolulu; counties of Kauai, Maui and Hawaii

1972

KAUAI

8973 Housing Units

99%   1%

83%   8%   9%

Lihue

Wailua

HONOLULU

174,050 Housing Units

Schofield 1.6 mg/d

99%   1%

Waipahu 2.2 mg/d

County Total

85%   14%   1%

Pearl City 4.4 mg/d

Ft. Kamehameha 4.1 mg/d

HONOLULU 60 million gallons per day

Kaneohe 2.5 mg/d

Kailua 3.2 mg/d

MAUI

13,888 Housing Units

99%   1%

44%   5%   51%

Lahaina 3.2 mg/d

Wailuku 2.5 mg/d

Kahului 2.0 mg/d

Lanai City

Kaunakakai

HAWAII

18,937 Housing Units

12%   88%

8%   23%   69%

Kailua
Keauhou

Hilo 7.0 mg/d

STATE TOTAL

Water 215,848 Housing Units

Public System or Private Company 98%

Other 2%

Sewerage

Septic Tank or Cesspool 23%

Other 2%

Public Sewer 75%

APPENDICES

Statistical Tables

Areas: State, Counties, and Islands

Place	Area in Square Statute Miles		
	Total	Land	Inland water
The State	6,450	6,425	25
Counties			
Hawaii	4,038.0	4,037.0	1.0
Maui	1,174.4	1,173.6	0.8
Honolulu	610.9	595.7	15.2
Kauai	627.1	619.1	8.0
Islands			
Hawaii	4,038.0	4,037.0	1.0
Kahoolawe	45.0	45.0	—
Molokini	0.006	0.006	—
Maui	728.8	728.2	0.6
Lanai	139.5	139.5	—
Molokai	261.1	260.9	0.2
Oahu	607.7	592.7	15.0
Kauai	553.3	548.7	4.6
Niihau	73.0	69.6	3.4
Lehua	0.380	0.380	—
Kaula	0.438	0.438	—
Nihoa	3.2	3.0	0.2
Northwestern Hawaiian Islands	0.298	0.298	—
Necker Island	0.091	0.091	—
French Frigate Shoals (12 islets)	0.088	0.088	—
Gardner Pinnacles	0.004	0.004	—
Maro Reef	Awash	Awash	—
Laysan Island	1.533	1.312	0.220
Lisianski Island	0.675	0.675	—
Pearl and Hermes Atoll (7 islets)	0.122	0.122	—
Kure Atoll	0.371	0.371	—
Green Island	0.354	0.354	—
Sand Island	0.017	0.017	—
Other nearby islands (not in the State)			
Kingman Reef	0.01	0.01	—
Palmyra Islands	3.854	0.837	3.017
Johnston Island	0.29	0.29	—
Midway Islands	2.0	2.0	—

Urban Areas

Island	Town	Land Area (acres)	Population 1970
Kauai	Hanamaulu	552	2,461
	Kapaa	2,591	3,794
	Kekaha	666	2,404
	Lihue	3,959	3,124
	Waimea	544	1,569
Oahu	Aiea	1,302	12,560
	Honolulu	53,696	324,871
	Kailua	4,470	33,783
	Kaneohe	4,316	29,903
	Pearl City	2,135	19,552
	Schofield Barracks	1,849	13,516
	Wahiawa	1,472	17,598
	Waipahu	1,815	22,798
Molokai	Kaunakakai	573	1,070
Lanai	Lanai City	328	2,122
Maui	Kahului	2,888	8,280
	Lahaina	870	3,718
	Lower Paia	560	1,105
	Makawao	652	1,066
	Pukalani	1,253	1,629
	Puunene	607	1,132
	Wailuku	1,499	7,979
Hawaii	Captain Cook	928	1,263
	Hilo	35,929	26,353
	Honokaa	882	1,555
	Pahala	652	1,507
	Papaikou	749	1,888

Coastline

County or Island	General Coastline (miles)	Tidal Shoreline (miles)
The State[1]	750	1,052
Counties:		
Hawaii	266	313
Maui	210	343
Honolulu	137	234
Kauai	137	162
Islands:		
Hawaii	266	313
Maui[2]	120	149
Kahoolawe[2]	29	36
Lanai[2]	47	52
Molokai[2]	88	106
Oahu	112	209
Kauai	90	110
Niihau	45	50
Kaula	2	2
Lehua	–	–
Northwestern Haw'n Is	25	25

1. Among the states and territories, Hawaii ranks fourth in general coastline and seventeenth in tidal shoreline.
2. The figures given here for the coastlines of the four islands of Maui County, totaling 284 miles, are not consistent with the official county total of 210 miles.

Channels

Channel	Approximate depth (feet below sea level)	Width (statute miles)	Adjacent Islands
Kaulakahi	2,400	16.9	Niihau and Kauai
Kauai	9,950	72.5	Kauai and Oahu
Kaiwi	2,260	25.3	Oahu and Molokai
Kalohi	360	9.0	Molokai and Lanai
Pailolo	840	9.0	Molokai and Maui
Kealaikahiki	930	17.5	Lanai and Kahoolawe
Alalakeiki	540	6.9	Maui and Kahoolawe
Alenuihaha	6,200	28.9	Maui and Hawaii

Major Mountains

Island and Mountain	Elevation (feet)	Island and Mountain	Elevation (feet)
Hawaii:		Oahu (cont.):	
Mauna Kea[1]	13,796	Tantalus[1]	2,013
Mauna Loa	13,677	Olomana Peak	1,643
Hualalai	8,271	Diamond Head	760
Kohala	5,480	Punchbowl	500
Kilauea (Uwekahuna)	4,090	Koko Head	642
Kilauea (Halemaumau rim)	3,646	Kauai:	
Kahoolawe:		Kawaikini	5,243
Luamakika	1,477	Waialeale	5,148
Maui:		Niihau:	
Haleakala (Red Hill)	10,023	Paniau	1,281
Haleakala (Kaupo Gap)	8,201	Kaula	550
Puu Kukui	5,788	Nihoa	910
Iao Needle	2,250	Necker Island	277
Lanai:		La Perouse Pinnacle	135
Lanaihale	3,370	Gardner Pinnacles	190
Molokai:		Maro Reef	Awash
Kamakou	4,970	Laysan Island	35
Puu Nana	1,381	Lisianski Island	20
Oahu:		Pearl and Hermes Atoll	–
Kaala	4,040	Midway Islands[3]	12+
Puu Konahuanui[2]	3,150	Kure Atoll	20
		Kingman Reef[3]	3
		Palmyra Islands[3]	6

1. Includes 19 cones over 11,000 feet, 5 of them over 13,000. The summit of Mauna Kea is between 29,400 and 30,000 feet above the ocean floor at the base of the Hawaiian chain.
2. Two distinct peaks. The lower has an elevation of 3,105 feet.
3. Not part of the State of Hawaii.

Highway Distances

Places	Statute Miles[1]	Places	Statute Miles[1]
Kauai		Lanai	
Lihue - Haena	38.0	Lanai City - Lanai Airport	3.3
Lihue - Lihue Airport	2.0		
Lihue - Poipu	11.8	Maui	
Lihue - Mana	33.0	Wailuku - Kahului	2.3
Lihue - Kalalau Lookout	41.5	Wailuku - Kahului Airport	5.3
		Wailuku - Makena	17.4
Oahu		Wailuku - Hana, via Kaupo	59.6
Honolulu - Ala Moana Center	1.6	Wailuku - Hana, via Keanae	53.9
Honolulu - Waikiki (Kalakaua - Lewers)	3.0	Wailuku - Haleakala Summit	39.4
Honolulu - Waimanalo, via Koko Head	21.2	Wailuku - Lahaina, via Kahakuloa	40.6
Honolulu - Waimanalo, via Nuuanu	12.8	Wailuku - Lahaina, via Olowalu	20.8
Honolulu - Kailua, via Nuuanu	12.5		
Honolulu - Kaneohe, via Kalihi	10.8	Hawaii	
Honolulu - Kahuku, via Kaneohe	39.0	Hilo - General Lyman Airfield	1.8
Honolulu - Kahuku, via Wahiawa	46.2	Hilo - Kalapana	26.1
Honolulu - Kaena Point, via Wahiawa	42.3	Hilo - Volcano House	31.0
Honolulu - Kaena Point, via Waianae	44.3	Hilo - Kailua, via Naalehu	125.2
Honolulu - Wahiawa	19.6	Hilo - Kailua, via Saddle Road	84.3
Honolulu - Pearl Harbor Shipyard	6.5	Hilo - Kailua, via Hamakua	92.9
Honolulu - Honolulu Airport	4.7	Hilo - Waimea, via Saddle Road	56.1
Waimanalo - Kahuku	36.2	Hilo - Waimea, via Hamakua	56.9
		Hilo - Kawaihae, via Hamakua	68.6
Molokai		Hilo - Upolu Point, via Hamakua	79.7
Kaunakakai - Maunaloa	16.5	Kailua - Keahole Airport	7.2
Kaunakakai - Hoolehua Airport	6.9		
Kaunakakai - Halawa	27.5		

1. Mileages between towns represent distances between post office buildings.

Largest Lakes

Island	Name of Largest Lake[1]	Category	Maximum Depth (feet)	Altitude (feet)	Area (acres)	Shoreline (miles)
Hawaii	Waiakea Pond	natural	(NA)[2]	sea level	27	2
Maui	Kanaha Pond	natural	(NA)	sea level	41	2
Kahoolawe	None					
Lanai	None					
Molokai	Meyer Lake	natural	5	2,021	6	1
Oahu	Wahiawa Reservoir	man-made	85	842	333	11
Kauai	Koloa Reservoir	man-made	23	233	422	3
Niihau	Halulu Lake	natural	(NA)	sea level	182	3

1. Excludes shoreline fish ponds and areas filled only during floods. The largest intermittent lake is Halalii Lake, Niihau (840.7 acres). Other important lakes include Lake Waiau, Hawaii (1.28 acres), and Violet Lake, Maui (3.0 acres). Lake Waiau (elevation 13,020 feet) is the highest lake in the United States.
2. NA = Not available.

Major Named Waterfalls

Island	Waterfall[1]	Height (feet) Sheer drop	Height (feet) Cascade	Horizontal Distance (feet)	Average Discharge (million gal./day)
Hawaii	Kaluahine	–	620	400	–
	Akaka	442	–	–	–
	Waiilikahi	320	–	–	6.6
	Hiilawe (3 falls)	–	300	200	–
	Rainbow	–	80	150	303.5
Maui	Honokohau	–	1,120	500	26.6
	Waihiumalu	–	400	150	–
	Waimoku	–	40	50	37.1
Molokai	Kahiwa	–	1,750	1,000	–
	Papalaua	–	1,200	500	–
	Wailele	–	500	150	–
	Haloku	–	500	200	–
	Hipuapua	–	500	300	–
	Olupena	–	300	150	–
	Moaula	–	250	200	19.7
Oahu	Kaliuwaa (Sacred)[2]	80	1,520	3,000	–
	Waihee (Wainea)	80	–	–	5.6
	Manoa	–	200	250	2.4
Kauai	Waipio (2 falls)	–	800	600	–
	Awini	–	480	500	–
	Hinalele	280	–	–	–
	Kapakanui	280	–	–	–
	Manawaiopuna	280	–	–	–
	Wailua	80	–	–	–
	Opaekaa	40	–	–	–
	Puwainui	20	–	–	90.9

1. Includes the largest named waterfall on each major island, either in height or average discharge; all other named falls 250 feet high or higher; and well-known smaller falls. Many unnamed falls have sheer drops of 200 feet or more.
2. Sheer drops refers to northernmost fall of a cascade of six falls

Major Streams

Island	Feature or Stream	Length or Avg. Discharge
Longest water feature (miles):		
Hawaii	Wailuku River	32.0
Maui	Kalalinui-Waiale Gulch	18.0
Kahoolawe	Ahupu Gulch	4.0
Lanai	Maunalei-Waialala Gulch	12.9
Molokai	Wailau-Pulena Stream	6.5
Oahu	Kaukonahua Stream (So. Fork)	33.0
Kauai	Waimea River-Poomaii Stream	19.5
Niihau	Keanauli-Puniopo Valley	5.9
Largest perennial stream (miles):[1]		
Hawaii	Wailuku River	22.7
Maui	Palikea Stream	7.8
Molokai	Wailau-Pulena Stream	6.5
Oahu	Kaukonahua Stream	30.0
Kauai	Waimea River	19.7
Streams with greatest average discharge (million gal./day):[2]		
Hawaii	Wailuku River	303.5
Maui	Iao Stream	54.1
Molokai	Pulena Stream	22.1
Oahu	Waikele Stream	26.8
Kauai	Hanalei River	186.0

1. Estimated on the basis of drainage area rather than stream runoff. Other major streams include Honokohau Stream, Maui (9.4 miles long); Halawa Stream (6.4), Waikolu Stream (4.7), and Pelekunu (2.3), all on Molokai; Waikele Stream (15.3), Kipapa Stream (12.8), and Waikakalaua Stream (11.8), all on Oahu; and Makaweli River (15.1), Wainiha River (13.8), Hanapepe River (13.3), and Wailua River (11.8), all on Kauai.
2. The three greatest in the State are from the Wailuku, Hanalei, and Wainiha rivers. The latter, on Kauai, averages 90.9 million gallons per day.

Airline Distances (Great Circle Distances in Statute Miles between Honolulu International Airport and Specified Places)

Place	Miles from Honolulu	Place	Miles from Honolulu
Hawaiian Islands:		Other Pacific locations (cont.):	
Cape Kumukahi, Hawaii[1]	236	Singapore	6,710
Hilo, Hawaii	214	Suva, Fiji	3,159
Ka Lae (South Cape), Hawaii	221	Sydney, Australia	5,070
Kailua, Kona, Hawaii	168	Taipei, Taiwan	5,046
Kahului, Maui	98	Tokyo, Japan	3,847
Lanai Airport	72	Vladivostok, U.S.S.R.	4,291
Molokai Airport	54	Wake Island	2,294
Lihue, Kauai	103	Wellington, N.Z.	4,738
Puuwai, Niihau	152		
Nihoa	283	North America:	
Necker Island	520	Anchorage, Alaska	2,781
French Frigate Shoals	556	Chicago, Illinois	4,179
Gardner Pinnacles	688	Cristobal, Canal Zone	5,214
Maro Reef	851	Los Angeles, California	2,557
Laysan Island	936	Mexico City, Mexico	3,781
Lisianski Island	1,065	Miami, Florida	4,856
Pearl and Hermes Atoll	1,208	Montreal, Quebec	4,910
Midway Islands	1,309	New York, N.Y.	4,959
Kure Atoll[1]	1,367	Portland, Oregon	2,595
		San Diego, California	2,610
Trust Territory of Pacific Islands:		San Francisco, California	2,397
Majuro, Marshall Islands	2,271	Seattle, Washington	2,679
Kwajalein, Marshall Islands	2,443	Vancouver, B.C.	2,709
Kolonia, Ponape, E.C.I.	3,087	Victoria, B.C.	2,668
Saipan, Mariana Islands	3,704	Tijuana, Mexico	2,616
Koror, Palau, W.C.I.	4,593	Washington, D.C.	4,829
Other Pacific locations:		Other world cities:	
Apra Harbor, Guam	3,806	Athens, Greece	8,277
Auckland, N.Z.	4,393	Bangkok, Thailand	6,585
Brisbane, Australia	4,743	Bombay, India	8,020
Djakarta, Indonesia	6,807	Cairo, Egypt	8,840
Haiphong, North Viet Nam	6,209	Calcutta, India	7,037
Hong Kong	5,541	Cape Town, South Africa	11,532
Johnston Island	820	Colombo, Ceylon	7,981
Kingman Reef	1,073	London, England	7,226
Manila, Philippines	5,293	Moscow, U.S.S.R.	7,033
Melbourne, Australia	5,513	Paris, France	7,434
Pago Pago, American Samoa	2,606	Peking, China	5,067
Palmyra Islands	1,101	Rio de Janeiro, Brazil	8,190
Papeete, Tahiti	2,741	Rome, Italy	8,022
Saigon, South Viet Nam	6,377	Santiago, Chile	6,861
Shanghai, China	4,934	Vienna, Austria	7,626

1. The great circle distance from Kure Atoll to Cape Kumukahi, Hawaii, is 1,523 statute miles. This distance represents the total length of the Hawaiian Archipelago.

Other Geographic Statistics

Island	Extreme Length (miles)	Extreme Width (miles)	Miles from Coast of Most Remote Point	Percentage of Area with Elevation: Less than 500 ft	Percentage of Area with Elevation: 2,000 ft or more	Percentage of Area with Slope: Less than 10 percent	Percentage of Area with Slope: 10 to 19 percent	Percentage of Area with Slope: 20 percent or more	Miles of Sea Cliffs with Heights of: 100 to 999 ft	Miles of Sea Cliffs with Heights of: 1,000 ft or more
The State	–	–	28.5	20.8	50.9	63.5	19.5	17.0	145	33
Hawaii	93	76	28.5	12.0	68.4	76.0	20.0	4.0	50	4
Maui	48	26	10.6	24.9	41.4	38.5	25.5	36.0	29	–
Kahoolawe	11	6	2.4	38.9	0	60.0	31.0	9.0	14	–
Lanai	18	13	5.2	24.8	6.3	61.0	23.0	16.0	13	1
Molokai	38	10	3.9	37.3	17.8	53.0	21.0	26.0	15	14
Oahu	44	30	10.6	45.3	4.6	42.5	45.5	45.5	3	–
Kauai	33	25	10.8	35.6	24.0	33.5	16.0	50.5	14	11
Niihau	18	6	2.4	78.2	0	68.0	19.5	12.5	7	3

Source: State Department of Planning and Economic Development, Statistical Report 67, *Geographic Statistics of Hawaii*, July 1, 1969 (updated to 1972 where necessary).

Conversion Factors

1 foot = 0.3048 meter
1 meter = 39.37 inches = 3.2808 feet
1 statute mile = 0.8684 nautical mile = 1.60934 kilometers
1 statute mile = 5,280 feet
1 nautical mile = 1.152 statute miles = 1.852 kilometers
1 kilometer = 0.621372 statute miles = 0.5399 nautical miles
1 fathom = 6 feet = 1.8288 meters
1 square kilometer = 247.106 acres = 100 hectares = 0.386103 square miles
1 square mile = 640 acres = 258.998 hectares = 2.58998 square kilometers
1 hectare = 2.47106 acres
1 acre = 43,560 square feet = 0.404685 hectare
1 nautical mile = 1,000 fathoms
1 league = 3 nautical miles
1 mile per hour = 1.467 feet per second = 0.447 meter per second = 1.610 kilometers per hour = 0.868 knot
1 meter per second = 3.600 kilometers per hour = 1.940 knots
1 knot = 1.152 miles per hour = 1.854 kilometers per hour = 0.515 meter per second
1 inch mercury = 25.4 millimeters = 33.8640 millibars
1 millimeter mercury = 0.03937 inch = 1.3332 millibars
1 millibar = 0.02953 inch = 0.75006 millimeter

Fahrenheit to Celsius

°F	0	1	2	3	4	5	6	7	8	9
+90	32.2	32.8	33.3	33.9	34.4	35.00	35.6	36.1	36.7	37.2
+80	26.7	27.2	27.8	28.3	28.9	29.5	30.0	30.5	31.1	31.7
+70	21.1	21.7	22.2	22.8	23.3	23.9	24.4	25.0	25.6	26.1
+60	15.6	16.1	16.7	17.2	17.8	18.3	18.9	19.5	20.0	20.6
+50	10.0	10.6	11.1	11.7	12.2	12.8	13.3	13.9	14.4	15.0
+40	4.4	5.0	5.6	6.1	6.7	7.2	7.8	8.3	8.9	9.5
+30	-1.1	-0.6	0.0	0.6	1.1	1.7	2.2	2.8	3.3	3.9
+20	-6.7	-6.1	-5.6	-5.0	-4.4	-3.9	-3.3	-2.8	-2.2	-1.7
+10	-12.2	-11.7	-11.1	-10.6	-10.0	-9.5	-8.9	-8.3	-7.8	-7.2
+ 0	-17.8	-17.2	-16.7	-16.1	-15.6	-15.0	-14.4	-13.9	-13.3	-12.8

Celsius to Fahrenheit

°C	0	1	2	3	4	5	6	7	8	9
+30	86.0	87.8	89.6	91.4	93.2	95.0	96.8	98.6	100.4	102.2
+20	68.0	69.8	71.6	73.4	75.2	77.0	78.8	80.6	82.4	84.2
+10	50.0	51.8	53.6	55.4	57.2	59.0	60.8	62.6	64.4	66.2
+ 0	32.0	33.8	35.6	37.4	39.2	41.0	42.8	44.6	46.4	48.2
– 0	32.0	30.2	28.4	26.6	24.8	23.0	21.2	19.4	17.6	15.8
-10	14.0	12.2	10.4	8.6	6.8	5.0	3.2	1.4	-0.4	-2.2

Nautical Charts (List of National Ocean Survey Charts for the Hawaiian Islands)

Chart No.	Title	Scale	Chart No.	Title	Scale
4000	Hawaiian Archipelago	1:3,121,170	4132	Oahu—Diamond Head to Pearl Harbor Entrance	1:20,000
4001	Hawaii to French Frigate Shoals	1:1,650,000	4133	Oahu—Ahua Point to Barbers Point	1:20,000
4100	Kauai	1:80,000	4134	Oahu—Kaneohe Bay	1:15,000
4101	Mahukona Harbor and approaches	1:5,000	4136	Port Waianae	1:10,000
4102	Hawaiian Islands	1:600,000	4140	West Coast of Hawaii—Cook Point to Upolu Point	1:80,000
4103	Hilo Bay	1:10,000		Keauhou Bay	1:5,000
4104	Maalaea Bay	1:10,000	4161	Paauhau Landing	1:5,000
4108	Port Allen	1:5,000	4162	Harbors and Landings, Hawaii	
4109	Honolulu Harbor	1:5,000		Punaluu Harbor, Honuapo Harbor,	
4110	Island of Oahu	1:80,000		Honokaa Landing, Kukuihaele Landing	1:2,500
4111	Nawiliwili Bay	1:5,000	4164	Kailua Bay—West Coast of Hawaii	1:5,000
4112	Hanamaulu Bay	1:2,500	4167	Kawaihae Bay—West Coast of Hawaii	1:10,000
4113	Hana Bay	1:5,000	4171	French Frigate Shoals Anchorage	1:25,000
4114	Approaches to Waimea Bay	1:10,000	4172	French Frigate Shoals	1:80,000
4115	Island of Hawaii	1:250,000	4173	Gardner Pinnacles and approaches	1:100,000
4116	Hawaii to Oahu	1:250,000		Gardner Pinnacles	1:20,000
4117	Oahu to Niihau	1:247,482	4174	Maro Reef	1:80,000
4118	Haena Point to Kepuhi Point	1:70,000	4175	Pearl and Hermes Reef	1:40,000
4120	Channels between Oahu, Molokai, and Lanai	1:80,000	4177	Kure Island	1:20,000
4121	Harbors of Molokai		4179	Hawaiian Islands—southern part	1:675,000
	Kaunakakai Hbr., Pukoo Harbor, Kamalo		4180	Hawaiian Islands—northern part	1:675,000
	Harbor, Kolo Harbor, Papohaku Roadstead	1:5,000	4181	Niihau to French Frigate Shoals	1:663,392
4122	Kaumalapau Harbor	1:2,500		Necker Island, Nihoa	1:20,000
4123	Kealakekua Bay to Honaunau Bay	1:10,000	4182	French Frigate Shoals to Laysan Island	1:653,219
4124	Kahului Harbor and approaches	1:30,000	4183	Laysan Island to Kure Island	1:642,271
	Kahului Harbor	1:10,000	4185	Midway Islands and approaches	1:180,000
4125	Approaches to Lahaina, Island of Maui	1:15,000	4186	Lisianski and Laysan Island	1:40,000
4130	Channels between Molokai, Maui,			West Coast of Laysan Island	1:10,000
	Lanai, and Kahoolawe	1:80,000	4188	Midway Islands	1:32,500
4131	Oahu—Waimanalo Bay to Diamond Head	1:20,000	9000	San Diego to Aleutian Islands and	
				Hawaiian Archipelago	1:4,860,700

SELECTED BIBLIOGRAPHY

Entries are grouped according to subject matter. The bibliography is intended only as a basic guide to source materials. No attempt has been made to give a comprehensive listing, nor the serial dates, of the many public documents, annual reports, and statistical publications available.

Geodesy

Chinen, J. J.
1958   *The Great Mahele: Hawaii's Land Division of 1848.* Honolulu: University of Hawaii Press.

Mitchell, H. C.
1930   *Triangulation in Hawaii.* U. S. Coast and Geodetic Survey, Special Publication 156.

Geology

Macdonald, G. A.
1972   *Volcanoes.* Englewood-Cliffs, N. J.: Prentice-Hall.

Macdonald, G. A., and Abbott, A. T.
1970   *Volcanoes in the Sea: The Geology of Hawaii.* Honolulu: University of Hawaii Press.

Macdonald, G. A., and Hubbard, D. H.
1970   *Volcanoes of the National Parks in Hawaii.* 5th ed. [n.p.] Hawaii Natural History Association.

Macdonald, G. A., and Kyselka, W.
1967   *Anatomy of an Island: A Geological History of Oahu.* B. P. Bishop Museum Special Publication 55.

Stearns, H. T.
1966a   *Geology of the State of Hawaii.* Palo Alto, Calif.: Pacific Books.
1966b   *Road Guide to Points of Geologic Interest in the Hawaiian Islands.* Palo Alto, Calif.: Pacific Books.

Wood, H. O.
1914   On the Earthquakes of 1868 in Hawaii. *Bulletin of the Seismological Society of America* 4:169-203.

Earthquakes

Macdonald, G. A., and Wentworth, C. K.
1952   The Kona Earthquake of August 21, 1951, and Its Aftershocks. *Pacific Science* 6:269-287.

Tsunamis

Eaton, J. P., Richter, D. H., and Ault, W. U.
1961   The Tsunami of May 23, 1960, on the Island of Hawaii. *Bulletin of the Seismological Society of America* 51:135-157.

Macdonald, G. A., Shepard, F. P., and Cox, D. C.
1947   The Tsunami of April 1, 1946, in the Hawaiian Islands. *Pacific Science* 1:21-37.

Shepard, F. P., Macdonald, G. A., and Cox, D. C.
1950   The Tsunami of April 1, 1946. *Scripps Institution of Oceanography Bulletin* 5:391-528.

Soils

Cline, M. G., and others
1955   *Soil Survey, Territory of Hawaii, Islands of Hawaii, Kauai, Maui, Molokai, and Oahu.* U. S. Soil Conservation Service, Soil Survey Series 1939, no. 25.

Foote, D. E., and others
In press *Soil Survey of the Islands of Kauai, Oahu, Maui, Molokai and Lanai, State of Hawaii.* U. S. Soil Conservation Service, Soil Survey Series.

Sato, H., and others
In press *Soil Survey of the Island of Hawaii.* U. S. Soil Conservation Service, Soil Survey Series.

United States, Soil Conservation Service, Soil Survey Staff
1960   *Soil Classification: A Comprehensive System, 7th Approximation.* Washington, D. C.

Water

Blumenstock, D. I., and Price, S.
1967   *Climates of the States: Hawaii.* U. S. Environmental Data Service, Climatography of the United States, no. 60-51.

Eckern, P. C., and others
1971   Hydrologic Systems in Hawaii. In *Systems Approach to Hydrology* (V. Yevjevic, ed.), pp. 186-200. Fort Collins, Col.: Water Resources Publications.

Stearns, H. T.
1967   *Geology of the Hawaiian Islands.* Reprint, with supplement. Honolulu: Dept. of Land and Natural Resources, State of Hawaii. (First published in 1946 as Division of Hydrography, Territory of Hawaii, Bulletin 8.)

United States, Water Resources Council
1968   *The Nation's Water Resources.* Washington, D. C.

The Ocean

Barkley, R. A.
1968   *Oceanographic Atlas of the Pacific Ocean.* Honolulu: University of Hawaii Press.

Chase, T. E., Menard, H. W., and Mammerickx, J.
1970   *Bathymetry of the North Pacific.* Scripps Institution of Oceanography, Technical Report IMR-TR 6.

Fan, P-F., and Grunwald, R. R.
1971   Sediment Distribution in the Hawaiian Archipelago. *Pacific Science* 25:484-488.

Macdonald, G. A., and Abbott, A. T.
1970   *Volcanoes in the Sea: The Geology of Hawaii.* Honolulu: University of Hawaii Press.

Malahoff, A., and Woollard, G. P.
1971   Geophysical Studies of the Hawaiian Ridge and Murray Fracture Zone. In *The Sea.* Vol. 4 (A. E. Maxwell, ed.), pt. 2, pp. 73-131. New York: Wiley-Interscience.

Moberly, R., Jr.
1968   Loss of Hawaiian Littoral Sand. *J. of Sedimentary Petrology* 38:17-34.

Moberly, R., Jr., and McCoy, F. W.
1966   The Sea Floor North of the Eastern Hawaiian Islands. *Marine Geology* 4:21-48.

Seckel, G. R.
1962   Atlas of the Oceanographic Climate of the Hawaiian Islands. U. S. Fish and Wildlife Service, Bulletin 193.

Climate

American Meteorological Society
1951   On the Rainfall of Hawaii: A Group of Contributions. Meteorological Monographs, vol. 1, no. 3.

Blumenstock, D. I., and Price, S.
1967   Climates of the States: Hawaii. U. S. Environmental Data Service, Climatography of the United States, no. 60-51.

Eckern, P. C., and Worthley, L. E., comps.
1968   Annotated Bibliography of Publications and Papers Relevant to Hawaiian Weather. Honolulu: Hawaii Institute of Geophysics.

State of Hawaii, Department of Land and Natural Resources, Division of Water and Land Development
1970   An Inventory of Basic Water Resources Data: Island of Hawaii. Report R34. Honolulu.

Taliaferro, W. J.
1959   Rainfall of the Hawaiian Islands. Honolulu: Hawaii Water Authority.
1961   A Key to Climatological Observations in Hawaii. U. S. Weather Bureau, Key to Meteorological Records Documentation 1.11.

United States, Weather Bureau
1962   Rainfall-frequency Atlas of the Hawaiian Islands. Technical Paper 43. Washington, D. C.
1963   Probable Maximum Precipitation in the Hawaiian Islands. Hydrometeorological Report 39. Washington, D. C.

Air Quality

Bach, W., and Lennon, K.
1972   Air Pollution and Health at Ala Moana Shopping Center in Honolulu. Hawaii Medical J. 31:104-113.

State of Hawaii, Department of Health
1972   Air Pollution Control. In Public Health Regulations, chapter 43. Honolulu.

State of Hawaii, Department of Health, Air Sanitation Branch
1972   State of Hawaii Air Pollution Control Implementation Plan. Honolulu. Mimeographed.

Plants

Carlquist, S.
1970   Hawaii: A Natural History. Garden City, N. Y.: Published for the American Museum of Natural History by Natural History Press.

Degener, O.
1933-1963   Flora Hawaiiensis. 6 vols. Honolulu. (Vol. 6 by O. Degener and I. Degener; additional vols. in preparation.)

1945   Plants of Hawaii National Park. Reprint. Ann Arbor, Mich.: Edward Brothers. (First published in 1930.)

Hillebrand, W.
1965   Flora of the Hawaiian Islands. Reprint. New York: Hafner Publishing Co. (First published in 1888.)

Neal, M. C.
1965   In Gardens of Hawaii. Rev. ed. B. P. Bishop Museum Special Publication 50.

Ripperton, J. C., and Hosaka, E. Y.
1942   Vegetation Zones of Hawaii. Hawaii Agricultural Experiment Station, Bulletin 89.

St. John, H.
1972   List and Summary of the Flowering Plants in the Hawaiian Islands. Pacific Tropical Botanical Garden (Koloa, Kauai), Memoir 1.

Mammals

Halloran, A. F.
1972   The Hawaiian Longhorn Story. Hilo, Hawaii: Petroglyph Press.

Kramer, R. J.
1971   Hawaiian Land Mammals. Rutland, Vt.: Charles E. Tuttle Co.

Payne, R. S.
1970   Songs of the Humpback Whale. Del Mar, Calif.: Communications Research Machines (LP stereo recording, 2 sides.)

Titcomb, M.
1969   Dog and Man in the Ancient Pacific. B. P. Bishop Museum Special Publication 59.

Tomich, P. Q.
1969   Mammals in Hawaii: A Synopsis and Notational Bibliography. B. P. Bishop Museum Special Publication 57.

Wirtz, W. O., II
1972   Population Ecology of the Polynesian Rat, Rattus exulans, on Kure Atoll, Hawaii. Pacific Science 26:433-465.

Birds

Alicata, J. E.
1969   Parasites of Man and Animals in Hawaii. Basel, Switzerland: S. Karger.

Berger, A. J.
1972   Hawaiian Birdlife. Honolulu: The University Press of Hawaii.

Fisher, H. I.
1948   The Question of Avian Introductions in Hawaii. Pacific Science 2:59-64.

Hawaii Audubon Society
1967   Hawaii's Birds. Honolulu.

Lewin, V.
1971   Exotic Game Birds of the Puu Waawaa Ranch, Hawaii. J. of Wildlife Management 35:141-155.

Richardson, F., and Bowles, J.
1964   A Survey of the Birds of Kauai, Hawaii. B. P. Bishop Museum, Bulletin 227.

Insects

Carson, H. L., and others
1970   The Evolutionary Biology of the Hawaiian Drosophilidae. In Essays in Evolution and Genetics in Honor of Theodosius Dobzhansky (M. K. Hecht and W. C. Steere, eds.), pp. 437-543. New York: Appleton-Century-Crofts.

Zimmerman, E. C., ed.
1948-   Insects of Hawaii. 12 vols. to date. Honolulu: University of Hawaii Press. (Vols. 1-8 by E. C. Zimmerman; vols. 10-12 by D. E. Hardy and others; vol. 9 by E. C. Zimmerman, forthcoming.)

Fish and Marine Invertebrates

Edmondson, C. H.
1946   Reef and Shore Fauna of Hawaii. B. P. Bishop Museum Special Publication 22.

Gosline, W. A., and Brock, V. E.
1960   Handbook of Hawaiian Fishes. Honolulu: University of Hawaii Press.

Hobson, E. S., and Chave, E. H.
1972 *Hawaiian Reef Animals in Fact and Legend.* Honolulu: The University Press of Hawaii.

Kay, E. A., ed.
1972 *A Natural History of the Hawaiian Islands: Selected Readings.* Honolulu: The University Press of Hawaii.

Archaeology

Green, R. C., ed.
1969 *Makaha Valley Historical Project: Interim Report No. 1.* Pacific Anthropological Records, no. 4. Honolulu: Dept. of Anthropology, B. P. Bishop Museum.
1970 *Makaha Valley Historical Project: Interim Report No. 2.* Pacific Anthropological Records, no. 10. Honolulu: Dept. of Anthropology, B. P. Bishop Museum.

Handy, E. S. C., and Pukui, M. K.
1958 *The Polynesian Family System in Ka-'u, Hawaii.* Wellington, N.Z.: Polynesian Society.

Highland, G. A., and others, eds.
1967 *Polynesian Culture History: Essays in Honor of Kenneth P. Emory.* B. P. Bishop Museum Special Publication 56.

Hommon, R. J., and Barrera, W. M., Jr.
1971 *Archaeological Survey of Kahana Valley, Koolauloa District, Island of Oahu.* Dept. of Anthropology, B. P. Bishop Museum, Report 1971-3.

Kamakau, S. M.
1961 *Ruling Chiefs of Hawaii.* Honolulu: Kamehameha Schools Press.

Newman, T. S.
1970 *Hawaiian Fishing and Farming on the Island of Hawaii in A. D. 1778.* Honolulu: Division of State Parks, Dept. of Land and Natural Resources, State of Hawaii.

Newman, T. S., and others
1970 *Hawaii Register of Historic Places: Bibliography of Hawaiiana.* Hawaii State Archaeological J. 70-3.

Tuggle, H. D., and Griffin, P. B., eds.
In press *Lapakahi: Excavations.* Social Science Research Institute, University of Hawaii, Asian and Pacific Archaeology Series.

History

Anthony, J. G.
1955 *Hawaii Under Army Rule.* Stanford, Calif.: Stanford University Press.

Beaglehole, J. C., ed.
1955-1967 *The Journals of Captain James Cook on His Voyages of Discovery,* 3 vols. Cambridge, England: At the University Press (published for the Hakluyt Society).

Bradley, H. W.
1942 *American Frontier in Hawaii: The Pioneers, 1789-1843.* Stanford, Calif.: Stanford University Press.

Daws, G.
1968 *Shoal of Time: A History of the Hawaiian Islands.* New York: Macmillan & Co.

Fuchs, L.
1961 *Hawaii Pono, a Social History.* New York: Harcourt, Brace & World.

Kuykendall, R. S.
1938-1967 *The Hawaiian Kingdom.* 3 vols. Honolulu: University of Hawaii Press.

Murphy, T. D.
1954 *Ambassadors in Arms: The Story of Hawaii's 100th Battalion.* Honolulu: University of Hawaii Press.

Wakukawa, E. K.
1938 *A History of the Japanese People in Hawaii.* Honolulu: The Toyo Shoin.

Population

Lind, A. W.
1967 *Hawaii's People.* 3rd ed. Honolulu: University of Hawaii Press.

Schmitt, R. C.
1968 *Demographic Statistics of Hawaii: 1778-1965.* Honolulu: University of Hawaii Press.

State of Hawaii, Department of Health
1972 *Statistical Report . . . the Statistical Supplement to the Descriptive Report.* 1970. Honolulu. (Annual.)

State of Hawaii, Department of Planning and Economic Development
1971 *Provisional Estimates of the Population of Hawaii, July 1, 1971.* Statistical Report 86. Honolulu.
1972a *Hawaii's In-migrants.* 1971. Statistical Report 89. Honolulu. (Annual.)
1972b *Statistical Boundaries of Cities, Towns, and Villages as Approved through December 31, 1971.* Report SB-A7. (Updated annually.)

United States, Bureau of the Census
1971a *Census of Population: 1970. General Population Characteristics.* Final Report PC(1)-B13: Hawaii. Washington, D. C.
1971b *Census of Population: 1970. General Social and Economic Characteristics.* Final Report PC(1)-C13: Hawaii. Washington, D. C.
1971c *Census of Population: 1970. Number of Inhabitants.* Final Report PC(1)-A13: Hawaii. Washington, D. C.
In press *Census of Population: 1970. Detailed Characteristics.* Final Report PC(1)-D13: Hawaii. Washington, D. C.

Urban Centers

Baker, H. L., and Dill, H. W.
1969 *Urbanization of Agricultural Land in Hawaii. J. of Soil and Water Conservation* 24.98-100.

Kornhauser, D. H.
1969 *Possible Elements of Portent for Asian Metropolitan Growth: Some Examples from Honolulu.* In *Modernization of the Pacific Region* (Report of the Malaysian Inter-congress Meeting of the Standing Committee on Geography, Pacific Science Congress, Kuala Lumpur, 1969), pp. 17-24.

Marshall Kaplan, Gans, Kahn, and Yamamoto
1971 *Housing in Hawaii: Problems, Needs, and Plans.* Prepared for the State of Hawaii, Dept. of Planning and Economic Development. Honolulu.

United States, Bureau of the Census
1971 *Census of Population: 1970. Number of Inhabitants.* Final Report PC(1)-A13: Hawaii. Washington, D. C.

Vargha, L. A.
1962 *Urban Development on Oahu, 1946-1962.* Land Study Bureau, University of Hawaii, Bulletin 2.
1964 *Urban Development on Oahu, 1962-1963.* Land Study Bureau, University of Hawaii, Bulletin 2, supplement 1.

Languages

Aspinwall, D. B.
1960 Languages in Hawaii. *Publications of the Modern Language Association* 75(no.4, pt.2): 7-13.
Carr, E. B.
1972 *Da Kine Talk: From Pidgin to Standard English in Hawaii.* Honolulu: The University Press of Hawaii.
Hörmann, B. L.
1960 Hawaii's Linguistic Situation: A Sociological Interpretation in the New Key. *Social Process in Hawaii* 24:6-31.
Reinecke, J. E.
1969 *Language and Dialect in Hawaii: A Sociolinguistic History to 1935.* Honolulu: University of Hawaii Press.
Tsuzaki, S. M.
1971 Coexistent Systems of Language Variation: The Case of Hawaiian English. In *Pidginization and Creolization of Languages* (D. Hymes, ed.), pp. 327-340. Cambridge, England: Cambridge University Press.
Tsuzaki, S. M., and Reinecke, J. E.
1966 *English in Hawaii: An Annotated Bibliography.* Honolulu: Pacific and Asian Linguistics Institute, University of Hawaii.

Religions

Comstock, W. R., ed.
1971 *Religion and Man.* New York: Harper & Row.
Gulick, O. R., and Gulick, A. E. C.
1918 *The Pilgrims of Hawaii: Their Own Story of Their Pilgrimage from New England and Life Work in the Sandwich Islands, Now Known as Hawaii.* New York: Fleming H. Revell Co.
Hunter, L. H.
1971 *Buddhism in Hawaii: Its Impact on a Yankee Community.* Honolulu: University of Hawaii Press.
Mulholland, J. F.
1970 *Hawaii's Religions.* Rutland, Vt.: Charles E. Tuttle Co.
Te Rangi Hiroa [P. H. Buck]
1964 *Arts and Crafts of Hawaii.* Section 11: *Religion.* Reprint. B. P. Bishop Museum Special Publication 45. (First published in 1957.)
Yzendoorn, R.
1927 *History of the Catholic Mission in the Hawaiian Islands.* Honolulu: Honolulu Star-Bulletin.

The Arts

Charlot, J.
1958 *Choris and Kamehameha.* Honolulu: Bishop Museum Press.
1963 *Three Plays of Ancient Hawaii.* Honolulu: University of Hawaii Press.
Elbert, S. H., and Mahoe, N., eds.
1970 *Nā Mele o Hawai'i Nei; 101 Hawaiian Songs.* Honolulu: University of Hawaii Press.

Frankenstein, A.
1961 *Angels Over the Altar: Christian Folk Art in Hawaii and the South Seas.* Honolulu: University of Hawaii Press.
Inouye, S.
1965 *The Art of Shugen Inouye.* Kyoto, Japan: Hozokan.
Martel, D. T.
1954 *The Honolulu Academy of Arts. Its Origins and Founder.* Master's thesis, University of Hawaii.
Neil, J. M.
1972 *Paradise Improved; Environmental Design in Hawaii.* American Association of Architectural Bibliographers, Papers, vol. 8
Roberts, H. H.
1967 *Ancient Hawaiian Music.* Republication. New York: Dover Publications. (First published in 1926 as Bulletin 29 of the B. P. Bishop Museum.)

The Economy

Bank of Hawaii
1971 *Hawaii '71: Annual Economic Review.* Honolulu.
First Hawaiian Bank
1971 *Hawaii in 1971.* Honolulu. (Annual.)
Shang, Y-C., Albrecht, W. H., and Ifuku, G.
1970 *Hawaii's Income and Expenditure Accounts, 1958-1968.* Honolulu: Economic Research Center, University of Hawaii.
United States, Bureau of the Census
1971 *County Business Patterns, 1970. CBP-70-13: Hawaii.* Washington, D. C.

Land Tenure

Baker, H. L., and others
1965 *Detailed Land Classification—Island of Hawaii.* Land Study Bureau, University of Hawaii, Bulletin 6.
1968 *Detailed Land Classification—Island of Molokai.* Land Study Bureau, University of Hawaii, Bulletin 10.
Ching, A. Y., and Sahara, T.
1969 *Land Use and Productivity Data State of Hawaii, 1968.* Land Study Bureau, University of Hawaii, Circular 15.
Eckbo, Dean, Austin & Williams
1969 *State of Hawaii Land Use Districts and Regulations Review.* Prepared for the State of Hawaii Land Use Commission. Honolulu.
Economic Research Associates
1969 *Hawaii Land Study: Study of Land Tenure, Land Cost and Future Land Use in Hawaii.* Los Angeles.
Horwitz, R. H., and Finn, J. B.
1967 *Public Land Policy in Hawaii: Major Landowners.* Legislative Reference Bureau, University of Hawaii, Report, 1967, no. 3.
Horwitz, R. H., and Meller, N.
1966 *Land & Politics in Hawaii.* 3rd ed. Honolulu: University of Hawaii Press.
Murabayashi, E. T., and others
1967 *Detailed Land Classification—Island of Kauai.* Land Study Bureau, University of Hawaii, Bulletin 9.
Nelson, L. A., and others
1963 *Detailed Land Classification—Island of Oahu.* Land Study Bureau, University of Hawaii, Bulletin 3.

Sahara, T., and others
1967 Detailed Land Classification—Island of Maui. Land Study Bureau, University of Hawaii, Bulletin 7.
1968 Detailed Land Classification—Island of Lanai. Land Study Bureau, University of Hawaii, Bulletin 8.

Agriculture

Bank of Hawaii
1971 Hawaii '71: Annual Economic Review. Honolulu.
County of Hawaii, Department of Research and Development
1969 Projection for Big Island Agriculture 1968-1973. Hilo, Hawaii.
Hawaiian Sugar Planters' Association
1971 Sugar Manual 1971. Honolulu. (Annual.)
State of Hawaii, Department of Agriculture
1971 Statistics of Hawaiian Agriculture, 1970. Honolulu. (Annual.)
State of Hawaii, Department of Planning and Economic Development
1969 The Life of the Land. Agriculture in Hawaii: Its Background, Problems and Potential. Honolulu.
State of Hawaii, Governor's Agriculture Coordinating Committee
1970 Opportunities for Hawaiian Agriculture. Agricultural Development Plan, State of Hawaii, 1970. Honolulu: Dept. of Planning and Economic Development, State of Hawaii.

Food Sources

Miller, C. D.
1947 Foods and Food Habits in the Hawaiian Islands. J. of the American Dietetic Association 23:766-768.
Miller, C. D., Bazore, K., and Bartow, M.
1965 Fruits of Hawaii. 4th ed. Honolulu: University of Hawaii Press.
Miller, C. D., Louis, L., and Yanazawa, K.
1946 Foods Used by Filipinos in Hawaii. Hawaii Agricultural Experiment Station, Bulletin 98.
Miller, C. D., Weaver, M., and Okita, S.
1949 Food Values of Portions Commonly Used; Hawaii Supplement to Bowes and Church. Honolulu: Home Economics Dept., University of Hawaii.

Commercial Fishing

Brock, V. E.
1965 A Proposed Program for Hawaiian Fisheries. Hawaii Marine Laboratory, Technical Report 6.
Shang, Y-C.
1969 The Skipjack Tuna Industry in Hawaii: Some Economic Aspects. Honolulu: Economic Research Center, University of Hawaii.
State of Hawaii, Department of Planning and Economic Development
1969 Hawaii and the Sea: A Plan for State Action. Honolulu.
State of Hawaii, Governor's Conference on Central Pacific Fishery Resources, Honolulu and Hilo, 1966
1966 Proceedings. Edited and with an introduction by T.A. Manar. Honolulu.

Forestry

Burgan, R. E., and Wong, W. H. C., Jr.
1971 Forest Products Harvested in Hawaii—1969. U.S. Forest Service, Research Note PSW-239.
Nelson, R. E.
1965 A Record of Forest Plantings in Hawaii. U.S. Forest Service, Resource Bulletin PSW-1.
1967 Records and Maps of Forest Types in Hawaii. U.S. Forest Service, Resource Bulletin PSW-8.
Nelson, R. E., and Wheeler, P. R.
1963 Forest Resources of Hawaii, 1961. Honolulu: Forestry Division, Dept. of Land and Natural Resources, State of Hawaii, in cooperation with Pacific Southwest Forest and Range Experiment Station, Forest Service, U.S. Dept. of Agriculture.

Manufacturing and Trade

Bank of Hawaii
1971 Construction in Hawaii—1971. Honolulu. (Annual.)
State of Hawaii, Department of Land and Natural Resources
1971 Report to the Governor 1969-1970. Honolulu. (Annual.)
State of Hawaii, Department of Land and Natural Resources, Division of Forestry
1962 A Multiple Use Program for the State Forest Lands of Hawaii. Honolulu.
United States, Bureau of the Census
1970 Census of Manufactures: 1967. Area Series. MC67(3)-12: Hawaii. Washington, D.C.

Tourism

Hawaii Visitors Bureau
1972a Annual Research Report. 1971. Honolulu.
1972b Visitor Reaction Survey 1971. Honolulu. (Annual summary of quarterly reports and annual supplement.)
Hawaiian Sugar Planters' Association
1971 Sugar Manual 1971. Honolulu. (Annual.)
Pineapple Growers Association of Hawaii
1971 Pineapple Fact Book: 1971. Honolulu. (Annual.)
State of Hawaii, Department of Planning and Economic Development
1969 Hawaii Tourism Data Book, 1969. Honolulu. (Updated annually in The State of Hawaii Data Book, below.)
1971 The State of Hawaii Data Book 1971: A Statistical Abstract. Honolulu. (Annual.)
1972 Tourism in Hawaii: Hawaii Tourism Impact Plan. 2 vols. Honolulu.

Transport

State of Hawaii, Department of Planning and Economic Development
1971 The State of Hawaii Data Book 1971: A Statistical Abstract. Honolulu. (Annual.)
United States, Army, Corps of Engineers
1970 Waterborne Commerce of the United States, Calendar Year 1969, Part 4: Waterways and Harbors, Pacific Coast, Alaska and Hawaii. Washington, D.C. (Annual.)
United States, Board of Engineers for Rivers and Harbors
1970 Ports of the Hawaiian Islands. Port Series, no. 50, pt. 2. Washington, D.C.

Communications

Bretz, R.
1971 A Taxonomy of Communication Media. Englewood-Cliffs, N.J.: Educational Technology Publications.
Broadcasting Publications, Inc.
1971 Broadcasting Yearbook, 1971. Washington, D.C.
State of Hawaii, Department of Defense, Civil Defense Division
1967 Telecommunications. In The State of Hawaii Plan for Emergency Preparedness. Vol. 2: Emergency Resources Management, chapter 12. Honolulu.

1972   Communications. In *The State of Hawaii Plan for Emergency Preparedness*. Vol. 1: *Operational Civil Defense*, chapter 4. Honolulu.

Education

American Council on Education
1946   *Hawaiian Schools: A Curriculum Survey, 1944-45.* Washington, D. C.
Cleveland, H.
1970   *The University of Hawaii: Prospectus for the Seventies.* Honolulu: University of Hawaii.
State of Hawaii, Department of Education
1971   *Facts & Figures: A Digest of Hawaii Public Education Data, 1970-1971.* Honolulu.
University of Hawaii, Academic Development Plan Committee
1969   *Academic Development Plan II for the University of Hawaii, March 1969.* Honolulu: University of Hawaii.
University of Hawaii, Land Grant Centennial Committee
1962   *Land Grant College for the Pacific, 1862-1962.* Honolulu: University of Hawaii.
Wist, B. O.
1940   *A Century of Public Education in Hawaii.* Honolulu: The Hawaii Educational Review.

Health

Schmitt, R. C.
1968   Medical Costs in Hawaii, 1859-1967. *Hawaii Medical J.* 27:236-239.
State of Hawaii, Department of Health
194?/-   *Hawaii Health Messenger.* (Bi-monthly.)
1972   *Statistical Report ...the Statistical Supplement to the Descriptive Report. 1970.* Honolulu. (Annual.)

Recreation

Freund, G.
1969   *Skin Diver's Guide to Hawaii.* Honolulu: Distributed by Pacific Sports.
Grigg, R. W., and Church, R.
1963   *Surfer in Hawaii: A Guide to Surfing in the Hawaiian Islands.* Dana Point, Calif.: John Severson Publications.
Hammel, F., and Levey, S.
1972   *Hawaii on $10 a Day.* 1972-1973 ed. New York: Arthur Frommer.
Kelley, J. M.
1965   *Surf and Sea.* New York: A. S. Barnes.
Kramer, R. J., and Walker, R. L.
1967   *Hunting in Hawaii.* Revised. Honolulu: Division of Fish and Game, Dept. of Land and Natural Resources, State of Hawaii.
MacKellar, J. S.
1968   *Hawaii Goes Fishing.* Rutland, Vt.: Charles E. Tuttle Co.
Morita, C. M.
1963   *Freshwater Fishing in Hawaii.* Honolulu: Division of Fish and Game, Dept. of Land and Natural Resources, State of Hawaii.
Sunset Editorial Staff
1971   *Hawaii: A Guide to All the Islands.* 4th ed. Research and text by N. Bannick. Menlo Park, Calif.: Lane Books. (First published in 1957.)

Services

Catton, M. M. L.
1959   *Social Service in Hawaii.* Palo Alto, Calif.: Pacific Books.
Fitzgerald, W. H., Force, R. W., and Kaeppler, A. L.
1969   *Directory of Asian-Pacific Museums.* Honolulu: Bishop Museum Press.
Health and Community Services Council of Hawaii
1972   *Directory of Social Resources: Health, Welfare, Recreation, Education.* January, 1972. Honolulu.
Luster, A. D. C., comp.
1970   *A Directory of Libraries and Information Sources in Hawaii and the Pacific Islands.* Edited by L. Engelberg. Indexed by D. H. Truitt. Hawaii Library Association J., vol. 27, no. 2.

Place Names

Alexander, W. D.
1903   *Hawaiian Geographic Names.* U. S. Coast and Geodetic Survey, Report for 1902, Appendix 7.
Coulter, J. W.
1935   *A Gazetteer of the Territory of Hawaii.* University of Hawaii, Research Publications 11.
Pukui, M. K., and Elbert, S. H.
1966   *Place Names of Hawaii.* Honolulu: University of Hawaii Press.
1971   *Hawaiian Dictionary; Hawaiian-English, English-Hawaiian.* Honolulu: University of Hawaii Press.
Sterling, E. P., and Summers, C. C.
1962   *The Sites of Oahu.* 6 vols. Honolulu: Bishop Museum Press.
Summers, C. C.
1971   *Molokai: A Site Survey.* Pacific Anthropological Records no. 14. Honolulu: Dept. of Anthropology, B. P. Bishop Museum.
Thrum, T. G.
1922   Hawaiian Place Names. In *A Dictionary of the Hawaiian Language* (by L. Andrews, revised by H. H. Parker), pp. 625-674. Honolulu: Board of Commissioners of the Public Archives of the Territory of Hawaii.
United States, Board on Geographic Names
1954   *Decisions on Names in Hawaii.* Cumulative Decision List 5403. Washington, D. C.

REFERENCES CITED

Ayer Directory 1970: Newspapers, Magazines and Trade Publications. Philadelphia: Ayerpress.

Burch, T. A.
1971 Health Statistics as Socio-environmental Indicators. In *Proceedings of the Conference on Socio-environmental Indicators.* Honolulu, 1971 (State of Hawaii, Dept. of Planning and Economic Development, pp. 26–39. Honolulu.

Cline, M. G., and others
1955 *Soil Survey, Territory of Hawaii, Islands of Hawaii, Kauai, Lanai, Maui, Molokai, and Oahu.* U. S. Soil Conservation Service. Soil Survey Series 1939, no. 25.

Ellis, W.
1783 *An Authentic Narrative of a Voyage Performed by Captain Cook and Captain Clerke... in Search of a Northwest Passage between the Continents of Asia and America.* Vol. 2. London: G. Robinson, J. Sewell and J. Debrett.

Fan, P-F., and Grunwald, R. R.
1971 Sediment Distribution in the Hawaiian Archipelago. *Pacific Science* 25:484–488.

Fitzgerald, W. H., Force, R. W., and Kaeppler, A. L.
1969 *Directory of Asian-Pacific Museums.* Honolulu: Bishop Museum Press.

Foote, D. E., and others
In press *Soil Survey of the Islands of Kauai, Oahu, Maui, Molokai and Lanai, State of Hawaii.* U. S. Soil Conservation Service, Soil Survey Series.

Howarth, F. G.
1972 Cavernicoles in Lava Tubes on the Island of Hawaii. *Science* 175 (4019):325–326.

Küchler, A. W.
1970 Potential Natural Vegetation of Hawaii. In *The National Atlas of the United States of America* (U. S. Geological Survey), p. 92. Washington, D.C.

Lind, A. W.
1967 *Hawaii's People.* 3rd ed. Honolulu: University of Hawaii Press.

Luster, A. D. C., comp.
1970 *A Director of Libraries and Information Sources in Hawaii and the Pacific Islands.* Edited by L. Engelberg. Indexed by D. H. Truitt. Hawaii Library Association J., vol. 27, no. 2.

Moberly, R., Jr.
1968 Loss of Hawaiian Littoral Sand. J. *of Sedimentary Petrology* 38: 17–34.

Morgan, T.
1948 *Hawaii. A Century of Economic Change, 1778–1876.* Cambridge, Mass.: Harvard University Press.

Neal, M. C.
1965 *In Gardens of Hawaii.* Rev. ed. B. P. Bishop Museum Special Publication 50.

Pukui, M. K., and Elbert, S. H.
1966 *Place Names of Hawaii.* Honolulu: University of Hawaii Press.

Ripperton, J. C., and Hosaka, E. Y.
1942 *Vegetation Zones of Hawaii.* Hawaii Agricultural Experiment Station, Bulletin 89.

Rothschild, W.
1893–1900 *The Avifauna of Laysan and the Neighbouring Islands.* 2 vols. London: R. H. Porter.

St. John, H.
1972 *List and Summary of the Flowering Plants in the Hawaiian Islands.* Pacific Tropical Botanical Garden (Koloa, Kauai), Memoir 1.

Sato, H., and others
In press *Soil Survey of the Island of Hawaii.* U. S. Soil Conservation Service, Soil Survey Series.

Schmitt, R. C.
1968 *Demographic Statistics of Hawaii: 1778–1965.* Honolulu: University of Hawaii Press.

State of Hawaii, Department of Planning and Economic Development
1971 *State Comprehensive Outdoor Recreation Plan.* Consultants: Marshall Kaplan, Gans, Kahn, and Yamamoto. Honolulu.

Stearns, H. T.
1946 *Geology of the Hawaiian Islands.* Division of Hydrography, Territory of Hawaii, Bulletin 8.

Te Rangi Hiroa [P. H. Buck]
1964 *Arts and Crafts of Hawaii.* Reprint. B. P. Bishop Museum Special Publication 45. (First published in 1957.)

Tsuzaki, S. M.
1971 Coexistent Systems of Language Variation: The Case of Hawaiian English. In *Pidginization and Creolization of Languages* (D. Hymes, ed.), pp. 327–340. Cambridge, England. Cambridge University Press.

United States Exploring Expedition
1844 *Atlas of Charts.* Vol. 2. From the Surveys of the Expedition... during 1838–1841. Charles Wilkes, leader. Philadelphia: C. Sherman and Sons.

United States, Soil Conservation Service, Soil Survey Staff
1960 *Soil Classification: A Comprehensive System, 7th Approximation.* Washington, D. C.

United States, Water Resources Council
1968 *The Nation's Water Resources.* Washington, D. C.

Wilson, S. B., and Evans, A. H.
1890–1899 *Aves Hawaiienses: The Birds of the Sandwich Islands.* London: R. H. Porter.

Zimmerman, E. C.
1957 *Insects of Hawaii.* Vol. 6: *Emphemeroptera, Neuroptera, Trichoptera.* Honolulu: University of Hawaii Press.

212

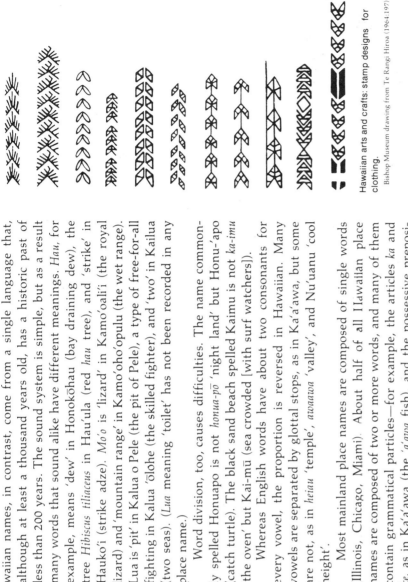

Hawaiian arts and crafts: stamp designs for clothing.
Bishop Museum drawing from Te Rangi Hiroa (1964:197)

THE PLACE NAMES

The spelling used on the reference maps and in the gazetteer of the Atlas differs from that used on the U.S. Geological Survey maps in that the glottal stops in Hawaiian place names are shown by apostrophes, and macrons are placed over long, stressed vowels. This is done to help persons not familiar with the places to pronounce their names correctly. As the number of speakers of Hawaiian as a mother tongue has steadily decreased, the pronunciation has become more and more anglicized. Fortunately, young people of Hawaiian ancestry are showing increased interest in the language of their forefathers, as are a great number of other islanders. Such persons, if they are to pronounce the names correctly, need these two symbols. Otherwise, how are they to know that the Moloka'i town Kala'e and the southernmost point in the United States, Ka Lae, do not rhyme? How are they to know that 'Ala'e on Hawai'i ends with a long and stressed final -'e, but that the crater 'Alae on the same island ends with final 'lae? Furthermore, unless the pronunciation is known, translation of a name is impossible.

For spellings and pronunciations the compilers of the Atlas have depended on *Place Names of Hawai'i*, now in preparation by Mary Kawena Pukui, Samuel H. Elbert, and Esther T. Mookini, as a revision and expansion of Pukui and Elbert's earlier *Place Names of Hawaii*. Names whose pronunciation is not known to the compilers are marked with asterisks. It is hoped that persons with knowledge of these names will inform the editors so that future editions may be corrected.

Once the pronunciation is known, translation of Hawaiian place names is in general easier, for example, than translation of American Indian names, which come from languages belonging to numerous families with complex sound systems. The Hawaiian names, in contrast, come from a single language that, although at least a thousand years old, has a historic past of less than 200 years. The sound system is simple, but as a result many words that sound alike have different meanings. *Hau*, for example, means 'dew' in Honokōhau (bay draining dew), the tree *Hibiscus tiliaceus* in Hau'ula (red *hau* tree), and 'strike' in Hauko'i (strike adze). *Mo'o* is 'lizard' in Kamo'oali'i (the royal lizard) and 'mountain range' in Kamo'oho'opulu (the wet range). Lua is 'pit' in Kalua o Pele (the pit of Pele), a type of free-for-all fighting in Kalua 'ōlohe (the skilled fighter), and 'two' in Kailua (two seas). (*Lua* meaning 'toilet' has not been recorded in any place name.)

Word division, too, causes difficulties. The name commonly spelled Honuapo is not *honua-pō* 'night land' but Honu-'apo (catch turtle). The black sand beach spelled Kaimu is not *ka-imu* 'the oven' but Kai-mū (sea crowded [with surf watchers]).

Whereas English words have about two consonants for every vowel, the proportion is reversed in Hawaiian. Many vowels are separated by glottal stops, as in Ka'a'awa, but some are not, as in *heiau* 'temple', *awaawa* 'valley', and Nu'uanu 'cool height'.

Most mainland place names are composed of single words (Illinois, Chicago, Miami). About half of all Hawaiian place names are composed of two or more words, and many of them contain grammatical particles—for example, the articles *ka* and *ke*, as in Ka'a'awa (the *'a'awa* fish), and the possessive prepositions *a* and *o*, as in Haleakalā (house of the sun) and Pu'u o Pele (hill of Pele). The most common prefixes are *hana-* and *hono-*, both meaning 'bay', as in Hanalei (*lei* bay) and Honolulu (sheltered bay).

Topographic terms commonly used in the place names follow:

wai 'stream, river, pond, fresh water', as in Waikīkī (spouting water)
pu'u 'hill, mound', as in Pu'unēnē (goose hill)
moku 'island, district', as in Mokumanu (bird island)
lua 'pit, crater', as in Kaluako'i (the adze pit)
lae 'cape, point, forehead' as in Ka Lae (the point)
mauna 'mountain, peak', as in Mauna Kea (white mountain) and Mauna Loa (long Mountain)
kai 'sea', as in Kailua (two seas)

A few adjectives occur frequently: *loa* 'long', *nui* 'large', *iki* 'small', and *ula* 'red' (by far the most common color found in the place names—which is not surprising, since red was the sacred Polynesian color and a symbol of royalty).

Post-contact iron hatchet head.
Drawing by T. Stell Newman

The place names may be classified as descriptive, legendary, cultural, transferred, and newly coined:

Descriptive names include the previously mentioned Honolulu, Mauna Kea, Mauna Loa, and Nuʻuanu, as well as Kawailoa (the long stream), Puʻu ʻUlaʻula (red hill), and many more.

Names with legendary associations include the names of gods and demigods of old, as Nā iwi o Pele (the bones of Pele) and Wai a Kāne (water of Kāne). On each island was a *heiau* called Hale o Lono, dedicated to worship of Lono, god of clouds, the sea, agriculture, and fertility. The island of Maui was named for the culture hero, Māui, who snared the sun in the crater of Haleakalā to lengthen the day so that his mother, Hina, would have time to dry her tapa. The island name must once have been Māui, but during the centuries it has been shortened to present-day Maui.

Kohelepelepe (fringed vagina) is an old name for Koko Crater. Kamapuaʻa, the pig god, attempted to ravish Pele at Kapoho, Hawaiʻi; Pele's sister, Kapo, had a flying vagina that she could send where she willed. She sent it to entice Kamapuaʻa, who straightway forgot Pele and followed the flying object to Koko Crater, Oʻahu, where it landed, left an imprint, and then flew away to Kalihi.

Names that show the cultural interests of the Hawaiians include words for objects of material culture and the names of plants and animals. We find *hale* 'house', *pā* 'fence, enclosure', *waʻa* 'canoe', *lei* 'garland', *lama* 'torch', and *koʻi* 'adze'.

Plant names, especially *kukui* 'candlenut' and *hau* 'Hibiscus tiliaceus', are extremely common: on each of the major islands is a place called Kukui. The kukui is the State tree, a symbol of enlightenment and wisdom because its nuts were used for small oil lamps. Other plants named frequently are *niu* 'coconut', *hala* 'pandanus', the *maile* vine, and the *lehua* flower. In all, at least 153 plant names have been noted.

Names of fish and other sealife are less common. They include *manō* 'shark', *puhi* 'eel', and such well-known fish as *ʻahi*, *ʻama*, *ʻanae*, *awa*, *kala*, *kūmū*, *uhu*, and *ulua*. Land animals named are *puaʻa* 'pig', *ʻīlio* 'dog', *ʻiole* 'rat', and the birds *pueo* 'owl', *ʻalae* 'mudhen', *ʻalalā* 'crow', and *ʻelepaio* 'flycatcher', as well as *manu* 'bird'.

Names brought from the homeland in the original Hawaiian migrations may have been numerous, but only a few survive that are definitely known as place names elsewhere. Hawaiʻi, Kaʻū, and ʻUpolu are cognate (that is, derived from a single source) with Savaiʻi, Taʻū, and ʻUpolu, all of them names of islands in Samoa. Cognates of Koʻolau (windward) and Kona (leeward) occur in most parts of Polynesia—for example, the Tokelau Islands, north of Samoa, and the Kingdom of Tonga, far to the south. Kahiki-nui on East Maui is cognate with Tahiti-nui in Tahiti and Tawhitinui in New Zealand. Except for Koʻolau and Kona, these names have no meanings in Hawaiian. Other important names without meanings and for which cognates have not been found in the South Sea islands include Kauaʻi and Molokaʻi.

Place names are continually being coined, especially by developers, who, in seeking names for their developments and new streets, unfortunately do not look for the old Hawaiian names, or endeavor to discover who were the original owners of the land. The area once known as Kaʻelepulu (the wet blackness) is now Enchanted Lake. Kokokahi (one blood) was the name given by Theodore Richards for an interracial camp. The name Lanikai is probably a mistake for Kailani (heavenly sea)—why would the area have been named 'marine heaven', the literal translation of Lanikai?

Hawaiian place names, then, hold other attractions than their pleasant and mellifluous sounds, for they describe the deeds of their culture heroes, and the close relationship of Hawaiians to their Polynesian cousins to the south.

S.H.E.

Gazetteer

Alphabetical listing of place names on the reference maps, pages 10 through 22.

The first letter and number at the right of each entry refer to the index of letters (along the left margins) and numbers (along the top margins) of each reference map. The number at the far right identifies the page where the entry appears. For example, **Hana**, Maui ... **D14 15** means that on page **15**, **Hana** can be found by looking in the square formed where **D** intersects with **14**.

Place names enclosed in parentheses are names in common use that are not recognized as the preferred ones. In each case, the more correct alternative is given alongside without parentheses; for example, **(Kamuela) Waimea**, Ha. Geographic labels in parentheses after place names (such as **hill** and **point**), are included to help identify the entry but are not commonly used as part of the name; for example, **Ahumoa (hill)**, Ha. Place names with no geographic label, with or without parentheses, are localities, villages, towns, or cities; for example, **Hilo**, Ha. Island abbreviations after each entry are as follows: Ha. = Hawaii, Ka. = Kauai, Kah. = Kahoolawe, Lan. = Lanai, Maui = Maui, Mid. = Midway Islands, Mol. = Molokai, Ni. = Niihau, NWHI = Northwestern Hawaiian Islands, Oahu = Oahu. The Midway Islands, while not part of the State of Hawaii, are included in the Gazetteer.

Pronunciation of Hawaiian names is aided by the inclusion of the glottal stop ', which indicates a stopping of sound, as between the vowel sounds in "oh oh!" in English, and by macrons over vowels—ā, ē, ī, ō, ū—which denote long stress. An asterisk preceding a place name indicates that pronunciation of that name is uncertain.

A

'Aahoaka (hill), Ka. ... C6 11
'Aahuwela (hill), Ha. ... G9 19
'Aka Ridge, Ka. ... D3 11
'Aikahi Gulch, Oahu ... B5 17
'Aakukui Valley, Ka. ... D3 11
'Aawela (hill), Ka. ... D4 11
Adams Bay, NWHI ... C4 22
'Ahia, Pu'u (hill), Ha. ... H6 18
'Ahihi Bay, Maui ... C5 17
'Ahihi Point, Ka. ... F8 14
'Ahiu, Kipuka (oasis), Ha. ... B7 11
'Ahole Rock, Maui ... N10 21
'Ahua Point, Oahu ... F13 15
'Ahualiku (peak), Ka. ... F5 12
'Ahualoa Gulch, Ha. ... D4 11
'Ahuimanu Stream, Oahu ... D8 17
'Ahulili, Pu'u (peak), Maui ... D6 11
Ahuloa, Ha. ... E12 15
'Aia Point, Ha. ... P3 20
Ahumoa, Ha. ... C4 17
'Aiamanu (hill), Ha. ... G6 18
Ahu o Laka Island, Oahu ... D7 17
'Ailii, Pu'u (hill), Ha. ... B2 14
Ahupi Bay, Kah. ... D7 17
'Ailii, Pu'u (hill), Lan. ... B3 14
Ahupi Iki Gulch, Kah. ... B3 14
'Alii Shores, Oahu ... F1 13
'Aika Cone, Ha. ... C5 16
'Aiaka'alala, Kipuka (Oasis), Ha. ... N6 20
'Aika Lava Flow, Ha. ... O3 20
'Aiea, Oahu ... N4 20
'Aiea, Pu'u (hill), Ha. ... C4 17
'Alo'i Crater, Ha. ... E6 12
Aiea Heights, Oahu ... E5 12
Aluea Rocks, Maui ... F7 12
Aiea Stream, Oahu ... C6 17
'Amuamu, Pu'u (hill), Ha. ... H8 19
'Aina Haina, Oahu ... Q3 20
'Amikopala (hill), Mol. ... N4 20
'Ainahou (hill), Ha. ... M11 21
'Ainahou (Lava Flats), Ha. ... C12 15
'Anahola, Ka. ... F6 17
'Ainakoa, Oahu ... E3 17
'Anahola Bay, Ha. ... E3 17
'Aina Moana (Magic Island), Oahu ... A3 16
'Anahola Stream, Ka. ... B6 11
'Ainaola Road, Ha. ... B7 11
Anahulu (hill), Ha. ... F3 17
'Ainapo Trail, Ha. ... B4 12
Anahulu River, Oahu ... B6 14
'Akahipu'u (hill), Ha. ... A6 16
Anakaluahine Gulch, Maui ... H14 19
Akahukaimu, Ha. ... D13 15
Ananoio, Mol. ... A2 16
'Akaka Falls, Ha. ... D6 11
*Anapalau Point, Ka. ... F12 19
Akaka, Kipuka (oasis), Ha. ... A4 16
Anapuka (cave), Maui ... A5 11
*Akasaki Camp, Ha. ... E12 15
Anapuka (cave), Mol. ... M7 18
'Akihi (mountain), Ha. ... 'Anini Beach, Ka. ...
'Akō'ako'a Point, Ha. ... 'Anini Stream, Ka. ...
Akōlea Road, Ha. ... D10 15
Andrade Camp, Ha. ... Anipe'ahi, Ha. ... M3 18
'Alae (peak), Mol. ... Annexation Hill, NWHI ...
Alae Crater, Ha. ... Anu, Pu'u (hill), Maui ... D7 14

Alakaha Point, Ha. ... D10 19
Alakahi Stream, Ha. ... E8 17
Alaka'i Swamp, Ka. ... B4 11
Alakukui Point, Ka. ... C7 11
'Alalā, Kipuka (oasis), Ha. ... J5 18
'Alalā, Pu'u (hill), Ni. ... B2 10
'Alalā Lava Flow, Ha. ... M6 18
Alalā Point, Oahu ... O3 20
'Alalākeiki Channel, Maui ... G8 12
Ala Moana Beach, Oahu ... B7 16
Alanahihi Point, Ha. ... D6 13
Alanaio Stream, Ha. ... A6 11
Alapi'i Point, Ka. ... A4 17
'Alau Island, Maui ... D14 19
'Alau, Pu'u (hill), Ka. ... B2 11
Auwae, Ha. ... E14 15
'Auwaiakeakua Gulch, Ha. ... C2 18
'Awaawapuhi Valley, Ka. ... C3 14
Awake'e Bay, Ha. ... H12 19
Awalua, Maui ... E12 15
Awāwakāhoa (stream), Ha. ... H12 19
'Awehi, Lan. ... F13 15
'Awehi (stream), Ha. ... B5 13
'Awehi Gulch, Lan. ... D4 11
Awili Point, Ka. ... F12 19
'Awini Falls, Ka. ... F12 19
Awini Pu'ali Gulch, Ha. ... B4 17

'Apa'apa'a, Pu'u (hill), Ha. ... B3 17
Apakue (hill), Ha. ... E8 19
'Apala, Pu'u (hill), Mol. ... A2 16
Apana Valley, Ni. ... C1 10
'Apole Point, Maui ... F11 15
'Apua Point, Ha. ... B5 17
'Apua Point, Ha. ... N11 21
Arched Rock, Ha. ... O3 20
'Au, Pu'u (hill), Mol. ... B7 16
'Au'au, Pu'u (hill), Ka. ... D6 13
'Au'au Point, Ha. ... E4 16
'Au'au Point, Ha. ... N3 20
Aukai, Pu'u (hill), Ka. ... D4 11

B

Baldwin Avenue, Maui ... C9 15
Barbers Point, Oahu ... F3 12
Barbers Point Housing, Oahu ... F4 12
Barbers Point Naval Air Station, Oahu ... F4 12
Bare Island, NWHI ... B4 22
Barking Sands (beach), Ka. ... C1 11
(Barking Sands) 'Ohiki
Lolo Beach, Oahu ... F1 13
Barking Sands Missile Range, Ka. ... C2 11
Bellows Air Force Station, Oahu ... E8 17
Bensaleux Reef, NWHI ... B1 22
Big Hill Camp, Ha. ... M4 18
(Black Sand Beach) Kaimū Beach, Ha. ... M14 21
Blonde Reef, NWHI ... C15 19
Blowhole (Hālona Point), Oahu ... F8 12
Brooks Shoal, NWHI ... B4 22
Bird Island, NWHI ... N5 20

C

C Village, Oahu ... F4 12
Camp H.M. Smith Naval Reserve, Oahu ... A2 13
15 3/4 Mile Road, Ha. ... L2 18
Carter Point, Ka. ... D6 11
Catlin Naval Reserve, Oahu ... C2 13
Chain of Craters, Ha. ... A5 11
Chain of Craters Road, Ha. ... M11 21
City of Refuge National
Historical Park, Ha. ...
(Coconut Island) Moku o Loe, Oahu ... D7 14

Cook Point, Ha. ... L2 18
Crater Hill, Ha. ... A6 11
Crater Reservoir, Maui ... C3 14
Crater Rim Road, Ha. ... M10 21
Crestview, Oahu ... C6 12
Crouching Lion, Oahu ... C6 12
Crown Terrace, Oahu ... F1 13

D

Devil Country, Ha. ... J4 18
Dewey Cone, Ha. ... K7 18
Diamond Head, Oahu ... F7 12
Dillingham Air Force Base, Oahu ... C2 12
Disappearing Island, NWHI ... B1 22
Disappearing Sands beach, Ha. ... J2 18
Dowsett Highlands, Oahu ... A6 13
Dowsett Reef, NWHI ... B3 22

E

East Loch, Oahu ... E5 12
Eastern Island, Mid. ... C1 22
Ehu, Pu'u (hill), Ka. ... B6 11
Ehu, Pu'u (hill), Maui ... C10 15
'Ekahanui Gulch, Oahu ... D4 17
'Eke Crater, Maui ... D5 17
Eke, Ha. ... B7 14
Ekuakapua'a, Ha. ... R6 20
'Eleao (peak), Oahu ... D6 12
'Ele'ele, Ka. ... E3 17
'Ele'ele, Pu'u (hill), Ha. ... L7 18
'Elehāhā Stream, Oahu ... B4 12
'Eleuweuwe Gulch, Mol. ... A4 16
Elevenmile Homestead, Ha. ... J13 19
'Enuhe, Pu'u (hill), Ha. ... O7 20
'Enuhe Ridge, Oahu ... O7 20
Eo, Pu'u (hill), Ha. ... C14 19
Eu, Pu'u (hill), Ka. ... B6 11
'Ewa, Oahu ... E4 12
'Ewa Beach, Oahu ... F12 19
'Ewa District, Oahu ... E4 12

F

Farrington Highway, Oahu ... D2 12
Fern Grotto, Ka. ... C6 11
Fernandez Village, Ha. ... E4 12
15 3/4 Mile Road, Ha. ... J12 21
(Fleming) Kapalua Beach, Maui ... A5 14
Ford Island, Oahu ... E5 12
Ft. De Russy Military Reserve, Oahu ... C2 13
Ft. Ruger Military Reserve, Oahu ... D7 13
Foster Village, Oahu ... D8 13
French Frigate Shoals, NWHI ... M3 18
Frigate Point, Mid. ... D7 12

G

Gambia Shoal, NWHI ... B1 22
Garden of the Gods, Lan. ... E2 16
Gardner Pinnacles, NWHI ... B3 22
Gaspars Dairy, Ha. ... L4 18
General Lyman Field
(Hilo Airport), Ha. ... H13 19
Gin Island, NWHI ... B4 22
Glenwood, Ha. ... L12 21
Gooney Spit Island, Mid. ... C1 22
Grass Island, NWHI ... D1 22
Great Crack, Ha. ... O8 20
Green Island, NWHI ... D1 22
Green Lake, Ha. ... K15 21

H

Ha'akoa Stream, Ha. ... E11 19
Hā'ao, Pu'u (hill), Ha. ... P6 20
Hā'ao Valley, Ni. ... C1 10
Hā'ele'ele Ridge, Ka. ... B2 11
Hā'ele'ele Valley, Ka. ... B6 11
Hi'ena, Ha. ... B3 17
Hā'ena, Ha. ... J14 19
Hā'ena, Ka. ... A4 11
Hā'ena Point, Ha. ... B3 17
Hā'ena Point, Ka. ... A4 11
Hā'ena Point, Ka. ... J14 21
Hā'ione Valley, Oahu ... E9 13
Hā'enokalele, Ha. ... D6 12
Hāhākea Gulch, Maui ... E13 15
Hāhālawe Gulch, Maui ... L7 18
Hā'ikū, Maui ... B10 15
Hā'ikū Point, Ha. ... E11 19
Hā'ikū Valley, Oahu ... E6 17
Haina, Ha. ... C8 17
Hainoa, Ha. ... O7 20
Hainoa Crater, Ha. ... H3 18
Haipua'ena Stream, Maui ... A4 16
Hā'iwahine, Pu'u (hill), Ha. ... G8 19
Hāka'a'ano, Mol. ... A7 16
Hakalau Bay, Ha. ... F12 19
Hakalau Stream, Ha. ... F12 19
Hakina Gulch, Mol. ... G10 19
Hakioawa, Kah. ... B1 16
Hakuhe'e Point, Maui ... A3 14
Hala Point, Ha. ... B7 14
Hālāli'i (cone), Maui ... L16 20
Hālāli'i (Lake), Ni. ... E11 15
Halapē Trail, Ha. ... C1 10
Hala'ula, Ha. ... N10 21
Hālawa, Ha. ... B4 17
Hālawa, Mol. ... B4 17
Hālawa, Cape, Mol. ... B2 13
Hālawa Bay, Mol. ... B8 13
Hālawa Bay, Mol. ... A8 16
Hālawa Point, Mid. ... C1 22

Kahi'u Point, Mol. A5 16
Kahiwa Falls, Mol. A7 16
Kahoaloha Valley, Ka. C2 11
Kahoana Valley, Ka. C2 11
Kaho'iawa Bay, Ha. G1 18
Kaho'iawa Point, Ha. G1 18
Kaholaiki Bay, Mol. A6 16
Kaholo Pali (cliff), Lan. F2 16
Kaholopo'ohina, Ha. D5 17
Kahoma Stream, Maui C6 14
Kahonua, Ha. L16 21
Kaho'olawe (island), Kah. -- 14
Kaho'olewa Ridge, Maui C6 14
Kaho'opulu (peak), Ka. B6 11
Kahuā (hill), Maui E10 15
Kahuā Ranch, Ha. C4 17
*Kahuaawi Gulch, Mol. B4 16
Kahuama'a Flat, Ka. B3 11
Kahuamoa (peak), Ka. D4 11
Kahuaolohu, Ha. Q7 20
Kahue Point, Ha. N12 21
Kahuihonu, Kīpuka (oasis), Ha. P6 20
Kahuku, Oahu A5 12
Kahuku (point), Ha. Q6 20
Kahuku Point, Oahu A5 12
Kahuku Ranch, Ha. Q5 20
Kahukupoko, Ha. R5 20
Kahului, Ha. H14 19
Kahului, Maui C8 14
E5 14
Kahului Airport, Maui C8 14
Kahului Bay, Ha. J2 18
Kahului Bay, Maui C8 14
Kahuna Falls, Ha. F12 19
Kahunali'i Valley, Ni. B2 10
Kahuwai Bay, Ha. F2 17
Kahuwai Crater, Ha. L15 21
Kahuwai Gulch, Mol. A3 16
Kaiaakea Point, Ha. E11 19
Kaiakekua (beach), Ha. Q3 20
Kaiehu Point, Mol. A3 16
Ka'ie'ie Stream, Ha. G12 19
Ka'ie'ie Waho Channel, Ka. E6 11
Kaihalulu Bay, Maui D14 15
Kaiholena (hill), Ha. D5 17
Kaiholena (hill), Ha. O6 20
Kaihuakala (peak), Maui E13 15
*Kaikipauula (peak), Ha. E8 17
Ka'ili'ili, Maui C10 15
Kā'iliki'i, Ha. R5 20
Ka'ilio, Pu'u (hill), Oahu D3 12
Ka'ili'o Point, Ka. A3 11
Kailua (Kona), Ha. J2 18
Kailua, Maui C11 15
Kailua, Oahu E3 12
Kailua Bay, Ha. J1 18
Kailua Bay, Oahu D8 12
Kailua Beach, Oahu D8 12
Kailua Gulch, Maui D10 15
Kailua Stream, Maui C11 15
Kailuapuhi, Oahu F3 13
Kaimalo'o (peak), Maui F9 14
Kaimū, Ha. M14 21
Kaimū Beach (Black Sand Beach), Ha. M14 21
Kaimū Stream, Ha. C5 17
Kaimukanaka Falls, Ha. D13 19
Kaimukī, Oahu C8 13
Kaimu'uwala, Ha. R4 20
Kaimu'uwala, Pu'u (hill), Ha. R5 20
Ka'inalimu Bay, Maui D14 15
Kaināliu, Ha. K2 18
Ka'inamanu (peak), Ka. B3 11
Ka'inapua'a, Pu'u (hill), Oahu B5 12
Kaiolohia Bay, Lan. D3 16
Kai'olu Bay, Ha. R6 20
Kai'opae Point, Ha. D3 17
Kaipapa'u Point, Oahu B6 12
Kaipapa'u Stream, Oahu B5 12
Kaipukaihina, Maui D8 14
Ka'iwa Point, Ka. E4 11
Ka'iwa Ridge, Oahu E8 12
Ka'iwa Stream, Ka. B5 11
Kaiwi Channel, Oahu F8 12
Kaiwi Point, Ha. F3 17
Kaiwi Point, Ha. J1 18
Kaiwiiwi, Pu'u (hill), Ha. G9 19
Kaiwiko'ele Stream, Oahu B4 12
Kaiwilahilahi Stream, Ha. E10 19
Ka Iwi o Pele (hill), Maui E14 15
Kaiwipo'o, Pu'u (hill), Oahu D6 12

Kākā Point, Kah. C4 14
Kaka'ako Gulch, Mol. A2 16
Kaka'a'u'uku Gulch, Mol. A3 16
Kakahai'a Fishpond, Mol. C5 16
Kakanihia, Pu'u (hill), Ha. D6 17
*Kakapa Bay, Ha. G1 17
*Kaki Point, Ka. D3 11
Kākio, Ha. R4 20
Kākio, Maui E14 15
Kākio Point, Ha. P2 20
*Kakipi Stream, Maui C10 15
Kākīwai (point), Ha. N10 21
Kala'alā'au Valley, Ni. C2 10
Kala'au o Kalakoni (point), Ha. K2 18
Kala'e, Mol. A5 16
Ka Lae (South Point), Ha. S5 20
Kalaeāhole (point), Lan. E1 16
Kalae'āmana (point), Ka. A7 11
Kalae'apuki (point), Ha. N13 21
Kalaehiamoe, Ha. M14 21
Kalaekapu (point), Mol. B8 16
Kalaekīki (point), Ka. E5 11
Kalaeloa, Maui F8 14
Kalaeloa (sandspit), Mol. C6 16
Kalaeloa Harbor, Mol. C6 16
Ka Lae Māmane (point), Maui F8 14
*Kalaemau (point), Mol. A5 16
Kalaemilo (point), Mol. A5 16
Kalaeoho'aikū (point), Ha. R6 20
Kalaeokahano (point), Lan. G3 16
Ka Lae o Kowali (point), Ka. A5 11
Ka Lae Pa'akai (point), Ha. N3 20
Ka Lae Pa'akai (point), Ha. R6 20
Kalahaku Pali (cliff), Maui E11 15
Kalāheo, Ka. D4 11
Kalāhiki Beach, Ha. M3 18
Kalāhū (mountain), Ka. B3 11
Kalāhū Point, Maui D13 15
Kala'i'ehā (hill), Ha. H8 18
Kālaipāloa Point, Oahu B6 12
Kalakala, Lan. E3 16
Kalākāo'o Stream, Ha. F11 19
Kalākohi Gulch, Maui C10 15
Kalalae Point, Ha. B5 17
Kalalau Beach, Ka. A3 11
Kalalau Foot Trail, Ka. A3 11
Kalalau Stream, Ka. A3 11
Kalaloa Point, Maui C12 15
Kalalua (crater), Ha. M13 21
*Kalaluanahelehela (peak), Ka. C4 11
Kalama (beach), Maui F12 15
Kalama Stream, Ka. C6 11
Kalama Valley, Oahu F8 12
Kalama Iki Gulch, Lan. F2 16
*Kalamalu (hill), Ha. H4 18
Kalāmanu, Ha. K15 21
*Kalanai Point, Oahu B5 12
Kalanaokuaiki Pali (cliff), Ha. M11 21
Kalaniana'ole Beach, Oahu E3 12
Kalaniana'ole Highway, Oahu F8 12
Kalanipu'u (hill), Ka. D6 11
Kalaoa, Ha. H2 18
Kalaoa Valley, Ni. C2 10
Kalapahāpu'u Gulch, Ha. D9 17
Kalapana, Ha. M14 21
Kalapana Trail, Ha. M12 21
Kalapawili Ridge, Maui E12 15
Kalauao Stream, Oahu E5 12
Kalaukani, Pu'u (hill), Ha. J3 18
*Kalauoa Stream, Oahu A2 13
*Kalauoo Stream Oahu A1 13
Kalaupapa, Mol. A5 16
Kalaupapa Peninsula, Mol. A5 16
Kālawamauna, Kīpuka (oasis), Ha. G5 18
Kalawao, Mol. A5 16
Kalawao County, Mol. *Note—same boundary as Kalawao District. Treated as part of Maui County for statistical purposes.* A5 16
Kalawao District, Mol. A5 16
Kale, Pu'u (hill), Ha. E7 17
*Kalea (point), Ha. L16 21
Kalehua, Ha. D8 17
Kale'ia (beach), Maui D8 14
Kalena, Pu'u (hill), Oahu D3 12
Kālepa, Ha. F9 19
Kālepa (hill), Ka. C6 11
Kālepa (peak), Ha. F9 17
Kālepa Gulch, Maui B7 14
Kālepa Point, Ha. L15 21
Kālepa Ridge, Ka. C6 11
Kale Pa'akai (point), Ha. J2 18

Kalepeamoa, Ha. R4 20
Kalepeamoa (hill), Maui E10 15
Kalepeamoa, Pu'u (hill), Ha. G8 18
Kalepolepo, Maui D8 14
Kaliali, Pu'u (hill), Ha. E6 17
*Kalialinui Gulch, Maui C9 14
Kalihi, Oahu B4 13
Kalihi Channel, Oahu D4 13
Kalihi Point, Ha. H1 18
Kalihi Stream, Oahu E6 12
Kalihikai Beach, Ka. A5 11
Kalihiwai, Ka. A5 11
Kalihiwai Bay, Ka. A5 11
Kalihiwai Reservoir, Ka. A5 11
Kalihiwai River, Ka. A5 11
*Kali'ipa'a, Ha. R5 20
Kaliko (peak), Ka. B5 11
Kalīpoa, Ha. R5 20
Kali'u, Pu'u (hill), Ha. L14 21
Kaliuwa'a (Sacred) Falls, Oahu C6 12
Kalohewahewa Stream, Ha. H11 19
Kalohi Channel, Lan. D2 16
Kalo'i Gulch, Oahu E3 12
Kaloko, Oahu F9 12
Kaloko Fishpond, Ha. H1 18
Kaloko Point, Ha. H1 18
Kaloko Reservoir, Ka. A6 11
Kaloko'eli Fishpond, Mol. C4 16
Kaloli Point, Ha. J14 21
Kalou Marsh, Oahu A4 12
Kalua, Maui E1 14
Kalua'aha, Mol. C7 16
Kaluaapuhi Fishpond, Mol. B4 16
Kaluahā'ula Ridge, Ka. C3 11
*Kaluahauoni (peak), Mol. B5 16
Kaluahine Falls, Ha. C6 17
Kaluaihākōkō (point), Maui E8 14
Kaluako'i Valley, Ka. D3 11
*Kalualea (mountain), Ka. D5 11
Kaluamakani, Ha. F8 17
Kaluanui (cape), Mol. A4 16
Kaluanui Stream, Oahu C5 12
Kaluanui Ridge, Oahu F9 13
Kaluaōhonu, Ha. R6 20
Kaluaokeli'iwa'a, Kīpuka (oasis), Ha. Q5 20
Kaluape'elua (gulch), Mol. D3 16
Kaluapuhi, Ha. Q6 20
Kaluapuhi, Ka. D3 11
Kaluapulani Gulch, Maui D10 15
Kālu'e (point), Ha. N10 21
*Kaluiu, Ha. H14 21
Kalulu, Maui F9 14
Kalulu (hill), Ha. H3 18
Kama'e'e Stream, Ha. F11 19
*Kamaha, Pu'u (hill), Ka. B4 11
Kamāhu'ehu'e Fishpond, Mol. C6 16
Kamāhuna (peak), Ka. B6 11
Kamaiki Point, Lan. F3 16
Kamaileunu Ridge, Oahu D2 12
Kama'ili, Ha. M15 21
Kama'ili Road, Ha. L15 21
Kamakai'a Hills, Ha. N9 21
Kamakalepo, Ha. R6 20
Kamakamaka Point, Ha. C8 17
Kamakeanu (peak), Ka. B4 11
Kamakoa Gulch, Ha. E4 17
Kamakou (peak), Mol. B6 16
Kāmala Point, Ka. E6 11
Kamali'i (hill), Ha. G3 17
Kamali'i Ridge, Ka. B6 11
Kamalino, Ni. C1 10
Kamalō, Mol. C6 16
Kamalō Gulch, Mol. C6 16
Kamalō Harbor, Mol. C6 16
Kamalomalo'o Stream, Ka. B7 11
*Kamalu Road, Ka. C6 11
Kamana, Pu'u (hill), Oahu D5 12
Kamanaiki Stream, Oahu E6 12
Kamanamana (point), Maui G9 14
Kamananui, Pu'u (hill), Oahu C3 12
Kamananui Stream, Oahu B4 12
Kamanawai Bay, Maui F12 15
Kamanawai Point, Maui F12 15
Kamanu, Ka. C5 11
Ka Manu, Pu'u (hill), Ka. A4 11
Kamā'oa Road, Ha. Q6 20
Kamā'ohe Bay, Ha. P2 20
Kama'ole, Maui E8 14
Kama'oli'i (cone), Maui E11 15
Kāmaulele (peak), Ka. D5 11
Kamawai, Ha. G3 18

Kamehame Hill, Ha. P8 20
Kamehame Ridge, Oahu F9 13
Kamehameha Heights, Oahu B5 13
Kamehameha Highway, Oahu A5 12
Kamehameha V Highway, Mol. C6 16
Kamiki Ridge, Lan. E3 16
Kamilo Point, Ka. D6 11
Kamiloaina, Kipuka (oasis), Ha. Q3 20
Kamilo Iki Valley, Oahu F9 13
Kamilo Nui Valley, Oahu F9 13
Kamiloloa, Mol. B4 16
Kamiloloa Gulch, Mol. B5 16
Kamio Point, Ha. R6 20
Kamoa, Pu'u (hill), Ha. D5 17
Kamoa Point, Ha. J2 18
Kamoamoa, Ha. N13 21
Kamoamoa, Pu'u (hill), Ha. M12 21
Ka Moa o Pele (cone), Maui E11 15
Kamōhio Bay, Kah. B3 14
Kamoi Point, Ha. Q3 20
Kamoku (hill), Ka. A6 11
Kamoku Flats, Mol. B5 16
Kamokuna (point), Ha. N13 21
Kamo'oali'i Lava Flow, Ha. N9 21
Kamo'oali'i Stream, Oahu G2 13
Kamo'oho'opulu Ridge, Ka. C6 11
Kamo'okoa Ridge, Ka. A5 11
Kamo'olāli'i Stream, Oahu E7 12
Kamo'oloa, Oahu C3 12
Kamo'oloa Stream, Ka. D5 11
(Kamuela) Waimea, Ha. D5 17
Kamuliwai, Ha. Q7 20
Kanaele Swamp, Ka. D4 11
Kanahā Rock, Mol. B8 16
Kanahā Stream, Maui C6 14
Kanahā Stream, Oahu B6 13
Kanahāhā, Ha. J4 18
Kanahau (peak), Maui E10 15
Kanahena, Maui F8 14
Kanahena Point, Maui F8 14
Kanaio, Maui F9 14
Kanakaleonui, Pu'u (hill), Ha. F9 19
*Kanakamilae, Ha. K3 18
Kanalo Valley, Ni. B2 10
Kanaloa (point), Maui G9 15
Kanalopaka Nui, Pu'u (hill), Ha. G6 18
Kanapou Bay, Kah. B4 14
Kāne, Pu'u (hill), Maui C7 14
*Kanealole Stream, Oahu B6 13
Kāneana Cave, Oahu C2 12
Kānehoa, Pu'u (hill), Oahu C6 12
Kānehoalani, Pu'u (hill), Oahu C6 12
Kāne'ilio Point, Oahu D2 12
Kānekanaka Point, Ha. E3 17
Kānekauhi'i Point, Ha. M3 18
Kāneloa Gulch, Kah. B3 14
Kanenelu Flat, Ha. O8 20
Kāne Nui o Hamo (crater), Ha. M11 21
Kāne'ohe, Oahu D7 12
Kāne'ohe Bay, Oahu D7 12
Kāne'ohe Marine Corps Air Station, Oahu D7 12
Kānewa'a Point, Ha. P2 20
Kaniahiku Village, Ha. L14 21
Kanikū Lava Flow, Ha. F3 17
Kānoa (hill), Ha. F12 19
Kānoa Fishpond, Mol. C5 16
Kanohina, Kipuka (oasis), Ha. Q3 20
Kanōnone Waterhole, Ha. Q4 20
Kanounou Point, Maui A6 14
Kanukuawa Fishpond, Mol. C5 16
*Kaoaini Fishpond, Mol. C5 16
Ka'ohe Ranch, Ha. N4 20
Kāohikaipu Island, Oahu F9 12
Ka'ōiki Pali (cliff), Ha. M9 21
Ka'ō'io Point, Oahu C6 12
Kaoma Point, Ha. B3 17
Ka'one, Pu'u (hill), Ha. N10 21
Kaonihu, Mol. A8 16
Ka'ōpala Gulch, Maui B6 14
Ka'ōpapawai Waterhole, Ha. M8 18
Ka'opeahina Fishpond, Mol. C7 16
Kapa'a, Ka. C7 11
E8 11
Kapa'a Park, Ha. B3 17
Kapa'a Stream, Ka. B6 11
Kapa'ahu, Ha. M13 21
Kapa'a Iki Point, Ha. B4 17
Kapa'akea (peak), Ha. F3 17
Kapa'akea Gulch, Mol. B5 16
*Kapa'alalaea Reservoir, Maui C10 15

Kapa'au (Kohala), Ha. B4 17
Kapāhili Gulch, Ka. D3 11
Kapaia, Ka. D6 11
Kapaia Reservoir, Ka. C6 11
*Kapāiloa (cape), Mol. A6 16
Kapaka, Ka. D3 11
Kapaka (mountain), Ka. A5 11
Kapakahi Gulch, Oahu F7 12
Kapaka Nui Falls, Ka. B5 11
Kapālama, Oahu C4 13
Kapālama Stream, Oahu E6 12
Kapalaoa, Ha. F3 17
Kapalaoa (peak), Ka. D4 11
*Kapālauo'a (head), Mol. A2 16
Kapale Gulch, Mol. A4 16
Kapalikōī (hill), Mol. B2 16
Kapalua Beach (village), Maui A5 14
Kapalua (Fleming) Beach, Maui A5 14
Kapana Bay, Ha. B4 17
Kapāo'o Point, Ha. O9 20
Kāpapa Island, Oahu D7 12
Kāpapa Pali (cliff), Mol. B6 16
*Kapapakikane, Mol. A5 16
Kapāpala Camp, Ha. N8 20
Kapāpala Cave, Ha. N8 20
Kapāpala Ranch, Ha. N8 20
Kapehu Stream, Ha. E11 19
Kapehu Stream, Ha. H11 19
Kapeku (hill), Ka. E4 11
Ka Pele, Pu'u (hill), Ha. G6 18
Ka Pele, Pu'u (hill), Ka. C2 11
Kapele, Pu'u (hill), Mol. A3 16
Kapi'a Stream, Maui E13 15
Kapīlau Ridge, Maui C7 14
Kapili Stream, Ha. E10 19
Kapilo Bay, Ha. M3 18
Kapō'ala'ala (hill), Ha. O5 20
Kapoho, Ha. K15 21
Kapoho, Lan. F4 16
Kapoho Crater, Ha. K15 21
Kapoho Gulch, Lan. F3 16
Kapoho Point, Oahu D8 12
Kapoho Point, Ha. L16 21
Kapoholimu'ele Gulch, Ha. E9 19
Kapu'a Bay, Ha. P3 20
Kapua Gulch, Lan. F3 16
Kapuahi a Pele, Mol. A4 16
*Kapue Stream, Ha. G11 19
Kapuhikani (point), Mol. B1 16
*Kapuka'amoi Point, Ka. A5 11
Kapukapaia Ridge, Ka. C3 11
Kapukapu, Pu'u (hill), Ha. N10 21
*Kapukapuahakea, Mol. B7 16
Kapukaulua, Maui B9 14
Kapukaulua, Mol. C5 16
Kapukaulua (point), Maui D13 15
Kapukuwahine, Mol. B1 16
Kapulau Point, Ha. O3 20
Kapūlehu, Kipuka (oasis), Ha. Q5 20
Kapulena, Ha. C7 17
Kapunakea, Maui C5 14
*Kapuniau Point, Ha. E3 17
Kau, Pu'u (hill), Ha. G6 18
Ka'ū Desert, Ha. M10 21
Ka'ū Desert Trail, Ha. N9 21
Ka'ū District, Ha. N5 20
Ka'ū Trail, Ha. N10 20
Kaua, Pu'u (hill), Oahu D3 12
Kaua'i (island), Ka. -- 11
Kaua'i Channel, Oahu B1 12
*Kauakio Bay, Maui E13 15
Kauakiu Point, Maui E13 15
*Kauapea Beach, Ka. A5 11
Kaua'ula Stream, Maui C6 14
Kau'eleau, Ha. L15 21
Kauhakō Bay, Ha. M3 18
Kauhakō Crater, Mol. A5 16
Kauhao Ridge, Ka. B2 11
Kauhao Valley, Ka. B2 11
Kauhiuhi, Ha. M9 21
Kauhoko (hill), Ka. D3 11
Kauhola Point, Ha. B4 17
Kauhuhu'ula Gulch, Ha. N7 20
Kauhu'ula, Ha. O8 20
Ka'uiki Head, Maui D14 15
*Ka'uili'i Point, Ha. B3 17
*Kauka, Pu'u (hill), Ha. M13 21
Kaukahōkū, Ha. K3 18
Kaukala'ela'e Point, Ha. K2 18
Kaukamoku Gulch, Kah. B3 14
Kaukanu, Pu'u (hill), Maui E13 15

L

Name	Ref	Pg
Kuapa'a Valley, Ka.	C2	11
Kū'au, Maui	B9	14
Kūē'ē, Ha.	O9	20
Kūheia, Kah.	A3	14
	J14	21
Kuhiō Bay, Ha.	H13	21
Kuhiō Highway, Ka.	B7	11
Kuhiō Village, Ha.	B4	11
Kūhua Gulch, Maui	D5	11
Kuhuoku (cliff), Ha.	D12	15
	P7	20
Ku'ia Stream, Ka.	R5	20
Kui'aha Gulch, Maui	D5	11
Kuiki (hill), Maui	B10	15
Kuki'i Point, Kah.	E12	15
Kuilei Cliffs, Oahu	A3	14
Kuilei Gulch, Ha.	F7	17
Kuka'i, Pu'u (hill), Maui	D7	17
Kīkaiau, Ha.	G1	18
Kūka'imanini Island, Oahu	C11	15
Kūka'iwa'a Point, Mol.	D9	19
Kukalau, Ha.	J1	16
Kūki'o Bay, Ha.	A4	12
*Kukoe, Pu'u (hill), Ha.	A5	16
Kuku, Ha.	A6	16
Kukui (peak), Ka.	B7	11
Kukui, Pu'u (hill), Maui	B5	14
Kukui, Fuʻu (hill), Ha.	E3	10
Kukui Bay, Maui	D9	18
Kukui Point, Ha.	O9	21
Kukui Point, Ha.	Q3	20
Kukui Village, Ha.	F4	10
Kukuihaele, Ha.	G1	17
Kukuihaele Landing, Ha.	K15	21
Kukui o Kanaloa (bluff), Mol.	P7	20
Kukuimui Ridge, Mol.	C5	11
Kuku'ula Bay, Ka.	E11	19
*Kuku'ula Point, Ha.	B14	19
Kukuku, Mol.		
Kula, Maui		
Kula Highway, Maui		
Kula'alamihi Fishpond, Mol.		
Kulalio, Pu'u (hill), Oahu		
Kulanalilia (peak), Maui		
Kīlanapahu (peak), Maui		
Kīlani (volcano), Ha.		
Kīlani Honor Camp, Ha.		
Kīlanhā'ko'i Gulch, Maui		
Kulaoka'e'a, Maui		
Kulaokalā'aloa, Maui		
Kuli'ou'ou Valley, Oahu		
Kiloa Point, Maui		
Kīloa Point, Oahu		
Kīloli (hill), Maui		
Kīlua (cones), Ha.		
Kumaha'ulula Point, Oahu		
Kumakali'i, Pu'u (hill), Oahu		
Kumimi, Pu'u (hill), Mol.		
Kumukahi, Cape, Ha.		
Kumukahi Channel, Ka.		
Kumekehu Point, Ha.		
Kumuweia Ridge, Maui		
Kunalele Valley, Ha.		
Kunia, Oahu		
Kunia Road, Oahu		
Kupapa'u Point, Ha.		
Kīpapa'ulua Gulch, Ha.		
Kīpaua Valley, Oahu		
Kīpeke Fishpond, Oahu		
Kipikipiki'ō Point, Oahu		
Kupolo, Mol.		
Kure Atoll, NWHI		
Kurtistown, Ha.		
Ku Tree Reservoir, Oahu		
Kū'unaka'iole (point), Ha.		
Ku'upāha'a Gulch, Ha.		

Name	Ref	Pg
Leinokano Point, Ha.	G6	18
Lei No Haunui Pali (cliff), Lan.	G3	16
Leleiwi Pali (cliff), Maui	E11	15
Leleiwi Point, Ha.	F13	21
Lelekea Bay, Maui	F9	14
Lēpau Point, Mol.	A7	16
Lepeamoa Rock, Ha.	M3	20
Lepo, Pu'u (hill), Ka.	C4	11
Līhau (peak), Maui	D5	11
Līhu'e, Ka.	D2	11
Līhu'e Airport, Ka.	E3	10
Līhu'e District, Ka.	D6	11
Līhu'e Point, Lan.	A5	16
Liliuoholo, Maui	C5	11
*Līliewa Crater, Ha.	E8	14
Lililoa, Ka.	L14	21
Lilinoe, Pu'u (hill), Ha.	L15	21
Līlī'ili, Pu'u (hill), Oahu	G8	18
Limahuli Stream, Ka.	A3	11
Limukoko Point, Ha.	B5	14
Lipoa Point, Maui	E5	11
Lisianski Island, NWHI	A6	14
Little Gin Island, NWHI	B2	22
Little North Island, NWHI	C1	22
Loa, Pu'u (hill), Ha.	D4	17
Lo'a, Pu'u (hill), Ka.	K2	18
Loa Point, Oahu	G9	18
Lo'alo'a (hill), Ha.	M3	18
Loe, Pu'u (hill), Ha.	H8	18
Loea Point, Ha.	D7	17
Lokoaku Pond, Ha.	P7	20
Loli River, Ka.	C5	14
Lōlia, Ha.	B14	15
Lōpā, Lan.	C6	14
Lōpā Gulch, Lan.	B14	10
Lou, Pu'u (hill), Ha.	C4	17
Lower Pā'ia, Maui	B7	14
Lower Village, Oahu	E3	17
Lua, Pu'u (hill), Ha.	D8	14
Lua'alaea Stream, Oahu	B9	14
Luahine, Pu'u (hill), Maui	B5	12
Luahinewai (pond), Ha.	B6	12
Lua Hohonu (pit), Ha.	C5	14
Lua Hou (pit), Ha.	C7	17
Luakē'ālia Lalo (peak), Kah.	B3	16
Luako'i Ridge, Maui	D6	17
Lualualei, Oahu	E10	15
Lualualei Beach, Oahu	A8	16
Lualualei Reservoir, Oahu	E9	15
Luamaha'ila (peak), Ka.	B7	16
Luamakika, Oahu	L9	21
Luamanu Crater, Ha.	A4	11
Luapalalauhala (crater), Ha.	F9	14
Luapō'ai (crater), Ha.	K10	21
Luapoholo, Ha.	K10	21
Luapū'ali (crater), Ha.	D8	14
Li'ua, Pu'u (hill), Ha.	A6	14
Lūhala Point, Ha.	E13	15
Lūkanaka, Pu'u (hill), Ha.	A6	14
Luluku Stream, Oahu	A10	13
Lumaha'i River, Ka.	A6	11
Lumiawai Waterhole, Ha.	F8	12
Līpe'a Kīpuka (oasis), Ha.	F8	12

M

Name	Ref	Pg
Ma'akua Gulch, Oahu	E13	15
Mā'alaea, Maui	C6	10
Mā'alaea Bay, Maui	G1	18
Ma'alehu, Mol.	C10	15
Ma'au, Pu'u (hill), Ha.	H6	18
Ma'au, Pu'u (hill), Ha.	K8	21
*Mā'eli'eli, Pu'u (hill), Oahu	D3	12
(Magic Island) 'Āina Moana, Oahu	B8	13
Magnetic Peak, Maui	D4	12
Mahaʻula, Ha.	N13	21
Maha'ula, Ha.	E10	19
Mahana, Mol.	A10	13
Mahana Bay, Ha.	C7	16
Mahanalua, Pu'u (hill), Lan.	F7	12
Māhanaluanui, Pu'u (hill), Maui	A1	22
Māhā'ulepū Road, Ka.	J13	21
Maheo, Pu'u (hill), Ka.	C5	12
*Maheo, Kīpuka (oasis), Ha.	E3	16
Māhie Point, Oahu	E7	17
Mahika Island, Ha.		
Mahiki Point, Ha.		

Name	Ref	Pg
Māhinahina, Maui	B5	14
Mahinakēhau Ridge, Ka.	B4	11
Mahinauli Gulch, Ka.	D3	11
Mahinui, Oahu	F9	14
Māhoe, Pu'u (hill), Maui	A7	16
Māhoelua (peak), Ha.	C4	17
Mahuka Bay, Ha.	D6	11
Mahukona Harbor, Ha.	B3	17
Mā'ihi Bay, Ha.	B6	11
Maiaki'i Stream, Ka.	E11	15
*Maile, Pu'u (hill), Maui	C5	11
*Mailehaehi (hill), Ha.	E8	14
Mā'ili, Oahu	L14	21
Mā'ili Point, Oahu	G8	18
Mā'ili Stream, Ha.	A3	11
Mā'ili'ili, Pu'u (hill), Oahu	D4	17
Major, Kīpuka (oasis), Ha.	A3	17
Maka'ākini Point, Ha.	A6	14
Maka'ala, Pu'u (hill), Ha.	B2	22
Maka'alae, Kah.	B4	22
Maka'alae Point, Maui	C1	22
Makaʻālia (hill), Ha.	D4	11
Makaha, Oahu	K2	18
Makaha Beach, Oahu	G9	20
Makaha Point, Ka.	M3	18
Mākaha Ridge, Ka.	H8	18
Mākaha Stream, Oahu	D7	17
Mākaha Valley, Ka.	F12	15
Makahalau, Ha.	H13	19
Makahalau, Pu'u (hill), Ha.	C3	11
Makahanu Pali (cliff), Ni.	L15	21
Makahau'ena (point), Ni.	C4	17
Makahiki Point, Ha.	F4	16
Makahoa Point, Ka.	F4	16
Makahoa Point, Oahu	R6	20
Makahoa Ridge, Ka.	E4	12
Makahū'ena Point, Ka.	B2	11
Makaiwa, Maui	A7	13
Makaiwa Bay, Ha.	B4	16
Makaiwa Gulch, Oahu	F2	17
Makaiwa Gulch, Oahu	L6	18
Makaiwa, Pu'u (hill), Oahu	L6	18
Makakilo City, Oahu	B3	14
Makakupu Gulch, Ha.	C6	14
Makalapa Crater, Oahu	F10	15
Makaleha, Oahu	D2	12
Makaleha (peak), Ka.	D2	12
Makaleha (stream), Oahu	D3	14
Makaleha Mountains, Ka.	M10	21
Makali'i (hill), Ha.	Q5	20
Makali'i Point, Ha.	Q5	20
Makaluapuna Point, Maui	L7	18
Makapu'u Beach, Oahu	Q5	20
Makamaka'ole (stream), Maui	D11	15
Makana (cliff), Ka.	L3	17
Mākanaka, Pu'u (hill), Ha.	G2	13
Makaohule Point, Ha.	A4	11
Maka o Kaha'i (point), Ka.	M4	18
Makapala, Ha.	K4	18
Makapili Rock, Ka.		
Makapipi Stream, West, Maui		
Makapu'u Beach, Oahu		
Makapu'u Head, Oahu		
Makapu'u Point, Oahu		
Makawao District (part), Kah.		
Makawao District (part), Maui		
Makawao, Maui		
Makawao District (part), Oahu		
Makaweli Landing, Ka.		
Makaweli River, Ka.		
Mākena, Maui		
*Makeolu (peak), Maui		
Maki'i, Oahu		
Makiki, Oahu		
Makiwa Gulch, Maui		
Mākole, Ka.		
Mākole'ā Point, Ha.		
Makua Gulch, Ha.		
Mākua Point, Ha.		
Mākua, Pu'u (hill), Maui		

Name	Ref	Pg
Mākua Stream, Oahu	C2	12
Makuaiki Point, Ka.	B4	11
Makuleia Bay, Maui	B2	11
Maku'u, Ha.	A6	14
	J14	21
Māla, Maui	C5	14
Māla'e, Oahu	E2	13
Māla'e Gulch, Mol.	C6	16
Māla'e Point, Ha.	C3	17
Malaekahana Stream, Oahu	B5	12
Malaeloa (point), Maui	D13	15
*Mālamalamaiki (peak), Ka.	B6	11
Mali, Pu'u (hill), Ha.	F8	17
Māliko Bay, Maui	H4	18
Māliko Gulch, Maui	C10	15
Mālua, Kīpuka (oasis), Ha.	Q3	20
Malu'aka (point), Maui	E2	
Maluhia Camp, Ha.	G12	19
Maluikeao, Ha.	L2	18
Māmala Bay, Oahu	M9	21
*Māmalahoa (peak), Ka.	F5	12
Māmalahoa Highway, Ha.	B4	11
Māmalu Bay, Maui	H4	17
Māmani, Kīpuka (oasis), Ha.	F12	15
Mamo, Pu'u (hill), Ha.	B2	14
Manā, Ka.	K4	18
Manā Point, Ka.	D3	17
Manā Road, Ha.	O6	
Manā Road, Ka.	D2	
Manaiki Stream, Oahu	C1	11
Manakai Stream, Oahu	C1	11
Manana Pali (cliff), Oahu	E7	17
Mānana Island (Rabbit I.), Oahu	D2	
Mānana Stream, Oahu	E6	12
Mananole Stream, Maui	B2	11
Manao, Pu'u (hill), Ha.	Q7	20
Manawahua, Pu'u (hill), Oahu	B2	11
Manawaiao (stream), Maui	A4	13
Manawainui, Maui	E7	17
Manawainui Gulch, Maui	A2	16
Manawainui Gulch, Maui	N10	21
Manawainui Gulch, Mol.	F9	22
Manawainui Stream, Maui	O3	20
Manawaipueo Gulch, Maui	D5	12
Mānā Waipuna Falls, Ka.	B7	14
Mānele, Lan.	A4	11
Mānele Road, Lan.	G6	18
Mānoa, Oahu	A5	12
*Mane one'o, Pu'u (hill), Mol.	B10	15
Mane opapa Gulch, Mol.	E5	11
Māniania Pali (cliff), Maui	F11	15
Mānienie'ula (ridge), Ka.	D7	14
Maniki Gulch, Oahu	F4	16
Manini, Pu'u (hill), Mol.	B4	17
Manō, Pu'u (hill), Ha.	E3	17
Manō Point, Ha.	F12	15
Mānoa, Oahu	C11	15
Mānoa Falls, Oahu	D4	11
Mānoa Stream, Ka.	E4	12
Manoloa (point), Ka.	F3	16
Manoloa Stream, Ha.	G1	18
Manu, Pu'u (hill), Ha.	A4	16
Manu, Pu'u (hill), Ha.	N7	20
Manu, Pu'u (hill), Lan.	B6	11
Manuahi Ridge, Mol.	E5	12
Manuahi Valley, Ka.	C3	12
Manuhonohono, Pu'u (hill), Ka.	B5	11
Manuka Bay, Ha.	D9	17
Manu'ōhūle, Maui	D4	11
Maro Reef, NWHI	C2	12
Maui (island), Ha.	A6	
Maui 'imae Ridge, Oahu	B7	14
Maukaloa Camp, Ha.	A3	11
Ma'ulili Bay, Maui	B7	17
Mauloa (hill), Ha.	P7	20
Maulua Bay, Ha.	A4	11
Maulua Stream, Ha.	F8	19
Maulua Trail, Ha.	F7	12
Mauna Alani (hill), Maui	F13	15
Maunaanu Waterhole, Ha.	F9	12
Maunaiki Trail, Ha.	F9	12
Mauna'iu, Kīpuka (oasis), Ha.	E11	19
Maunakapu (mountain), Oahu	D6	17
Mauna Kea (mountain), Ha.	M12	21

Name	Ref
Wahiawā, Oahu	D4 12
Wahiawā (hill), Ka.	A8 12
Wahiawā (stream), Ka.	D4 11
Wahiawā Bay, Ka.	E4 11
Wahiawā District, Oahu	C4 12
Wahiawā Reservoir, Oahu	D4 12
Wahikuli Gulch, Maui	A14 12
Wahilauhue Gulch, Mol.	B2 16
Wahiloa Falls, Ha.	C6 14
Wahinemakanui (island), Ha.	G11 19
Wai a Hewahewa Gulch, Mol.	J14 19
Wai'ahi Stream, Ka.	H9 11
Wai'ama Stream, Ha.	G11 19
Waiāhole Ditch, Oahu	D6 12
Waiāhole Ditch Tunnel, Oahu	D5 12
Waiāhole Stream, Oahu	D6 12
Waiahuakua Stream, Ka.	A3 11
Waiahulu Stream, Ka.	F11 19
Waiahulu, Kipuka (oasis), Ha.	P4 20
Waiakapū Stream, Maui	B4 16
Wai'aka, Ha.	D5 17
Wai'akea, Ha.	B3 17
Wai'akea Camp, Ha.	D5 17
Waiākea Stream, Ha.	J9 21
Wai'aka Ridge, Ka.	G12 19
Wai'aka Stream, Ka.	C5 11
(Wai'alae Bay) Maunalua Bay, Oahu	F7 12
Wai'alae, Oahu	B7 12
Wai'ale'ale (peak), Ka.	A5 12
Wai'ale Gulch, Oahu	C5 11
Waia Kāne (spring), Mol.	A2 16
Wai a Kāne Gulch, Mol.	B3 16
Waiakanonula (peak), Ha.	B2 16
Waiakapuhi (islet), Maui	G9 14
Waiakala'e Gulch, Mol.	A6 16
Waiākea Reservoir, Ka.	B4 16
Waikakala'e Gulch, Mol.	D3 17
Waikakala'e Stream, Ka.	D2 11
Waiākōlea Pond, Ha.	M14 21
Waia Kōlea Stream, Ka.	B3 11
Waiakala'e Gulch, Mol.	D10 15
Waiakala'e Pond, Ha.	C8 14
Waiakukini (pond), Ha.	G2 16
Waiakala'e (peak), Ka.	G2 16
(Wai'alae Bay)	D15 19
Waiaiehu Stream, Ha.	J9 21
Wai'alae Camp, Ha.	G12 19
Waiaiele Falls, Ha.	B3 16
Wai'alae Stream, Ka.	D2 11
Wai'alae Iki, Oahu	C9 13
Wai'alae Nui, Oahu	A7 13
Wai'alae Nui Gulch, Oahu	B8 13
Wai'ale Gulch, Oahu	D10 15
Wai'ale Reservoirs, Maui	C8 14
Wai'ale'ale (peak), Ka.	E3 17
Waiākea Bay, Ha.	C5 11
Waiale'ale (peak), Ka.	A4 12
Wai'alae'ia Stream, Mol.	A5 12
Waiālua, Ha.	B7 16
Waialua, Mol.	C3 12
Waialua, Oahu	C3 12
Waiālua Bay, Oahu	B3 12
Waialua District, Oahu	C3 12
Waialua Stream, Mol.	B7 16
Waianae, Oahu	D2 12
Waianae District, Oahu	D2 12
Waianae Range, Oahu	D2 12
Wai'ānapanapa Cave, Maui	D13 15
Wai'ānuenue Falls, Maui	C6 14
Wai'ānuenue Falls, Ka.	C4 11
Waianukole, Maui	C5 14
Waiapele Bay, Ha.	P8 20
Wai'au, Lake, Ha.	G8 18
Wai'au Stream, Ha.	H12 19
Waawa Stream, Ka.	E5 12
Waaehu, Maui	B8 14
Waiehu, Mol.	A6 16
Waiehu Point, Ha.	E12 19
Waiehu Point, Maui	B8 14
Waiehu Stream, North, Maui	C7 14
Waiehu Stream, South, Maui	C7 14
Waiemi Falls, Ha.	G11 19
Waihali Gulch, Maui	N7 20
Waihe'e, Maui	B7 14
Waihe'e, Oahu	A5 16
Waihee Point, Ha.	B7 14
Waiʻānmau Stream, Mol.	B7 14
Waihe'e Falls, Oahu	B4 12

Name	Ref
Waihe'e Point, Maui	B7 14
Waihe'e Reef, Maui	B7 14
Waihe'e River, Maui	B7 14
Waihe'e Stream, Oahu	A7 13
Waihi'i Gulch, Mol.	A3 16
Waihi'umalu Falls, Maui	E13 15
Waihohonu Stream, Ka.	B3 11
Waiho'i Valley, Maui	E13 15
Waihou, Ha.	D5 11
Waikū, Ha.	K3 18
Waikapū Stream, Maui	B5 11
Waikāne, Oahu	C6 12
Waikapū Stream, Maui	C6 12
Waiki'i, Ha.	C7 18
Waikīkī, Oahu	D7 13
Waikiki Beach, Oahu	F6 12
Waikoko Stream, Ka.	C5 11
Waikōloa Stream, Ha.	D7 17
Waikōloa, Pu'u (hill), Ha.	D5 17
Waikolu Stream, Mol.	D7 17
Waikolu, Ha.	D4 17
Wailau Gulch, Maui	A7 16
Wailena Gulch, Maui	B7 14
Wailau, Ka.	A7 16
Wailau Foot Trail, Mol.	B7 16
Wailau Stream, Mol.	B6 16
Wailau Valley, Ka.	C2 11
Wailaulau Gulch, Maui	F11 15
Wailea, Ha.	E8 14
Wailea, Maui	E8 14
Wailea Bay, Ka.	C6 11
Wailea Point, Oahu	E13 15
Wailea Cove, Maui	C6 11
Wailele Falls, Mol.	A6 16
Wailele Falls, Oahu	B5 12
Wailena Gulch, Maui	B7 14
Wai'ōla'i Gulch, Maui	C6 11
Wailua, Ka.	C6 11
Wailua, Maui	C12 15
Wailua, Oahu	C6 11
Wailua Iki Stream, East, Maui	D12 15
Wailua Nui Stream, West Maui	D12 15
Wailua River, Ka.	E13 15
Wailua River, North Fork, Ka.	C5 11
Wailua River, South Fork, Ka.	C6 11
Wailua Reservoir, Ka.	C6 11
Wailua Falls, Ka.	C6 11
Wailua Stream, Maui	C9 13
Wailuku District, Maui	C8 14
Wailuku Heights, Maui	C8 14
Wailuku River, Ha.	C7 14
Wailuku Stream, Ha.	H11 19
Wailupe, Oahu	D13 19
Wailupe Gulch, Oahu	F7 12
Waima Point, Ka.	E3 17
Waimaha'iha'i, Maui	E8 14
Waimalu, Oahu	A1 13
Waimalu Stream, Oahu	E8 14
Waimānalo, Oahu	E3 12
Waimānalo Bay, Oahu	F3 12
Waimānalo, Pu'u (hill), Ha.	R5 20
Waimānalo Beach (town), Oahu	E8 12
Waimānalo Gulch, Oahu	E3 12
Waimānalo Stream, Oahu	E8 12
Waimano Stream, Oahu	D5 12
Waimanu Bay, Ha.	C6 17
Waimanu Gap, Ha.	C6 17
Waimanu Stream, Ha.	C6 17
Waimanu Valley, Ha.	C6 17
Waimea, Ka.	D2 11
Waimea (Kamuela), Ha.	D5 17
Waimea (Maunawai), Ha.	B4 12
Waimea Bay, Ka.	D2 11

Name	Ref
Waimea Bay, Oahu	B4 12
Waimea Canyon, Ka.	C3 11
Waimea District (part), Ka.	C3 11
Waimea District (part), Ni.	C2 10
Waimea River, Ka.	D5 11
Waimea-Kohala Airport, Ha.	D5 17
Waimoku Falls, Maui	E13 15
Wainaku, Ha.	B4 17
Wainaku Camp, Ha.	H12 19
Waine'e, Maui	A4 11
Wainiha, Ka.	A4 11
Wainiha River, Ka.	A4 11
Wainiha Pali (cliff), Ka.	B4 11
Waiohinu, Ha.	Q6 20
Wai'ohiwi Gulch, Maui	C10 15
Wai'ohula Spring, Ha.	P8 20
Waiohuli, Ha.	E9 14
Waiohuli, Maui	E9 14
Wai'ōkala, Mol.	A7 16
Waiokamilo Stream, Maui	D12 15
Waiokapua, Ka.	C1 11
Waiokole Falls, Maui	C12 15
Waiolani Stream, Oahu	F6 12
Waiōli Stream, Ka.	A4 11
Wai'ōma'o Stream, Oahu	B8 13
Waiopae Gulch, Lan.	F3 16
Wai'ōpae (lakes), Ha.	L16 21
Waipahoehoe Gulch, Ha.	G10 19
Waipahoehoe Gulch, Ha.	C4 17
Waipahoehoe Stream, Ha.	C6 17
Waipahu, Oahu	B11 15
Waipa Stream, Ka.	B2 11
Waipahee Stream, Ka.	A6 11
Waipa'o Gulch, Maui	F11 15
Waipahi Point, Ha.	A4 11
Waipahi, Ha.	J13 21
Waipahu Gulch, Maui	G12 19
Waipi'o, Acres, Oahu	E14 15
Waipi'o, Ha.	C6 17
Waipi'o Bay, Maui	D4 12
Waipi'o Bay, Ha.	C6 17
Waipi'o Falls, Ha.	B2 17
Waipi'o Pali (cliff), Ha.	B11 19
Waipi'o Peninsula, Oahu	Q6 20
Waipi'o Stream, Ha.	E5 12
Waipuka Point, Maui	C6 17
Waipi'o Stream, Maui	C6 17
Waipuhi (bay), Ha.	D8 14
Waipu'ilani Gulch, Maui	Q7 20
Waipuna Point, Maui	E9 14
Waipunahoe Gulch, Ha.	C6 17
Waipunalei Trail, Ha.	E10 19
Waita Reservoir, Ka.	D5 11
Waitū Bay, Maui	C6 11
Waitū (hill), Ka.	C6 11
Wauha Bay, Maui	F11 15
Wawa'ula Point, Ha.	F12 15
Wai'ula'ula Gulch, Ha.	D4 17
Waiulili Stream, Maui	D6 17
Waiwelawela Point, Ha.	O9 20
Wala'ōhia Gulch, Ha.	B4 17
Wailulua Point, Maui	E3 17
Wanaapoa Islands, Oahu	B4 12
Wao'ala Gulch, Maui	F11 15
Waolani Stream, Oahu	B5 13
Wawahiwa'a Point, Ha.	H1 18
Wāwā'ia Gulch, Mol.	H1 18
Wawionu Bay, Ha.	C3 17
Wāwāloli Beach, Ha.	H1 18
Wawu (point), Maui	B9 14
Wekea Point, Maui	F10 15
Wekiu (hill), Ka.	B6 11
Weli Point, Ka.	E4 11
Weliweli, Ha.	F3 17
Weliweli Point, Ha.	F3 17
Welles Harbor, Mid.	I1 22
Weloka, Ha.	E11 19
West Cove, NWHI	C3 22
West Loch, Oahu	E4 12
West Maui Mountains, Maui	C6 14
Whale Island, NWHI	A4 22
Wheeler Air Force Base, Oahu	D4 12

Name	Ref
Whitmore Village, Oahu	C4 12
Wilhelmina Rise, Oahu	C8 13
Wiliwilinui Ridge, Oahu	B9 13
Wilson Tunnel, Oahu	E7 12
Woodlawn, Oahu	B7 13
Wood Valley, Ha.	B7 13
Wood Valley Camp, Ha.	N8 20